THE CAMBRIDGE C(

Incorporating the most recent resea... .., scholars in Italy, the UK, Ireland, and North America, this collection of essays foregrounds Boccaccio's significance as a pre-eminent scholar and mediator of the classical and vernacular traditions, whose innovative textual practices confirm him as a figure of equal standing to Petrarch and Dante. Situating Boccaccio and his works in their cultural contexts, the *Companion* introduces a wide range of his texts, paying close attention to his formal innovations, elaborate voicing strategies, and the tensions deriving from his position as a medieval author who places women at the centre of his work. Four chapters are dedicated to different aspects of his masterpiece, the *Decameron*, while particular attention is paid to the material forms of his works: from his own textual strategies as the shaper of his own and others' literary legacies, to his subsequent editorial history, and translation into other languages and media.

GUYDA ARMSTRONG is Senior Lecturer in Italian at the University of Manchester and is author of *The English Boccaccio: A History in Books* (2013).

RHIANNON DANIELS is Lecturer in Italian at the University of Bristol and is author of *Boccaccio and the Book: Production and Reading in Italy 1340–1520* (2009).

STEPHEN J. MILNER is Serena Professor of Italian at the University of Manchester. He is co-editor, with Catherine E. Léglu, of *The Erotics of Consolation: Desire and Distance in the Late Middle Ages* (2008) and editor of *At the Margins: Minority Groups in Premodern Italy* (2005).

A complete list of books in the series is at the back of the book

THE CAMBRIDGE
COMPANION TO
BOCCACCIO

EDITED BY

GUYDA ARMSTRONG, RHIANNON DANIELS,
AND STEPHEN J. MILNER

*Greto Olyson Reconsidering
Unreliability: Fallible and
Untrustworthy Narrators*

Lessico decameronine Brogentini, forni

*CALABRESS: Feminism and the
Packaging of Boccaccio's
Fiammetta (r.184)*

*(Olson : the language of Women as Written
by men)*

CAMBRIDGE
UNIVERSITY PRESS

CAMBRIDGE
UNIVERSITY PRESS

University Printing House, Cambridge CB2 8BS, United Kingdom

Cambridge University Press is part of the University of Cambridge.

It furthers the University's mission by disseminating knowledge in the pursuit of
education, learning and research at the highest international levels of excellence.

www.cambridge.org
Information on this title: www.cambridge.org/9781107609631

© Cambridge University Press 2015

First published 2015

Printed in the United States of America by Sheridan Books, Inc.

A catalogue record for this publication is available from the British Library

Library of Congress Cataloguing in Publication data
The Cambridge Companion to Boccaccio / edited by Guyda Armstrong, Rhiannon Daniels,
Stephen J. Milner.
pages cm. – (Cambridge Companions to Literature)
Includes bibliographical references and index.
ISBN 978-1-107-01435-0 (hardback)
1. Boccaccio, Giovanni, 1313–1375 – Criticism and interpretation.
2. Literature and society – Italy – History – To 1500. I. Armstrong, Guyda, editor.
II. Daniels, Rhiannon, editor. III. Milner, Stephen J., editor.
PQ4294.C34 2015
853′.1 – dc3 2014048678

ISBN 978-1-107-01435-0 Hardback
ISBN 978-1-107-60963-1 Paperback

CONTENTS

FIGURES

CONTRIBUTORS

BEATRICE ARDUINI is Assistant Professor of Italian at the University of Washington. Her research deals with medieval Italian literature and Dante studies, particularly the tradition of Dante's unfinished *Convivio* in manuscripts and early printed editions, and the study of Boccaccio's activity as copyist and editor of Dante's works. She has published on these and other topics in *Romance Philology*, *Textual Cultures*, and *Medioevo Letterario d'Italia*, among other journals, and contributed chapters to *Dante in the Long Nineteenth Century: Nationality, Identity and Appropriation*, and *The Politics of Poetics: Poetry and Social Activism in Early-Modern through Contemporary Italy*.

GUYDA ARMSTRONG is Senior Lecturer in Italian at the University of Manchester. Her research focuses on the reception of Boccaccio in translation from the medieval period to the present day, translation in early modern print cultures, and the history and future of the book. She is the author of *The English Boccaccio: A History in Books* (2013), and is currently preparing a critical edition of sixteenth- and seventeenth-century English translations of Boccaccio for the MHRA.

CORMAC Ó CUILLEANÁIN is Professor of Italian at Trinity College, Dublin. An occasional crime writer and translator, he is joint editor of *Translation and Censorship* (2009) and *Translation Right or Wrong* (2013). His new English version of the *Decameron* (2004) was based on the 1886 translation by John Payne.

RHIANNON DANIELS is Lecturer in Italian at the University of Bristol. Her research focuses on the reception of Boccaccio in the Middle Ages and Renaissance, the history of the book, and the history of reading. She is author of *Boccaccio and the Book: Production and Reading in Italy 1340–1520* (2009). Her current book-project is on the reception of the *Decameron* and print culture in sixteenth-century Italy.

PIER MASSIMO FORNI is Professor of Italian Literature at Johns Hopkins University. He received his 'Laurea in lettere e filosofia' from the University of Pavia and his doctorate in Italian literature from the University of California at Los

Angeles. Among his publications of Boccaccian interest are *Forme complesse nel 'Decameron'* (1992), *Adventures in Speech: Rhetoric and Narration in Boccaccio's 'Decameron'* (1996), and *Parole come fatti: la metafora realizzata e altre glosse al 'Decameron'* (2008). He co-edited with Renzo Bragantini the *Lessico critico decameroniano* (1995).

TOBIAS FOSTER GITTES is Associate Professor at Concordia University's Liberal Arts College (Montréal). He received his BA from Yale University (1987) and his PhD from Columbia University (2000). Dr Gittes specializes in Italian literature of the Middle Ages and early Renaissance. In addition to articles on Dante, Boccaccio, and Cervantes he has published a book on Boccaccio's myth-making activity: *Boccaccio's Naked Muse: Eros, Culture, and the Mythopoeic Imagination* (2008).

DAVID LUMMUS is Assistant Professor of Italian at Stanford University. His research focuses on late medieval Italian literature and early Renaissance humanism in Latin and the vernacular, especially on the interrelationship between politics and poetry and on the mythographic tradition between the twelfth and sixteenth centuries. He has published articles on Boccaccio's *Genealogia deorum gentilium*, *Buccolicum carmen*, and *Decameron*, and on Boccaccio's intellectual relationship with Petrarch.

MARILYN MIGIEL is Professor of Italian at Cornell University. She is known for her feminist readings of medieval and Renaissance Italian literature, and in particular for her book *A Rhetoric of the 'Decameron'* (2003), which received the Modern Language Association's Howard Marraro Prize in 2004. Currently, she is working on a book on the ethical dimension of the *Decameron*; several chapters of this book in progress have been published in recent years in *Heliotropia*, the online journal of Boccaccio studies.

STEPHEN J. MILNER is Serena Professor of Italian at the University of Manchester. A graduate in History from Cambridge, he undertook his PhD at the Warburg Institute, University of London. Amongst his recent publications are *The Erotics of Consolation: Desire and Distance in the Late Middle Ages* (2008) co-edited with Catherine E. Léglu; *At the Margins: Minority Groups in Premodern Italy* (2005), and *Artistic Exchange and Cultural Translation in the Italian Renaissance City* (2004) co-edited with Stephen J. Campbell.

F. REGINA PSAKI is Giustina Family Professor of Italian Language and Literature at the University of Oregon. She publishes on Boccaccio, Dante, and medieval courtly genres, translating chivalric romances from French and Italian: *Il Tristano Riccardiano* (2006), *Le Roman de la Rose ou de Guillaume de Dole* (1995), and *Le Roman de Silence* (1991). With Gloria Allaire she co-edited *The Arthur of the Italians* (2014); with Thomas C. Stillinger she co-edited *Boccaccio and*

Feminist Criticism (2006). Her current project is *The Traffic in Talk about Women: Misogyny and Philogyny in the Middle Ages.*

BRIAN RICHARDSON is Emeritus Professor of Italian Language at the University of Leeds and a Fellow of the British Academy. His publications include *Print Culture in Renaissance Italy: The Editor and the Vernacular Text, 1470–1600* (1994), *Printing, Writers and Readers in Renaissance Italy* (1999), *Manuscript Culture in Renaissance Italy* (2009), and an edition of Giovan Francesco Fortunio's *Regole grammaticali della volgar lingua* (2001). He is directing (2011–15) a project on oral culture in early modern Italy, funded by the European Research Council.

MASSIMO RIVA is Professor and Chair of Italian Studies at Brown University. He recently published a collection of essays, *Pinocchio digitale: Post-umanesimo e iper-romanzo* (2012) and co-edited (with Michael Papio and Francesco Borghesi) Giovanni Pico della Mirandola's *On Human Dignity* (2012). He is the founder and co-editor of the *Decameron Web* and directs the *Virtual Humanities Lab* at Brown University.

GUR ZAK is Lecturer in Comparative Literature at the Hebrew University of Jerusalem. His Book *Petrarch's Humanism and the Care of the Self* was published by Cambridge University Press in 2010. He is currently working on a book-project on ethics and literary form in the Italian Renaissance from Boccaccio to Poliziano. His recent publications include articles for the *Oxford Handbook of Medieval Latin Literature* and the *Cambridge Companion to Petrarch.*

This book is designed for multiple audiences: those who are coming to Boccaccio for the first time, or who may have only a passing acquaintance with his work, those studying his texts as undergraduate or postgraduate students, and those scholars interested in the production and reception of Boccaccio's works from the medieval to the modern day. Although our Companion is relatively simple in form – a collection of short chapters which each take on key aspects of Boccaccio's life and works – we hope to give a sense of the complex interrelation between his texts, the social and literary contexts which conditioned their composition, and their subsequent reception in the centuries since. Boccaccio was a writer who mastered all the medieval language arts and showed a keen interest in literary theory and the interpretation of texts. Equally at home writing poetry, prose, and letters, he also produced commentaries on classical and vernacular texts, wrote encyclopaedic collections of mythological and historical biographies, and avidly collected classical, patristic, and contemporary writings in his own autograph notebooks.

In our Companion we aim to reflect the richness and breadth of Boccaccio's textual production and the abundance of critical responses and adaptations that it subsequently generated, and which continue to flourish. The studies in this volume seek to provide a new and more nuanced consideration of Boccaccio, not merely as the author of deservedly renowned literary works, but as the pre-eminent cultural mediator of his age. Our approach as editors and contributors is conditioned by our complementary intellectual formations and our overlapping areas of expertise as *boccaccisti*, who combine concerns with the social and rhetorical practices of late medieval Italy with the material production of texts and their complex literary voicing. We have deliberately tried to transcend the artificial but abiding disciplinary barriers between literary and historical approaches to medieval Italian studies in order to propose a new perspective on Boccaccio. Consequently the focus is not simply on the literary works, but aims to bring together the social (that is, Boccaccio's own social networks and social practices), with the material facts of his textual cultures (the books which Boccaccio himself made, and the way they express their own intertextual networks). In this way the aim is to re-read the historical record and the historiographical tradition in order to propose a new way of thinking about Boccaccio, which is grounded in both his historic contexts and his multiple reception contexts, and informed by the latest critical work.

The book is divided into four parts which foreground different, but equally important, strands of the cultural context which we consider vital for an understanding of Boccaccio's leading role within multiple, overlapping cultural networks. Part I is concerned with essential features of Boccaccio's practice as both the writer and maker of books, with chapters on his life as pre-eminent cultural mediator (Armstrong, Daniels, and Milner), his material and textual practices in the production and editing of his texts (Arduini), and his literary strategies in the construction and addressing of his narrative and historic audiences (Daniels). Part II takes his most famous work, the *Decameron*, as its focus, framing it within literary, socio-political, and gendered perspectives, with chapters on its narrative form (Forni), its relation to Boccaccio's poetics, here figured as encompassing both prose and verse (Lummus), its implication within contemporary social practices (Milner), and its gender contestations (Psaki). Part III foregrounds Boccaccio's liminal position on the threshold between the late Middle Ages and the beginning of the Renaissance, with chapters on his intellectual relationships with his predecessor Dante (Armstrong) and his near-contemporary Petrarch (Zak), on his key role in sponsoring the revival of interest in classical humanism (Gittes), and on his engagement with gender difference and the voicing of women in a selection of minor and Latin works (Migiel). Finally, Part IV focuses attention on Boccaccio's reception history, with chapters on the editorial history of his works post-1800 (Richardson), on their translation into other languages and reception contexts (Ó Cuilleanáin), and on the transmedial afterlife of the *Decameron* (Riva).

Throughout the volume we have aimed to foreground certain fundamental themes and approaches which we judge crucial to the study of Boccaccio in the twenty-first century. First and foremost is our attention to the material and historical record: we focus on the works not just as literary texts, but as texts which are shaped, transmitted, and transformed in their containers, from Boccaccio's own autograph manuscripts right up to the distributed digital media forms of today. Our attention to the historic likewise encompasses both the material object – for example in the archival record of Boccaccio's civic life – and an interrogation of the conventional historiography of Boccaccio studies, which has customarily seen him in relation to Dante and

Petrarch, rather than as a historical protagonist of considerable importance in his own right. Finally, we highlight Boccaccio's literary and intellectual innovations, especially in the context of his writings for and about women, and as a humanist, alongside a recognition of the importance of providing an assessment of Boccaccio which moves beyond a narrow literary focus.

We see the Companion itself as a mediating text which consciously seeks to combine the romance philological tradition of Italian scholarship on Boccaccio, with the Anglophone literary-critical approach, and recent work in book-historical studies. This volume is the first English-language study to incorporate the most recent codicological and archival advances in its chapters and editorial apparatus, whilst simultaneously providing interpretative studies of key themes in Boccaccio's work and reception history. In this guise the Companion locates itself between the two landmark publications of the 2013 anniversary year: the catalogue of the exhibition held at the Biblioteca Medicea Laurenziana in Florence, *Boccaccio autore e copista*, and the North American *Boccaccio: A Critical Guide to the Complete Works*, the former providing the first full codicological survey of all Boccaccio's autographs and glossed manuscripts, and the latter with new essays on the full range of Boccaccio's authored texts.[1] Our aim is to combine the best of these approaches, in order to animate new discussions in Boccaccio studies.

It only remains for us to thank all those who have helped us along the way. First and foremost, our thanks go to our contributors, for their enthusiastic engagement with the project, their vast learning, generosity of spirit, and most of all their patience at the protracted delivery of this volume. We hope the results are worth the wait. Invaluable guidance and sustenance throughout the project has been provided by David Wallace, Brian Richardson, and Simon Gilson; we are also extremely grateful to our editors at Cambridge University Press, in particular Linda Bree and Anna Bond, who saw this project through to completion. Thanks go also to all those who read different parts of the book at various stages, including the anonymous readers for Cambridge University Press and those who fed into individual chapters during the writing process. As editors we would especially like to thank David Wallace, Kenneth P. Clarke, Simon Gilson, Ruth Glynn, and Tristan Kay for their input into our individual and co-authored chapters. Throughout we have been sustained by the energy and expertise of our wider academic communities: at the Villa I Tatti and Florentine archives, in particular Evan MacCarthy, Nicoletta Marcelli, and Sanam Nadar; all those who participated in our 'Locating Boccaccio in 2013' conference in Manchester with whom we have had such stimulating discussions; our friends at the John Rylands Library, University of Manchester, for their help with the Locating

Boccaccio exhibition and for supplying the images and photographic permissions for this volume, especially Julianne Simpson and the staff of the Centre for Heritage Imaging and Collection Care; and finally our colleagues at the Universities of Bristol and Manchester, for their continued friendship, support, and advice.

NOTE

1 *Boccaccio autore e copista*, ed. by Teresa De Robertis and others (Florence: Mandragora, 2013); *Boccaccio: A Critical Guide to the Complete Works*, ed. by Victoria Kirkham, Michael Sherberg, and Janet Levarie Smarr (Chicago: Chicago University Press, 2013).

LIST OF MANUSCRIPTS

We now know of seventeen Boccaccio autograph manuscripts, three of which are currently separated into different volumes, making twenty-two in total. Eleven further manuscripts are now known to have been glossed by Boccaccio, and there also exists one private letter, written to Leonardo del Chiaro in 1366. There is also one antigraph of the *Decameron* (a copy prepared under the supervision of Boccaccio), which represents an earlier editorial stage of the text prior to that of the autograph manuscript now in Berlin.

Below we have listed in order Boccaccio's autograph manuscripts, divided into works of his own composition and archive books containing copies of works by others. There follows a list of manuscripts copied by other people and glossed by Boccaccio; and finally, a list of other manuscripts mentioned in the essays in this volume. Please note that the texts listed in the *Zibaldoni* below are not comprehensive, and we have given only those works transcribed by Boccaccio which are mentioned in this book.

For full descriptions of all of these manuscripts, see the exhibition catalogue *Boccaccio autore e copista*, ed. by Teresa De Robertis and others (Florence: Mandragora, 2013). For the datings we have drawn on the 2013 catalogue and on Marco Cursi's *La scrittura e i libri di Giovanni Boccaccio* (Rome: Viella, 2013).

Abbreviations

Florence, Biblioteca Medicea Laurenziana	BML
Florence, Biblioteca Nazionale Centrale	BNC
Florence, Biblioteca Riccardiana	BR
Paris, Bibliothèque nationale de France	BNF
Vatican City, Biblioteca Apostolica Vaticana	BAV

Autograph manuscripts

Works of Boccaccio's own composition

Title	Location	Date
Allegoria mitologica	Florence, BML, 29. 8	*c.* 1340
Argomenti to Dante's *Comedy* (*Brieve raccoglimento*)	Toledo, Biblioteca Capitular, Zelada 104. 6 (To)	late 1350s–early 1360s
	Florence, BR, 1035 (Ri)	1360s
	Vatican City, BAV, Chigi L. VI. 213 (Chig)	1360s
Buccolicum carmen	Florence, BR, 1232	*c.* 1367; revised until 1375
Carmina (Latin poems):		
I. 'Tu qui secura procedis' (*Elegia di Costanza*)	Florence, BML, 29. 8	*c.* 1341
II. 'Postquam fata sinunt' (to Checco di Meletto Rossi)	Florence, BML, 29. 8	*c.* 1347–8
III. 'Tempus erat placidum' ('Faunus', to Checco di Meletto Rossi)	Florence, BML, 29. 8	*c.* 1347–8
v. *Ytalie iam certus honos* (to Petrarch)	Vatican City, BAV, Chigi L. V. 176	1360s
VIII. 'Finis adest' (concluding rubric to Dante's *Comedy*)	Florence, BR, 1035 Vatican City, BAV, Chigi L. VI. 213	1360s 1360s
Decameron	Berlin, Staatsbibliothek Preussischer Kulturbesitz, Hamilton 90 (B)	*c.* 1370
De Canaria	Florence, BNC, Banco Rari 50	early 1350s
De mulieribus claris	Florence, BML, 90 sup. 98^I (L^I)	*c.* 1373
Epistole (Latin Epistles):		
I. 'Crepor celsitudinis' (to the Duke of Durazzo)	Florence, BML, 29. 8	*c.* 1339–40
II. 'Mavortis milex' (to Petrarch)	Florence, BML, 29. 8	*c.* 1339–40
III. 'Nereus amphytritibus' (addressee unknown)	Florence, BML, 29. 8	*c.* 1339–40
IV. 'Sacre famis' (addressee unknown)	Florence, BML, 29. 8	*c.* 1340
VI. 'Quam pium' (to Zanobi da Strada)	Florence, BML, 29. 8	*c.* 1348

Title	Location	Date
VIII. ///'expetentem arciquelocum' (first part missing; to Zanobi da Strada?)	Florence, BNC, Banco Rari 50	*c.* 1350–3
IX. 'Longum tempus' (to Zanobi da Strada, 13 April 1353)	Florence, BNC, Banco Rari 50	*c.* 1353
Genealogia deorum gentilium	Florence, BML, 52. 9	1360s
Teseida delle nozze d'Emilia	Florence, BML, Acquisti e doni, 325	1348–50
Trattatello in laude di Dante: First redaction	Toledo, Archivo y Biblioteca Capitulares, Zelada 104. 6	late 1350s or early 1360s
Second, shorter, redaction (first compendium)	Vatican City, BAV, Chigi L. v. 176	1360s
Private letter to Leonardo del Chiaro	Perugia, Archivio di Stato, Carte del Chiaro	20 May 1366

Boccaccio's archive books: compilations and copies of works by others

In the case of partial autographs, the date refers to Boccaccio's scribal interventions. Manuscripts that have been divided into separate volumes are presented below as separate tables, giving the contents and locations of their constituent parts.

Parchment notebook (*Zibaldone membranaceo*): Florence, BML, 29. 8 + BML, 33. 31[1]

'Zibaldone Laurenziano', includes Boccaccio, *Epistles* I–IV: *Allegoria mitologica*, 'Postquam fata sinunt', *Faunus* (1st redaction), *Elegia di Costanza*; *Notamentum*; Dante, *Epistles* XI, III, XII; Dante, *Eclogues*; 'Letter of Ilaro'; Andalò del Negro, *Tractatus spere materialis*; Juvenal; Walter Map; Jean de Meun; Petrarch, *Bucolicum carmen*, II ('Argus'); Petrarch, metrical Epistles I. 14, I. 4, I. 13, I. 12; Giovanni del Virgilio, *Eclogue* to Albertino Mussato; Giovanni del Virgilio's exchange with Guido Vacchetta; verses by St Thomas; Cicero excerpts; Greek alphabet and epigram	Florence, BML, 29. 8	Copied in three different phases: before 1330 (fols 26r–45r), 1330–4 (fols 2r–25v), 1338–48 (fols 46r–77r). Fol. 45v probably dates to 1367.

'Miscellanea Laurenziana', includes Pseudo-Virgil, *Culex, Dirae*; Persius, *Satires*; *Lamentatio Bertoldi*; Tetrastich in honour of St Miniato; Lovato Lovati, verses on Tristan and Isolde; Lydia; Ovid, *Ibis, Amores*; *Priapeia*; excerpts from Martial, Ausonius	Florence, BML, 33. 31	1338–48

Paper notebook (*Zibaldone Magliabechiano*): Florence, BNC, Banco Rari, 50 + Kraków, Biblioteca Czartoryskich, 2566[2]

'Zibaldone Magliabechiano', includes Boccaccio's Epistle IX to Zanobi da Strada; Epistle VIII; *De Canaria*; Paolino da Venezia, *Compendium* or *Chronologia magna*; Sallust, *De coniuratione Catilinae*; excerpts from Pliny; Seneca, *Florilegio*	Florence, BNC, Banco Rari 50	Dating is uncertain and varies between end of 1330s to mid-1350s.
Transcription of Petrarch's *Familiares*, XVIII. 15, sent to Boccaccio by Petrarch in November 1355, formerly fol. 115 of the 'Zibaldone Magliabechiano'	Kraków, Biblioteca Czartoryskich, 2566 (fol. 43)	After 1355

Florence, Biblioteca Riccardiana 627 (partial autograph) + London, British Library, Harley 5383 + Biblioteca Riccardiana 2795[VI]

Paulus Orosius, *Historiae adversus paganos*; Paul the Deacon, *Additamentum ad Eutropii Breviarium ab Urbe condita* (partial autograph: fols 29r–102v)	Florence, BR, 627	*c.* 1350
Paul the Deacon, *Historia Langobardorum* (up to Book VI, chapter 24)	London, British Library, Harley 5383	*c.* 1350
Paul the Deacon, *Historia Langobardorum* (from Book VI, chapter 24 onwards)	Florence, BR, 2795[VI]	*c.* 1350

Toledo Dante anthology:

Boccaccio, *Trattatello* (1st redaction); Dante, *Vita nova, Comedy* with Boccaccio's *Argomenti*, Dante, 15 canzoni (Latin rubrics; Homer portrait)	Toledo, Archivo y Biblioteca Capitulares, Zelada 104. 6 (To)	late 1340s to mid-1350s

Riccardiano Dante anthology:

Dante, *Comedy* with Boccaccio's *Argomenti*; Boccaccio, Latin poem *Finis adest longi Dantis cum laude laboris*; Dante, 15 canzoni (Vernacular rubrics; 7 illustrations)	Florence, BR, 1035 (Ri)	*c.* 1360

Dante and Petrarch anthology: Vatican City, BAV, Chigi L. VI. 213 + Vatican City, BAV, Chigi L. V. 176

Trattatello (2nd redaction); Dante, *Vita nova*; Cavalcanti, *Donna mi prega* and gloss by Dino del Garbo; Boccaccio, *Ytalie iam certus honos*; Dante, 15 canzoni; Petrarch, *Rerum vulgarium fragmenta* in Forma Chigi	Vatican City, BAV, Chigi L. V. 176	1363–6
Dante, *Comedy* with Boccaccio's *Argomenti*; Boccaccio, Latin poem *Finis adest longi Dantis cum laude laboris* (Longer vernacular rubrics)	Vatican City, BAV, Chigi L. VI. 213	1363–6
Martial, *Liber spectaculorum, Epigrammata*; John of Salisbury, *Entheticus in Policraticum*; Juvenal, *Satires*, x. 22, Latin verses	Milan, Biblioteca Ambrosiana, C 67 sup.	1370–2
Statius, *Thebaid*, with commentary by Lattanzio Placido (partial autograph)	Florence, BML, 38. 6	12th–13th century; B's interventions 1340–5.
Terence anthology: epitaph and life of Terence; *Andria, Eunuchus, Heautontimorumenos, Adelphoe, Hecyra, Phormio*	Florence, BML, 38. 17	1340–5, with later additions
Apuleius anthology: *Apologia, Metamorphoseon libri, Florida, De deo Socratis*	Florence, BML, 54. 32	1350–5, with later additions
Joseph of Exeter, *Ylias Frigii Daretis*	Florence, BML, Ashburnham App. 1856	*c.* 1355
Aristotle, *Nicomachaean Ethics*, Robert Grosseteste's Latin translation, with commentary by Thomas Aquinas (partial autograph)	Milan, Biblioteca Ambrosiana, A 204 inf.	1340–5

Manuscripts glossed by Boccaccio

The dates of Boccaccio's glosses are provided where available.[3] To the eleven glossed manuscripts noted by De Robertis (p. 329), we have also added two manuscripts sent from Boccaccio to Petrarch: the Dante manuscript, which contains textual variants in Boccaccio's hand ('Vat'), and the manuscript of Augustine's *Enarrationes in Psalmos,* which contains an autograph note in which Boccaccio names himself and gives the date.

Apuleius anthology: *Apologia, Metamorphoseon libri, Florida*	Florence, BML, 29. 2	1330s
Montecassino manuscript of Varro, Cicero, and Pseudo-Cicero: Varro, *De lingua latina;* Cicero, *Pro Cluentio;* Pseudo-Cicero, *Rhetorica ad Herennium*	Florence, BML, 51. 10	*c.* 1355
Flavius Josephus, *Antiquates Iudaicae,* Pseudo-Hegesippus, *Historiae*	Florence, BML, 66. 1	*c.* 1355
Juvenal, *Satires; Vita Iuvenalis; Accessus Satirarum; Vita Iuvenalis*	Florence, BML, 34. 39	undated
Lucan, *Pharsalia*	Florence, BML, 35. 23	undated
Ovid anthology: *Heroides, De somno, Fasti, Tristia, Ars amatoria, De medicamine faciei;* Pseudo-Ovid, *De nuce, De pulice, De speculo medicaminis, De Philomela;* Faltonia Proba, *Centones vergiliani*	Florence, BR, 489	undated
John of Wales, *Compendiloquium de vita et dictis illustrium philosophorum*	Florence, BR, 1230	undated
Petrarch's copy of Pliny, *Naturalis historia*	Paris, BNF, lat. 6802	late 1350s– early 1360s
Petrarch's copy of Claudian (Boccaccio contributes a drawing of a laurel-crowned head in profile with manicule)	Paris, BNF, lat. 8082	probably 1351
Petrarch's copy of Augustine, *Enarrationes in Psalmos*	Paris, BNF, lat. 1989^{1-2}	1355
Petrarch's copy of Paolino da Venezia, *Compendium sive Chronologia magna*	Paris, BNF, lat. 4939	*c.* 1355–6
Petrarch's historical miscellany, *Liber de regno Siciliae*	Paris, BNF, lat. 5150	*c.* 1356–60
Dante Alighieri, *Comedy* (gift to Petrarch)	Vatican City, BAV, Vat. lat. 3199 ('Vat')	*c.* 1350

Other manuscripts mentioned in this volume

Boccaccio's works

Decameron, copied by Giovanni di Agnolo Capponi (antigraph)	Paris, BNF, It. 482 (P)	*c.* 1360
Decameron and *Corbaccio*, copied by Francesco d'Amaretto Mannelli	Florence, BML, 42. 1 (Mn)	1384
Decameron	Florence, BML, 42. 3 (L²)	*c.* 1450–75
Decameron, illuminated by Taddeo Crivelli	Oxford, Bodleian Library, Holkham misc. 49	1475–1500
De mulieribus claris	Vatican City, BAV, MS Urbinate lat. 451 (Vu)	1450–1500
De casibus virorum illustrium	Vatican City, BAV, Ottoboniano Lat. 2145 (Vo)	1373–1400
Amorosa visione	Florence, BR, 1066	pre-1433

Works by other authors

Persius manuscript, from which Boccaccio copies into *Miscellanea Laurenziana*	Florence, BML 37.19	11th century
Cantare di Fiorio e Biancifiore	Florence, Biblioteca Nazionale Centrale, MS Magliabechiano, VIII. 1416	*c.* 1343

NOTES

1 For a full table of contents of the parchment *Zibaldone* according to its original ordering, see *Boccaccio autore e copista*, pp. 305–13.
2 For a full table of contents of the paper *Zibaldone*, see *Boccaccio autore e copista*, pp. 316–26.
3 On Boccaccio's copying practices, and a chronology of his copying and glossing activity, see *Boccaccio autore e copista*, pp. 329–35.

LIST OF EDITIONS AND TRANSLATIONS

All works of Boccaccio's are quoted in English translation. For those who wish to consult the works in the original languages, we also supply references to the relevant source text to enable readers to locate the appropriate passage. In referencing Boccaccio's works, we have used the critical editions published in the Mondadori series *Tutte le opere di Giovanni Boccaccio*, ed. by Vittore Branca, 10 vols (Milan: Mondadori, 1964–98), which have long been recognized as the standard editions, and which are widely available in university libraries. New editions continue to be published, and we have noted these where relevant. Each critical edition is referenced individually in the list of editions, below, with shortened forms given in the individual chapters.

There are likewise a vast number of Boccaccio translations available. For this Companion, we have used Harry McWilliam's well-loved translation for the *Decameron*, which was first published in 1972 by Penguin and revised for a second edition in 1993. This translation pays particular attention to the rendering of Boccaccio's authorial paratexts, such as titles and rubrics, which aligns with our own editorial attention to the materiality of the book-object and the mechanisms of Boccaccio's narrative strategies. All translations of the *Decameron*, unless specified otherwise, are taken from the most recent reprint of McWilliam's revised 1995 translation (below), with page numbers signalled within the individual chapters. For Boccaccio's other works, we have used the English translations signalled below, unless authors have provided their own renderings.

The transmission and reception history of Boccaccio is complex and unruly, and this textual instability is reflected in the many forms and names by which his works have been known over time. The table below provides a list of the critical editions and English translations referenced in each chapter, listed alphabetically. Texts are presented by the name by which they are best known in the original languages (Italian or Latin), and we note alternative titles as they are used within chapters. We have also provided an English translation of each title here, but refer to them with their Italian or Latin titles in the individual chapters. The table is thus directed towards both Boccaccio scholars and those who are coming to Boccaccio for the first time.

Title of work and English translation	Critical edition and preferred translated edition
Allegoria mitologica or *De mundi creatione* (*Mythological Allegory*)	*Allegoria mitologica*, ed. by Manlio Pastore Stocchi, in *Tutte le opere*, v. 2 (1994), 1091–1123
Amorosa visione (*Amorous Vision*)	*Amorosa visione*, ed. by Vittore Branca, in *Tutte le opere*, III (1974), 1–272; *Amorosa visione*, trans. by Robert Hollander, Timothy Hampton, Margherita Frankel, with an intro. by Vittore Branca (Hanover, NH: University Press of New England, 1986)
Argomenti (verse summaries of Dante's *Comedy*)	*Argomenti e rubriche dantesche*, ed. by Giorgio Padoan, in *Tutte le opere*, v. 1 (1992), 147–92
Buccolicum carmen (*Eclogues*) I: 'Galla' II: 'Pampinea' XIV: 'Olympia' XV: 'Phylostropos'	*Buccolicum carmen*, ed. by Giorgio Bernardi Perini, in *Tutte le opere*, v. 2 (1994), 689–1090; *Eclogues*, trans. by Janet Levarie Smarr (New York: Garland, 1987)
Caccia di Diana (*Diana's Hunt*)	*Caccia di Diana*, ed. by Vittore Branca, in *Tutte le opere*, I (1967), 1–43; *Diana's Hunt, Caccia di Diana: Boccaccio's First Fiction*, ed. and trans. by Anthony K. Cassell and Victoria Kirkham (Philadelphia: University of Pennsylvania Press, 1991)
Carmina (Latin poems): I. *Elegia di Costanza* (*Elegy of Costanza*) or *Verba puelle sepulte* V. *Ytalie iam certus honus* (*Already certain honour of Italy*)	*Carmina*, ed. by Giuseppe Velli, in *Tutte le opere*, v. 1 (1992), 375–492
Comedia delle ninfe fiorentine or *Ameto* (*Comedy of the Florentine Nymphs*)	*Comedia delle ninfe fiorentine*, ed. by Antonio Enzo Quaglio, in *Tutte le opere*, II, 665–835
Consolatoria a Pino de' Rossi (*Consolatory Letter to Pino de' Rossi*)	*Consolatoria a Pino de' Rossi*, ed. by Giorgio Chiecchi, in *Tutte le opere*, v. 2 (1994), 615–87

Corbaccio

Corbaccio, ed. by Giorgio Padoan, in
Tutte le opere, V. 2 (1994), 413–614
Giovanni Boccaccio, *The 'Corbaccio',
or 'The Labyrinth of Love'*, trans. by
Anthony K. Cassell, rev. edn
(Binghamton: Medieval and
Renaissance Texts and Studies, 1993)

*De casibus virorum illustrium (The
Fates of Illustrious Men)*

De casibus virorum illustrium, ed. by
Pier Giorgio Ricci and Vittorio
Zaccaria, in *Tutte le opere di
Giovanni Boccaccio*, 10 vols (Milan:
Mondadori, 1983), IX;
Giovanni Boccaccio, *The Fates of
Illustrious Men*, trans. and abridged
by Louis Brewer Hall (New York:
Frederick Ungar, 1965)

*De montibus, silvis, fontibus, lacubus,
fluminibus, stagnis seu paludibus et
de diversis nominibus maris (On
Mountains, Forests, Springs, Lakes,
Rivers, Marshes or Ponds and on the
Different Names of the Seas)*

*De montibus, silvis, fontibus, lacubus,
fluminibus, stagnis seu paludibus et
de diversis nominibus maris*, ed. by
Manlio Pastore Stocchi, in *Tutte le
opere*, VIII, 1815–2149

*De mulieribus claris (On Famous
Women)*

Giovanni Boccaccio, *Famous Women*,
ed. and trans. by Virginia Brown
(Cambridge, MA: Harvard University
Press, 2001)

De mundi creatione, see *Allegoria
mitologica*
*De origine, vita, studiis et moribus viri
clarissimi Dantis Alighierii Florentini
poete illustris et de operibus
compostis ab eode* see *Trattatello in
laude di Dante*
*De vita et moribus domini Francisci
Petracchi de Florentia* or *Vita
Petracchi (On the Life and Mores of
Francesco Petrarca of Florence* or *Life
of Petrarch)*

Vite di Petrarca, Pier Damiani e Livio,
ed. by Renata Fabbri, in *Tutte le
opere*, V. 1 (1992), 879–962

Decameron

Decameron, ed. by Vittore Branca, in
Tutte le opere, IV (1976)
Giovanni Boccaccio, *The 'Decameron'*,
trans. by G. H. McWilliam, 2nd edn
(London: Penguin, 2003)

Elegia di Costanza, see *Carmina*

Elegia di madonna Fiammetta (*Elegy of madonna Fiammetta*)

Elegia di madonna Fiammetta, ed. by Carlo Delcorno, in *Tutte le opere*, v. 2 (1994), 1–412

Esposizioni sopra la Comedia di Dante (*Expositions on Dante's Comedy*)

Esposizioni sopra la 'Comedia' di Dante, ed. by Giorgio Padoan, in *Tutte le opere*, VI (1965)

Boccaccio's Expositions on Dante's 'Comedy', trans. with introduction and notes by Michael Papio (Toronto: University of Toronto Press, 2009)

Epistole (Latin Epistles) and *Lettere* (Letters):
II: to a 'Valorous soldier of Mars'
IV: addressee unknown
X: to Petrarch
XV: to Petrarch
XVIII: to Niccolò Orsini
XIX: to Jacopo Pizzinga
XXII: to Mainardo Cavalcanti
XXIII: to Fra Martino da Signa

Giovanni Boccaccio, *Epistole e lettere*, ed. by Ginetta Auzzas and Augusto Campana, in *Tutte le opere*, v. 1 (1992), 493–856

Filocolo

Filocolo, ed. by Antonio Enzo Quaglio, in *Tutte le opere*, I, 45–675

Filostrato

Filostrato, ed. by Branca, in *Tutte le opere*, II (1964), 1–228

Genealogia deorum gentilium (*Genealogy of the Pagan Gods*)

Genealogia deorum gentilium, ed. by Vittorio Zaccaria, in Giovanni Boccaccio, *Tutte le opere di Giovanni Boccaccio*, ed. by Vittore Branca, 10 vols (Milan: Mondadori, 1998), VII–VIII, 1–1813;

Giovanni Boccaccio, Genealogy of the Pagan Gods, Volume 1 (Books 1–v), ed. and trans. by Jon Solomon (Cambridge, MA: Harvard University Press, 2011);

Boccaccio on Poetry: Being the Preface and the Fourteenth and Fifteenth Books of Boccaccio's 'Genealogia Deorum Gentilium', trans. by Charles G. Osgood (Indianapolis: Bobbs-Merrill, 1956)

Life of Dante, see *Trattatello in laude di Dante*

Ninfale fiesolano (*Nymphal of Fiesole*)   *Ninfale fiesolano*, ed. by Armando Balduino, in *Tutte le opere*, III (1974), 273–421

Rime (*Poems*)   *Rime*, ed. by Vittore Branca, in *Tutte le opere*, V. 1 (1992), 1–374

Teseida delle nozze d'Emilia (*Theseid of the Marriage of Emilia*)   *Teseida delle nozze d'Emilia*, ed. by Alberto Limentani, in *Tutte le opere*, II, 229–664

Trattatello in laude di Dante or *De origine, vita, studiis et moribus viri clarissimi Dantis Alighierii Florentini poete illustris et de operibus compostis ab eodem* or *Vita di Dante* (*Treatise in praise of Dante* or *Concerning the origins, life, studies and habits of that most great man and illustrious poet Dante Alighieri, and the works composed by him* or *Life of Dante*)   *Trattatello in laude di Dante*, ed. by Pier Giorgio Ricci, in *Tutte le opere*, III (1974), 423–538

Life of Dante, trans. by Philip Wicksteed (London: Oneworld Classics, 2009)

Verba puelle sepulte, see *Carmina*

Vita Petracchi, see *De vita et moribus domini Francisci Petracchi de Florentia*

Zibaldone laurenziano and *Miscelleanea laurenziana* or *Zibaldone membranaceo* (*Laurentian Notebook* and *Laurentian Miscellany* or *Parchment Notebook*)   *Lo Zibaldone Boccaccesco, Mediceo Laurenziano Pluteo XXIX, 8: riprodotto in facsimile*, ed. by Biblioteca Medicea Laurenziana, with preface by Guido Biagi (Florence: Olschki, 1915)

Zibaldone Magliabechiano or *Zibaldone cartaceo* (Magliabechian Notebook or *Paper Notebook*)

CHRONOLOGY

Boccaccio's life	Boccaccio's texts	Political and cultural events
1313 June/July. Born in Florence or nearby Certaldo to Boccaccio di Chellino, a merchant broker with the Florentine Bardi company.		1313 Petrarch's father, ser Petracco, moves from Tuscany with his family to Avignon.
1320s Tutored in elementary curriculum of grammar and arithmetic by Giovanni Mazzuoli da Strada, father of Boccaccio's friend Zanobi da Strada.		1321 Dante dies in Ravenna. 1323–6 Petrarch studies law in Bologna before returning to Avignon.
1327 Leaves Florence to join his father in Naples as an apprentice merchant working for the Bardi bank.		1328 Boccaccio's father, Boccaccio di Chellino, appointed *Consigliere* (Counsellor) to King Robert of Naples.
1330 Begins his studies in canon law at the University in Naples where Cino da Pistoia lectures in civil law. Frequents the court circles of King Robert of Naples.	1330s Begins to compose Latin *carmina* and vernacular *rime* to which he adds throughout his career; starts to copy classical and medieval texts into his *Zibaldone Laurenziano* and *Zibaldone Magliabechiano*.	1334 Andalò del Negro, astronomer and geographer at Angevin court in Naples and associate of Boccaccio, dies. 1334 Construction of the campanile of Florence cathedral begins.

c. 1333–8 *Caccia di Diana, Filostrato,* and *Filocolo.*

1337 1.3 million florins lent to Edward III of England by Florentine Bardi and Peruzzi companies.

1338 Giovanni Villani's chronicle describes the magnificence of Florence at the height of its power, one of the five largest and richest urban centres in Europe, with an estimated population of *c.* 90,000.

1340–1, winter. Returns to Florence with father in the wake of the collapse of the Bardi bank caused by Edward III defaulting on his bank loans.

c. 1339–40 Letter in Neapolitan dialect to Francesco de' Bardi, a Florentine merchant in Gaeta; four allegorical epistles in Latin; *Allegoria mitologica.*

1341 *Comedia delle ninfe fiorentine.* Possible start date of *De vita et moribus domini Francisci Petracchi de Florentia.*

1340 Florence hit by the plague, *c.* 15,000 die. The coup led by the Bardi magnate family fails.

1341 Petrarch crowned Poet Laureate in Rome after spending previous months as the guest of King Robert at the Angevin court in Naples.

1342 Walter of Brienne, the French military leader and nephew of King Robert of Naples, is appointed *Signore* (ruler) of Florence with the support of the city's elite.

1343 *Amorosa visione.*

1343 King Robert of Naples dies. Walter of Brienne expelled from Florence after ten months. Boccaccio's magnate friend, Pino de' Rossi, is instrumental in the expulsion. A broad-based popular government is instituted as the elite's power wanes.

c. 1344 *Elegia di madonna Fiammetta.* The *Ninfale fiesolano* also dates from the post-Neapolitan period but no precise date is attributed.

1344 Banking crisis in Florence resulting in the eventual bankruptcy of the Bardi, Peruzzi, and Acciaiuoli companies.

1345, September. Boccaccio di Chellino elected *Gonfaloniere di compagnia* (standard-bearer) for the Nicchio district in the quarter of Santo Spirito for four months.

1346 At the court of Ostagio da Polenta in Ravenna.

1347 At the court of Francesco Ordelaffi in Forlì.

c. 1346 Begins *Buccolicum carmen.*

1348 Boccaccio returns to Florence; his father and stepmother die in the plague. He is elected one of six communal *Ufficiali delle gabelle* (indirect tax collectors) for six months.

1350, September. Boccaccio is mandated by the *Capitani* of the *Compagnia della madonna di Orsanmichele* to deliver a charitable gift of 10 florins to Dante's

1348 Fictional date of the *Decameron*. First dated evidence for circulation of the text is 1360. Boccaccio continues to edit the text through the 1370s.

c. 1348–50 *Teseida delle nozze d'Emilia.*

1348 Black Death strikes Florence, killing over half the population. The elite in Florence recover influence under the leadership of the Parte Guelfa.

daughter, Sister
Beatrice, in Ravenna.
Acts as guarantor on
Jacopo Pucci's election
as one of the *Signori* of
Florence.

October. First encounter
with Petrarch at the
gates of Florence.

November. First known
commission as
communal ambassador
to the Romagna.

1350s Boccaccio copies
De Canaria into the
Zibaldone
Magliabechiano: a text
based on the letters of
Florentine merchants
involved in expedition
to the Canary Islands
in 1341.

1350 The Jubilee year
sees mass pilgrimages
to Rome.

Early 1350s Elected one
of two *Camerlinghi
della Camera del
comune* (Communal
treasurers) in 1350.
Registers and witnesses
the sale of Prato to
Florence by
procurators acting for
Niccolò Acciaiuoli and
King Robert of Naples.

Elected as *Difensore del
contado* (Overseer of
the territorial state)
(1351), *Ufficiale delle
gabelle del pane*
(Collector of indirect
taxes on bread)
(1352–3), *Ufficiale di
torre* (Communal
overseer of public
works and the city's
streets and bridges)
(1353–4), *Ufficiale dei
difetti* (Auditor of
mercenary troops)
(1355).

1353, July. Boccaccio
writes famous letter of
reproach to Petrarch
for subjecting himself
to Visconti tyrants
(Epistle x).

1353 Petrarch accepts
patronage of Giovanni
Visconti in Milan.

1354, May–June. Undertakes a mission to Pope Innocent VI in Rome as communal ambassador.

1355, April. Sends Petrarch an 11th-century manuscript of Augustine's *Enarrationes in Psalmos* (*Expositions on the Psalms*).

1359, June. Communal ambassador to Lombardy with brother Jacopo.

c. 1355? *Corbaccio.* Also dated to *c.* 1365? Begins first redaction of *De casibus virorum illustrium* and *De montibus.*

1359–60 Begins *Genealogia deorum gentilium.*

Mid-1350s–late 1360s Makes his three Dante compilations, including a biography, prose rubrics, and verse summaries.

1360, 13 July. First mention of existence of a manuscript of Boccaccio's *Decameron* in a letter by Francesco Buondelmonti.

1356 Battle of Poitiers. Death of Walter of Brienne.

1358 Parte Guelfa revives the practice of *ammonizione* (prohibitions) to discredit and ban opponents from office holding.

1360, December. Failed Magnate coup led by Pino de' Rossi and involving several of Boccaccio's close friends. Some executed and others, including Pino, exiled.

1361, July. Gifts house in the *popolo* of Santa Felicità to his younger brother Jacopo.

1362–3 Attempts to return to Naples using his connections with Niccolò Acciaiuoli.

1364, January. Included on the scrutiny lists for the three major civic councils by the Parte Guelfa, although he was never formally elected.

1361, January. *Consolatoria a messer Pino de' Rossi.* Begins first redaction of *De mulieribus claris* around this time.

1362 *Vita di san Piero Damiani* (Life of Saint Peter Damian) sent to Petrarch together with Epistle XI.

1361 Zanobi da Strada dies.

1364–5 Elected *Ufficiale dei castelli* (Overseer of fortifications).

1365, August–September. Communal ambassador to Pope Urban V, the College of Cardinals, and the Doge of Genoa together with Francesco Bruni. Makes first will and testament before leaving.

1367, April. Serves on arbitrational panel to evaluate the quality of the work undertaken on the tabernacle of Orsanmichele.

October. Elected *Ufficiale della condotta* (Overseer of mercenary troops).

November. Communal ambassador to Pope Urban V in Rome.

1373, 23 October. Begins first public lectures on Dante's *Comedy* in the Florentine Badia, paid for by the commune.

1374, 28 August. Latin version of Boccaccio's will, originally written in a vernacular autograph copy, is underwritten by notary ser Tinello de Pasignano.

1370 Drafts and revises autograph copy of the *Decameron* (Berlin, MS Hamilton 90).

1373–4 *Esposizioni sopra la Comedia*.

c. 1374 writes his own epitaph (*Carmina* x).

1373 Florentine population estimated at 55,000.

1374, 18 July. Petrarch dies in Arquà.

1375, 21 December. Boccaccio dies in Certaldo.

1377 Boccaccio's brother, Jacopo, takes legal action to secure restitution of the notebooks containing Boccaccio's *Esposizioni sopra la Comedia*.

1375 Coluccio Salutati becomes Chancellor of Florence and the Florentine 'War of the Eight Saints' against the Papacy begins.

1378 Rebellion of Florentine woolworkers, the *Ciompi*, who remove the Parte Guelfa elite from power; many of Boccaccio's friends are driven from Florence.

PART I

Locating Boccaccio

I

GUYDA ARMSTRONG, RHIANNON DANIELS, AND
STEPHEN J. MILNER

Boccaccio as cultural mediator

Networks

Was Boccaccio the most networked man in Trecento Italy? Simply posing this question allows us to begin to visualize the vast web of social, cultural, textual, political, and familial relations across which he operated. Boccaccio's literary standing alongside Dante and Petrarch as one of the three crowns of Italian literature is already familiar to us: he is the author of the world-famous story collection, the *Decameron*, at once the emblematic document of the Black Death in Europe and a repository of artful, erotic enterprises; he is also a proto-humanist, a learned friend, a follower of Petrarch, and an author of encyclopaedic scholarly works. But these familiar (predominantly literary) truisms give no sense of the scale of his astonishing achievements as a cultural mediator, his extraordinary interconnectedness, his revolutionary syntheses of intellectual domains, his social mobility, and political alignment. Even in his own time his mediating agency extended far beyond the bounds of the literary.

In a life spanning three-quarters of the century and which was lived the length of the Italian peninsula, Boccaccio was a poet and a reader, an author and an editor, an orator and a glossator, a merchant and an ambassador, a politician and a priest. To get a real sense of his reach and significance, we must abandon traditional biographical accounts and their linear timelines in favour of alternative models. Social network analysis shows that we are all single points in connected networks of association. Indeed with the advent of new digital media forms, we are increasingly used to locating ourselves in our own social networks, stretching across time and space, which we can now map with speed and complexity, tracing, registering, and (geo)locating our histories, friendships, encounters, and interests. Boccaccio was similarly well connected, and by viewing him as an actant in a social network, we can explore the multiplicity and complexity of the many relationships he had with different people (who are not simply limited to other authors), institutions, places, events, and domains of knowledge (not only literary, but also religious, political, and clerical). The breadth of his experiences, the extent of his networks, and the density of their interconnections make him a key nexus of mediation and exchange: a symbol for – and in fact a physical dealer in – literary and political transactions, inside and outside his texts. The network model would surely not seem unfamiliar to an author who created his own visualizations of social relations within his manuscript copies of the *Genealogia deorum gentilium* and whose own complex literary forms and multimedial reception history render him ideally suited to digital media as it continues to evolve (see Figure 1.1).[1]

Just as Boccaccio meets and mingles with many people, so his culture is a combinatorial one, in which a multiplicity of sources, languages, registers, and geographies link and combine. His literary works are underpinned by a complex mesh of sources which he collected and transcribed in vernacular dialects (both Florentine and Neapolitan), and Latin (both classical and medieval). We should remember that, as an office-holder in the Florentine commune, he was equally expert in the languages and registers of civic documentary cultures; he was also a trained canon lawyer, and later, a lay priest, equally adept in legal and clerical forms of mediation and intercession. Boccaccio's position in multiple, overlapping, networks enabled him to mediate between these different social and cultural domains, and create new textual forms, which in turn become new points in other networks.

To date scholarship has largely examined Boccaccio as a mediator within a literary context: his authorial self in the *Decameron* explicitly presents himself as a go-between and procurer.[2] But in his civic life, Boccaccio is also a procurer and broker: a man who borrowed and lent classical and vernacular texts, exchanged words as a communal ambassador and private correspondent, gave official and personal gifts, and oversaw the pecuniary transactions of the common wealth as city treasurer. His textual practices as a mediator are similar in both civic and literary domains: he is a record-keeper and underwriter of communal registers, he collects and distributes monies, lists (and enlists) as auditor of the city's mercenary companies; likewise in his literary life he lists, compiles, and copies texts into his *Zibaldoni*, as well as auditing the contents of libraries in search of classical texts, as he did so successfully in 1355 when he discovered previously unknown works by Cicero, Tacitus, and Varro at Montecassino. The transactional terminology found in his *texts* in this way derives from the everyday lexis of his working *contexts*, where his narrative pose as literary procurer literally reflects his paid employment as a communal one.

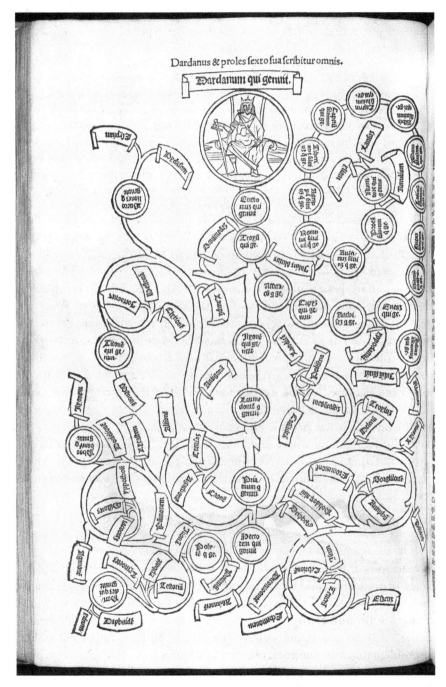

Figure 1.1 Proto-network visualization in an early printed edition of the *Genealogia*, after Boccaccio's autograph diagrams (Paris: Denis Roce, N. Hornken et sociorum, 1511), fol. 47v.

In his *Textual Cultures of Medieval Italy*, Will Robins has noted the habitual distinctions which obtain for different types of texts produced in late medieval Italy:

> Approaches to medieval textuality, especially editorial methods... customarily distinguish between two general species of texts: first, documentary 'acts' produced in the course of institutional administration (especially when an act stands as an official record or executive order), which are caught up in a tight web of legal, political, governmental, and archival apparatuses; and second, texts which are not juridical or contractual (for example, literary texts or scientific writings), and which harness narrative or discursive or expressive modes for bringing writers and readers into shared textual practices.[3]

Adhering to such distinctions is especially limiting in this case, since Boccaccio himself worked across both systems. Why has the civic, documentary record of Boccaccio's work been so obscured in favour of a historically deracinated study of his literary texts alone? Even the material forms of his books have been a minority interest until very recently, in comparison with the amount of attention paid to the content of the text. After all, 'texts (medieval or otherwise) consist of both an immaterial aspect (structured in the minds of readers and writers through literary form, propositional content, and conceptual patterns) and a material aspect (vocalized sound, ink on a page, etc.)'.[4] Why, indeed, has his autobiography for so long been premised on his literary texts, when many traces of the actual life lie in the archive? From the combined perspective of literary scholars and historians, it has become apparent that the material text-object is the natural meeting point where disciplines converge, as the manuscript record (albeit different kinds of manuscript record) becomes the means by which essential clues about Boccaccio's literary and socio-political interactions are revealed.

Mobilities

Boccaccio is above all else *mobile*: he moves within and between a wide range of contexts, as do his texts both during his life and in their multimedial afterlives. Textual scholars now talk about the fluid, mobile text, which changes form and function as it circulates and is republished in various media.[5] The canonical, authorized, critical edition is no longer the stable, unproblematized monument it once was. Boccaccio scholars themselves have moved away from a dogmatic attribution of chronological dating to a more fluid understanding of the mobility of Boccaccio's own texts, recognizing that he was an author who constantly revised and reworked the same texts across his life, leaving traces of multiple redactions both in autograph copies as well as embedded within the wider manuscript tradition. New technology now renders the reading of such three-dimensional works possible through the archaeological analysis of the different strata of ink deposits inscribed in the overwriting of the parchment and paper record.[6] Boccaccio himself, as author and scribe, makes the mobility of texts his signature compositional manoeuvre: his citational mechanisms move his sources into his own works, while his miscellany autograph manuscripts such as the *Zibaldone membranaceo*, or his copies of other authors' texts, such as his Dante compilations, reveal the ways in which he groups and collates sources, and how their internal juxtapositions and design decisions externalize his immense learning. As a cultural processor and early adopter, he acts as a literary mediator par excellence as he imports his sources into his writings, recombines them, and exports them out again to his readers (both historic and imagined).

But if the texts are mobile, then Boccaccio himself is even more so, in an extraordinary life of extraordinary social, geographical, and cultural range. Boccaccio's cultural mediation – in his literary work and his social worlds – arises from and is an expression of the various contexts within which he operated, contexts which are themselves more mixed and mobile than has sometimes been thought. For example, the reductive and traditional critical dichotomy often established in Boccaccio's biography between 'mercantile Florence' and 'chivalric Naples' underplays the complex political and cultural interrelations between the two centres. While there are certainly marked political and linguistic differences between them (Florence a republican commune, Naples a monarchy and the seat of King Robert of Anjou's court; one Tuscan-speaking, one French), in some ways Boccaccio's Naples was as mercantile and classical as his Florence was chivalric and French. Boccaccio is thus a product of this social, geographical, and cultural hybridity, and his ability as a mediator is a consequence of his facility in moving within and between these worlds.

We can learn much about this foundational hybridity and mobility from the career of Boccaccio's father, Boccaccio di Chellino. Boccaccio's father was a 'new man', a migrant from the country to the city who was granted Florentine citizenship and access to public office in 1320. He became a member of the major guild of bankers and money-changers, a councillor to the merchant court of the *Mercanzia*, and, during his political life, served as both a Prior of Florence and one of the standard-bearers (*Gonfalonieri*) of the city's popular militia charged with the city's security. As a member of the mercantile *popolo*, as opposed to the Magnate class of the old feudal aristocracy, it was his business interests that took him to Paris on two occasions in 1313 and 1332, whilst his transfer to Naples in late 1327 – as the main agent for the Florentine Bardi bank – also placed him in the world of aristocratic court culture. In fact, it was Boccaccio di Chellino's role in mediating between the Angevin court and communal Florence during the tenure of King Robert's son Carlo, Duke of Calabria, as *Signore* of Florence in 1326, that in all likelihood resulted in his transfer to Naples the following year. Once there, he acted as a broker in securing loans for the Neapolitan treasury and obtaining supplies for the army of the Duke of Calabria.

Boccaccio's transfer to Naples as a teenager to serve as an apprentice to his father in the Bardi bank, therefore, was a direct consequence of the interpenetration of mercantile and court cultures. In many ways the move prefigured his own professional career as civic office-holder and mediator between Naples and Florence. He, too, experienced the signorial rule of an Angevin military captain over Florence when the city's elite invited the French mercenary captain and Duke of Athens, Walter of Brienne, to assume signorial powers over the city in 1342. He, too, mediated between Naples and Florence as the communal treasurer who oversaw the sale of Prato to Florence by the King of Naples in February 1351. He, too, was involved in raising troops, but in this case for his fellow Florentines, in his role as overseer of the city's mercenary captains and their horse and infantry in the 1350s.[7]

The social mobility these relationships permitted to the second generation of the Florentine mercantile 'new men' is best illustrated by the career of Boccaccio's Florentine friend and associate, Niccolò Acciaiuoli, who also transferred to Naples to work for the family's banking company in 1331. Not only was Niccolò elevated to the post of Grand Seneschal of Naples by King Robert, but he was also made a knight, the highest social rank a king could confer. The assumption of the courtly attributes of chivalric culture by the growing class of communal knights in Florence illustrates perfectly the blurring of traditional social distinctions, as the revival of Magnate fortunes and the renaissance of the 'comune nobiliare' (commune led by the patrician elite) in Florence resulted in political instability and the perennial possibility that Florence's communal status could be threatened should it become a permanent Neapolitan protectorate under royal rule.

In a telling indication of the complexity of social relations at this time, the chronicler Marchionni di Coppo Stefani noted that the leading families in Florence during the rule of the Duke of Athens in 1342 were horrified that his French courtiers and soldiers, themselves representatives of the European feudal class, enjoyed better relations with the lower-class Florentines (the so-called *Ciompi*) than did the city's noble families; the word *Ciompo* being the artisan's response to the French invitation to drink, which was prefixed by the salutation *Compar*, meaning friend or ally. The 1340s–1370s in Florence were characterized, therefore, by tensions between an increasingly assertive and articulate urban aristocracy and a guild-based *popolo* both inhabiting the same social space in which chivalric and communal practices, values, and literary cultures ebbed and flowed, overlapping, merging, and clashing in what has been termed the fourteenth-century dialogue of power in Florence.[8]

Boccaccio makes no overt statements concerning his own social and political alignment in the struggle between the merchant 'new men' fresh from the countryside, the longer-established mercantile families of the *popolo grasso*, and the still-older aristocratic lineages. However, it is telling that he looked to court cultures for employment, first in Ravenna at the court of Ostagio da Polenta, and then at the court of Francesco Ordelaffi in Forlì. It was only in 1348, with the onset of the Black Death, that Boccaccio returned to Tuscany for the remainder of his life. Boccaccio died three years before the uprising of the *popolo minuto* and *Ciompi* woolworkers of 1378, but it is notable that it was his friends and neighbours from his own quarter of Santo Spirito, and the colleagues with whom he worked during his diplomatic missions, who suffered at their hands. Many saw their houses torched and their social standing challenged by the *Ciompi*'s own cohort of sixty communal knights, created in recognition of services to the *popolo* rather than as the result of any aristocratic or Magnate lineage. Boccaccio's associates and peers belonged to the social elite of knights, lawyers, and members of the Parte Guelfa, who sought to reform Florentine foreign policy to realign it with Angevin Naples and the Papacy, and to reduce the influence of the rising business class and guild regime. They represented the oligarchy that had controlled the government and economy of the city pre-1343. At their head were families with established Neapolitan (and Boccaccian) connections: the Bardi, Rossi, Acciaiuoli, Peruzzi, and Castellani, all led by Lapo da Castiglionchio, himself another close associate of Boccaccio who shared his literary and rhetorical interests.

Within the unstable political world of Florence in the mid-fourteenth century, Boccaccio was closely associated with major political upheavals. The Bardi, for example, led a Magnate attempt to overthrow the popular communal regime in 1340, whilst several of Boccaccio's closest friends, including fellow communal ambassador and knight, Pino de' Rossi, were involved in factional struggles within the elite and were either hanged or exiled for participation in a plot against the prevailing regime in 1360. It was after this incident that Boccaccio noticeably withdrew from the political world of communal office-holding for nearly five years. Such was the complex and unstable social reality which conditioned Boccaccio's textual practices and which he, in turn, read and represented in his works: a dense network of social relationships, professional associations, and communal roles across which flowed official and personal correspondence and through which passed texts of various types with Boccaccio acting as go-between.

Understood in these terms, Boccaccio's activities as a man of letters run parallel with his activities as a communal office-holder and his participation in the textual economy of the communal chancery and its associated documentary culture. One consequence of the rapid growth of the administrative offices and bureaucracy of the Florentine commune in the mid-fourteenth century was an explosion in governmental record-keeping as the complexity of social regulation and statutory reform increased. As a Florentine communal office-holder, diplomat, and cultural attaché from the 1340s onwards, Boccaccio was embedded in the administrative machinery of the commune and participated in its own official mediating practices. The increasing focus on the archival witness to Boccaccio's presence in these communal records and the conventions of communal record-keeping shows the continuity and interrelation between the practices of textual production and circulation in the communal and literary realms, and the correlation between communal and literary registers.

Similarly, the practices of recording, compiling, copying, listing, and corresponding were as civic as they were literary. The book-keeping and accounting skills Boccaccio learnt in Naples, therefore, were put to use in a variety of appointments from the late 1340s to the late 1360s, covering roles as diverse as *Ufficiale delle gabelle* (Collector of indirect taxes) in 1348, *Difensore del contado* (Overseer of the territorial state) in 1351, *Camerlingho della Camera del commune* (Communal treasurer) in early 1351, *Ufficiale del pane* (Collector of taxes on bread) in 1352–3, *Ufficiale di torre* (Communal overseer of public works and the city's streets and bridges) in 1354, *Ufficiale dei difetti* (Auditor of mercenary troops) in 1355, and *Ufficiale della condotta* (Communal overseer of the armed forces) in 1368 (see Figure 1.2). All these offices required the keeping of records, the collating of accounts, the rogation of registers, the constant switching between Latin and the vernacular, and the supply and use of the self-same materials of paper, parchment, ink, and quills that Boccaccio used in his literary production. Amongst the payments listed during Boccaccio's tenure as Communal Treasurer, for example, is the sum of twenty-two lire to one Filippo di Giovanni, *cartolaio* (stationer), for the supply of office stationery.[9] In the same capacity, Boccaccio oversaw payments to Antonio Pucci as town crier and Andrea Lancia as ambassador,

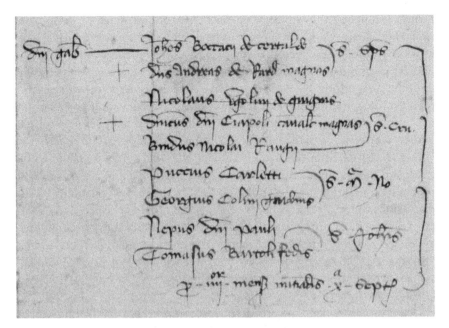

Figure 1.2 Giovanni Boccaccio extracted for a four-month term as one of eight *Ufficiali delle gabelle*, communal tax collectors, September–December 1348 (Archivio di Stato di Firenze, *Capitoli registri*, 28, fol. 77r.)

both of whom were also writers, compilers, and translators whose textual and oral practices straddled the civic and the literary, the vernacular and the classical. Accounting for Boccaccio, therefore, is as much a financial as a literary activity. Boccaccio's financial affairs as listed in the 'libro delle mie ragioni' that he mentions in his will coexisted alongside his other famous literary testimony, the 'libro di ragionamenti' we know as the *Decameron*.

Reconsidering the interrelation between Boccaccio's literary voicing and the verbal economy of the commune also serves to highlight the overlap and creative synergies between the two activities and the interpenetration of his poetic, rhetorical, and dictaminal practice. To date the archive has rendered no speeches given or diplomatic letters written by Boccaccio as a communal diplomat and cultural ambassador. We know he was sent on ambassadorial commissions to the Emperor Ludwig of Bavaria in 1351, to Padua to invite Petrarch to take a position at the Florentine *Studio* in 1352, to Pope Innocent VI in Avignon in 1354, and to Pope Urban V in 1365 and 1367. As communal spokesperson he was mandated to speak on behalf of the commune as *portavoce* of the Florentine body politic. Set-piece orations by fellow ambassadors and friends sent on similar missions such as Lapo da Castiglionchio and Luigi Gianfigliazzi have survived and furnish examples of the kinds of epideictic rhetoric expected on such occasions. Boccaccio would also have sent back diplomatic reports during such missions, although the record-keeping and archive practices of the communal chancery did not begin to collect such correspondence systematically until the early 1390s. He would also have been expected to provide an oral report to the relevant magistracy on his return. We know that as a communal official he attended the commune's deliberative assemblies as a formal witness who testified to the faithful recording of the debates and subsequent voting as registered in the so-called *Libri fabarum*, a role also fulfilled by Pucci and Lancia. In the legal realm he both appointed and acted as a legal procurator, granting and accepting powers of attorney in relation to legal discussions concerning the affairs of friends and family, whilst as a commentator on visual culture he was also a member of the arbitrational committee appointed to deliberate over the merits of the work undertaken on Andrea Orcagna's gothic tabernacle of the Orsanmichele in 1367, having commissioned two altarpieces himself for the church of SS Jacopo e Filippo in Certaldo a year earlier.

Given the prominence afforded virtuoso preachers in his literary works and his own labour in collecting both tracts of the *ars predicandi* (art of preaching) tradition and numerous holy relics during his many travels, it is tempting to imagine Boccaccio as preacher. He was, after all, a trained canon lawyer versed in the arts of rhetoric and dialectic and he would doubtless have witnessed King Robert perform one of his numerous sermons whilst growing up and studying in Naples, the 289 known incipits testifying to the king's propensity for public oratory.[10] We know that Boccaccio secured a Papal bull from Innocent VI in 1360 which referred to him as a 'clerico fiorentino' (Florentine cleric) and granted him permission to hold ecclesiastical benefices, a privilege which allowed him to exercise pastoral ministry over a specific jurisdiction. As yet, the archive has rendered no definitive information concerning the possibility of a Boccaccio *predicatore* (preacher), but his final will and testimony lists all the apparatus of priestly ministry which would have been used in the celebration of the mass: breviary, chasuble, stole, maniple, and associated altar furniture, including the cushions on which liturgical books would have rested.[11] Evidence of the vestments and accoutrements of religious practice remained even if the voice, as yet, is not heard.

Reconstructing these networks of association and practice helps furnish the context for Boccaccio's literary activity and provides a framework, a cultural *cornice*, which allows us to make sense of the complex interrelation and overlapping of his mediating practices. The continual imbrication of his communal and literary roles and interests can be seen, for example, by taking one year alone: 1350. In this year Boccaccio was mandated as a Florentine ambassador to the Romagna, undertook a parallel cultural mission on behalf of the Company of Orsanmichele to deliver a charitable gift of ten florins to Dante's daughter, Sister Beatrice, in Ravenna, and was then sent as the Florentine cultural attaché to meet Petrarch at the city's borders when he visited Florence in October. This famed historic encounter is an emblematic moment of cultural mediation and exchange, as Boccaccio introduced Petrarch to his learned Florentine circle of friends, Zanobi da Strada, Francesco Nelli, Lapo da Castiglionchio, and most probably both Luigi Gianfigliazzi and Francesco Bruni. They in turn were able to show Petrarch previously unknown rhetorical texts including Quintilian's *Institutiones* and some Ciceronian orations, texts Petrarch would later request in early 1351, in exchange for a copy of Cicero's *Pro Archia*, the oration Petrarch discovered in 1333 and which he held to be the foundational manifesto of classical scholarship in its legal defence of poetry. No moment better symbolizes the fusion of legal, rhetorical, and literary concerns in both form and content and their transmission across networks at once official and personal. And these diplomatic, social, and textual exchanges were reciprocated: just as Boccaccio hosted Petrarch in his own house when he passed through Florence on his way to Rome in 1350, so Florentine émigrés and associates hosted Boccaccio when he undertook missions beyond the city, as, for example, when Francesco Bruni put him up in Avignon in 1354 and on his return to Naples in 1355, affective bonds being cemented during official business.

Boccaccio's activity as a consumer and transmitter of texts is integral to our understanding of his literary practice. His literary innovations as the inventor of new rhyme forms and literary genres drive out of his processing of the multiple forms of documentary cultures – both literary and non-literary – which travel into and out of his literary works. Boccaccio's personal experience of both Florence and Naples, and the cultures of commerce and exchange operating along the mercantile and chivalric networks connecting cities inside and outside the peninsula, created an exceptionally rich textual culture on which he could draw. What some scholars have termed the 'invasion' of French culture in the twelfth century gave rise to an influx of new literary and scholarly genres, including – but not limited to – the study of classical *auctores* (authorities), vernacular romances, epic poetry, the *fabliau* tradition, instruction in the notarial arts, *dictamina*, and legal commentary. Brunetto Latini's encyclopaedic *Li Livres dou trésor* rubbed shoulders with manuscript copies of the French *Li Fait des Romains*, and collections of Occitan poetry. Both the dynastic families of the magnate class, steeped in the values of chivalry and the codes of honour and vendetta characteristic of the aristocratic nobility, and the increasingly assured merchant class of the popular regime with its burgeoning civic bureaucracy were keen consumers of these traditions: tapping into the same fields of reference with different audiences and purposes in mind.

Boccaccio's education reflects this cultural hybridity and its inherent flexibility of genres, registers, and languages. In Florence he learnt the rudiments of Latin grammar from Giovanni Mazzuoli da Strada (the father of Boccaccio's friend and fellow humanist, Zanobi), which was followed by his Neapolitan apprenticeship in the arts of vernacular book-keeping and arithmetic under his father's mercantile tutelage. Later, he spent almost six years studying canon law at the Neapolitan *Studium* with the famous Tuscan exile and lawyer-poet, Cino da Pistoia. The illusion of genteel courtly pursuits as expressed through Boccaccio's Neapolitan literary production (for example, the *Caccia di Diana, Filocolo, Filostrato*) gives no account of his implication in the complex business interests and military-political and legal concerns of the Neapolitan state. But beyond the fictions, we should not forget, as noted above, that Boccaccio grew up working in a Florentine expatriate business community that underwrote the financial and logistical workings of the imperial court, and which included in its number both the Acciaiuoli and Peruzzi families. If King Robert 'the wise' looked to Florence for financial muscle, he also looked beyond Naples to recruit leading minds to the Angevin court as part of his enlightened patronage. These included the astronomer Andalò del Negro from Genoa; the royal librarian and literary commentator Paolo da Perugia; the Augustinian theologian and classicist Dionigi da San Sepolcro, who had taught in Paris and Avignon and acted as Petrarch's confessor; the Bolognese chancellor and Dante commentator Graziolo de' Bambaglioli, who came to Naples on his exile in 1334; and the Venetian cleric, geographer, and political writer Fra Paolino Minorita, amongst many more. Boccaccio was thus located right in the middle of this eclectic community of migrant scholars and poets, whose expertise covered francophone culture, the vernacular lyric, classical literature, science and natural philosophy, and legal commentary.

This unusually rich mix both informs his literary ambitions and accounts for the ease with which he moves between an astonishing range of subjects in his writings, as an author of vernacular and Latin, prose romances and *novelle*, epic and lyric poetry, scholarly encyclopaedias and biographical compendia. From the early experiments in Dantean terza rima (*Caccia di Diana*) to later Petrarch-scale scholarly compilations (*De mulieribus claris, De casibus virorum illustrium, Genealogia, De montibus*), Boccaccio is in constant dialogue with literary traditions (classical or vernacular, homiletic or political, to name but a few), as well as drawing on compositional practices which had a wider sociological relevance within the commune, such as legal formulae and the art of rhetoric, to create a multi-faceted and nuanced model of authorship.

Textual mediations

Within his literary texts, Boccaccio performs his attentiveness to mediation and dialogue via a complex interplay of narrative voices, which he – unusually for his day, and especially in comparison to Dante and Petrarch – genders both male and female. The manner in which male narrators mediate the text for the benefit of their female audiences performs a central role. Most famously, he gave the *Decameron* the subtitle 'Prince Galahalt', establishing a literary genealogy with the knight who acted as go-between in the ill-fated chivalric affair between Lancelot and Guinevere, whose story in turn inspired the infamous lovers confined to Dante's *Inferno*, Paolo and Francesca, to commit their own adultery. The illicit, erotic, dimension to this act of procurement, combined with an authorial voice that is frequently labelled as ambiguous and self-effacing, has tended to result in the idea of mediation as a slippery and untrustworthy narrative mode. This has dominated a reading of Boccaccio's canon to the detriment of appreciating the sophistication of his ability to submerge and efface himself in multiple text-types and authorial modes. The attention to female voicing is a similarly problematic feature of Boccaccio's posthumous reception. While his engagement with the question of women and representations of various female subject-positions within his works is surely one of the principal factors which has contributed to his mass popularity, and perhaps even to his survival, by the same measure his 'female' content is the factor which has confined his reputation to a subordinate position relative to his masculine, and therefore more 'serious', literary cousins, Dante and Petrarch, and which has also, historically, created distortions in his traditional literary biography.

Boccaccio's extraordinary mediation skills within his literary and scholarly texts are thus also prominently located in the contested territories of gender studies. The *Decameron* is his best-known and most overt performance of literary mediation understood in terms of relations between the sexes, but he also wrote works explicitly concerned with first-person female voicing (*Elegia di madonna Fiammetta*), the scholarly cataloguing of women of cultural import (*De mulieribus*), and a text which contains a vituperative invective documenting the manifold flaws and fundamental inferiority of women (*Corbaccio*). Rather than merely considering gender within the world of the text (and thus always mediated by the historical author) we can also use it as part of a broader sociological focus which illuminates both Boccaccio's contemporary contexts and afterlife survival. In the context of Petrarch's Latin rendering of Boccaccio's Griselda story (*Decameron*, x. 10), David Wallace has noted how Petrarch's works are powerfully gendered towards an elite, male, Latin-literate network of readers, thereby 'perform[ing] powerfully gendered, social work' which excludes women even while they are the subject matter.[12] It would be facile indeed to argue that Boccaccio's writings were not part of these self-same masculine networks, and thus it becomes even more urgent to deduce why Boccaccio socializes his texts through and to female audiences, interlocutors, and characters.

The uniqueness of Boccaccio's achievements in voicing his polyphonic gendered narratives derives directly from his command of vernacular and classical poetic and prose genres. Women are the prism through which he *reads* literary production: they are the means through which he explores notions of writing and reading, the negotiation between work and leisure, pleasure and duty, and the erotics of the literary exchange. Here, as in so much else in his career, there is a clear continuity between his earliest and later works. His instinct to break new generic ground, using female subjects, can be seen from his very first literary work, the *Caccia di Diana*, through to his later Latin non-fictional production of the *De mulieribus*, and his encyclopaedic antifeminist text, the *Corbaccio*. Sole among the *tre corone*, he prioritizes the Latin and French vernacular amatory genres, which by tradition allow the exploration of a gendered exchange of views, and their reworked presence can be found across his oeuvre: the subject of women as construed in the francophone tradition of the debates of the *querelle des femmes* and the *jeux partis* situated in the staging of the questions of love in the *Filocolo*, or the courtly tale-telling of the *Decameron*; the classical elegy of Ovid's *Heroides* reworked in the *Fiammetta*; the low-register sex wars of the *fabliaux* replayed in *Decameron novelle* and the tricks of the widow in the *Corbaccio*. In Boccaccio, women serve as the expression of genre, and the act of textual generation; they are in the frontline of his authorial explorations of uses of reading (knowledge) and its licit expression; sometimes hated, sometimes celebrated, but a perennial point of tension and discussion.

Much ink has been expended on the question of Boccaccio's feminism, which has risen and then declined as a theme in Boccaccio studies as academic feminisms have evolved over the past forty years or so. Yet, proportionally, very little has yet been spilled on Boccaccio's historical women, or the agency of women associated with the production, dissemination, reception, and survival of these texts. This aspect of his life, and work, has been historically skewed, firstly, by scholarly lack of interest in the subject until relatively recently, and secondly, and more importantly, by the problematic slippage on the part of critics between Boccaccio's literary 'autobiography' and the actual events of his life. Scholarship has now abandoned the centuries-old trope of his supposed love affair with 'Fiammetta', the illegitimate daughter of King of Naples, but the notion of a personal 'conversion narrative' still endures, which reads his turn to writing Latin compilatory works in later life, and especially the strident invective in the *Corbaccio*, as a result of a romantic reverse at the hands of a feckless widow.

We know, of course, that the lives of medieval women do not register in the archive in the same way as do those of men, who are office- and property-owners, yet the critical disregard to date for the women in his life (as opposed to the 'women' in his works) means that it is even harder to locate this fundamental issue within the material evidence which survives. The gaps and absences in the historical record, coupled with the partiality of archival research, leave us wondering not only who and where Boccaccio's mother is located, but also who and where the mother of his own (many) children might be found. Yet even in the absence of hard data, we can nevertheless get a sense of the negative spaces in the network and connect together fragments of metadata. Hence in the context of gender, for example, we can open up the discussion to wider expressions of female agency than just the actions of the fictional women in the texts.

Indeed, the gendered co-ordinates of his networks of contacts are inscribed in Boccaccio's writings just as much as are his citations from his favourite *auctores*. History's obsession with the illegitimate princess Maria d'Aquino as the real-life model for Fiammetta has sometimes obscured the realities of Boccaccio's elite female readers in Naples in the 1360s and 1370s, where for example we find Andrea Acciaiuoli as the dedicatee for the *De mulieribus*. Mainardo Cavalcanti's female relatives are implicit in the discussion concerning the suitability of the *Decameron* as reading matter for women (the subject of the notorious letter Boccaccio writes to Mainardo apparently forbidding his womenfolk to read his works), and there is also evidence that Queen Giovanna (herself the subject of the last life in the *De mulieribus*) owned a copy of the *De casibus*, the oldest surviving manuscript witness to this text.[13] Radiating out from these early contexts, over time, more and more women feature in the ongoing dialogues and dissemination of Boccaccio's works through translation and adaptation: Christine de Pizan, who takes on the *De mulieribus* in her *Cité des Dames*; the printing nuns of San Jacopo di Ripoli, who produce an incunable *Decameron* in 1483; and Marguerite de Navarre, who composed her own *Heptaméron* in imitation of Boccaccio's *Decameron*. These instances are individually well known, but have not yet been joined up and integrated into the master narratives of

Boccaccio's afterlife. For women as authors, translators, printers, artists, or scholars, therefore, there is an index of production and reception that still remains to be written.

Whilst some aspects of Boccaccio's mediating role continue to be valorized, revisited, and contested, other parts of the network are currently in darkness or may never come to light. The invisibilities in Boccaccio's social network and the occlusions of humanistic scholarship are not a uniquely gendered problem in Boccaccio studies. Despite the representation of so many classes and nations in the *Decameron*, there is no sustained subaltern voice and experience.[14] For example, the actual participation of lower-class characters in the diegesis – when Licisca and Tindaro interrupt the *brigata* in the introduction to Day VI – is played purely for comic effect. Likewise, in stark contrast to the vibrant and complex literary portrait which we can draw for Boccaccio as poet, the evidence for the kaleidoscopic textual processing which he undoubtedly performed in the role of communal office-holder is conspicuously sketchy. It is not possible to do more than gesture at his combinatory textual practices in a non-literary context because this remains at present a dark part of the network. We have only the epistles and letters which Boccaccio authored as a private individual to other private individuals, and these, more often than not, represent an intertextual mingling between the public and the private, the literary and the non-literary. Increasing attention continues to be paid to Boccaccio's implication in the textual economy of the Florentine commune and its processes of documentary production and circulation, and it is hoped that more documents directly evidencing financial and political transactions issued in his name, or records of orations that he delivered on his ambassadorial missions, may yet come to light.

This volume cannot therefore offer any quick solutions to the gaps in the historical record, or effect a wholesale refocusing of critical attention on to specific aspects of his work and reception; but in paying particular attention to the material and the contextual, we aim to raise critical awareness of the uneven visibility of Boccaccio's mediations to date, and emphasize the ample scope which exists for further interrogation of his multiple reception contexts as we continue to explore his cultural and literary significance.

NOTES

1 The 'Decameron Web' hosted by the Department of Italian Studies at Brown University is an early example of Boccaccio's digital reception: http://www.brown .edu/Departments/Italian_Studies/dweb/index.php; as the medium matures, more sophisticated models continue to emerge, such as the digital networking project

'Kindred Britain', where Nicholas Jenkins describes genealogy as the 'first self-conscious use of network understanding', in his introduction: 'Originating Kindred Britain'; http://kindred.stanford.edu/#.

2 Francesco Bruni, *Boccaccio: l'invenzione della letteratura mezzana* (Bologna: Il Mulino, 1990).

3 William Robins, 'Introduction', in *Textual Cultures of Medieval Italy*, ed. by William Robins (Toronto: University of Toronto Press, 2011), pp. 3–9 (p. 5).

4 Robins, 'Introduction', p. 4.

5 John Bryant, *The Fluid Text: A Theory of Revision and Editing for Book and Screen* (Ann Arbor: University of Michigan Press, 2002). Part IV of this Companion examines the fluidity of Boccaccio's work in a range of reception contexts.

6 William E. Coleman, '*Teseida delle nozze d'Emilia*', in *Boccaccio autore e copista*, ed. by Teresa de Robertis and others (Florence: Mandragora, 2013), pp. 89–93.

7 Z. Zafarana, 'Boccaccio di Chellino' and N. Sapegno, 'Boccaccio, Giovanni', in *Dizionario biografico degli italiani* (Rome: Istituto della encyclopedia italiana, 1968), X, 835–8; 838–56.

8 John M. Najemy, *A History of Florence 1200–1575* (Oxford: Blackwell, 2006), pp. 124–55.

9 Archivio di Stato di Firenze, Camera del Comune, Camarlinghi, Uscita 75, fol. 12v.

10 Darleen N. Pryds, *The King Embodies the Word: Robert d'Anjou and the Politics of Preaching* (Leiden: Brill, 2000), p. 126.

11 Laura Regnicoli, 'Documenti su Giovanni Boccaccio', in *Boccaccio autore e copista*, pp. 385–93 (p. 392).

12 David Wallace, '*Letters of Old Age*: Love between Men, Griselda, and Farewell to Letters (*Rerum senilium libri*)', in *Petrarch: A Critical Guide to the Complete Works*, ed. by Victoria Kirkham and Armando Maggi (Chicago: University of Chicago Press, 2009), pp. 321–30 (p. 325).

13 See MS Vo in List of manuscripts.

14 David Wallace, 'Humanism, Slavery and the Republic of Letters', in *The Public Intellectual*, ed. by Helen Small (Oxford: Blackwell, 2002), pp. 62–88.

2

BEATRICE ARDUINI

Boccaccio and his desk

We have a reasonable understanding of some of the main events in Boccaccio's biography and work continues to be done to trace his network of literary influences. Though it is well known that Boccaccio was a prolific writer and a conscientious scribe and note keeper, there is still much to be learned about the processes by which he gathered, processed, and created texts, from his youth in Naples to his mature output in Florence. Boccaccio's activity as a scribe of his own works, and as a copier of others' works – documented within what are referred to as autograph manuscripts – has left a large legacy of codices. This chapter will use these autographs to consider what was on his desk in terms of tools and materials, and the techniques of his writing practice. It will describe the particularities of Boccaccio's scribal practice, such as his choice of support material, script, layout, and decoration, as well as the features of the physical structure and presentation of his autograph manuscripts and how they compare with contemporary manuscripts, since these can offer information about how Boccaccio processed texts and produced his works. While we do not have hard evidence of texts written in Dante's hand, the wealth of Boccaccio's extant manuscript production gives us the best evidence for this study. The material record, provided by the texts he chose to include in his transcriptions and by the traces of his readings in commentaries, glosses, and illustrations, triggers thoughts about his own way of gathering, processing, and creating texts, and of influencing and controlling the publication and readership of his works.

Boccaccio's extant autograph manuscripts date from as early as 1333 to the mid-1370s. Marco Cursi has recently listed and dated seventeen codices transcribed by Boccaccio, as well as another eleven manuscripts which he annotated, in addition to a single letter addressed to Leonardo del Chiaro.[1] The extant autographs are characterized by the variety of textual typologies adopted by Boccaccio, ranging from his own literary works written in both Latin and Italian, including the *Decameron*, copied into the autograph manuscript Berlin, Staatsbibliothek Preußischer Kulturbesitz, MS Hamilton

90, which is the source of all modern editions; copies of classical works, such as Martial's *Epigrams*, and the rare *Liber spectacolorum*, in Milan, Biblioteca Ambrosiana, MS C 67 sup.; a vernacular letter; compilations of material, including anthologies of works by and about Dante, as well as his *Zibaldoni* (described as 'working notebooks' by Claude Cazalé Bérard) – manuscripts containing notes, compendia, and excerpts of texts by different authors, written by Boccaccio for himself, with annotations and extensive marginal glosses.[2] There are three of these notebooks, two of which were once joined together: the pair of parchment manuscripts known as the *Zibaldone Laurenziano* (Florence, Biblioteca Medicea Laurenziana, MS 29.8) and *Miscellanea Laurenziana* (Florence, Biblioteca Medicea Laurenziana, MS 33. 31); the third notebook is made of paper and known as the *Zibaldone Magliabechiano* (Florence, Biblioteca Nazionale Centrale, MS Banco Rari 50).[3] New autograph manuscripts continue to be discovered, including most recently a copy of Paul the Deacon's *History of the Lombards*, which contains a gloss by Boccaccio cross-referencing the plague in Florence of 1348.

The contents of Boccaccio's desk

Following contemporary scribal practices, Boccaccio's desk would have contained writing tools such as pens, ink, and a penknife for sharpening his pen and for erasing mistakes made in copying. All literate people prepared their own pens, but unfortunately medieval instructions for the cutting of pens have not survived. We know that the best pens were made of goose feathers, which are strong yet flexible. We do, however, have a number of medieval recipes for making ink, which was thicker and more glutinous than modern commercial ink. Although there were two completely different types of ink (carbon ink and metal-gall ink, usually iron gall), most late medieval manuscripts were written with iron gall. Holding a knife in one hand and resting it against the surface of the parchment would have also helped steady the writing material. Cursi points out that in the autograph copy of the *Decameron* Boccaccio resorts to erasure to eliminate a rubric which was originally written below the summary of *novella* 1. 6 (fol. 9v), rather than to correct single, unwanted, words.[4] He also employs a method of correcting in which he places dots under unwanted letters or strikes through them, and then writes the correct letters above the original, uncorrected, ones.[5]

Medieval pictures of scribes often show two inkhorns on the right side of the desk, and some illustrations also show portable pen cases and inkpots made of leather for scribes who travelled or for storage between writing sessions. One inkpot was for black ink and the other for red ink, which was used for headings, running-titles and initials, and rubrics. Red ink was also used to introduce a text and to break the page into visual sections. In his autograph copy of the *Decameron*, Boccaccio used red ink for the rubrics of the days and the tales, and he traced little guide-letters for another hand to execute the large decorated capital letters in red, which correspond to four lines of text and tell the days apart, and the smaller capital letters in red and turquoise which mark the beginnings of the tales and the *ballate*; these are only two lines of text high. As Armando Petrucci notes, in at least one case the rubricator misread Boccaccio's guide-letter and decorated a capital U, instead of a capital S.[6] Boccaccio did not correct the mistake, and the capital S was reinstated by a later hand, but this accident shows that the system of presentation of a text can be reshaped not only by the copier, who coincides with the author of the text in the case of MS Hamilton 90, but also by the rubricator.

Copying and annotating were clearly part of Boccaccio's cultural and artistic programme, and his decision to act as his own copyist, instead of employing a professional scribe as Petrarch usually did, reveals his awareness and appreciation of the relationship between the presentation and content of the text. In MS Hamilton 90 Boccaccio's use of different sized and colour-coded capital letters expresses the hierarchies on the page. A third and smaller type of capital, which occupies only one line of text, signals the changes in the narrative voices within the tales, such as the beginning of the story after the narrator's opening words and the reflections by the narrator from the *brigata* at the beginning, or exceptionally, at the end of the *novella*. For medieval audiences this careful hierarchy of decorative initials would have been an important orientation device. The material dimension of Boccaccio's sophisticated system of voicing is now recognized in the latest edition of the *Decameron*, which reproduces the system of initials from MS Hamilton 90 using three different sizes of initial printed in bold type.[7]

Boccaccio, as a scribe, would be sitting with the copy from which he had to reproduce the text (referred to as the exemplar) set on a lectern just above his writing-desk. In addition to there being slots for the pens and inkhorns, the manuscripts were held open by the scribe with his knife, and also by weights hanging from each end of a string, similar to those used in today's libraries. Scribes sat very upright at the writing desk, often, judging from pictures, on tall backed chairs. Quill pens are most effective when held at right angles to the writing surface because the ink flows better, and this is easier to achieve on a tilted desk. Since the quill was held more vertically than a modern pen, the movement was all from the arm and the hand did not touch the page, unlike using a modern pen, which requires more finger control. Writing was therefore a tiring practice, especially for the formal, careful scripts used in high-quality works. For example, Martin Eisner suggests that it could have taken Boccaccio forty-five workdays to copy out Dante's *Comedy*.[8] We can only imagine the toll it took on Boccaccio, who copied out the *Decameron* found in MS Hamilton 90, as well as undertaking to gloss Dante's *Comedy* for public readings in the Church of Santo Stefano in Badia in Florence, towards the end of his life. As a result, MS Hamilton 90 contains more transcription errors than one would expect from an autograph manuscript.

In fourteenth-century Italy Boccaccio could choose between parchment and paper for his writing materials. Paper had become a relatively common material by this date, although parchment was linked to works of higher status. Parchment was made from animal skin, usually calfskin, sheepskin, or goatskin, which was prepared to make it suitable for writing upon. Medieval paper, on the other hand, was obtained from linen rags and ship sails, which made it much stronger and more durable than modern wood-pulp paper, and Italian paper in particular could be very refined, durable, and expensive. The major advantage of paper, compared with parchment, was that it could be supplied in sheets of an exact format. Many scribes, however, still believed that paper would not survive as well as parchment, which may explain why Boccaccio copied most of his own works on to parchment. Interestingly, Rhiannon Daniels suggests that there may be some correlation between size and the quality of the support material that Boccaccio used. It appears, in fact, that the parchment of his smallest autographs, which Daniels identifies with the codices of *De mulieribus*, the *Buccolicum carmen*, and with the Chigi codex which includes texts by Dante and Petrarch (Vatican City, Biblioteca Apostolica Vaticana, MS Chigi L. V. 176), is of higher quality – a very thin and refined Italian parchment – than that used for the other autographs.[9]

Parchment could be reused, either for financial reasons or because of lack of support material, by scraping off a previous text in so-called palimpsest manuscripts, which is the case of two of Boccaccio's autograph notebooks (*Zibaldone Laurenziano* and *Miscellanea Laurenziana*), which originally formed a single volume and are made in part with leaves from a thirteenth-century parchment gradual. The only one of his autographs to be made from paper is the so-called *Zibaldone Magliabechiano*, which was compiled over a thirty-year period.

Boccaccio built up his library in different stages by searching for, buying, borrowing, and copying manuscripts. During his youth in Naples between 1327 and 1341 he was in contact with scholars of the Angevin court, such as the royal librarian, Paolo da Perugia, and he had the opportunity to study classical texts from the monastic library of Montecassino, such as the *Priapeia* transcribed in the *Miscellanea Laurenziana*. His activity as a copier of his and others' works has often been explained by his supposedly difficult financial situation, but in fact Boccaccio's practices in reading, copying, and glossing are part of his working methods, as shown by the influence of other sources on some of his works, such as the *Teseida delle nozze d'Emilia*.[10] Moreover, his decision not to employ a professional scribe put Boccaccio in a position of control over the material and presentational features of the works he transcribed, whereas Petrarch, who employed professional scribes, often complained about contemporary scribal practices.[11]

Boccaccio searched for codices during his travels and diplomatic missions, but also called upon friends to help him find texts. For instance, in his early letter 'Sacre famis' (1339–40), which survives along with three other letters in his *Zibaldone Laurenziano*, Boccaccio informs a friend that he has recently acquired a copy of Statius' *Thebaid* and asks him if he might borrow one of his friend's manuscripts that contains glosses on that work, in order to transcribe them and better understand the classical author. This is a testimony of how volumes typically circulated between educated friends in Florence. Boccaccio's letters have often been considered as mere literary exercises in the *ars dictaminis* (art of letter writing): the themes of friendship, book learning, and sharing in the 'Sacre famis', in particular, are tropes of the epistolary genre. But David Anderson has found independent confirmation of the content of the letter in Boccaccio's glosses on Statius' *Thebaid* and in his *Teseida*, and re-established the importance of the 'Sacre famis' as a witness to his practices.[12] The letter, written in Naples toward the end of the period in which Boccaccio lived there, mentions the request to borrow and copy a manuscript containing glosses on Statius' *Thebaid*, which differs from the commentary Boccaccio added to his copy of the *Thebaid* (Florence, Biblioteca Medicea Laurenziana, MS 38. 6).

Boccaccio built up an extensive private library, although not all of it remains. The text of Statius quoted in Boccaccio's *Genealogia deorum gentilium* also reveals another copy of Statius which is now lost. A 1451 inventory of Boccaccio's manuscripts, then held at the library of the Florentine convent of Santo Spirito, listed 107 books, most of which remain untraceable. In his will, in fact, Boccaccio left his Latin codices to Fra Martino da Signa, prior of the Augustinian convent, and requested that his volumes be included in the convent library. The close relationship between the Augustinian prior and Boccaccio revealed in his will is also testified by one of Boccaccio's letters (*Epistle* XXIII), where the poet explains to Martino da Signa the allegorical meaning of his *Buccolicum carmen* (1372–4). Shortly after Fra Martino da Signa's death in 1387, Boccaccio's books went into the library of the convent, forming an important resource for contemporary scholars, as he wished.

Characteristic features of Boccaccio's writing practices

As the scribe, rubricator, and sometimes illustrator of his own and others' works, Boccaccio could choose the script and layout of the texts. The script in which he transcribed his manuscripts is an important element that helps illuminate his cultural preferences and his perception of the status of his copies. Since the nomenclature used to describe the development of script can vary greatly between palaeographers of different nationalities, we can simply divide the scripts that Boccaccio used into the gothic system and the pre-humanistic system.[13] The stages in the development of Boccaccio's script are captured within his manuscript tradition, ranging from juvenile forms, dating from when he was a schoolboy in Florence, through to a script modelled on Petrarch's semi-gothic bookhand in his later years. Up until the mid-1330s, Boccaccio was using a small-sized gothic bookhand with tentative letter forms, as can be seen in parts of the *Zibaldone Laurenziano*, but it seems that he exercised an increasing amount of control over his letter forms and the layout he selected for his manuscripts towards the end of his Neapolitan period and return to Florence.[14] In his mature years, during which Boccaccio composed scholarly works in Latin, as well as the *Corbaccio* in Italian, which was structured with Latin rubrics, and continued to edit the works of others, his handwriting developed and became more closely modelled on Petrarch's handwriting style (see Figure 2.1).

The creation of the so-called semi-gothic bookhand, understood as a transitional phase between Italian gothic scripts and the humanistic scripts, has been attributed to Petrarch, who had always praised the 'decorum' and 'majesty' of classical, pre-gothic handwriting: in a 1355 letter to Boccaccio he thanked him for a manuscript of Saint Augustine's works, which he appreciated for its sober and clear ancient handwriting (*Familiares*, XVIII. 3). Petrarch eliminated Italian gothic elements from his script and revived earlier Caroline forms. His graphic reform resulted in a compact script in which single letters are generally separated and aligned, in both bookhand and cursive forms. Bocaccio was among the circle of friends and disciples influenced by Petrarch's reform, and adopted a semi-gothic script for autographs containing his own texts. In particular, Boccaccio may have decided to transcribe the *Decameron* in a large-sized parchment manuscript (MS Hamilton 90), similar to scientific-academic codices, and in semi-gothic bookhand, to ensure that it reached the cultural and social elite. The presentational features of

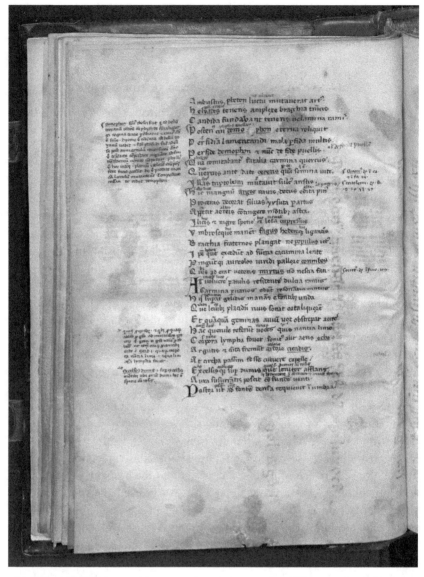

Figure 2.1 Pseudo-Virgil, *Culex*, with autograph marginal glosses in the *Miscellanea Laurenziana*: Florence, Biblioteca Medicea Laurenziana, MS 33.31, fol. 19v.

MS Hamilton 90 suggest that in his maturity Boccaccio was interested in promoting a rather different readership of the *Decameron* than that represented by the consumers of texts written in mercantile script (*mercantesca*), a documentary script employed in trade by Florentine merchants in the late thirteenth and fourteenth centuries, characterized by very compressed letters and the repeated use of ligatures and abbreviations.[15]

The development of Boccaccio's punctuation can also be used to date the forms of his handwriting: scholars have pointed out the difference in use between his early and later autographs. In the parchment notebooks (the *Zibaldone Laurenziano* and *Miscellanea Laurenziana*), as well as in the first two sections of the paper notebook (*Zibaldone Magliabechiano*), all of which were intended mainly for his private reading, Boccaccio uses only two punctuation signs: a comma (\\) and *punctus* (.). In his mature scripts (witnessed in MS Hamilton 90, for example), he adds a comma beneath a *punctus* (in a sign similar to a semicolon), as well as a *punctus* with a comma above it.[16] The use of these four main punctuation marks shows a more precise separation of the different parts of his discourse: the comma, for example, signals minor logical and syntactic partitions, whereas the *punctus* concludes a period, and the *punctus* with the comma above it marks the conclusions of different parts of the texts, or the end of a tale, rubric, or stanza. Boccaccio's mature prose is marked, therefore, by his simplified and rationalized use of punctuation.[17]

Boccaccio's commentaries on his copies of classical authors (such as Terence, Persius, and Statius) and vernacular authors (such as Dante) reveal his reading and compositional practices as well as his learning.[18] Boccaccio's commentaries either take the form of interlinear glosses, placed near the text and dependent upon it for their grammatical construction, or they are placed in the margins in the unruled space on both sides of the page. Boccaccio's glossing practice therefore differs significantly from late-antique glosses, which are typically written in separate ruled columns, often accompanied by paragraph marks and large capital letters. Boccaccio also calls attention to notable passages by using signs such as manicules (pointing hands), drawings, and C-shaped (or semicircular) division marks.[19] The MS C 67 sup. (see Figure 2.2) shows Boccaccio's taste for satire in his later years when the author writes in the vernacular 'Frate Cepolla' next to Martial's epigram IX. 35, where the Latin poet presents a sly character, Filomuso, who reminds Boccaccio of his own astute friar (Friar Cipolla in *Decameron*, VI. 10).[20]

Before beginning to write, Boccaccio would have had to rule the leaves of his manuscript. Throughout the Middle Ages, scribes pricked small holes in the margins of the leaves to guide their horizontal and vertical ruling. In the early period, ruling was done in drypoint, that is, it was made by pressing a knife or a stylus made of metal or bone into the page. By the fourteenth century, ruling in ink had become quite common, but fifteenth-century humanist scribes frequently reverted to the practice of ruling in

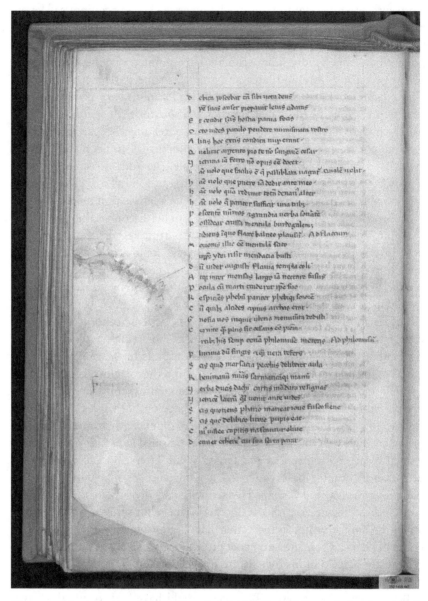

Figure 2.2 Marginal autograph note 'Frate Cepolla' in Milan, Biblioteca Ambrosiana, MS C 67 sup., fol. 88v.

drypoint as part of their conscious revival of classical scribal and codicological features. Boccaccio, however, did not adopt this practice, and when transcribing both poetic text and marginal glosses from a manuscript ruled by drypoint, he respected the proportions of the original leaves but placed

28

his glosses in the unruled space of the margins, contrasting the different position of the narrative in classical commentary with his own, using single words or phrases that did not require a ruling of their own.

In terms of layout, the autographs of the *Teseida* and *Buccolicum carmen* are the only copies whose texts are arranged in a single column. It is possible that Boccaccio decided to follow this design for works in verse, as the *Teseida* is written in *ottava rima* and the *Buccolicum carmen* in hexameters. Prose texts, such as the *Decameron* and Boccaccio's own epistles, all follow instead the two-column pattern, excluding the two redactions of his *Trattatello in laude di Dante*. Since in the Chigi codex (MS Chigi L. V. 176) the *Trattatello* coexists with other texts in verse, such as Dante's *Vita nova*, *Comedy*, and *canzoni*, as well as with poems by Guido Cavalcanti and Petrarch, Daniels suggests that the epigraphic tradition – in which inscriptions are normally displayed in a single-column or full-page layout – may have been influential, since Boccaccio was creating virtual monuments to commemorate Dante and ensure the circulation of his works.[21] Boccaccio also acted as an illustrator within his autograph manuscripts. Although his authorship of the illustrations of the *Inferno*'s first seventeen cantos is now discredited, and are thought to have been added by a later artist, Boccaccio included drawings in other autographs, such as the thirteen half-figure portraits found in the *Decameron* (MS Hamilton 90), and five drawings in his transcription of Martial's *Epigrams* (MS C 67 sup.), among which is the bust of a girl very similar to the portrait of Neifile on fol. 31v of MS Hamilton 90 (see Figure 2.3).[22]

Boccaccio as compiler

Boccaccio positions himself as a central figure in the transmission of the works of others, for example in the anthologies Chigi L. V. 176 and Chigi L. VI. 213, now held in two separate manuscripts but which were originally part of the same volume. In these once-conjoined codices we find a unique miscellany which includes the *Trattatello*, *Vita nova*, fifteen of Dante's poems (the 'canzoni distese'), Petrarch's *Rime*, Guido Cavalcanti's *Donna mi prega* (with Dino del Garbo's commentary), Boccaccio's Latin carmen *Ytalie iam certus honos*, and Dante's *Comedy*. This choice of works reveals Boccaccio's intentions of promoting the early vernacular literature which flourished in Tuscany, as well as his own pivotal role in divulging and advancing Tuscan literature.[23]

Other manuscript evidence shows that Boccaccio was engaged in this compilatory activity from an early age. His working notebooks exemplify his practices in copying and annotating classical and contemporary authors,

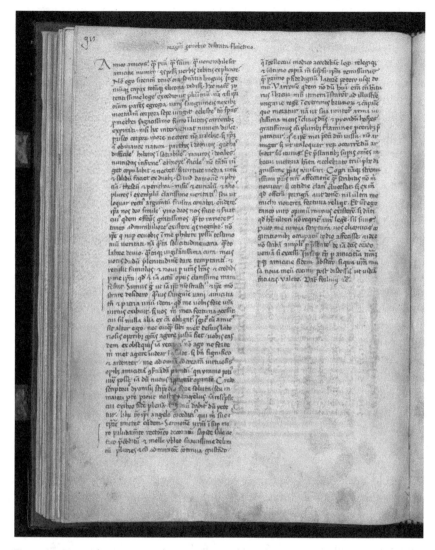

Figure 2.3 Two-column autograph transcription of *Epistle* VI in Florence, Biblioteca Medicea Laurenziana, MS 29.8, fol. 50v.

as well as his experiments in composing his first literary texts alongside and sometimes in imitation of them. The *Zibaldone Magliabechiano* (MS Banco Rari 50) contains a compendium of historical texts, collected in order to be reused in literary writings, patiently glossed and elegantly transcribed; we can also see numerous corrections in Boccaccio's hand, especially in the section of the *Compendium* or *Chronologia magna* by Paolino da Venezia (fols 163v–263v), where in the margins Boccaccio corrects and criticizes the

Venetian chronicler for his contradictions and lack of analysis of historical facts.[24]

The complex composite nature of the *Zibaldoni* makes it difficult to date these manuscripts as a whole or to order their texts chronologically. The *mise-en-page* varies from text to text between a two-column or single-column layout, and Boccaccio often includes notes or tentative compilations in the large margins. Since the links between the *Zibaldone Laurenziano* and *Miscellanea Laurenziana* have been recognized, based on their shared reuse of pages taken from a late thirteenth-century Beneventan liturgical codex, a more certain dating has been proposed for the various parts of this originally unified manuscript, which is now thought to extend from the late 1320s up to about 1348. We see the evolving interests of a literary man in training, copying for himself, which explains why the quality of the script and layout has not always been judged as consistent; the volume reflects Boccaccio's first attempts to follow Petrarch's graphic models through to his maturation, while the fasciculation is irregular, with the coexistence of quires and single leaves.

The two parchment notebooks differ from the relatively cohesive contents of the paper *Zibaldone Magliabechiano*. In contrast to this, the *Zibaldone Laurenziano* seems to be characterized by its heterogeneity of content, which has a scholastic bent. It includes astronomical works by Andalò del Negro, medieval texts with a moral and historical content, and a mosaic of texts that combines erudition and literature, a typical trait of Boccaccio that has no equivalent in Petrarch's manuscripts. Instead, it follows a different kind of practice which is closer to the anthology of historical texts, rhymes, and *formulae dictandi* (rhetorical models) collected by the Paduan pre-humanist scholar Lovato Lovati and by Francesco da Barberino's autographs (Vatican City, Biblioteca Apostolica Vaticana, MSS Barberiniano latino 4076 and 4077), which contain miscellanies of Latin and vernacular texts including Boccaccio's verses *Ad Africam domini Francisci Petrarche* and *Life of Petrarch*.[25]

The compilation of texts in the *Miscellanea Laurenziana* is also exceptional because several of its minor texts have been handed down to us through this manuscript and very few others. Examples include the tetrastich (four-line stanza) in honour of St Minias (fol. 3v), the *Lamentatio Bertoldi* (fol. 3v), a scholastic cento made up of classical and middle-Latin quotations, and the sole extant fragment of Lovato Lovati's poem on Tristan and Isolde (fol. 46r). Boccaccio's hand has been identified not only in the text, but also in the numerous marginal and interlinear notes, which provide evidence of his scribal and decorative skills. The manicules depicted in a variety of gestures and positions are also in Boccaccio's own hand

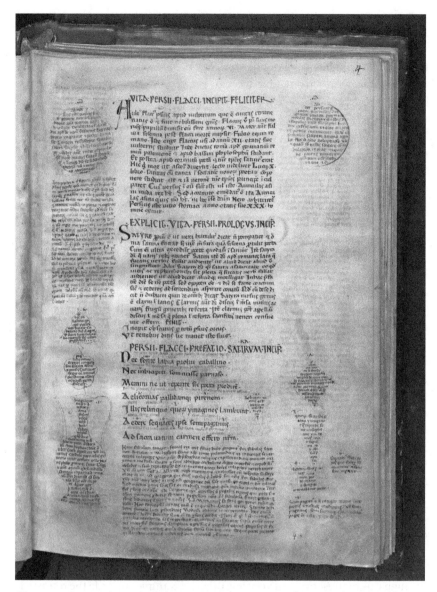

Figure 2.4 Autograph marginal glosses arranged as geometric figures in Florence, Biblioteca Medicea Laurenziana, MS 33.31, fol. 4r.

(fol. 12). We know that Boccaccio copied his Persius in the *Miscellanea Laurenziana* from another manuscript also now held in the Laurenziana library in Florence (MS 37. 19), making it possible to follow Boccaccio's pen and his literary interests and to test his reliability as a scribe. The first leaf of Persius' transcription shows Boccaccio's originality: while the exemplar arranges the materials in a chaotic way on the page, Boccaccio's autograph presents a series of geometric figures in the margins of fol. 4r, within which the glosses are arranged. The most striking figure is the outline of a jug, and the two shorter *Vitae* are enclosed in circles on each side and are labelled *aliter* ('differently'). Although there is a profusion of geometric and diamond-shaped figures, a flower and a trilobite leaf on the left margin, the neat arrangement of the glosses, numbered consecutively for each folio, is a great improvement over the disorderly array in the exemplar (see Figure 2.4).[26]

It is clear that Boccaccio's choice of the texts he collected, transcribed, and annotated in his *Zibaldoni* reveals his literary tastes and the development of his interests in different genres: the moral-historical narrative, the renewal of the bucolic genre, and the *ars dictaminis* (art of letter writing). Even more significantly, the texts collected in the *Zibaldoni* outline the dynamics of Boccaccio's creative research, which is characterized by his interest in intertextuality and collections. At the same time, these collections of texts point outwards to show other parts of his oeuvre, including the sources for some of his more famous works. The references to the Pseudo-Hegesippus' Latin texts in the *Zibaldone Magliabechiano* lead to the practical joke of the angel Gabriel in *Decameron*, IV. 2; several notes anticipate chapters in *De casibus virorum illustrium*; and the transcription of the elegiac comedy *Lydia* in the *Miscellanea Laurenziana* leads to Nicostratus and Pyrrhus's tale (*Decameron*, VII. 9).[27]

Boccaccio's *Zibaldoni* thus illuminate his method of reading the Latin and vernacular traditions and how he incorporates them into his own literary production. Despite the scarcity of direct information he provides us with on his writing processes, his extant autographs reflect the wide array and complexity of his cultural enterprises. In his pursuit of classical texts and in making editorial choices when copying from his Latin and vernacular exemplars, in particular in the case of Dante's and Petrarch's works, Boccaccio anticipates the philological activities of later humanists such as Coluccio Salutati and Lorenzo Valla, while in his manuscript culture he is indebted to the fourteenth-century Tuscan tradition for his very decision to create a miscellany.

NOTES

1 Marco Cursi, *La scrittura e i libri di Giovanni Boccaccio* (Rome: Viella, 2013), pp. x; 129–34. See List of manuscripts in this volume.

2 Claude Cazalé Bérard, 'Boccaccio's Working Notebooks (*Zibaldone Laurenziano, Miscellanea Laurenziana, Zibaldone Magliabechiano*)', in *Boccaccio: A Critical Guide to the Complete Works*, ed. by Victoria Kirkham, Michael

Sherberg, and Janet Levarie Smarr (Chicago: University of Chicago Press, 2013), pp. 307–18; Marco Petoletti, 'Gli zibaldoni di Giovanni Boccaccio', in *Boccaccio autore e copista*, ed. by Teresa De Robertis and others (Florence: Mandragora, 2013), pp. 291–326.

3 See List of manuscripts in this volume.

4 Marco Cursi, *Il 'Decameron': scritture, scriventi, lettori. Storia di un testo* (Roma: Viella, 2007), p. 162.

5 Armando Petrucci, 'Il manoscritto berlinese Hamiltoniano 90. Note codicologiche e paleografiche', in Giovanni Boccaccio, *Decameron: edizione diplomatico-interpretativa dell'autografo Hamilton 90*, ed. by Charles S. Singleton (Baltimore: Johns Hopkins University Press, 1974), pp. 647–61 (p. 655).

6 Petrucci, 'Il manoscritto berlinese', p. 648.

7 Maurizio Fiorilla, 'Nota al testo', in Giovanni Boccaccio, *Decameron*, ed. by Amadeo Quondam, Maurizio Fiorilla, and Giancarlo Alfano (Milan: BUR Rizzoli, 2013), pp. 121–3.

8 Martin Eisner, *Boccaccio and the Invention of Italian Literature: Dante, Petrarch, Cavalcanti, and the Authority of the Vernacular* (Cambridge: Cambridge University Press, 2013), p. 27.

9 Rhiannon Daniels, *Boccaccio and the Book: Production and Reading in Italy 1340–1520* (London: Legenda, 2009), p. 140.

10 David Anderson, *Before the Knight's Tale: Imitation of Classical Epic in Boccaccio's 'Teseida'* (Philadelphia: University of Pennsylvania Press, 1988).

11 Armando Petrucci, *La scrittura di Francesco Petrarca* (Vatican City: Biblioteca Apostolica Vaticana, 1967), pp. 62–9.

12 David Anderson, 'Boccaccio's Glosses on Statius', *Studi sul Boccaccio*, 22 (1994), 3–134 (pp. 57–62).

13 Daniels, *Boccaccio and the Book*, pp. 26–9.

14 Marco Cursi, 'Le scritture di Boccaccio nel loro svolgimento diacronico', in his *La scrittura e i libri*, pp. 15–82.

15 Daniels, *Boccaccio and the Book*, p. 79.

16 Patrizia Rafti, 'Lumina dictionum: interpunzione e prosa in Giovanni Boccaccio', *Studi sul Boccaccio*, 29 (2001), 3–66; 27 (1999), 81–106; 25 (1997), 239–73; 24 (1996), 59–121; Patrizia Rafti, 'Riflessioni sull'*usus distinguendi* di Boccaccio negli Zibaldoni', in *Gli zibaldoni di Boccaccio: memoria, scrittura, riscrittura. Atti del Seminario internazionale di Firenze-Certaldo (26–28 aprile, 1996)*, ed. by Michelangelo Picone and Claude Cazalé Bérard (Florence: Cesati, 1998), pp. 283–306.

17 Cursi, *La scrittura e i libri*, pp. 47–9.

18 Anderson, 'Boccaccio's Glosses on Statius', p. 100.

19 See Anderson, 'Boccaccio's Glosses on Statius', pp. 98–114.

20 Cursi dates MS C 67 sup. to 1370–2 in his *La scrittura e i libri*, pp. 31; 47–9.

21 Daniels, *Boccaccio and the Book*, p. 42.

22 Victoria Kirkham, 'A Visual Legacy (Boccaccio as Artist)', in *Boccaccio: A Critical Guide*, pp. 321–40; Francesca Pasut, 'Boccaccio disegnatore', in *Boccaccio autore e copista*, pp. 51–9.

23 Domenico De Robertis, 'Il "Dante e Petrarca" di Giovanni Boccaccio', in his *Il codice chigiano L. V. 176 autografo di Giovanni Boccaccio: edizione fototipica* (Rome: Archivi Edizioni, 1974), pp. 7–72. See also Chapter 8 in this volume.

24 Cazalé Bérard, 'Boccaccio's Working Notebooks', pp. 312–14.
25 Denis Dutschke, 'Il libro miscellaneo: problemi di metodo tra Boccaccio e Petrarca', in *Gli zibaldoni di Boccaccio*, pp. 95–112 (p. 103).
26 Dorothy M. Robathan, 'Boccaccio's Accuracy as a Scribe', *Speculum*, 13 (1938), 458–60.
27 Vittore Branca, 'Parole di apertura', in *Gli zibaldoni di Boccaccio*, pp. 6–7.

3

RHIANNON DANIELS

Boccaccio's narrators and audiences

Scholarship has long promoted the idea that Boccaccio's career is marked by a distinct ideological shift from a vernacular, erotic, and pro-feminist poetics to a Latinizing, scholarly, and misogynistic stance, with his meeting with Petrarch in 1350 seen as a pivotal moment in this development. This view is now starting to be unpicked in favour of emphasizing continuities and developments in Boccaccio's literary production. The fashioning of narratorial personas and the audiences which they address is a key part of this discussion of authorial style and intention, since the dramatized first-person voice often announces the aims of the work. Each of Boccaccio's literary works, whether written in Italian or Latin, poetry or prose, includes at least one narrating voice who tells the story to a listener or reader. This voice is usually at its most audible at the beginning and end of the text and acts as a framing device, both defining the limits of the work's contents, and directing it outwards: to its fictional audiences within the text and anticipated historical flesh-and-blood audiences outside the text.

Historically, Boccaccio scholars have been reluctant to distinguish narrating voices operating within the bounds of the fictional text from the voice of the historical author operating outside it. Narrators appear to be convincing stand-ins for Boccaccio-the-historical-author not because they are fully rounded characters but because they have been read as fragments of a whole. Apparent consistencies operating in the presentation of narrators in the vernacular works, which contrast with a different, but parallel, scholarly narratorial model developed in the Latin works, have been pieced together to create the biography of a single Author-Narrator. Narrators of the vernacular fictions are linked by their use of amorous experience as a premise for telling their stories, with variations in the development of these love affairs appearing to map on to the chronology of the texts. Thus, for example, in the first fiction, the *Caccia di Diana*, the Narrator depicts himself as already fully in the throes of love, looking for shelter 'against the blows of Love that were piercing my heart with bitter pangs' (1. 4–6; p. 99).

In the *Filocolo*, the Narrator provides more context for his experience of love, with details of the precise hour and location in which he saw his lady for the first time (1. 17–22). By the time we reach the later *Decameron* and *Corbaccio*, the love affair is over. The sense that we are reading the development of a single narrator's story across multiple works, rather than separate and unrelated narratorial instances, is reinforced by a recurring address to the Narrator's beloved. The fragmented appearances of this receiving figure have been subsumed under the *senhal* 'Fiammetta', which complements the composite figure of the Author-Narrator, whose explicit hope is that Fiammetta will understand more perfectly his feelings for her, and – implicitly – cede to them. The barely sublimated erotic aim is largely responsible for the historical interpretation of these vernacular fictions as immoral, and the reluctance to distinguish between fictional narrator and historical author has thus framed Boccaccio as an immoral author.

More recently, the literary-critical field of narratology has given us the tools and vocabulary to distinguish clearly between the historical flesh-and-blood Boccaccio, the multiple authorial and narrating voices which can operate within the same text, and a corresponding array of receivers of different types. The *Decameron* is the perfect example of a text containing numerous narrators and audiences whose architecture has been meticulously examined and labelled: thus we can identify that the Primary Narrator operates in the outer (extradiegetic) level of the text, most obviously in the Proem, Introductions to Day I and IV, and Conclusion. This Narrator can also be held responsible for the shorter introductions and conclusions to each day, and the rubrics which precede each *novella*. The *brigata* function as secondary (intradiegetic) narrators, since the stories they recount to one another constitute the main narrative (diegesis). Characters within the *novelle* also tell stories on occasion and become tertiary (hypodiegetic) narrators. On the receiving end of these narratives are equivalent levels of audience, ranging from the women addressed by the Primary Narrator, to the nine members of the *brigata* listening to the tale told by the tenth member, to the characters within the *novelle* listening to their fellow characters. However, this type of analysis, with its focus on formal structures within the text, tends to ignore the social context in which texts are performed. The way in which the narrative act of communication is played out within the text is accompanied by an equally complex layering of actors and receivers operating outside the text, encompassing not only a historical author and readership, but also the many different agents involved in the creation of text-objects: scribes, printers, editors, publishers, designers, illustrators, and so on, all of whom have the potential to exert control over the way in which we access the voices within the text.

This chapter draws on elements of structural analysis in order to consider Boccaccio's authorial strategies through the multiple figures of his narrators and the range of equivalent narratees who make up the audience for a text. At the same time, Boccaccio's texts are understood as inherently performative, and rooted in the art of rhetoric, which is fundamentally concerned with the relationship between author and audience:

> A rhetorical approach to a text must concern itself not only with the author's intentions, but also with all the features implicated in the text as a persuasive or argumentative use of language: the structure of the text as a means of communication, the nature and response of the audience or reader, the text's relation to other discourses, and the social and political contexts of the interaction between author, text, and reader, as well as a historicist concern with the differences between a modern reception of the text and its original performative conditions.[1]

Rather than treat individual works in isolation, one of the aims of this chapter is to underscore the currents of continuity which run the length of Boccaccio's career and characterize his authorial practice, and therefore the chapter will begin with a comparative evaluation of examples taken from the *Decameron* and *De casibus virorum illustrium*. A second, equally important aim is to consider the variety of authorial roles adopted by Boccaccio in the context of the different genres in which he experimented. The role of the audience, and the associated question of reception, is problematized through a discussion of the fluidity of the boundaries between fictional and non-fictional worlds within the communications circuit joining author, text, and consumer.

Narrators in the *Decameron* and *De casibus virorum illustrium*

In Boccaccio's lifetime the term 'auttore' (author) could encompass various authorial roles. In the thirteenth century St Bonaventure had described four of these:

> the scribe [*scriptor*] is subject to materials composed by other men which he should copy as carefully as possible... The *compilator* adds together or arranges the statements of other men, adding no opinion of his own... The *commentator* strives to explain the views of others, adding something of his own by way of explanation. Finally, and most importantly, the *auctor* writes *de suo* [in his own right] but draws on the statements of other men to support his own views.[2]

Within the *Decameron*, one of the most explicit descriptions of the Narrator's role occurs in the Conclusion, where the Primary Narrator steps in to defend his finished work from anticipated criticisms:

> I could only transcribe the stories as they were actually told, which means that if the ladies who told them had told them better, I should have written them better. But even if one could assume that I was the inventor as well as the scribe of these stories (which was not the case), I still insist that I would not feel ashamed if some fell short of perfection.   (Conclusion, 16–17; p. 800)

Here the Narrator is clearly labelling himself not as the *auctor* or inventor of original work, but as a *scriptor* or scribal transmitter of existing stories. This appears such an unlikely reality that we mistrust the narratorial voice, building the ironic, tongue-in-cheek authorial image frequently associated with Boccaccio. While we can interpret the Narrator's self-professed mediating function in the context of the *Decameron*'s subtitle as a 'Prince Galahalt' or go-between, it is also important to remember that this slippery defence of moral integrity is an authorial role which is entirely consistent with the Narrator's claims at the beginning of the work. Here we are told that the story he has to tell was transmitted to him by someone else: 'one Tuesday morning (*or so I was told by a person whose word can be trusted*) seven young ladies were to be found in the venerable church of Santa Maria Novella' (Introduction to Day I, 49; p. 13; emphasis added). While we never discover who this trustworthy person is, the fiction of the oral source is appropriate for a collection of stories which are represented as oral productions. Amedeo Quondam points out that the Narrator of the Proem uses a verb closely linked with oral performance to describe his activity ('raccontare' [to tell stories]), rather than a verb signalling written performance (i.e. 'scrivere' [to write]), arguing that this emphasizes the ambiguity between author (*auctor*) and transcriber (*scriptor*).[3]

However, this is not the only role assumed by the Narrator of the *Decameron*: there are clear suggestions that some compilatory work has taken place at the level of the diegesis. At the end of VII. 1, the storyteller Emilia asks her audience to choose between two different endings. Conferring responsibility on the reader is a habit common to compilers, which finds an echo in the Primary Narrator's exhortation to readers to use the rubrics supplied at the head of each *novella* in order to navigate their own paths through the text:

> And the fact remains that anyone perusing these tales is free to ignore the ones that give offence, and read only those that are pleasing. For in order that none

of you may be misled, each of the stories bears on its brow the gist of that
which it hides in its bosom.   (Conclusion, 19; p. 801)

Raising the issue of the freedom that historical readers have to choose how
they read within the fictional world reveals that the Narrator is aware of
the transmission process, but also anxious about his inability to control
it. The implicitly passive nature of the scribal and compilatory roles that
dominate the *Decameron* needs to be tempered by the more active roles of
commentator and *auctor*. The rubrics can be read as mini-commentaries on
the stories they introduce, guiding their audience by highlighting particular
characters and scenes, and – we imagine – authored ('invented') by the
Narrator when he translated his oral source into a written document. These
two modes of operating – authorial and commentarial – come together
with particular force when the Narrator breaks into the frame narrative at
the beginning of Day IV: here, the defence of his subject matter functions
as a clearly structured piece of exegesis in the manner of a commentary,
which culminates in the action of an *auctor* who tells his own *novella*.
Underplaying these more active roles of *commentator* and *auctor* endows
Boccaccio's authorship with an apparently light touch which should not
blind us to the seriousness of his intentions. In this context we must not lose
sight of the material container which transmits the text. A fourteenth-century
audience may well have had a much clearer sense of the interplay between
these different authorial positions, since Boccaccio established a tradition of
signalling the distinction between narrating voices visually, using a carefully
orchestrated hierarchy of decorative initials. The latest critical edition has
taken steps to restore the original prominence of the initials found in the
autograph manuscript by including printed equivalents.[4]

Multiple authorial strategies are adopted in *De casibus* as they are in the
Decameron, although they are used to very different effect. This is appropriate to the difference in genre, since within the art of rhetoric, the style of a text
must be suited to the audience whom the author is seeking to persuade. The
scholarly credentials of the Narrator of *De casibus* are emphasized through
the foregrounding of the compilatory mode. Indeed, the dramatized act of
compilation makes up the frame-story: the Narrator sits in his study and
has a vision in which a series of figures present themselves for selection and
demand his attention. The scribal function is reduced, and the compilatory
act underlined, as the Narrator himself witnesses and selects from among
the examples presented to him, without the need for an additional mediating
figure.

In order to vary the style of narration and maintain audience interest, the
compilatory mode fluctuates along the scale which includes active authorial

modes at one end and passive scribal modes at the other. Thus, in Book I, when Thyestes and Atreus quarrel over whose story should be told (literally performing the idea of multiple and potentially conflicting versions of stories which is only hinted at in the *Decameron*), their aggressive behaviour threatens to transform the Narrator into a scribal conduit, as he seems powerless to intervene. Indeed, rather than select one version over another, he prefers simply to move on to the next biography. In Book IX, however, the Narrator performs a struggle for authorial control with Brunhilde, Queen of the Franks, disputing which version of her story is correct. His ability to counter Brunhilde's arguments effectively is a rhetorical device designed to strengthen his own authorial position, which is then bolstered further when he changes tactics to solicit audience compassion for his own cause, commenting: 'I have written her story, writing, I confess, without using enough trustworthy evidence; and so, if it is revealed that I have related something that is not true, it should be laid to the great effectiveness of her speaking' (IX. 1. 30; p. 226). The evident similarity between this technique and the virtually identical combination of combative argumentation and disavowal of responsibility used by the Narrator in the Conclusion to the *Decameron* to defend his decision to relate stories told by women warns us against reading the claims literally, and points us instead towards a display of rhetorical prowess.

The Narrator of *De casibus* is not only a compiler and occasionally a scribe, but also an author and commentator on his own work. As the Narrator had offered his own example of a *novella* in the Introduction to Day IV of the *Decameron*, so the Narrator of *De casibus* includes the story of Philippa of Catania, which is a mix of his own direct observation and other people's sources (IX. 25). While in the *Decameron* the Narrator steps in to defend and explain his activity at select and infrequent moments, the *De casibus* Narrator maintains a steady degree of self-reflection and explanation of his authorial activity, with continual references to the process of recording and transcribing oral sources, as well as overt commentary on the lessons to be drawn from the examples provided. These disquisitions on topics such as pride, deceit, and lust lend the work its directness of tone, which contrasts so dramatically with the *Decameron*. Rather than suggest that readers navigate their own personal course through the text by selecting an order of reading according to the rubrics, here the Narrator maintains a much tighter control over the order of reading and offers section divisions simply as a means of taking stock and as a memory device in line with scholastic practices. These brief examples illustrate the range of authorial modes on which Boccaccio was drawing in order to effect a sensitive balance between the purpose and style of his subject matter in relation to intended audiences.

Strategies of authorization

Throughout his literary career, Boccaccio is acutely aware of his 'newness' as an author, and therefore of the importance of endowing his works and his authorial image with an appropriate status. This was an issue which affected the reception of both vernacular and Latin works, and Boccaccio employed numerous strategies for self-authorization which can be traced across his oeuvre.

One of these is a concern to situate himself within an established tradition of authoritative authors ('*auctores*'). This is manifested in many works through the narrator explaining that he is reworking existing models and themes.[5] In the *Decameron* the Narrator cites three modern poets, Guido Cavalcanti, Dante Alighieri, and Cino da Pistoia, in order to authorize his vision of a new literature: a vision which is echoed materially in Boccaccio's promotion of Dante as a modern classic, framed by Cavalcanti and Petrarch in his manuscript compilations.[6] This roll-call of poets is placed in the Introduction to Day IV (§33), when the Narrator is apparently at his most vulnerable because he is subject to criticism, but is also demonstrating rhetorical skills by masterfully commenting on his own work in order to authorize his undertaking. The poets are carefully chosen to show that the Narrator is part of a recent, but nevertheless established, tradition of writing about love. It is a risky strategy precisely because of his fellow poets' relative novelty (Guido, Dante, and Cino are barely more than a generation older than Boccaccio): indeed, in the *Genealogia deorum gentilium*, Boccaccio felt it was necessary to include an entire section justifying the use of modern authors, including Dante and Petrarch (xv. 6). The Narrator's comments show that the genre of the *Decameron* justifies the risk and would have rendered a different set of examples inappropriate: if it had been a history book, he could have included examples from antiquity (*Dec.*, Introduction to Day IV. 34).

Aligning himself with a mixture of classical and modern authors was appropriate within the *Filocolo*, however, since it is a reworking of both classical and romance genres. Here, he advises his book to leave aside a host of previous authors – Virgil, Lucan, Statius, Ovid, and Dante – and to follow the 'low road' and concentrate on giving pleasure only to his lady (v. 97). This modest proposal is perfectly in line with the Narrator's erotic aims, but it also attests to his carefully orchestrated self-authorization. While the *auctores* are listed explicitly with the aim of disassociating them from the *Filocolo*, the implicit message must be that we should make Boccaccio the sixth *auctor* in the list. The inclusion of Dante as the only other 'modern' should alert the reader to the clear resonances with Dante's own 'bella scola' ('lovely school') and inclusion of himself as the 'sixth amongst such great wisdom'.[7] This is a theme which Boccaccio will pick up again in the *Amorosa visione*, where Dante is shown as the central figure in a group of illustrious classical authors, among whom also appear Virgil, Lucan, Statius, and Ovid, depicted with 'their gaze bent . . . fervently upon the ladies' (Canto v; p. 23).

Boccaccio's sense of poetic hierarchy is at its most sensitive in relation to Dante and Petrarch, whom he manipulates as characters designed to endorse his own activities. Thus Dante appears to the Narrator in *De casibus* IX to speak briefly, but assertively, in praise of his skills as an author. Dante-character authorizes Boccaccio's endeavour by introducing another character whom Dante wishes the Narrator to include in his set of biographies. In a process of inspired circular self-authorization the Narrator expresses his inability to do justice to the biography of Dante himself, an intertextual homage to Dante's own use of the ineffability *topos* in relation to his divine journey, and Beatrice in particular. This is ironic, since we know that another narrator 'belonging' to Boccaccio has written precisely that biography of Dante (known as the *Trattatello in laude di Dante*).[8] Likewise, in *De casibus* VIII, the Narrator has a vision of Petrarch who comes to exhort him to continue working hard, including, as part of the encouragement, another roll-call of illustrious ancients whom Boccaccio should seek to emulate: Moses, Aristotle, Virgil, Scipio, the Catos, Plato, and Homer.

Praising himself through the mouths of others, in line with the rhetorical art of *sermocinatio*, is one of many methods which Boccaccio employs to authorize himself, since his self-fashioning as an author and narrator is heavily flavoured with modesty. Thus, for example, the Narrator of the *Genealogia* describes in detail the difficulties of the compilatory and exegetical task ahead, which he insists he is unable to accomplish (I. Preface). This serves, in fact, to highlight what the Narrator *has* achieved, since any reader reading the preface will undoubtedly be (literally) feeling the weight of the completed fifteen books. Modestly referring to his poetry as an activity which confines him to the low roads, far distant from the high places of poetic glory, becomes a Boccaccian *topos*.[9] In a similar vein narrators comment on the humble appearance of their books, most expansively in Book IX of the *Elegia di madonna Fiammetta*, but also in *Filostrato*, IX. 6.

Using the metaphor of travel for narration also becomes part of the act of self-authorization framed within the modesty *topos*, included within the vernacular works (for example, *Filocolo*, V. 97 and *Decameron*, VI. 1), but played out most extensively in the Latin works (for example, *Genealogia*, I. Preface, I. 40; IV. Preface; V. Preface). Throughout *De casibus*, the Narrator's frequent reflections on the process of writing using the journey analogy function as a magnified and fractured scribal *explicit*: scribes frequently signed off their work by complaining about the length of time it had taken and the difficulty of the task, thereby implicitly seeking praise for having withstood these trials. Reflecting on the length of the journey and its challenges draws the readers' attention to the skill of the Narrator in travelling so far successfully.

The tone used by the Narrator varies even within the same work, and therefore while it is appropriate that modesty and humility usually mark the opening parts of the text, elsewhere the Narrator's sense of his place within the poetic tradition is more confidently expressed. Thus in the chapters in *De casibus* where the Narrator defends the status of poetry and his own practice as a poet, he seems comfortable drawing an analogy between the needs of Homer, Virgil, and himself for a solitary life in order to compose poetry, without needing to dress it up in modest denials (Book III). Similarly, in the *Comedia delle ninfe*, he is happy to compare his own relationship to his dedicatee with a set of illustrious precedents including Virgil and Augustus, Gaius Herrenius and Cicero, Horace and Maecenas (Chapter L).

From fictional to historical audiences and back again

The fictional audiences posited within Boccaccio's texts have frequently received attention in relation to their gender, with a particular focus on the idle ladies of the *Decameron* and Boccaccio's muse, Fiammetta. An autobiographical reading of the vernacular fictions posits a continuous relationship between Boccaccio-narrator and Fiammetta-reader. In practice, however, the audience for these texts is more complicated than this picture allows. As an addressee, Fiammetta is only named explicitly as 'Fiammetta' in the *Teseida*, and alluded to as 'dear flame' ('cara Fiamma') in the *Amorosa visione* (sonnet I). The lovers who are addressed in other works implicitly become pseudonyms for Fiammetta by virtue of the same desire to create a consistent biography that exists for the Author-Narrator. Beyond these women in the spotlight there are glimpses of other, unnamed, but often carefully defined, groups of male and female addressees. For example, in the *Decameron*, a collective audience comes to the fore when the Narrator defends his work against criticisms in the Introduction to Day IV and Conclusion. These might include female readers, but the objection that he is spending too much time writing about women suggests that these are male. The *Filostrato* is dedicated to Filomena but the Narrator reserves a helpful warning for an audience of young men to beware the kind of women in whom they put their trust (VIII. 29), and in the *Filocolo* (I. 2), *Ninfale fiesolano* (4), *Fiammetta* (Prologue; Book IX), and *Corbaccio* (412) the narrator distinguishes between different male and female audiences, each of whom receives specific guidance.

Multiple audiences also operate alongside one another in the Latin texts. Although in real terms the pool of potential readers must be restricted to the educated elite thanks to the language of transmission, this does not seem to mean that the narrators expect smaller numbers of readers or a greater degree of sophistication in reading techniques. The grand aim of *De casibus* is to benefit the state, by means of guiding the behaviour of illustrious princes, whose improved conduct will thereby benefit the greater population under their control. Layered over this audience, and overlapping with it, is another audience of the 'wise', whom the Narrator exhorts to correct his work at the end of Book IX, but this seems to concern the Narrator less than the minimally educated public that needs morals drummed into it. The Narrator of the *Decameron* explains to his unschooled female audience 'you have need of a lengthier form of address than those who have sharpened their wits with the aid of their studies' (Conclusion, 21; p. 801), and thus by extension we might conclude that one of the fictional audiences for *De casibus* is also minimally educated. The Narrator's concern with diversely educated reading publics is particularly evident at the beginning of Book II, when he writes:

> There are many who rely on things that are transitory. They scarcely feel the constantly roaring wind, and, of course, they do not hear words spoken quietly. These people, I think, should always continually be hit with the blows of impressive examples. As a constant flow of water will penetrate the hardest stone, so an adamantine heart is softened by a long narration. And to those [for] whom these examples suffice, I give thanks that I have worked thus far with their good grace. But I shall continue to satisfy the others.
>
> (Introduction to Book II. 3; p. 48)

The *Genealogia* is also directed at multiple fictional audiences of varying levels of sophistication. It was ultimately written at the request of King Hugo and therefore dedicated to a single reader, but Boccaccio's fictionalized account of the King's officer attempting to persuade him to undertake the task is supplemented by frequent references to plural 'readers', suggesting that the Narrator visualized a wider audience of like-minded scholars. In Book XV. 12. 2 these male, scholarly audiences are made explicit: 'my audience is neither children nor the lazy rabble, but, as I say, a most learned

King and such men of higher studies as this work may reach from the hands of your Serene Highness, O Prince' (p. 126). And yet, as in *De casibus*, he also anticipates a public of less educated readers: 'I ask my more accomplished readers to remember that they were once untrained and so accept in patience a statement made somewhat fuller for the benefit of their juniors' (XV. 12. 5; p. 136), as well as addressing a series of critical readers described as the enemies of poetry (Books XIV and XV). There are clear parallels here with the Introduction to Day IV and Conclusion in the *Decameron*, although in the *Genealogia* the nature and characteristics of these critics are described and vilified with greater rhetorical force and at greater length, as befits this scholarly work. Thus, as we have seen a range of authorial strategies at play, so these can be mapped on to groups of different readers within the same work, each of which may require some modulation of technique – even within the same text – in relation to the threefold function of literature to delight, entertain, and also affect an audience. From this perspective, the audience is not an extrinsic factor, but integral to the creation and success of a literary work.

Beyond these fictional audiences the author's ultimate aim is to make a published work available to a historical audience. However, the distinction between fictional and non-fictional audiences is not always as clear-cut as we might first imagine and can be a question of critical interpretation. For example, the Narrator's reference to critical readers in the Introduction to Day IV of the *Decameron* is variously seen as a reflection of a historical reading public operating outside the text which has accessed published instalments of the as yet unfinished work, deliberately circulated by the author, or can be read as an entirely fictional device constructed in order to allow Boccaccio to display his accomplished skills in 'subiectio' (stating the opponent's objection, known as 'hypophora'), and therefore part of his ongoing concern with the defence of literature which also surfaces in *De casibus* and is developed most fully in the *Genealogia*.[10]

While the history of the composition and publication of the *Decameron* is still unclear, we do know that Boccaccio continued to revise many of his texts – including the *Decameron* – throughout his lifetime, thereby releasing multiple redactions of his works into the public arena and creating plenty of scope for historical audiences to participate in the creative process. There is, firstly, a distinction to be drawn here between the creation of fictional scenarios and themes which could be designed to influence and guide the way in which historical readers approach the text, and secondly, cases in which historical readers have intervened either directly or indirectly to influence the nature of the fiction during its creation. In both cases, the audience – whether anticipated or real – is an integral part of the process of composition.

Thus in the first situation we could list the many different ways in which Boccaccio attempts to steer an intended historical audience – both *who* should be reading and *how* they should be reading – by using the layers of audience interpretation embedded in the theme of a *brigata* telling and receiving stories, not only in the *Decameron*, but also through similar frame-stories, including the *Filocolo*, *Comedia delle ninfe fiorentine*, *Corbaccio*, and *De casibus*. Guidance on strategies for reading can also be deduced from Boccaccio's decision to append his own commentary to the *Teseida*, and from the recycling of Paolo and Francesca's experience of the dangers of seductive literature which are scattered across Boccaccio's works, from Florio and Biancifiore reading in the *Filocolo*, through the subtitle of the *Decameron*, the dedication in the *Teseida*, and the reading choices of female characters in the *Fiammetta* and *Corbaccio*.

Boccaccio seems particularly alert to the 'problem' of reader-response (in other words, that the meaning of a text is located within a reader's interpretation rather than within authorial intention), and acknowledges it at the same time as attempting to guide his audiences. In the *Genealogia*, his invitation to future readers to correct the text recognizes that this is a standard *topos*, while at the same time carefully distinguishing between different types of potential reading public:

> Conscious as I am that my errors are matters of negligence, I meekly crave your pardon, and humbly beseech your distinguished Eminence [King Hugo] to supply these defects out of your own lofty genius, making necessary excisions, emendations, corrections of style, and all, such as your fair judgment may suggest. Perhaps, as usual with kings, you are too busy with more important matters to find leisure for this work. If so, then ... I beseech all honest, holy, and devout Catholics, into whose hands this book falls, and particularly my eminent teacher, the far-famed Francis Petrarch, piously and kindly to remove any errors which I may have made unawares, and alter them to sacred truth.
>
> (xv. Conclusion, 2–3; pp. 141–2)

In the second situation outlined above – the extent to which historical readers influence the creation of fictional works – this influence can be defined as either active or passive. For example, Boccaccio wrote a series of eclogues over a period of thirty years, only finally collecting them together in 1372, leaving plenty of opportunity for friends and fellow scholars such as Petrarch and Donato degli Albanzani (to whom the *Buccolicum carmen* is finally dedicated) to read and comment on their progress, thereby actively influencing

47

their creative development. *De mulieribus* was also composed and revised over a period of many years, and its dedicatee, Andrea Acciaiuoli, could be cited as an example of a 'passive' historical audience. Boccaccio added the dedication to Andrea in an intermediate phase of the composition, in order to curry favour after he was invited to Naples by Andrea's brother. Thus she could be said to have altered subsequent forms of the work without having any direct contact with it prior to publication, granting her a less visible form of agency than the men with whom Boccaccio discussed his writing.

In general, Boccaccio did not often choose to dedicate his works to non-fictional dedicatees. Indeed, he preferred to maintain a position of independence, writing: 'I am too proud and obstinate to dedicate even one poem to anybody unrequested, except to God, to whose glory all works should be ascribed;... only a request, or friendship, would move me' (*Genealogia*, xv. 13. 3; p. 140). The only other instances of historical figures who might be described as dedicatees are King Hugo, who requested that Boccaccio compose the *Genealogia*, Niccolò di Bartolo del Buono, to whom the *Comedia delle ninfe fiorentine* is dedicated in friendship, and the second redaction of the *De casibus*, dedicated to Boccaccio's friend and patron Mainardo Cavalcanti.

Dedications authorize a text, helping to deflect criticism of both the author and his work through their association with a figure who has an established social and/or cultural stature. They also act as a bridge between the world of fiction and the text's future in the public realm. The presentation of the dedicatee allows the author to offer a template for reading practice, based on connections between the style and contents of the text and the abilities of its idealized first reader. Thus, the narrator of *De mulieribus* takes great pains to establish the suitability of its female dedicatee in relation to the biographies of famous women contained therein:

> For as I reflected on your character, both gentle and renowned; your outstanding probity, women's greatest ornament; and your elegance of speech; and as I noted your generosity of soul and your powers of intellect far surpassing the endowments of womankind;... considering all this, I felt that you deserved comparison with the most excellent women anywhere, even among the ancients. (Dedication, 5; pp. 3–5)

The narrator then continues to set out instructions for reading:

> You will find, at times, that an appropriate recital of the facts has compelled me to mix the impure with the pure. Do not skip over these parts and do not shy away from them, but persevere in your reading. As on entering a

garden you extend your ivory hands towards the flowers, leaving aside the thorns, so in this case relegate to one side offensive matters and gather what is praiseworthy. (Dedication, 9; p. 5)

To what extent these instructions were followed by Andrea and the historical audiences beyond her is the concern of scholars tracing the reading history of *De mulieribus*. As the only text containing a historical female dedicatee, its reception history is one of the most intriguing, not least because of the difficulty we have in uncovering evidence for female readerships in the period. Glimpses of female readers are often transmitted indirectly through men, and this additional filter provides considerable interpretative difficulties. Boccaccio himself offered a tantalizing suggestion that women may have been reading his works when he wrote a letter to Mainardo Cavalcanti (*Epistle* XXII) asking him to forbid female readers access to his texts. However, not only is it a matter of personal interpretation whether Boccaccio's modesty and self-damning criticism should be taken at face value, it is also difficult to know whether this is any reflection of a historical audience, or a rhetorical position-statement from an author acutely conscious of his own reputation. Similarly, while there are very few records of female book owners, some women undoubtedly had access to books belonging to the men in their households, which they may have been able to read themselves and from which they were read to by others. Aristocratic women could benefit from courtly lending libraries: inventories of fifteenth-century libraries belonging to the House of Montefeltro in Urbino, the Visconti family in Milan, and the Este family in Ferrara demonstrate that these all contained copies of *De mulieribus*. There is evidence from a century later that courtly women were interested in the genre of literature in defence of women stimulated by Boccaccio's text, since a close friend of Isabella d'Este, Margherita Cantelmo, commissioned a text entitled *De mulieribus* from Mario Equicola. But there is little or no direct evidence of women reading *De mulieribus* in Italy in manuscript or print in the first century or so after its publication, whether from critical comments made in letters, journals, or other literary texts, or which we can trace from marks of reading and ownership found within the books themselves.

Clearly neither fictionalized female audiences nor the presence of dedications to non-fictional women discouraged male audiences. There is plenty of evidence that men both owned and read *De mulieribus* in the decades immediately following publication. Boccaccio's instructions for reading to Andrea Acciaiuoli could therefore either be imitated, or ignored as inappropriate for men, as the humanistically educated reader Ludovico Sandeo chose to do in the latter half of the fifteenth century.[11] Rather than embracing the whole of the text, Sandeo chose to read in the selective manner encouraged by the Narrator of the *Decameron*, transcribing into his manuscript copy only those biographies which appealed to him, acting as a secondary compiler of Boccaccio's compilatory text.

Conclusion

The social context of the performance of the text is fundamental to understanding the ways in which Boccaccio's authorial strategies operate. A narrator cannot tell his or her story if there is no one there to hear it, and therefore the receiving audience determines and defines a narrator's professed – and implicit – intentions. The arousal of compassion within the audience, a recurring feature in Boccaccio's vernacular texts, functions not only as a component of the text's erotic intention, but as an indication of Boccaccio's sensitivity to the art of rhetoric – which involves the interplay between text and context – and the conventions of genre. In order for rhetoric to function adequately, the teller of the story must create an affective response in the listener or reader. Thus, in Boccaccio's stories about love, it is entirely consistent that the narrator should have experience of his subject-matter in order to signal his credibility for the task, and correspondingly, that the narrators of the Latin works should gain authority by being figured as knowledgeable scholars. The modes adopted by the narrator are thus determined by generic practice and function independently of any autobiographical schema.

NOTES

1 M. A. R. Habib, *A History of Literary Criticism and Theory: From Plato to the Present* (Oxford: Blackwell, 2008), p. 98.
2 Alastair Minnis, *Medieval Theory of Authorship: Scholastic Literary Attitudes in the Later Middle Ages*, 2nd edn (Philadelphia: University of Pennsylvania Press, 2010), pp. 94–5.
3 Giovanni Boccaccio, *Decameron*, ed. by Amedeo Quondam, Maurizio Fiorilla, and Giancarlo Alfano (Milan: BUR Rizzoli, 2013), pp. 14–15.
4 *Decameron*, ed. by Quondam, Fiorilla, and Alfano, pp. 121–3.
5 For example: *Filostrato*, Proem, 27; *De mulieribus claris*, Preface, 1–3.
6 See Chapter 8 in this volume.
7 *The Divine Comedy of Dante Alighieri*, ed. and trans. by Robert M. Durling, 3 vols (Oxford: Oxford University Press, 1996), I, 74–75; IV, 102.
8 See List of manuscripts and Chapter 8 in this volume.
9 See, for example, *Decameron*, IV. 3; *Filocolo*, V. 97. 7; *Comedia delle ninfe fiorentine*, LI; *Elegia di madonna Fiammetta*, IX.

10 'Hypophora occurs when we enquire of our adversaries, or ask ourselves, what the adversaries can say in their favour, or what can be said against us; then we subjoin what ought or ought not to be said – that which will be favourable to us or, by the same token, be prejudicial to the opposition': *[Cicero] ad C. Herennium: de ratione dicendi (Rhetorica ad Herennium)*, with a translation by Harry Caplan (Cambridge, MA: Harvard University Press, 1964), IV. xxiii. 33, 311. The *Rhetorica ad Herennium* is among the works glossed by Boccaccio in Florence, Biblioteca Medicea Laurenziana, MS 51.10: see List of manuscripts in this volume.

11 Rhiannon Daniels, *Boccaccio and the Book: Production and Reading in Italy 1340–1520* (London: Legenda, 2009), pp. 146–8.

PART II

Literary Forms and Narrative Voices

4

PIER MASSIMO FORNI

The *Decameron* and narrative form

What is the *Decameron*? Even someone well acquainted with the masterpiece by the sage of Certaldo may still hesitate when answering such a basic question. To say what the *Decameron* is *not* is easy. It cannot be called a novel because it is not a long work of unified narrative prose. It is, however, the work of someone who did write novels and was able to transpose the feeling of a novel into a *novella* (witness for instance tales such as Alatiel's (II. 7) and Messer Torello's (X. 9)). Although made of narrative units of the *novella* genre, the *Decameron* is not a collection of tales – or at least not *only* that. Such a definition would not do justice to the sophisticated system of connections between and among tales. Written mostly in prose, it also features parts in poetry, but it is unlike any prosimetrum ever written. Let us then simply say that the *Decameron* is an aggregate of micro-texts which, without sacrificing their autonomy, form a larger entity, a macro-text. The book purports to be a truthful retelling of tales originally narrated by a group of ten young men and women who flee Florence in 1348, seeking shelter on the surrounding hills from the plague epidemic. Its narrative form made of multiple voices (eleven in total, counting the author's) gives the book its overarching structure.

Aimed at giving the impression of a comprehensive account of the human experience (a totality effect) the *Decameron* owes much to Dante, who had shown the way first of all by demonstrating that the young literature in the Florentine vernacular was ready to produce work of such an ambition to compete with the classics – that Francesca could vie with Virgil's Dido. This exciting feeling of both potential and actual achievement is what brought Dante to fashion his self-congratulatory self-co-optation among the great spirits of antiquity in *Inferno* IV. If we remember Dante and Boccaccio today, it is because of their courage and indeed their daring in becoming mythographers of modernity, thus opening the road to realism, which became the *via aurea* of all of modern narrative.

There is no mistaking the fact that Dante's work was the first to lay open the panorama of the common and multiplex world of human reality... Without the *Commedia* the *Decameron* could not have been written... What he [Boccaccio] owes to Dante is the possibility of making such free use of his talent, of attaining the vantage point from which it is possible to survey the entire present world of phenomena, to grasp it in all its multiplicity, and to reproduce it in a pliable and expressive language.[1]

Erich Auerbach's words from his seminal monograph on Western realism are still among the most effective, if not *the* most effective conceptualization of Dante's and Boccaccio's realism. 'To survey the entire present world of phenomena, to grasp it in all its multiplicity' aptly defines the gravitational pull exerted by realism on the two writers. But both Dante and Boccaccio went beyond that. Not only was Boccaccio persuaded by Dante that a great vernacular work could and should be rooted in the sense of empirical, everyday reality. Just as he was a gifted conjurer of reality effects – to use Roland Barthes's term – Boccaccio was also most proficient in exploiting totality effects.[2] He did this in part by ordering the book's contents with criteria of correspondence, opposition, and complementarity. While on Day I we find tales showcasing the protagonists' moral failings, on the last the narrators try to outdo one another by presenting stories of increasingly admirable deeds. While the stories of Day I highlight the power of the word, those of Day II are action-based. While on Day II fortune intervenes heavily in determining the shape of human affairs, on Day III human ingenuity and resourcefulness prevail. Days IV and V deal with tragic loves and loves with a happy ending respectively. Throughout the book the ten narrators in the frame-tale respond to one another's tales. This happens in an overt manner when they state that the tale they have just heard brought to their mind the one they are about to tell. Filomena's introduction to her tale in Day I is a typical example:

Neifile's story was well received by all the company, and when she fell silent, Filomena began at the queen's behest to address them as follows: The story told by Neifile reminds me of the parlous state in which a Jew once found himself. Now that we have heard such fine things said concerning God and the truth of our religion, it will not seem inappropriate to descend at this juncture to the deeds and adventures of men. So I shall tell you a story which, when you have heard it, will possibly make you more cautious in answering questions addressed to you. (I. 3; pp. 41–2)

To quote Marcel Janssens: 'The reception proves to be productive and creative in that it influences the making of other narratives. Reception and production are connected in a circular process which constitutes the making of the *Decameron*.'[3]

A covert example of production rooted in reception involves one of the best-known tragic tales and one of the most charming ones in the day of happily-ending love-stories. In Day IV, the day of the loves with a tragic ending when the unhappy lover Filostrato rules, Fiammetta opens the narrative rituals with the sombre story of Tancredi and Ghismonda (IV. 1). The tale's major narrative sequences include: a jealous father who witnesses his daughter's lovemaking; the father ordering the killing of her lover; the father having the lover's heart excised and presented to the young woman in a golden cup; and finally, the daughter taking her own life. In Day V, the day of loves ending happily presided over by Fiammetta, Filostrato chooses to tell a story which harks back to the one of Tancredi and Ghismonda told by Fiammetta the day before. This is the cheerful story of the nightingale in which a father catches his daughter Caterina and her lover Ricciardo *in flagrante delicto* but contains his indignation while reviewing the advantages of showing leniency (V. 4). Bloodshed is eventually averted and a wedding ensues. The story's decisive moment happens when the young lovers waking up in each other's arms become aware of the looming presence of the girl's father.

We should not let the dramatic rendering of the events prevent us from observing their linguistic texturing: 'He [Ricciardo] felt as though his heart was being ripped out.'[4] To convey Ricciardo's distress at being discovered in quite embarrassing and risky circumstances, Boccaccio could have chosen many other suitable analogies. He however, picked one which brings us back to the tragic fate of Guiscardo in the first story of the previous day – more precisely to the excision (non-metaphorical, to be sure) of his heart. For a moment in the comedic Ricciardo we see the tragic Guiscardo. Whether we are in the presence of an intentional reference or whether the choice of words is 'innocent', the effect does not escape the attentive reader. As Giovanni Getto observed:

> These symmetrical, or rather bipolar situations seem to be due, at least in part, to the intention of collecting all of reality, in its contrasting or complementary aspects . . . It is not a reality fastidiously picked which Boccaccio relished, but neither is it one which is chaotically assembled. His formula is instead that of a total reality arranged according to a perspective which conveys the sense of a most varied totality.[5]

We should observe, at least in passing, that the rewriting of tragic *novella* IV. 1 as comedic V. 4 can be seen as a parody or more precisely as a self-parody. As Carlo Delcorno has shown persuasively, parody is a core component of Boccaccio's imagination.[6]

The illusion is one of dealing with a book that not only is a world in itself, but in which the whole world is contained, with the totality of human experience in it. This is what allows Dante and Boccaccio to have their place on Homer's shelf, to be joined in due time by the likes of Proust and Joyce. The interconnections are not all of the totality-making kind and their purpose varies from one occurrence to another. It is one of the critic's tasks to suggest what their function may be. At any rate, twentieth-century Boccaccio scholars have made it abundantly clear that any critical approach to any tale needs to include a preliminary account of how such a tale participates in the structural and rhetorical complexity that characterizes the book. In what Day does the tale appear? Who is its narrator and why? What is its position within the sequence of the Day's tales? How does it fit within the small corpus of remaining nine tales presented by its narrator? In what other ways does it relate to other tales and to the frame-tale? Do its characters appear in other tales as well? (Calandrino, for instance, is the character who returns most often in the book, there being four tales of his antics: VIII. 3; VIII. 6; IX. 3; IX. 5.) Are the tales situated in no particular order or do they form a mini-macro-text? In the end, to a book written in the vernacular, in whose contents there is no dearth of sex and laughter and whose preferred mode of expression is realism, complexity brought much-needed respectability. One basic element of complexity comes to the work from its being the product of eleven fictional voices: that of the author and the ten members of the *brigata.*

The author reserves for himself three places in which to address his readers directly: the Proem, Introduction to Day IV, and Conclusion make Boccaccio's macro-text one of the very first appearances of authorial self-commentary in European literary history. The Proem expounds the circumstances that caused the writing, defines the work, and identifies its audience. As we peruse it we catch a glimpse of fourteenth-century bourgeois society where young women are relegated under the strict control of parents, brothers, and husbands. The author, who received life-saving help from the conversations with his friends while in the throes of a passionate love, is now delivered from those bonds. Thus, the time has come to pay his debt of gratitude:

> And who will deny that such encouragement, however small, should much
> rather be offered to the charming ladies than to the men? For the ladies, out
> of fear or shame, conceal the flames of passion within their fragile breasts,
> and a hidden love is far more potent than one which is worn on the sleeve,
> as everyone knows who has had experience of these matters. Moreover they
> are forced to follow the whims, fancies and dictates of their fathers, mothers,

brothers and husbands, so that they spend most of their time cooped up within the narrow confines of their rooms, where they sit in apparent idleness, wishing one thing and at the same time wishing its opposite, and reflecting on various matters, which cannot possibly always be pleasant to contemplate. And if, in the course of their meditations, their minds should be invaded by melancholy arising out of the flames of longing, it will inevitably take root there and make them suffer greatly, unless it be dislodged by new interests. Besides which, their powers of endurance are considerably weaker than those that men possess.

(Proem, 9–12; p. 2)

Having swiftly evoked the place and mood of the women's domestic seclusion, he offers the details of his plan:

I intend to provide succor and diversion for the ladies, but only for those who are in love, since the others can make do with their needles, their reels and their spindles. I shall narrate a hundred stories or fables or parables or histories or whatever you choose to call them, recited in ten days by a worthy band of seven ladies and three young men, who assembled together during the plague which recently took such heavy toll of life . . . In these tales will be found a variety of love adventures, bitter as well as pleasing, and other exciting incidents, which took place in both ancient and modern times. In reading them, the aforesaid ladies will be able to derive, not only pleasure from the entertaining matters therein set forth, but also some useful advice. For they will learn to recognize what should be avoided and likewise what should be pursued, and these things can only lead, in my opinion, to the removal of their affliction. If this should happen (and may God grant that it should), let them give thanks to Love, which in freeing me from its bonds, has granted me the power of making provision for their pleasures. (Proem, 13–15; p. 3)

The pro-feminist nature of the *Decameron* is in full display also in the next privileged spot from which the author addresses his readers: the Introduction to Day IV. Here he responds to the supercilious readers who have taken him to task for writing frivolous tales about women and for women. His response is that the Muses who inspire him are not those residing on Mount Parnassus, but rather real women in real life. His love of women – he claims – is bred in the bone and it is just about the most natural thing in the world. He goes on to illustrate the force of erotic impulse with a light-hearted moral fable. Born and raised in the wilderness, completely innocent of the ways of the world, and never having seen a town before, a young hermit one day finally finds himself walking the streets of Florence. All being new to him and a source of awe and marvel, the young man keeps asking his father what the things he sees are. When father and son stumble upon a group of pretty girls returning from a wedding the son is immediately smitten by the comeliness of those creatures unknown to him. Naturally, he wants to know what they are called. To protect his son's chaste mind the father tells him that they are evil and are called goslings. But having already completely forgotten all the other marvels of Florence the young man already has eyes only for the girls: '"Oh, father, do please get me one of those goslings."' (IV. 24; p. 287). When the father reiterates that the goslings are evil, the son insists in his request:

> 'You can say what you like, father, but I don't see anything evil about them. As far as I am concerned, I don't think I have ever in my whole life seen anything so pretty or attractive. They are more beautiful than the painted angels that you have taken me to see so often. O alas! if you have any concern for my welfare, do make it possible for us to take one of these goslings back with us, and I will pop things into its bill.' (IV. 28; p. 287)

Although the father has the last word he must admit defeat: '"Certainly not", said his father. "Their bills are not where you think, and require a special sort of diet." But no sooner had he spoken than he realized that his wits were no match for Nature, and regretted having brought the boy to Florence in the first place' (IV. 29; p. 287). The moral of the story is that nature defeats culture. Whether we like it or not this is what real life is. The invitation to be realistic when considering the basic traits of human nature blooms into a manifesto of realism:

> The Muses are ladies, and although ladies do not rank as highly as Muses, nevertheless they resemble them at first sight, and hence it is natural, if only for this reason, that I should be fond of them. Moreover, ladies have caused me to compose a thousand lines of poetry in the course of my life, whereas the Muses never caused me to write any at all. It is true that they have helped me, and shown me *how* to write; and it is possible that they have been looking over my shoulder several times in the writing of these tales, however unassuming they may be, perhaps because they acknowledge and respect the affinity between the ladies and themselves. And so, in composing these stories, I am not straying as far from Mount Parnassus or from the Muses as many people might be led to believe. (IV. 35–6; p. 289)

This is one of the crucial pronouncements not only in the *Decameron* but in the whole of Boccaccio's literary production. It begins with an accommodating inclination by paying tribute to both women and Muses, only to dismiss abruptly the latter in the very next sentence: not even one verse did they inspire in him. Here the pendulum swings again with the author's admission that some assistance came to him from the Muses. In the strong closing sentence the dichotomy Muses/women seems to dissolve. In essence, the author conveys the message that although he may not need the Muses, his work is nevertheless comparable in quality to that which is said to have been inspired by them. Boccaccio is demanding here the respect he believes he deserves as a writer of genius. The Conclusion provides the author with another opportunity to defend his work. This time, however, he is not doing battle with hostile critics. He proactively addresses his audience of women, imagining their possible objections to his work. Among these is his having taken too many liberties in the writing of his tales. Part of his reply focuses not on the tales themselves, but rather on the circumstances in which they were told, reiterating the fiction that he is not their author, but only their scribe:

> Furthermore it is made perfectly clear that these stories were told neither in a church... nor in the schools of the philosophers, in which, no less than anywhere else, a sense of decorum is required, nor in any place where either churchmen or philosophers were present. They were told in gardens, in a place designed for pleasure, among people who, though young in years, were none the less fully mature and not to be led astray by stories, at a time when even the most respectable people saw nothing unseemly in wearing their breeches over their heads if they thought their lives might thereby be preserved.
>
> (Conclusion, 7; p. 799)

Another possible objection allows him to remind his readers one more time for whom and to what purpose the book was conceived and written:

> I suppose it will also be said that some of the tales are too long, to which I can only reply that if you have better things to do, it would be foolish to read these tales, even if they were short. Although much time has elapsed from the day I started to write until this moment, in which I am nearing the end of my labours, it has not escaped my memory that I offered these exertions of mine to ladies with time on their hands, not to any others; and for those who read in order to pass the time, nothing can be too long if it serves the purpose for which it is intended.
>
> (Conclusion, 20; p. 801)

Dante built with his *Comedy*, later called 'divine', a gothic cathedral as a shrine to a woman who was the object of his idealizing love and who never ceased to be a source of inspiration. Beatrice is the woman like no other whose excellence in virtue and intellect makes her the worthy celestial trustee of a genius who knew all too well that he was one. Boccaccio, who considered Dante his first *maestro* among the moderns, followed him to the extent that his imagination allowed him, building with his human comedy a secular mausoleum to all women. Ostensibly written for women, its action set in motion by women and its stories, mostly narrated by women, frequently presenting women in the role of protagonists: this is how Giovanni Boccaccio imagines his world and at its core he places women. There is no book in the history of early Italian literature, or perhaps in Italian literature *tout court*, in which women are more predominantly represented. There is not a Giovanna, Andrea, or Fiammetta here who commissions the book or to whom the book is dedicated: for example, Boccaccio considers Queen Giovanna of Naples as a possible dedicatee for *De mulieribus claris*, before dedicating it to the Neapolitan noblewoman, Andrea Acciaiuoli; the *Teseida* is dedicated to Fiammetta. The *Decameron* does not belong to this or that woman, real or imaginary, but to all. After the Proem, the first glimpse of the centrality of women to the project of the book is detectable in the Introduction to Day I. We are at the very beginning of the frame-tale action taking place in the church of Santa Maria Novella in Florence, and the spotlight is on the women: in particular, the initiative of fleeing the plague-ridden city comes from Pampinea, the most authoritative female figure in the group. It is she who, upon arrival at the *locus amoenus* (pleasant place) where they will reside, proposes the telling of stories as the preferred pastime for the hot hours of the day. On account of her crucial role at the beginning of the frame-tale Pampinea represents a major inspirational force for the *brigata*. As such, she is a good example of the kind of Muse to whom the author pledges his allegiance in the Introduction to Day IV. This is Pampinea proposing the notion of an escape from Florence:

> And if we return to our homes, what happens? I know not whether your own experience is similar to mine, but my house was once full of servants, and now that there is no one left apart from my maid and myself, I am filled with foreboding and feel as if every hair of my head is standing on end. Wherever I go in the house, wherever I pause to rest, I seem to be haunted by the shades of the departed, whose faces no longer appear as I remember them but with strange and horribly twisted expressions that frighten me out of my senses... Besides, unless I am mistaken we shall not be abandoning anyone by going away from here; on the contrary, we may fairly claim that we are the ones who have been abandoned, for our kinsfolk are either dead or fled, and have left us to fend for ourselves in the midst of all this affliction, as though disowning us completely. (Introduction to Day I, 59–70; pp. 15–16)

This is a dismal picture indeed, but it is because the very fabric of society is unravelling that Pampinea and her six female companions for the very first time are in charge of their own lives. Without the plague the young women of the *brigata* might find themselves in seclusion within their homes like the prospective female readers of the book. Instead, they are no longer forced 'to follow the whims, fancies and dictates of their fathers, mothers, brothers and husbands' and to 'spend most of their time cooped up within the narrow confines of their rooms' (Proem, 10; p. 2). Florence may be in the throes of the pestilence, but at the same time to them it feels as though it is benefiting from an epoch-making season of deliverance. The death of fathers, mothers, brothers, and husbands makes the idyllic and self-regulated retreat of the *brigata* possible, which in turn makes it possible for the female readers to picture themselves freely enjoying an alternative world beyond the stifling confines of their domestic walls. 'Our kinsfolk are either dead or fled' (Introduction to Day I, 69; p. 16): a *frisson* of parricide informs Boccaccio's *Decameron*. Identifying with the female protagonists of the frame-tale, the intended female readers can find in the description of plague-ridden Florence excitement mixed with horror. Horror is an obvious response. The excitement comes when the contemplation of it allows them to indulge a fantasy of emancipation.

As I have observed elsewhere, a landmark in the development of early Italian narrative is the canonization of the *cornice* – the framing device – thanks to the astounding success of Boccaccio's *Decameron*. The loosely structured anthology of stories (the *novelliere aperto*, such as the *Novellino*) is superseded by the *novelliere chiuso* with its all-encompassing meta-story. Likewise, similar developments can be observed within lyric poetry, where the fragmentary collection evolves into the prosimetrum (Dante's *Vita nova*) and the *canzoniere* (Petrarch's *Rime*). The development of innovative modes of collection, structuring, and closure characterizes the progress of literary forms as they evolve, and thus the maturation of Italian literature is marked by its mastery of what semiologists call the macro-text.[7] It was a choice that allowed authors to utilize occasional texts, injecting new meaning in them and making them part of more complex and ambitious writing projects. When it comes to building the work of his full maturity as a writer, Boccaccio certainly looks at Dante's *Comedy*. But the structure he derives from the vernacular work of his other great *maestro*, Petrarch. As a macro-text, the *Decameron* is his *Canzoniere*. This is not to say that the *Decameron* is a derivative exercise. Once we have established the connections with his great *maestri*, the *Decameron* stands on its own, with its own moral and aesthetic timbres as any masterpiece does.

NOTES

1 Erich Auerbach, *Mimesis: The Representation of Reality in Western Literature* (Princeton: Princeton University Press, 1974), p. 220.

2 Roland Barthes, 'L'Effet du Réel', *Communications*, 8 (1968), 84–9.

3 Marcel Janssens, 'The Internal Reception of the Stories within the *Decameron*', in *Boccaccio in Europe: Proceedings of the Boccaccio Conference, Leuven,*

December 1975, ed. by Gilbert Tournoy (Leuven: Leuven University Press, 1977), pp. 135–48.

4 Own translation. In Italian: 'parve che gli fosse il cuore del corpo strappato' (v. 4. 42); McWilliam's translation reads: 'he almost died of fright' (p. 397).

5 Giovanni Getto, *Vita di forme e forme di vita nel 'Decameron'* (Turin: Petrini, 1986), p. 202 (my translation).

6 Delcorno, 'Ironia/Parodia', in *Lessico critico decameroniano*, ed. by Renzo Bragantini and Pier Massimo Forni (Turin: Bollati Boringhieri, 1995), pp. 162–91.

7 Pier Massimo Forni, *Adventures in Speech: Rhetoric and Narration in Boccaccio's 'Decameron'* (Philadelphia: University of Pennsylvania Press, 1996), p. 2.

5

DAVID LUMMUS

The *Decameron* and Boccaccio's poetics

At the end of his Latin treatise on myth, the *Genealogia deorum gentilium*, Boccaccio delineates his understanding of poetry as a useful art: '[poetry] offers us so many inducements to virtue, in the warnings and teachings of poets whose care it has been to describe with sublime talent and utmost honesty, in exquisite style and diction, men's meditations on things of heaven' (xiv. 6. 8).[1] Whereas such a declaration of poetics is relatively unsurprising for a medieval reader of poets such as Virgil, Dante, or Petrarch, at first glance it seems difficult to apply it to Boccaccio's own works, especially the morally ambiguous *Decameron*, but also his early works, each of which explores the nature of human desire in a language that oscillates between the erudite and the plebeian. The sense of lowliness that results from the popular origins of Boccaccio's poetic practice seems out of place in this definition of poetry's moral utility and aesthetic sublimity. In order to understand the complex poetic system according to which Boccaccio's *Decameron* succeeds in overcoming the humble, even debased, nature of its material, we must retrace in broad strokes the history of his poetics from the point of view that he provides in the *Genealogia*.

Exquisite speech: the mechanics of Boccaccio's poetry

For Boccaccio, poetry distinguishes itself from other forms of discourse by its beauty. In the *Genealogia*, following Petrarch's definition of poetry in the *Epistolae familiares* (*Familiar Letters*) x. 4 and that of Isidore of Seville in *Etymologiae* (*Etymologies*) viii. 7, Boccaccio incorrectly traces the origins of the Latin word for poetry (*poesis*) not to the Greek word for 'making' (from *poiéō*), but to the Greek word for quality (*poiótēs*), which he understood as meaning 'exquisite discourse' (xiv. 7. 2; p. 40). In the production of this kind of speech there are two key elements, a poetic fervour and an artistic skill, that together render ordinary speech inspired and sublime. The result of this kind of speech is a fiction that hides truth beneath an allegorical veil – a truth that, when disclosed, can have sublime effects:

> Poetry . . . is a sort of fervour of exquisite invention, either in speech or writing, of that which you have invented or found. It proceeds from the bosom of God, and few, I find, are the minds in which this gift is born; indeed so wonderful a gift it is that true poets have always been extremely rare. The effects of this fervour of poetry are sublime: it impels the soul to a longing for speech; it brings forth strange and unheard-of inventions; it composes these meditations in a fixed order, it adorns the whole composition with unusual interweaving of words and ideas, and it conceals the truth in a fair garment of fiction . . . It can arm kings, marshal them for war, launch whole fleets from their docks, even describe the sky, land, and sea, adorn virgins with flowery garlands, portray human character in its various aspects, awake the idle, stimulate the dull, restrain the rash, subdue the criminal, and distinguish excellent men with the praise that they deserve. (XIV. 7. 2; pp. 39–40, modified)

Thus, for Boccaccio, poetry is a means to a sublime moral, political, and even contemplative end that depends on inspiration, technical ability, and the employment of allegorical discourse. The aesthetic ordering of poetic language recreates mimetically the marvellous ordering of the natural world in order to spur readers and listeners both to action and to contemplation.

Besides the effects of poetry and the artifice of its production, one of the main questions that this passage raises concerns the divine origins of poetic inspiration. In the same tradition as the aesthetic theory espoused by Virgil in *Inferno*, XI. 103–5, which maintains that 'our art follows Nature "as the learner does his master" . . . "for your art is nearly like God's grand-daughter"', Boccaccio creates a tenuous link between art and God through Nature.[2] The poetic fervour that originates in the bosom of God seems to render poets vessels for the word of God. The etymology of one of the Latin words for poet, 'vates', was commonly understood to be derived from 'vas Dei', vessel of God, which was also a way of referring to Christ, the perfect embodiment of God on earth. For Boccaccio, however, if the poetic word 'proceeds from the bosom of God', it is because poetic creation emerges from the material of the natural world of history, or 'Natura naturata'. The poet imitates the creative function of God in nature, or 'Natura naturans', aesthetically organizing his words in the creation of poetic worlds like the gardener his flowers. In this way, poetic creation looks on to the divine through the filter of nature and creates links between human experience and the creator. These links reside within the closed, veiled discourse of recondite and highly ornate speech, or poetry.

Whereas the sublime effects of poetry are guaranteed by the semantic depth of allegorical discourse, the beauty of poetry resides for Boccaccio in its ordering. The exquisiteness of poetic speech derives from 'song in an age hitherto unpolished', after which poets applied to their words 'measured periods', 'the standard of fixed rules', and 'a definite number of feet and syllables' (*Genealogia*, XIV. 7. 4; p. 41). During the course of his own poetic career Boccaccio explores the expressive possibilities of both Latin and the vernacular in a more or less allegorical kind of fiction that is founded nevertheless on verisimilar human experiences. He makes use of a vast variety of poetic schemes, tropes, metres, and macro-textual structures in order to open a dialogue with his readers about natural, ethical, and theological truths.

Boccaccio's first real poetic work, from the early 1330s, the *Caccia di Diana*, was composed in the eleven-syllable lines of Dante's *terza rima* (a–b–a–b–c–b–c–d–c). Loosely modelled on Dante's lost *sirventese*, praising the sixty most beautiful women of Florence, mentioned in Chapter VI of the *Vita nova*, the *Caccia* represents Boccaccio's first effort at combining a courtly literature about love with the tradition of moral allegory in the interpretation of classical myth. He playfully combines Dante's stilnovistic language of love with the moralized Ovidian transformation of fifty-eight women of the Neapolitan court. By modelling his poem of moral metamorphosis through love on a poem that Dante did not include in his own narrative of self-transformation, Boccaccio is situating his own work as marginal with respect to Dante's poetry. Boccaccio was also explicitly combining the vernacular poetics of Dante's *Comedy* with Ovid's mythical content; both authors would remain key points of reference for Boccaccio's poetics throughout his career. Later on, in the *Amorosa visione*, Boccaccio will again make use of *terza rima* in a more explicit effort to vernacularize the classical tradition, according to the form of the *Comedy*, and to put into dialogue the content and themes of classical and medieval literature, from Ovid, Virgil, and Homer to the courtly literature of France and the love poets of Sicily and Tuscany. In both of these works Boccaccio shows a predilection for figures such as the acrostic and anaphora, and even for numerological signification. Boccaccio's language in these poems is highly affected and influenced both by classical authors such as Ovid and by vernacular lyric poets such as Dante. In them, especially, readers get a sense of the artificiality and recondite knowledge latent in the poetic ordering of knowledge.

Composed around the same time as the *Caccia di Diana*, the *Filostrato* tells the story of Troiolo and Criseida in the rhyming stanzas of *ottava rima* (a–b–a–b–a–b–c–c). Boccaccio's invention and development of the literary octave derives from a popular metrical form in which the medieval *cantare*, or vernacular romance, was recounted. Boccaccio establishes the form as literary by virtually eliminating its redundant four-part structure (i.e. 2 + 2 + 2 + 2) in favour of the more versatile two-part structure (usually, 4 + 4 or 6 + 2), which renders the stanza more flexible and capable of handling both lyric and narrative moments.[3] With a balanced bipartite structure, Boccaccio was able to express more freely and with more syntactical complexity the emotions of his characters, such as in the following example from Criseida's lament in the *Filostrato*:

> Oimè lassa, trista e dolorosa,
> ch'a me convien portar la penitenza
> del tuo peccato! Cotanto noiosa
> vita non meritai per mia fallenza.
> O verità del ciel, luce pietosa,
> come sofferi tu cotal sentenza,
> ch'un pecchi ed altro pianga, com'io faccio,
> che non peccai e di dolor mi sfaccio?
>
> (IV. 94; p. 135)

[Alas, weary, sad and pained that I must bear the penitence for your sin! I did not deserve such a vexing life for my mistake. O truth of heaven, light of pity, how can you suffer such a sentence, that one sins and the other suffers, as I do, who did not sin and am now undone with pain?]

Another form of the bipartite structure, with a semantic unity expressed in the first six lines, followed by a contrast or concluding phrase of two lines, allowed for a more complex Latinate syntax in the narration of events. This form can be seen in the following description of Troiolo's search for Diomedes at the end of the *Filostrato*:

> E spesse volte insieme s'avvisaro
> con rimproveri cattivi e villani,
> e di gran colpi fra lor si donaro,
> talvolta urtando, e talor nelle mani
> la spada avendo, vendendosi caro
> insieme molto il loro amor non sani;
> ma non avea la Fortuna disposto
> che l'un dell'altro fornisse il proposto.
>
> (VIII. 26; p. 223)

[And often they both saw each other and met with evil and villainous reproaches, and they struck each other with great strength, sometimes clashing, sometimes with their sword in their hands, each madly giving the other his due; but Fortune had not disposed for the one to decide the end of the other.]

We can compare these two stanzas from Boccaccio's poem with one from the popular *Cantare di Fiorio e Biancifiore*, which Boccaccio would retell in prose in the *Filocolo*. This version of the *Cantare* comes from the oldest of the datable *cantari* manuscripts, copied around 1343 (although the story was told in *cantare* form in Italy from at least the thirteenth century):

> E preson la cristiana molto bella
> da poi che le avean morto lo marito.
> Ella dicea: 'O lasa, tapinella,
> dolorosa, son giunta a mal partito!'
> Gran gioia ne fazea la gente fella,
> guardandola nel viso colorito:
> davanti a lo re la presentaro,
> e' quel presente ben lo tene caro.[4]

[And they took the very beautiful woman after they had killed her husband. She said: Alas poor little me, sadly I have reached an evil end! Great joy did the bad men take, looking at her flushed face. They presented her to the king, and he took that present and held it close.]

The *cantare*'s melodic singsong rhythm is avoided for the most part in Boccaccio's version of the octave, with its complex syntactical and rhythmic structures which reinforce his poems' status as literary artefacts meant to be read and studied.

Later on, at the beginning of the 1340s, Boccaccio would definitively institute the *ottava rima* as the metrical form of the vernacular epic, by again intermixing the material of classical epic and the themes of courtly and stilnovist love poetry in the *Teseida*. *Terza rima* was associated with the Dantesque moralizing dream vision and the prosimetrum was a form for autobiographical philosophical reflection, in the tradition of Boethius's *De consolatione philosophiae* (*On the Consolation of Philosophy*) in Latin and Dante's *Vita nova* in the vernacular. *Ottava rima*, however, was more suited to the combination of classical epic and love poetry, since it had already been employed in popular culture to recount the love-epic of the medieval romance. In the years immediately prior to the composition of the *Decameron*, Boccaccio would go on to compose the *Ninfale fiesolano*, again in octaves. Here Boccaccio attempts to compose a pastoral aetiological poem with the language and form of popular poetry. It is an adaptation of the model of Ovid's *Metamorphoses* to new poetic forms in a 'pseudo-popular' and impressionistic language that is more limpid and versatile than his earlier attempts.[5] This development resulted in the establishment of the octave as the vernacular version of the hexameter, capable of expressing in verse a broad range of human experience, from the horrors of war to the passions of love.

Boccaccio's main innovations, however, lie in the creation of a vernacular prose that could absorb the multiplicity of themes that had been the realm of verse in the classical and medieval traditions. The first instance of his work in literary prose is the *Filocolo*, also connected to the tradition of Old French romance and popular *cantari*, which tells the story of Floris and Blancheflour. To a greater extent than the octave, prose allows Boccaccio to retell this well-known story of love within a learned apparatus that engages with classical and medieval poetic sources at the same time as it exploits the encyclopaedic tradition of the medieval *summa*. The prose of the *Filocolo* is still immature compared to that of the *Decameron*, in that the language is not as capable of expressing with ease both an internal reality of sentiment and an external reality of events.

The *Comedia delle ninfe fiorentine* engages with the classical tradition (Virgil, Ovid, Apuleius) and with Dante's *Comedy* through the form of the pastoral prosimetrum, alternating between prose and *terza rima*. The allegorical meditations of the portions in verse are in clear contrast with the prose sections, whose language oscillates between 'eccentric' and 'archaic' and 'plebeian and vernacular'.[6] With the prose of the *Elegia di madonna Fiammetta*, Boccaccio succeeds at developing a language capable of representing the psychological complexities of human sentiment. Here again, however, the language is affected and calculated, inasmuch as it imitates and transforms the tragic tone of Seneca's tragedies and the elegiac tone of Ovid's *Heroides*, pitting them against one another in an effort to create a tragic-elegiac register in the vernacular.

Boccaccio's work expands the literary range of the Tuscan vernacular by melding the forms of popular literature and of the limited vernacular tradition with classical themes and content, creating a hybrid language that bridges the popular with the erudite. In the *Buccolicum carmen*, his major work of Latin poetry, too, Boccaccio chooses the form of the eclogue, written in dactylic hexameters, which the late antique grammarian Servius had described as the lowest of the styles practised by the Roman poet Virgil. Boccaccio's Latin pastorals situate his work as the modern-day standard-bearer of the ancient *modus humilis*, or low style, as it aligns him with the Virgil of the *Bucolics*, not of the *Aeneid*. His Latin resembles most closely that of Virgil, although there are resonances throughout of other late antique and medieval bucolic poets as well as of Dante's *Comedy*.[7] The Latin Boccaccio's humble stance allows him to be considered together with the vernacular Boccaccio, inasmuch as both are concerned with finding poetic forms and languages in consonance with the multiplicity of human experience.

Throughout his prose works in the vernacular and in Latin Boccaccio follows to a varying extent the medieval Latin prose style of the *cursus*, a system of rhythmic phrase endings. By 1351, after his meeting with Petrarch, Boccaccio follows less and less the rules of medieval prose composition, modelling instead his Latin prose on the classical style of Cicero and Livy. As far as his vernacular works are concerned, by the time of the *Decameron*, Boccaccio's use of the *cursus* as a model is sporadic and almost casual.[8] Furthermore, the origin of Boccaccio's prose in medieval *cantari* led him to employ versified prose in which attentive readers can hear various metres, including eleven-syllable and seven-syllable lines (hendecasyllables and septenaries), and other metres. Boccaccio's poetic career leads to the conclusion that, for all of the formal differences between prose and verse, both forms can be subsumed beneath the category of 'poetry'.[9] In fact, in conclusion to his definition of poetry in the *Genealogia*, he does not differentiate between rhetoric and poetry in terms of form, but instead in terms of purpose and intention. For Boccaccio, the study of rhetoric, along with the other liberal arts, was necessary for the poet, but rhetoric was not synonymous with poetry. In response to those who equate the two arts, Boccaccio declares: 'Although rhetoric has also its own inventions, it has no part among the coverings ('integumenta') of fiction, for whatever we compose beneath the veil of allegory ('sub velamento') and set forth exquisitely, is poetry and poetry alone' (XIV. 7. 8; p. 42, modified). The difference between the language of the poet and that of the orator resides in the poet's inspired intention to communicate truth beneath a beautiful fictional covering.

Summary Table of Works and Forms

Title	Form
Caccia di Diana	Allegorical poem in *terza rima*
Filostrato	Romance in *ottava rima*
Filocolo	Romance in prose
Teseida	Romance/Epic in *ottava rima*
Amorosa visione	Allegorical dream vision in *terza rima*
Comedia delle ninfe fiorentine	Allegorical pastoral prosimetrum (prose + *terza rima*)
Elegia di madonna Fiammetta	Sentimental novel in prose
Ninfale fiesolano	Pastoral aetiological poem in *ottava rima*
Decameron	Framed collection of short stories in prose
Corbaccio	Allegorical dream vision in prose
Buccolicum carmen	Collection of Latin eclogues in dactylic hexameters

History and allegory: the development of Boccaccio's poetics

In addition to his innovations across a wide range of literary forms and registers Boccaccio demonstrates a concerted effort to expand poetry's possibilities for meaning. Indeed, for Boccaccio, poetic language is intricately connected to literary form. In another definition of the work of poets from the *Genealogia*, Boccaccio concedes to his critics that poets are 'tale-tellers' ('fabulosos homines'). He goes on to define poetry as the composition of tales, or 'fabulae', and traces the etymology of the term 'fabula' back to the verb '*for, faris*, hence "conversation," which means only "talking together"' (XIV. 9. 3–4; p. 47). The exquisite speech of poets is connected to the dialogic language of conversation and commerce, but also to the speech of Christ and the exemplary stories (*exempla*) often recounted for moral edification in sermons and in tractates. Key to the moral function of these tales was allegorical discourse, known as *figura* for the Bible and *integumentum* for secular texts, which prized the internal philosophical meaning of texts over the fictional outer covering.

Following the late antique philosopher Macrobius,[10] Boccaccio goes on to describe four kinds of tale within this system of meaning: (1) the animal tale of Aesop, whose outer layer is entirely fantastic, but whose inner layer contains moral truths; (2) the mythic tale, whose outer layer mixes the fantastic with the true and whose inner truth is both human and divine; (3) the verisimilar tale, used by epic poets like Virgil and comic poets like Plautus and Terence, which is more similar to history ('historia') than to fiction ('fabula') since the story's meaning is found in the letter; and (4) the kind of old-wives' tale that contains no truth at all (XIV. 9. 5–8, pp. 48–9).

With the exception of this last brand of tale, Boccaccio writes, each kind of fiction can be found not only in the poetry of Graeco-Roman authors, but also in the Bible itself, especially in the words of the prophets, of Solomon, and of Christ. Again linking beauty and morality, Boccaccio declares that 'such is the value of fables that the unlearned may enjoy the fictional covering while the talents of the learned may work on the hidden truths; and thus in one reading the latter are edified and the former delighted' (XIV. 9. 15). Adapting the Horatian dictate from the *Ars poetica* (343) that the best writers mix the useful with the delightful ('miscuit utile dulci'), Boccaccio divides the two effects of poetry according to the capabilities of readers, assigning the delightful to the unlearned and the useful to the learned. This division at the core of Boccaccio's poetic theory will be essential to understanding the poetics of the *Decameron*, but it is useful to review first the process of poetic development that brought him to this point. Within the course of his career Boccaccio experimented especially with the second and third kinds of storytelling that he delineates in the *Genealogia*, developing historical and mythic fables, often either blending the two within an allegorical interpretative structure or inserting allegorically charged moments (such as dreams or visions) into the narratives.

Throughout Boccaccio's oeuvre there is a consistent engagement with the historical world as the realm of human interaction and of contact between human and superhuman forces. Yet the Latin term used to describe this kind of poetic world, *historia*, denotes both a narrative form and, in its adjectival acceptation *hystorialis*, a specific level of exegesis. In patristic and later medieval modes of interpreting the Bible there were four exegetical levels: the historical, the moral, the allegorical, and the anagogical, where the allegorical level signalled the way in which the Old Testament prefigured the events of the New Testament and the anagogical level the prefiguration of future Christian history, such as the afterlife or the apocalypse. Non-biblical texts could be interpreted in a similar manner, with the exception that, unlike the Bible, the historical level was fictional and that often there was only a single (usually moral) figural interpretation. Dante, however, in the letter to Cangrande pointed out the four levels of allegory of the *Comedy*, with the radical claim that the truth of the poem follows the paradigm of the Bible. By focusing on the historical foundations of allegorical discourse, both in its representation and in its interpretation, Boccaccio is in accord with Dante and other late medieval interpreters, who located the origin of figurative meaning in a literal, or historical, interpretation of a text. History offered the assurance (or illusion) of objectivity for interpretation and allowed for the autonomy of texts from often-spurious exegetical apparatuses.

Boccaccio's earliest fictions oscillate between overtly allegorical fiction and the history-like representations of medieval romance, which were linked to the same kind of mixed verisimilar poetics as ancient epic. The *Caccia di Diana* is an allegorical narrative poem with clear historical referents in the Neapolitan court of Boccaccio's time, while the *Filostrato* is a pseudo-historical narrative with foundations in the medieval romance tradition. Boccaccio's authorial stance in the *Filocolo* is one of historical recovery: the popular tale of love and marriage is framed by Fiammetta's injunction to save the story from the hands of the ignorant (i.e. the composers of the popular *cantari*). With the *Teseida*, Boccaccio blends the two forms of representation at the same time as he separates them. The epic is accompanied by a series of glosses written by the author himself in order to establish the modes of the poem's interpretation between the historical (glosses that explain the materiality of ancient culture) and the allegorical (glosses that explain the significance of various gods).

In his Florentine fiction, with works such as the *Ninfale fiesolano* and the *Comedia delle ninfe fiorentine*, but also the *Amorosa visione*, Boccaccio moves from a recognizably historical and verisimilar representation of a past world (whether Troy, Athens, or Naples) to a more openly fantastic world of the mythical past populated by nymphs and heroes. The dream vision of the *Amorosa visione* mediates between the two forms of poetry by staging the protagonist/narrator's encounter with ekphrases of gods and men in a moral-allegorical journey through literary history. These works represent, on the one hand, a turn towards the mythic, and, on the other, the recognition of a historical, human element within mythical allegories. The *Elegia di madonna Fiammetta* is a blend of the verisimilar story of a historical, embodied individual with the possibility of allegorical interpretation expected from mythical discourse. The characters that populate Boccaccio's early historical and mythical fictions are roughly verisimilar figures that also have allegorical meanings. As his career progresses and his literary language becomes more versatile, the worlds and characters that he creates gain in complexity.

In the *Decameron*, Boccaccio continues to be concerned with similar questions of poetics: with the formation of a literary vernacular capable of expressing the complete range of embodied human experience, with forms of verisimilar representation, and with the metaphorical language at the heart of allegorical discourse. Although the *Decameron* is unique among Boccaccio's works for its scope and variety, it is the culmination of the poetic work that preceded it.

Embodied histories and sublime interpretations: the poetics of the *Decameron*

Boccaccio's language in the *Decameron*'s prefatory sections, self-defences, and conclusion is highly ornate, with roots in the medieval rhetorical tradition, while the language of the tales of the first nine days is extremely varied and representative of an objective historical reality recognizable by its readers as verisimilar. Boccaccio adapts his style and language to the various contexts of each narrative moment. In Day x, the influence of the *cursus* of the medieval rhetorical tradition returns, signalling the higher aspirations of the storytellers. Erich Auerbach, in *Mimesis*, examined Boccaccio's prose style in the *Decameron* and came to the conclusion that, while it fails to elicit the *pathos* of Dante's *Comedy*, it succeeds in imitating the language of life in the *piazza* as no other work before it.[11] The linguistic variety and fluid style of the *Decameron*'s tales belie the artistry behind them in their very simplicity. With the help of a historically and geographically rooted language Boccaccio can give the illusion of representing reality objectively in his stories. He was not interested in merely representing reality for its own sake, however, but in offering these pleasurable stories to his readers so that they could reflect on reality according to their own intellectual abilities.

In the Proem to the *Decameron* Boccaccio declares that his work will be a compilation of 'stories or fables or parables or histories' recounted in order to cure lovesick ladies, whose leisure both condemns them to contemplate endlessly their state of unhappiness and permits them to read lovely stories in the vernacular (Proem, 13; p. 3). The women's lovesickness is framed by the literal disease of the plague of 1348, which, Boccaccio writes, had led women to show their naked bodies to male servants in order to be cured (Introduction to Day I, 29). The tales of the *Decameron* return to a ground zero of poetic signification, where there are no Muses dressed in the sublime veils of allegory, but instead the nude bodies of women set before the gaze of the examining physician. By staging his audience as women and himself as the doctor capable of curing them, Boccaccio overtly restricts the poetic value of the tales to the purposes of delight and seemingly abandons all pretentions to utility for the men of universities, cloisters, and courts. In fact, in the Conclusion (§7), at the end of the 100 tales, Boccaccio points out that his stories were told in a garden and should not be held to the same criteria as the sermons of the clergy or the discourses of the learned. The question begged by Boccaccio's authorial stance as a man writing for women in a place of aesthetic pleasure is whether or not there is a poetics of the *Decameron* that allows for anything other than the joy of its readers. Or in other words, is there a vernacular poetics that can provide anything but solace?

To begin to answer this question, I would like to examine two points within the frame of the *Decameron* in which Boccaccio pre-empts potential attacks that he might receive from critics: the Introduction to Day IV and the Conclusion. At stake in both defences of the work is the nature of a poetic language founded on verisimilitude. In the first response to critics who accuse him of an inappropriate use of the language of desire, Boccaccio responds with the story of the widower Filippo Balducci and his son, who has grown up in isolation and without a mother on the top of Mount Asinaio. In an effort to save his son from the pain that derives from the love of women, Filippo has given him no knowledge of the world of desire. During his first trip to Florence, however, the son is overcome by a marvel for the things of the world and asks his father to name each and every thing with which they come into contact. When he sees a group of women for the first time the son asks his father what they are called; Filippo responds metaphorically,

'Goslings' (Introduction to Day IV, 23; p. 287). Unaffected by the father's effort to avert his desire by changing the name of its object, the son responds by saying that he wants to take one home with him so that he can 'pop things into its bill' (§28; p. 287). The father is forced to take up the inadvertent sexual metaphor of the gosling's bill in his retort: 'Their bills are not where you think, and require a special sort of diet' (§29; p. 287).

Filippo's failure to control his son's desire with figurative language leads into Boccaccio's conclusion that the father's 'wits were no match for Nature' (§29; p. 287). The tale of Filippo Balducci is meant to show that metaphorical language cannot circumvent the natural desires behind the son's naming of the things of the world, because the meaning expressed by language follows a speaker's intentions. Boccaccio does not necessarily advocate that his readers should blindly follow their natural appetites, but he recognizes that the figurative language of poetry does not have the power to change things merely by renaming them. Boccaccio thus defends the language of the *Decameron*, which represents as if unveiled the desires and pitfalls of an embodied world.

Similarly, in the Conclusion, Boccaccio defines his verisimilar poetics in terms of the realist artistic style of his day. In response to those who would accuse him of having taken too many liberties with his language, Boccaccio writes that it should be considered no more improper of him to have used 'one or two trifling expressions . . . too unbridled' than it is for those who use the transparently pornographic metaphors of everyday speech to describe sexual anatomy (§6; p. 798).[12] His own language, like the women who show their nude bodies to physicians, exposes the metaphors whose outer appearance gives the illusion of good taste; like the tales he tells with it, his language is verisimilar even as it is figurative. In order to justify this stance, Boccaccio invokes the authority of naturalist painters, who do not shy away from sexual realism:

> Besides, no less latitude should be granted to my pen than to the brush of the painter, who without incurring censure, of a justified kind at least, depicts Saint Michael striking the serpent with his sword or his lance, and Saint George transfixing the dragon wherever he pleases; but that is not all, for he makes Christ male and Eve female, and fixes to the Cross, sometimes with a single nail, sometimes with two, the feet of Him who resolved to die thereon for the salvation of mankind. (§§5–6; p. 799)

Boccaccio's realism, even when it transgresses the boundaries of a socially appropriate sexual vocabulary, is similar to that of the painters of fourteenth-century Italy, who are given licence to depict with verisimilitude the religious figures of Christianity, from the saints to Christ himself, even when those very images represent either the sexuality of Christ and Eve or objects with highly sexual figurative connotations (i.e. 'nail', 'sword', 'lance'). In this passage, Boccaccio highlights the ambiguity of the sacred and the profane in his style. Just as sacred images may potentially be interpreted lewdly, so lewd language contains the potentiality of the sacred. Boccaccio thus defends his engagement with the world through a naturalist, poetic language that represents the world in its embodied nudeness. As is true for painting, however, the more *realistic* a representation, the more evident is the intervention of the artist's talents.

Thus when faced by the tales of the *Decameron* that recount, in the vernacular language of the town-square, the moral and sexual freedom of an increasingly secular world, we are asked to consider them in the same way in which we would treat religious iconography: as both historical and figurative representations. This poetics, in line with his thought on poetry in the *Genealogia*, seems contrary to Boccaccio's declaration in the Proem that his stories are merely for the pleasure of his lovesick female readers. There is, however, a connection between these real women and his pretensions for poetic authority that becomes clear in another passage from the defence in the Introduction to Day IV. Here he declares that if he is writing for and of women, then he should not be condemned for it, because he is doing something similar to the love poets of the previous generation. His women, he says, are not so different from the muses who live on Mount Parnassus, but since 'one cannot actually live with the Muses, any more than they can live with us', he must content himself with their embodied representation as women (§35; p. 289). In fact, he says that:

> the Muses are ladies, and although ladies do not rank as highly as Muses, nevertheless they resemble them at first sight... And so, in composing these stories, I am not straying as far from Mount Parnassus or from the Muses as many people might be led to believe. (§35; p. 289)

Boccaccio's women are embodiments of the Muses – and he gives the impression that real women are to be preferred precisely because they are present and embodied. In the *Decameron* the poetics of the historical world, populated with sexed and desiring bodies that speak in a specifically female-gendered vernacular language, is linked to the sublime lyrical poetics of Dante, Cino da Pistoia, and Guido Cavalcanti, whom he invokes here in his defence. Only through the mechanism of the frame can Boccaccio bridge the gap between the tales of historical, embodied life and the lyric reflection on divine matters.

The question of the poetic production of meaning in the *Decameron* is best addressed by turning back to the theory of genres in the *Genealogia*, in which

Boccaccio declares that old wives' tales are meaningless. In the chapter of the *Genealogia* that follows this initial definition, Boccaccio redeems somewhat the usefulness of such tales:

> it must be believed that not only great men – who were brought up on the milk of the Muses, frequented the homes of philosophy, and have been hardened by sacred studies – have always placed the most profound meanings in their poems, but also that there is nowhere such a delirious old woman who, around the household fire among the wakeful on winter nights, makes up and recites stories of Hell, or fairies, or nymphs, and the like (from which these inventions are often composed), and does not intend beneath the pretext of the stories, in accordance with the powers of her modest intellect, some meaning, sometimes not at all ridiculous; a meaning through which she would like to cause terror in children, delight girls, or tease the old, or at least show the powers of Fortune.
>
> (XIV. 10. 7; p. 54, modified)

This kind of tale seems to be the model for the stories of the *Decameron*, at least as far as concerns the *brigata*, who tell each other stories to pass their free time with pleasure.[13] By embedding the 100 tales within the multiple diegetic layers of the frame – the members of the *brigata*, the source who reports the stories, the narrator for women, and the author of the book – different kinds of utility, or meaning, can be gleaned from the different levels of discourse.

The ironic distance between author and tale created by the frame of the *Decameron* acts not only to detach Boccaccio's authorial intentionality from the import of the tales, so that the intentions of the ten fictional storytellers become separated from those of narrator and author. It also allows the reactions of the members of the *brigata* to exist on a separate plane from those of the *Decameron*'s readership. The popular stories of the *Decameron* can take on more sublime meanings in different interpretive contexts, if they are seen as related to the historical foundation of allegorical discourse. The ambiguity created by the multiple diegetic levels causes a crisis of interpretative authority, which calls into question the effectiveness of all external hermeneutic systems and gives the text autonomy.

The initial interpretative level of the *Decameron* is based on a poetics of the verisimilar, which Fiammetta defends in her critique of Neifile's tale at the beginning of the fifth tale of Day IX. In the fourth tale, Neifile had recounted a story that inverted the historical attributes of its characters – both named Cecco. In the opening remarks of her own story, the last of the Calandrino tales, Fiammetta describes the importance of verisimilitude for pleasure:

'I could easily have told it [the story] in some other way, using fictitious names, had I wished to do so; but since by departing from the truth of what actually happened, the storyteller greatly diminishes the pleasure of his listeners, I shall... tell it in its proper form.'   (IX. 5. 5; p. 669)

As Fiammetta represents it, the poetics of the *brigata*'s stories is founded upon the verisimilar narration of events in a corresponding realistic language.

The second layer of interpretation corresponds to the moral utility that a plague-ridden society might glean from the tales. It is in turn embedded in the fiction of the consolation of lovelorn ladies, whose spiritual malady is embodied by the political and ethical breakdown of the city. This exegetical level is demonstrated most clearly in the description of the garden in the Introduction to Day III:

> In the central part of the garden (not the least, but by far the most admirable of its features), there was a lawn of exceedingly fine grass, of so deep a green as to almost seem black, dotted all over with possibly a thousand different kinds of gaily-coloured flowers, and surrounded by a line of flourishing, bright green orange- and lemon-trees, which, with their mature and unripe fruit and lingering shreds of blossom, offered agreeable shade to the eyes and a delightful aroma to the nostrils. In the middle of this lawn there stood a fountain of pure white marble, covered with marvellous bas-reliefs. From a figure standing on a column in the centre of the fountain, a jet of water, whether natural or artificial I know not, but sufficiently powerful to drive a mill with ease, gushed high into the sky before cascading downwards and falling with a delectable plash into the crystal-clear pool below. And from this pool, which was lapping the rim of the fountain, the water passed through a hidden culvert and then emerged into finely constructed artificial channels surrounding the lawn on all sides. Thence it flowed along similar channels through almost the whole of the beautiful garden, eventually gathering at a single place from which it issued forth from the garden and descended towards the plain as a pure clear stream, furnishing ample power to two separate mills on its downward course, to the no small advantage of the owner of the palace.   (§§8–10; pp. 190–1)

This passage is a visualized description of how the pleasure principle of the *Decameron*'s tales is connected to utility beyond the boundaries of the text. The flowered field corresponds to the flowers of speech and rhetoric that make up its narratives. The description of the font at the centre of the garden is reminiscent of Boccaccio's declaration in the *Genealogia* that poetic inspiration arises from the 'bosom of God'. The flowers and trees of the garden are not only aestheticized versions of the natural world, but also the sensorial stimulations of the work of art. The water that spurts out from the artistically wrought statue both nourishes the beauty of the garden and flows beyond its confines, where it will work for the landowner. Like the tales of the *Decameron*, composed of artistically nourished flowers of speech, the garden is an aesthetically wrought representation of the world of creation, with its same bounties and dangers. The frame of the *Decameron* separates the world of pleasure and beauty from the world of utility and work, just as much as it links them, acting as both the water channels and the walls of the garden.

If the poetics of the *Decameron* suggests a connection between aesthetics and ethics in consonance with Boccaccio's theory of poetry in the *Genealogia*, then it also offers the opportunity to reflect on higher matters through the ballads that conclude each day. Like a prosimetrum, the *Decameron* gives rise to a tension between the linguistic and historical verisimilitude of the prose tales and the contemplative language and themes of lyric poetry in the ballads. One example of how the frame dramatizes this tension is again from Day III. In this day's concluding ballad, Lauretta sings of the travails of a woman, whose true love dies and goes to reside 'in heaven... before Him who created us' (§17). The rest of the poem concerns her regret at having settled for the love of the young man despite her desire to reside with her lover on high. Her initial experience of love is framed by the notion of divine love, as her beauty is described in terms of its connection to God, who destined her 'to show men here on earth | some sign of [His] eternal grace' (§13; p. 281). The lyrics of the ballad, written in a language reminiscent of stilnovist poetry and of Dante's *Comedy*, show the tenuous metaphorical connection between human and divine love. Like the tales of the *Decameron*, the lyric moments of the ballads, which are themselves popular songs accompanied by instruments and embodied by dance, can be interpreted in multiple ways. The *brigata*'s reaction to this particular ballad points to the ambiguity of interpretation inherent even in the language of the lyric:

> Here Lauretta ended her song, to which all had listened raptly and which all had construed in different ways. There were those who took it, in the Milanese fashion, to imply that a good fat pig was better than a comely wench. But others gave it a more sublime, more subtle and truer meaning, which this is not the moment to expound. (§18; p. 283, modified)

Whereas the literal Milanese-style interpretation fits the context of the *brigata*'s purpose, the author refuses to report the sublime interpretation because it belongs outside the garden-world of the work. The poetics of the *Decameron* depends on a layered discourse that separates the author and reader from the storytellers, placing the onus of the production of meaning on the reader.

The basic linguistic and narrative verisimilitude of the tales of the *Decameron* betrays an artistically wrought representation of the world of creation. By framing the stories within multiple contexts, Boccaccio is able to suggest a connection between the everyday language of an embodied, historical reality and the rarefied lyric artifice that veils sublime truths. With the *Decameron* Boccaccio fully develops the poetics tested in his earlier works, in which he endeavoured to combine the historical narratives and popular language of the vernacular tradition with the language and forms of poetry inherited from Roman antiquity. Almost always ostensibly concerned with pleasure and beauty, Boccaccio engages obliquely with sublime allegorical meanings from the embodied perspective of history. The broad gamut of Boccaccio's poetic production shows his commitment to expanding the range of the literary Tuscan vernacular and to creating a new vernacular poetics capable of reaching multiple types of readers, from the intellectual to the merchant, stimulating in them reflection on things human and divine.

NOTES

1 Trans. by Osgood, pp. 38–9, modified. Whenever I have made minor changes to cited translations, I have noted it 'modified'. Unless marked with page numbers, the translations are my own.

2 *The Divine Comedy of Dante Alighieri*, ed. by Robert M. Durling, 3 vols (Oxford: Oxford University Press, 1996), I, 174–5; Boccaccio, *Esposizioni*, XI. 71; p. 469.

3 Branca, 'Introduzione', in *Filostrato*, in *Tutte le opere*, II (1964), 3–13 (p. 11).

4 Florence, Biblioteca Nazionale Centrale, MS Magliabechiano, VIII. 1416; *Cantari del Trecento*, ed. by Armando Balduino (Milan: Marzorati, 1970), pp. 19–21; 38; *Il cantare di Fiorio e Biancifiore*, ed. by Vincenzo Crescini, 2 vols (Bologna: Commissione per i testi di lingua, 1969), I, 16–24.

5 Armando Balduino, 'Introduzione', in *Ninfale fiesolano*, in *Tutte le opere*, III (1974), 269–89 (p. 281).

6 Antonio Enzo Quaglio, 'Introduzione', in *Comedia delle ninfe fiorentine*, in *Tutte le opere*, II (1964), 667–77 (p. 674).

7 Janet Levarie Smarr, 'Introduction', in *Eclogues* (New York: Garland, 1987), pp. viii–lxxvi.

8 Vittore Branca, *Boccaccio medievale e nuovi studi sul 'Decameron'*, rev. edn (Florence: Sansoni, 1996), p. 51.

9 Branca, *Boccaccio medievale*, p. 71.

10 Macrobius, *Commentarii in somnium Scipionis*, I. 2. 7–11, in *Commentary on the Dream of Scipio*, trans. by William Harris Stahl (New York: Columbia University Press, 1990), pp. 84–5.

11 Erich Auerbach, *Mimesis: The Representation of Reality in Western Literature*, Fiftieth-Anniversary Edition, trans. by W. R. Trask (Princeton: Princeton University Press, 2003), pp. 203–31.

12 Giuseppe Mazzotta, *The World at Play in Boccaccio's 'Decameron'* (Princeton: Princeton University Press, 1986), p. 70.

13 Millicent Marcus, *An Allegory of Form: Literary Self-Consciousness in the 'Decameron'* (Saratoga: Anma Libri, 1979), pp. 4–5; James C. Kriesel, 'The *Genealogy* of Boccaccio's Theory of Allegory', *Studi sul Boccaccio*, 36 (2009), 197–226 (p. 223).

6

STEPHEN J. MILNER

Boccaccio's *Decameron* and the semiotics of the everyday

The *Decameron* is without doubt Boccaccio's most famous work and the text that has had the greatest influence on the western storytelling tradition. Variously describing it as a 'mercantile epic' and 'the human comedy', such characterizations have sought to position the *Decameron* relative to the more chivalric epics of medieval Carolingian and Arthurian romances and the *Divine Comedy* of Dante Alighieri.[1] Yet while the *mise-en-scène* of these works was the courtly world of questing knights and stricken damsels, and a vision of social life after death as described by Dante-author, Boccaccio's masterpiece is celebrated for its mundane setting in the socio-political world of late medieval Italy. Set against the backdrop of civic disintegration caused by the Black Death of 1348 as witnessed by Boccaccio-author and described by his fictional narrator, the 100 *novelle* of the *Decameron* are told by a *brigata* of ten speakers over ten days in the Florentine countryside and feature a multiplicity of associational forms – communal, courtly, monarchical, clerical, monastic, and even hermetic – in keeping with the variegated social and political geography of the late medieval Italian peninsula. Over half the stories are set in Florence and Naples and their surrounding regions, reflecting Boccaccio's own familiarity with those settings and their social worlds, whilst the travels and travails of many of the tale's protagonists take them across seas and mountains to Britain (II. 3, II. 8), Crete (IV. 3, V. 1), Cyprus (I. 9), Corfu (II. 4), Portugal (II. 7), Turkey (II. 9), Paris (III. 9), the Holy Land (X. 9), and even as far as northern China (X. 3). Yet despite such geographical range, what the *novelle* have in common is a shared concern with communicative practice and the dynamics of social interaction and verbal exchange within and between the various speech communities imagined.

In what follows, the aim is to show how Boccaccio's *Decameron* is both a product of and intended participant in the social world in which it imagines itself circulating. Approached from this critical perspective, the *Decameron* can be read as a performative rather than a constative text, embedded in the verbal and communicative practices that characterized the oral and textual cultures of late medieval Italy. To read it as merely descriptive, or reflective, of the quotidian experience of the peninsula's inhabitants and their adventures in foreign lands would be reductive and overlook the ludic imbrication of the text as a whole into the same social world it seeks to describe. For the *Decameron*'s complex narrative architecture, and its conscious fashioning as a purposeful text addressing a known social constituency to a specific end (as stated in the text's Proem) renders it an extended speech act which addresses the threefold function of rhetorical composition in seeking to win over an audience: to educate, to entertain, and to move (*docere, delectare, movere*).[2] Read in these terms, the *Decameron* assumes the guise of a rhetorical work of poetic invention, rather than a chronicle-style account of daily life or a *summa* of comic, tragic, and satirical tales.

The textual and oral cultures of late medieval Italy and the *Decameron*

One consequence of the growing complexity of the bureaucratic, diplomatic, and mercantile networks that linked the major cities in late medieval Italy and their overseas markets was an explosion in the production of documentation and texts of all kinds. A plethora of 'how to' instruction manuals were written on the late medieval *artes*, furnishing advice on the composition of accounts, contracts, letters, texts, and speeches from the *ars notaria* (drawing up of legal documents), the *ars predicandi* (the composition of sermons), and *ars concionandi* (instruction in the composition of public speeches), to the *ars dictaminis* (the writing of letters).[3] In addition, the widespread dissemination and circulation of works of classical rhetorical theory and exemplary speeches furnished further guidance in securing the applied skills that were highly prized in a social world that placed so much emphasis on persuasion, negotiation, deliberation, and decision-making.

A commensurate increase in the number of texts concerning the reading arts and textual interpretation is also evident in the growing commentary tradition on biblical, patristic, legal, grammatical, and rhetorical texts, and the increasing sophistication of late medieval textual exegesis. As his own education, writing, and diplomatic career make clear, Boccaccio was steeped in this textual and oral culture as a writer as well as a commentator and compiler of classical and medieval texts. His particular interest in rhetoric and its shaping of both oratory and poetics is apparent in his own writings about literary invention, especially in Book XIV of the *Genealogia deorum gentilium*, and from his avid collecting of doctrinal texts and set-piece speeches. In addition to introducing Petrarch to Quintilian's *Institutiones* and discovering Cicero's *Pro Cluentio* and the pseudo-Ciceronian *Rhetorica ad Herennium* at Montecassino in 1355, he left a library to the monastery at Santo Spirito which contained numerous rhetorical works as well as a copy of Alan of Lille's *De arte predicandi* and Geoffrey of Vinsauf's *Poetria nova*.[4]

Not surprisingly, both the literary form and the narrative content of the *Decameron* is informed by these compositional arts, and their precepts are regularly deployed by able practitioners within the tales themselves: by ser Ciappelletto the unreliable notary (I. 1), Guido Cavalcanti the sharp-tongued poet (VI. 9), Friar Cipolla the virtuoso preacher (VI. 10), and in the commentary of the unnamed vengeful scholar (VIII. 7). The use of the term *cornice* to describe the structural framing device which acts as container of the 100 *novelle* also points to the obvious parallels between the verbal and artistic forms of symbolic practice which are present throughout the text. Boccaccio's inclusion of Giotto (VI. 5) and Bruno and Buffalmacco, both of whom appear in more than one tale (VIII. 3, VIII. 6, VIII. 9, IX. 3, IX. 5), indicates his awareness of the complementarity of verbal and visual artistry in creating fictive worlds. Significantly, given the Horatian invocation 'ut pictura poesis' ('as is painting, so is poetry'), the scene of a young company entertaining themselves in a garden amidst the piled corpses which surround them in the 'Triumph of Death' fresco cycle at the Campo Santo in Pisa is often attributed to the real-life Buonamico Buffalmacco and cited as the source for Boccaccio's textual, rather than pictorial, framing of the same conceit.[5] Similarly, the artistry of many protagonists within the *novelle* themselves is apparent in the ingenuity with which they make use of symbols and material objects to communicate their secret desires to the objects of their illicit affections through non-verbal communication.

As an accomplished practitioner of the late medieval language arts and a fine textual and pictorial exegete, therefore, Boccaccio was alive to the affective potency of symbolic forms, verbal and visual, and undoubtedly aware of the increasing importance of the management of speech within the oral world of the Italian urban centres. Tracts written by lawyers and clerics alike, such as Albertano da Brescia's *Liber de doctrina dicendi et tacendi* of 1245 and Domenico Cavalca's *Pugnilingua* and *Frutti della lingua* from the 1330s, enjoyed huge success together with other advice books on the verbal economy of day-to-day life which addressed the key question of the relation of words and deeds (*detti e fatti*) in the social realm. Boccaccio's friend Paolo da Certaldo, who hailed from the same small town outside Florence and, within the city, lived in the same neighbourhood of the Gonfalone del Nicchio in the quarter of Santo Spirito, compiled his own collation of over 380 maxims that proffer advice on how best to navigate the exigencies of everyday life. Many of them related specifically to the prudential control of the tongue. Entitled *Libro di buoni costumi*, or *Book of Good Practices*, its maxims and pieces of homespun advice evoke a strong sense of a highly socialized culture characterized by face-to-face interaction, and strong familial and affective ties. The concern with honour, reputation, and social standing is indicative of a social world in which people observed, judged, commented, and gossiped about other people's business. To cite some examples: 'It is better to stand with a good man despite your legs hurting than sit on a bench with an evil one'; 'If you don't know how to talk well, shut up and you will be considered more wise'; 'A spoken word is like a thrown stone. Think, and think again, therefore, before you say out loud what you're thinking and the results it could have, both good and bad'; 'To prevent gossip always turn up'; 'If your friend tells you his secrets, it is either a sign he loves you or idiocy and madness'; and, almost echoing Day IX story 6, 'In whichever house you stay, leave the women alone and steal nothing.'[6]

A central concern of such works was the trustworthiness of one's associates, the nature of true friendship, and the dangers of unguarded speech. This focus on strategic symbolic interaction and the interpretation of conduct in order to understand the nature of social relations has been the subject of much recent social history of the Italian peninsula and the Florentine commune in this period. What such studies have revealed is a social world characterized by a strong sense of doubt and conflict in the face of competing commitments and obligations. In the highly socialized cities of medieval Italy what have been termed the 'obscurity of motives' and the 'duplicity of social relations' are recurring themes. In the words of Ronald Weissman, a historical anthropologist of late medieval and Renaissance Florence, 'The face value of social exchanges hid many layers of meaning, even during exchanges between friends.'[7] The 'importance of being ambiguous', to borrow his phrase, applied especially to verbal commitments in communities characterized by an excess of community, enabling individuals both to define and to protect themselves within highly regimented and structured social worlds. It is into precisely this kind of verbal economy that Boccaccio launches the *Decameron*, the ambivalence of the Narrator's voice and Boccaccio's narrative strategies ensuring its studied ambiguity.

The *Decameron* as ambiguous fiction

At the formal level, interpreting the work should be relatively straightforward as Boccaccio gives it all the features found in explicatory commentaries. He begins his text by using a commentary-style preface (*accessus ad auctores*) of the kind that is normally used to support and facilitate the reading of classical, biblical, and legal texts. The Proem and Introduction to Day I contain all the component elements expected in a typical *accessus*: the title of the work (*titulis operis*), an introduction to the author (*vita auctoris*), an explanation by the commentator of his reasons for writing the work (*intentio scribentis*), the subject matter it contains (*materia operis*), and the text's usefulness or function for its intended readership (*utilitas*). Similarly, when we reach the end of the text, Boccaccio has the Narrator add a 'Conclusione dell'autore' which functions as a rhetorical epilogue (*peroratio*) to refresh the memory and influence the emotions of the reader/listener in order to secure a successful outcome by soliciting sympathy for the writer/speaker's cause (*conquestio*). What such conquest could entail, however, only becomes fully apparent as the work draws to its end.

Yet despite containing all the standard formal elements used to facilitate the exposition and interpretation of a text, and despite adding numerous paratextual rubrics and conclusions to each tale and each day, Boccaccio seems intent on deliberate obfuscation when moving through the various parts of the text's opening. Unlike the commentator whose role was to open out (*aprire*) the meaning of a text, Boccaccio confuses his multiple readers through elaborate textual doubling.[8] His use of rhetorical and poetic allegory, insinuation, and figurative allusion all stand in opposition to grammar and dialectic's claims to render language a transparent and literal medium. The rhetoric of the *Decameron*, when compared with the aims of grammar and dialectic, is presented as an adulteration of language in its betrayal of the faithful relation of sign to signified, and its unmooring of fixed referentiality, a theme which becomes the leitmotif of the whole text. The *Decameron* thus becomes an adulterous text in more ways than one, as its literary form performs the subject matter of many of its stories.

Hence Boccaccio gives his work two titles (*Decameron* and *Prencipe Galeotto*); he uses the ironic distance furnished by a literary Narrator to evade any responsibility for what is written; he has his surrogate provide two reasons for writing down the stories (as a gift to his friends and as consolation for lovelorn women), and has him describe the subject matter as 'varied' and claim the utility of the work lies in teaching the female readers he claims to be addressing what to do and what not to do without saying what that might entail and why. What follows is a complex network of narrative voices and layers: of tales told within the framework of another tale by a fictional Narrator who claims to be a mere collator (*compilator*) and transcriber (*scriptor*) of stories told him 'by a person whose word can be trusted' ('da persona degna di fede') (Introduction to Day I, 49; p. 13).[9] In effect, the whole text is presented as an extended piece of unverifiable gossip with Boccaccio as author hiding behind a series of aliases that he uses to ventriloquize his fictional characters, both female and male. He even has his Narrator claim that he changed the names of the members of the *brigata* in order to protect their reputations should they subsequently be identified as participants in the events narrated, thereby doubling the fictive layering (Introduction to Day I, 50; p. 13). By the time we reach the Conclusion the Narrator tells us he does not even trust himself: 'distrusting my own opinion (which in matters concerning myself I trust as little as possible)' (§27; p. 802). Boccaccio's evasive and untrustworthy Narrator, it would seem, is only reliable in his unreliability.[10]

This deliberate obfuscation on Boccaccio's part creates a fictional world that replicates the complexity of the verbal economies of actual speech communities. The struggle for coherence and the search for guidance in making sense of the *Decameron* is on a par with the struggle for coherence and making sense in community as evidenced in the maxims and guidance found in the contemporary advice books examined above. Boccaccio places the reader in the same position as he has the Narrator place his nominal female readers, and the same position many of the protagonists in individual *novelle* find themselves in as they seek to interpret and make sense of their situations and what is being represented to them. From the very outset, therefore, the text requires we question the motives (*intentio*) of Boccaccio as author, the motives he attributes to his Narrator, the motives of the *brigata* as interlocutors, and the motives of the protagonists within the individual tales recounted when reading the text.

This task is rendered more problematic by the *Decameron*'s fundamental ambivalence as a work of realist fiction, hovering between the narrative poles of history and fable. Its much-vaunted 'realism', as discussed by Erich Auerbach in his classic study of the tale of Frate Alberto (IV. 2), is a consequence of its narrative verisimilitude: its plausible but fictive representation of a social reality peopled by characters acting in known or familiar social settings and speaking in familiar conversational registers.[11] Boccaccio's use of known associates as protagonists in some of the tales, as noted above and as apparent in the tale of Cisti the baker and Geri Spina (VI. 2), only adds to the text's verisimilitude, what in rhetorical terms is known as the narrative *argumentum*. Boccaccio's authorship lies in the *Decameron* being both a thing made (*fictio*) and a thing made up (*inventio*). By weaving together the fabulous, plausible, and historical to produce a text of realist fiction, the *Decameron* challenged, and still challenges, its readers to evaluate its plausibility and ponder its classification as a work of vernacular prose as the reader is given no clear guidance as to what type of texts he or she is dealing with. Indeed, the fictional Narrator simply states his intention 'to narrate a hundred stories or fables or parables or histories or whatever *we* choose to call them' (Proem, 13; p. 3; emphasis added).

In the Proem, Boccaccio positions his Narrator squarely in post-Plague Florence as a man only recently recovered from the pains of unrequited love for a woman he describes as beyond his reach. Whilst accepting responsibility for his 'immoderate passion' (Proem, 3; p. 1), the Narrator thanks his friends whose 'agreeable conversation' ('piacevoli ragionamenti') and 'admirable expressions of sympathy' ('laudevoli consolazioni') (Proem, 4; p. 1) helped save his life. In writing the text, he expresses the hope that the debt of gratitude will be repaid, but then chooses to dedicate the collection of entertaining stories to an imagined social constituency and reading public of lovelorn women 'cooped up within the narrow confines of their rooms' as being in greater need of consolation than their male counterparts. His promise to make 'provision for their pleasures' (Proem, 15; p. 3) is the first implication that his intentions might not be as pure as they seem.

The ordering of the storytelling, with each speaker expected to tell one tale per day and each day overseen in turn by a different member of the *brigata* acting as king or queen for the day, is often cited as a nostalgic evocation by Boccaccio of the monarchical court of Naples. The fact that the *Decameron*'s own micro-community of ten interlocutors, seven women and three men, is described by the Narrator as being drawn exclusively from the upper ranks of the Florentine patrician class – 'each was a friend, a neighbour, or a relative of the other' and all 'were intelligent, gently bred, fair to look upon, graceful in bearing, and charmingly unaffected' (Introduction to Day I, 49; p. 13) – clearly echoes the type of noble community found in the *Caccia di Diana* written in Naples in 1333–4. The servants and support staff who accompany the *Decameron*'s *brigata* on their two-week escape to their country retreats remain largely invisible throughout the text, apart from a brief eruption from the kitchens below at the start of Day VI, which appropriately initiates a consideration of the theme of verbal licence when addressing social superiors. This reinforces the sense of social privilege and aristocratic haughtiness.

Yet significantly, the regulation of the storytelling also replicates the aspirations apparent in the ordering of Florence's own civic councils in the Statutes of the *Capitano del Popolo* and *Podestà* of 1322–5, whereby the regular rotation of office, the maintenance of silence when listening to fellow speakers, the outlawing of standing up, interrupting, or insulting other speakers were key to securing the prudential and impartial deliberations of a self-determining community.[12] Boccaccio's innovation in constituting his idealized fictive speech community in the *Decameron*, however, lies in combining the two political cultures and in foregrounding women as both participants and decision-makers in the social world he evokes.

In the Introduction to Day I, Boccaccio deliberately sets the harmonious community of the *brigata* against the backdrop of a fractured social world ravaged by the plague. Indeed, Boccaccio has the Narrator present a portrait of negative community, in which all the normative bonds of affective association and civic order are dissolved and the holy-trinity of social ties – 'relations, friends, and neighbours' ('parenti, amici, vicini') – are systematically unpicked as 'all respect for the laws of God and man had virtually broken down and been extinguished in our city' (Introduction to Day I, 23; p. 7).[13] Whilst the contrast between the living hell of Florence and the idyllic setting of the storytelling reported to us by the Narrator could not be more stark, the political implications of the text in terms of furnishing a model of communal regeneration and social practice are far from clear.

Allegory, allegoresis, and the obscurity of the *Decameron*

Discerning readers of medieval poetry and prose were attuned to the four senses of biblical exegesis (the literal, allegorical, moral, and anagogical) and were similarly aware of the different roles and authority (*auctoritas*) implied in the composition of texts: from being a scribe, copier, collector, and compiler, to a collator, commentator, and author, and often more than one at the same time.[14] When it came to the interpretation of allegory in texts – the work of allegoresis – the act of reading was understood as a hermeneutical process whereby the veil of fiction was drawn back to reveal the true sense of the figures used, their 'under-meaning' (*hyponoia*). In the *Geneologia* Boccaccio praises Dante's interpretative virtuosity 'as he often unties with amazingly skilful demonstration the hard knots of holy theology' (XIV. 10. 3; p. 53). The Bible itself was after all a complex and ambiguous text (*scriptum obscurum et ambiguum*) whose meaning was made clear by the exegetes.[15] Commentary and interpretation, therefore, were fundamentally concerned with disambiguation and clarification of meaning. Similarly, the ideal of perspicuity and clarity of both purpose and language were identified as key qualities of poetic and rhetorical composition in the Horatian and Ciceronian traditions. Yet when allegory was used as a trope in writing, it fell under the purview of the rhetoricians in keeping with the etymology of allegory as 'other-speaking'.[16] It was this sense of saying one thing and meaning another, as Quintilian defined it, that gave licence to writers and speakers to present double meanings through the use of images, words, figures, and symbols, what Dante famously referred to as the 'beautiful lie' ('bella menzogna') (*Convivio*, ɪɪ, ɪ) of poetry and literature.

There was also something both seductive and intriguing, in the Latin sense of 'entangled', about enigmatic texts that combined innuendo, allusion, and figurative usage, and called for commentary and interpretation on the part of the reader. Boccaccio's *Decameron* sits firmly in this tradition as a text that self-consciously plays with the supposed narratological vices of obscurity and mendacity (*obscuritas* and *mendacium*). It is lengthy, periodically verbose, seemingly fragmented and discontinuous, and mendacious in its periodic improbability. Boccaccio's use of what he terms in the *Genealogia* the 'disguises of fiction' (*integumenta fictionum*), to mask his Narrator's intent is part of the challenge issued to his readers, making the task of interpreting his text a labour in its own right (*Genealogia*, xɪv. 7. 8; p. 42). His deliberate enigmatic voicing of his multiple narrators and his extensive use of allegory render him a master of double-speak. Rather than clarifying, his extended metaphors, double entendres, and insinuations in the *Decameron* are offered as a provocation to encourage the fascination and stimulate the hermeneutical impulses of his readers.

Boccaccio had already given over a whole chapter of his defence of poetry in the *Genealogia* to the contention that the allegorical and figurative language of the poets was not to be condemned: 'The obscurity of poetry is not just cause for condemning it' ('Damnanda non est obscuritas poetarum') (*Genealogia*, xɪv. ɪ2. ɪ; pp. 58–62). Indeed, he states that 'I have time and time again proved that the meaning of fiction is far from superficial . . . and as its superficial aspect is removed, the meaning of the author is clear' (*Genealogia*, xɪv. 9. 5; p. 48). Yet he was also very keen that the work of interpretation should be done by the intelligent reader rather than be put on a plate by the poet/commentator: 'surely it is not one of the poet's various functions to rip up and lay bare the meaning which lies hidden in his inventions' (*Genealogia*, xɪv. ɪ2. 8; p. 59). This work of discovery, or revelation, is the task of the reader, and to master such arts required application and study: 'You must read, you must persevere, you must sit up nights, you must enquire, and exert the utmost powers of your mind' (*Genealogia*, xɪv. ɪ2. ɪ7; p. 62). Those unable to make sense of texts are given short shrift: 'my only advice is for them to go back to the grammar schools, bow to the ferule, study, and learn what licence ancient authority granted the poets in such matters, and give particular attention to such alien terms as are permissible beyond common and homely use' (*Genealogia*, xɪv. ɪ2. ɪ3; p. 6ɪ). In this sense Boccaccio makes a virtue of the *Decameron*'s ambiguous voicing, a quality deemed a cardinal sin in most contemporary poetic precept literature, passing the hard work of disambiguation to the reader rather than the writer.

Yet within the *Decameron*, Boccaccio does actually furnish some tools to help in interpreting his text by providing multiple subtexts. In the medieval commentary tradition, the interpretative gloss was literally a subtext which sat underneath the authorized text. After all, the word 'intelligence' derives from *intus* and *leggere* 'to read between or beneath the surface' and hence 'under-stand'. To return to rhetoric, the human ability to com-prehend as well as app-rehend is the difference between the faculties of the intellec-tive and sensitive soul, and the space in which human will, the ability to choose and exercise judgement, resides. The intellectual form of persuasion appealed to the intellect (rational soul) and was largely carried out in the narration of events and the structuring of arguments (*narratio* and *argumen-tatio*). By contrast, the affective form of persuasion appealed to the emotions (the sensitive soul) and was carried out by entertaining and establishing an empathy with the audience (*delectatio* and *conciliatio*) through a prologue (*exordium*) and the use of humour and the power of a speaker's personal charisma or ethos.

In seeking to educate his readership in modes of interpretation, therefore, Boccaccio has his Narrator assume the function of teacher to his implied readership, engaging both their reason and emotion when instructing them in the art of textual reading as a form of code-breaking: part teacher (*docere*), part seducer (*movere*). To understand his text, intelligent readers need to realize that the commentary function lies in the subtexts that run through Boccaccio's *cornice* and the paratextual material that frames each day and each tale. This studied double-speak, which insinuates the idea of a subtext into the mind of the reader, is apparent from the two-faced address of the work's double title. The direct address of the main title aligns the *Decameron* with the patristic commentary tradition, as is clear from the etymology of the word itself. Drawn from the Greek 'δέκα', meaning 'ten', and 'ἡμέρα' meaning 'day', it echoes the medieval *Hexameron*, a genre of authorized exegetical commentary in which patristic writers commentated and expounded the meaning of Genesis, the text which provides the account of God's six-day authorship of the world. In the indirect address constituted by the text's subtitle, Boccaccio provides an alternative surname, or familiar nickname, for both the book and its author: 'Prencipe Galeotto' (Prince Galahalt). The reference is to the character in the Arthurian legend of the Round Table held responsible for bringing together Lancelot and Guinevere in their illicit tryst. The name is clearly derived from Francesca's speech in Dante's *Inferno* v where she holds both the text and its author responsible for her fateful affair with Paolo, 'Galeotto fu il libro e chi lo scrisse' ('This book was Galahault – pander-penned, the pimp!') (*Inferno*, v. 137).[17] This morally ambiguous figuring of the author and the book as erotic mediators, procurers, and go-betweens is significantly found in the text's very first subtext, the Dantean allusion working under the cover of patristic commentary.

This juxtaposition of the commentary tradition of the foundational text in the history of making and naming with such a famous instance of the affective power of reading sees education and affect combine forces as Boccaccio builds his own fictional world. Yet unlike God, who as maker, *auctor*, signified through things, humans were held to signify through symbols, the medium of language understood as the 'literal sense'. This is Boccaccio's medium, and the partiality and unreliability of human signing is starkly illustrated in the very first *novella* of the collection, the story of Ser Ciappelletto, 'probably the worst man ever born' (I. 1, 15; p. 26). Told by Panfilo and overseen by Pampinea, it comes replete with its own mini-*cornice*, or interpretative frame, and is a case study in the ambivalence of rhetorical figuring. Boccaccio has Panfilo run through the places of invention in describing how Ciappelletto embodied the seven deadly sins, prior to recounting Ciappelletto's own fraudulent deathbed confession in keeping with the conventions of medieval hagiography. His credulous confessor then spreads the word concerning Ciappelletto's 'saintly' life through his preaching, with the result that Ciappelletto becomes the subject of a local cult, the former sinner being reputed a saint. That Ciappelletto was a notary is doubly significant given the story's subject, for the main work of notaries was to draw up and rogate (guarantee) legally binding contracts. As authorizers of texts and underwriters of testimony, they ensured people did what they said they were going to do, enforcing the trust function in social relations: in the words of a much-cited late medieval Tuscan proverb, 'karta si face, perch' omo è fallace' ('Get it in writing; you can't trust anyone'). Yet despite the normative function of a notary, Ciappelletto is reported to have taken 'great delight in giving false testimony' and would have taken it as a personal slight 'if one of his legal deeds were discovered to be other than false' (I. 1, 10–11; p. 25).

Boccaccio's interpretative framework for this tale destabilizes the reliability of the text by foregrounding the limits of human comprehension, the ease with which we misread what is represented to us and our fallibility in appointing the wrong advocates as our intercessors in the afterlife. As Panfilo states, 'Common opinion deceives us', yet God, whose omniscience means he sees and understands everything without the need for any form of explication, pays 'more attention to the purity of the supplicant's motives' (I. 1. 5;

p. 24) than the rightness of their appointment of appropriate go-betweens. His ability to forgive us 'when we appoint as our emissary (*mezzano*) one who is His enemy' (I. I. 90; p. 37) shows God's ability to see, through the agency of the divine intellect, the purity of intention (*intentio*) over the mistaken appointment of corrupt mediators on the basis of false witnesses and unreliable testimony. The *Decameron*'s symbolic economy, by contrast, is clearly man-made: rhetorical and manufactured. It requires interpretation and interrogation, but its truth-value can never be fixed due to the latent potential for symbols to carry both a surface and an implied meaning. The work commences with an exemplary tale, therefore, which warns the reader to question the reliability and trustworthiness of the world of mundane signs.

In much the same way as the Florentine commune was divided into guilds that practised a range of mercantile arts and required a test of competence prior to matriculation, the *Decameron* can be read as a text which seeks to establish a *brigata* of artful readers, a literary guild, and sets itself as both a primer and a test with the aim that its readers will eventually matriculate into the guild of subtle readers, practitioners of the hermeneutics of the everyday, fellow 'furbi' constantly reading between the lines, constantly seeking to under-stand, by looking beyond the represented world to the intentions (*intentio*) of fellow citizens and their trustworthiness. As contemporary chronicles and letters make clear, Florentines were avid readers of the everyday and were encouraged to observe and interpret the reliability of their civic officials through 'syndication', a legal procedure which allowed ordinary folk to denounce the practices of officials deemed to be in breach of their obligation to work for the good of the commune rather than personal gain (this was the process which saw Dante exiled). As a guide to the poetics of the everyday, the *Decameron*'s readers could find advice on the arts of both reading and writing, both looking beyond the surface of texts to subtexts as signposted in subtitles and the glosses of the Narrator's interventions. The *Decameron*'s educative function and form, it could be plausibly argued, was to produce artful meaning-makers and insightful readers in the social world.

In this respect, one particular character never graduated into the community of urbane readers: Calandrino. The series of stories involving his escapades in the company of his 'friends' Bruno and Buffalmacco are the only ones in which the same characters appear in more than one *novella* (VIII. 3; VIII. 6; IX. 3 and IX. 5). Calandrino is presented as the stereotypical simpleton, or 'sciocco', who is ridiculed for his lack of urbanity and sophistication in his credulous acceptance of what he is told. It is precisely his literal-mindedness that lands him in such difficulty and provides such entertainment for Bruno and Buffalmacco, who as artists understand the ability of symbolic forms, both literal and pictorial, to create impressions and effect action. His belief in the magic properties of the heliotrope, in the idea he had stolen a pig from himself, that he had become pregnant, and that a magic scroll would help him conquer a young girl, all result from his being too impressionable and easily led and his not questioning the motives of others.

Numerous tales within the main corpus of the 100 *novelle* revolve around the ability of participants to encode and decode meanings through the strategic use of signs, both verbal and non-verbal. Secret signs and exclusive speech, understood as a mutually comprehensible code shared by just two actants, become the necessary means of communicating untoward social activity within a highly socialized world. In the tale of King Agilulf and his groom (III. 2), the crafty young servant erases the sign that would identify him as the person who had just had sex with the King's unknowing wife by clipping the hair of all the other servants in the same place as the King had clipped his, thinking he was asleep. In keeping with the kind of advice on when to speak and when stay silent as found in Albertano da Brescia's tract on the same subject, Masetto da Lamporecchio pretends to be a deaf mute in order to gain access to a convent as a gardener prior to having sex with the brides of Christ (III. 1). The wife of Messer Francesco Vergellesi, on the other hand, overcomes the silence imposed upon her by her husband and succeeds in communicating her desires for Zima through sighs and gestures whilst he, acting as ventriloquist, speaks her words (III. 5). In a *novella* told by Filomena who describes Florence as a city 'where fraud and cunning prosper more than love or loyalty', a deliberately 'unnamed' lady skilfully reverses the normative function of the confessional in using its confidentiality to confide her love for a young man (III. 3, 5; p. 206). Similarly, many protagonists demonstrate their narrative virtuosity in their ability to invent (*inventio*) *post factum* justifications for untoward social action by furnishing convincing alternative readings to explain away their infidelity. Day VII specifically focuses on the tricks played by women on their husbands 'either in the cause of love or for motives of self-preservation' (VII. 1; p. 484). Similarly, verbal ingenuity and quick-wittedness are celebrated in Day VI, which is given over wholly to 'those who, on being provoked by some verbal pleasantry, have returned like for like, or who, by a prompt retort or shrewd manoeuvre, have avoided danger, discomfort or ridicule' (VI. 1; p. 444).

Many other *novelle*, in keeping with the *Decameron* itself, depend on forms of doubling and the use of surrogates to carry meaning. The wife of

Bernabò da Genova disguises herself as a man to save her skin (II. 9); Tedaldo disguises himself as a pilgrim in order to secure access to his mistress (III. 7); Ricciardo Minutolo succeeds in having sex with the wife of Filippello Sighinolfo by substituting himself for her husband in a public baths (III. 6); Gilette of Narbonne impersonates a young Florentine woman in order to entrap her wandering husband (III. 9); and Monna Sismonda escapes punishment by placing a servant girl in her bed after an illicit liaison with a young man named Roberto (VII. 8). Similarly, many *novelle* themselves contain stories that require interpretation on the part of the protagonists, echoing Boccaccio's claims in the *Genealogia* that literary fiction is a valid medium for communicating truths. Melchizedek the Jew avoids a trap through telling of a story about the three rings (I. 3); Madonna Oretta saves the blushes of a knight by making a veiled analogy between good horsemanship and good storytelling (VI. 1); and Bergamino reprimands Can Grande della Scala for his parsimony with a story about Primas and the Abbot of Cluny (I. 7). All depend for their efficacy on the ability of the listeners to interpret their meaning.

As in the *Comedy*, the progression in the *Decameron* is an interpretative one, a quest that reaches its culmination in the epilogue or Conclusion of the text. Here too, Boccaccio has his Narrator deploy another form of rhetorical double-speak, literally putting down (*subiectio*) the objections he voices on behalf of potential critics who may claim the tales recounted are unseemly and inappropriate for a female audience. From start to finish, therefore, Boccaccio maintains the *Decameron*'s narrative ambiguity. In denying that he has spoken out of turn or taken liberties, Boccaccio's Narrator makes direct reference to the language of the street, asserting that 'it was no more improper for me to have written them than for men and women at large, in their everyday speech, to use such words as *hole*, and *rod*, and *mortar*, and *pestle*, and *crumpet*, and *stuffing*, and any number of others' (Conclusion, 5; p. 799). Significantly, many of these words appear in allusive form in the *novelle* just recounted. Yet by now, the sheer weight of metaphorical allusion, and its authorial denial, is staged in such a ludic manner that the knowing reader, primed and alert to double meanings and subtexts from her/his reading of all that has gone before, can dismiss the superficial assertion that the thing signified has just one signifier. The lewd allusion implied in the Narrator's claim that his neighbour was a keen admirer of his linguistic skills would not have been lost on those who had learnt the lessons of the work's subtexts. In returning to his intended audience of noble young ladies, Boccaccio's Narrator has no problem accepting responsibility for his textual literalism, but is much more reluctant to admit to any hidden meanings, passing the responsibility in finding other senses in the text as a whole, and in individual stories, exclusively to his readers. The continuing acceptance of this invitation is reflected in the vast critical literature his text continues to provoke.

Conclusion

As a late medieval symbolic interactionist, Boccaccio pays detailed attention to the way in which shared symbols are made to work as carriers of meaning in the social realm.[18] As a social performance of studied ambiguity deploying the tools of late medieval composition and exegesis, the *Decameron* is without equal: a text that embodies and comments upon strategies of simulation and dissimulation, of insinuation and circumlocution. If the *Decameron*, understood as a primer in the semiology of the everyday, has one lesson, it is that the life of signs and their use in the world of social interaction is one fraught with ambiguity and ambivalence. The result is a magisterial 'social' commentary, or guide, to reading the world as text and to authoring a meaningful self. What kind of self can actually be fashioned on the basis of the text's contents depends upon the reader's own disposition and educated judgement (*arbitrium*). Boccaccio's use of the term 'ragionare' to denote both storytelling and reasoning reinforces the instrumentality granted to fictional stories in informing decision-making. This generative dimension of the text was in keeping with the thrust of late medieval language arts, which sought to move from comprehension to composition, calling texts and selves into being through the agency of invention, or what we may care to call late medieval self-fashioning.

In this respect, Boccaccio's text is far from prescriptive and, in collapsing the distinction between literature and social action, stands as one of the most important humanistic and civic texts of the late medieval world. For Boccaccio, both the art of communal living and the art of poetry involved learning the skills of disguise (*figura*) and discovery (*inventio*), of subversion of, and compliance with, social and poetic rules in a process that fused life styles and literary styles. For rather than unveiling the allegories of theology and philosophy to reveal universal truths, Boccaccio deliberately uses allegory, displaced meanings, to veil the ambiguous nature of his fictional characters' intentions in the here and now. In this sense the *Decameron* can be read as a symbolic reversal of Dante's *Comedy*: rather than revealing divine truths and the nature of social life after death through the medium of a prophetic poetry, Boccaccio has his surrogate Narrator conceal dubious intentions beneath obscure and mundane prose. Similarly, he parodies Boethius's advice in the *Consolation of Philosophy*, replacing the Stoic contemplation of disembodied philosophical truths with the implication that better forms of consolation can be found in physical communion. Such a reading is wholly in keeping with Boccaccio's belief in the potential sublime effects of poetic composition, although the anticipated outcome is an embodied rather than transcendental sublimity. In questioning the prescriptive norms of social regulation as policed by the church and state, he authors a participatory text that playfully advocates the benefits of coming together through the agency of studied ambiguity.[19] Therein lies his humanity.

By way of my own authorial conclusion, and as self-appointed exegete providing one possible key to the reading of the *Decameron*, it is clear that any attempt to unravel the deliberate narrative entanglements of the text is doomed from the outset. Any clarification of a deliberately ambiguous work simplifies in the very act of disambiguation, even if the disambiguation is to stress the text's ambiguity. Boccaccio's skill lies in keeping so many meanings in play and placing the onus on the reader to make sense when seeking to render the text meaning-ful. The benefit of any lessons learnt will be proportional to the subtlety of the reading made. In the words of the unreliable Narrator, readers 'will learn to recognize what should be avoided and likewise what should be pursued' (Proem, 14; p. 3). This is the fundamental question of meaningful human action in both the philosophical and theological traditions: 'Like all other things in this world, stories, whatever their nature, may be harmful or useful, depending upon the listener' (Conclusion, 8; p. 799).

In this sense, Boccaccio's text acts as a preceptive 'social' grammar, furnishing examples and teaching lessons (both in the *cornice* and in the *novelle* themselves) that are worthy of imitation when composing a social self. While some readers may mirror Calandrino's literal-mindedness in accepting what is said at face value, the intention to educate more intelligent textual exegetes through the course of the text privileges the skill of reading between the lines in the search for meaning. By taking the truisms of popular advice books and reworking them through the complex doctrine of literary allegory as doublespeak, Boccaccio produced a text which challenges its readers to question its motives and interpret its meaning in exactly the same way citizens were challenged as readers of the semiotics of the everyday.

NOTES

1 Vittore Branca, *Boccaccio: The Man and his Works*, trans. by Richard Monges and Dennis J. McAuliffe (New York: New York University Press, 1976), pp. 216 and 276–307; Francesco de Sanctis, *History of Italian Literature*, trans. by Joan Redfern, 2 vols (Oxford: Oxford University Press, 1930), I, 335–49.

2 Heinrich Lausberg, *Handbook of Literary Rhetoric: A Foundation for Literary Study*, trans. by Matthew T. Bliss, Annemiek Jansen, and David E. Orton and ed. by David E. Orton and R. Dean Anderson (Leiden: Brill, 1998), pp. 112–19.

3 Studies of specific medieval textual genres are published in the series *Typologie des sources du Moyen Âge occidental (TYP)* (Turnhout: Brepols, 1972–).

4 Teresa De Robertis, 'L'inventario della *parva libraria* di Santo Spirito', in *Boccaccio autore e copista*, ed. by Teresa De Robertis and others (Florence: Mandragora, 2013), pp. 403–9; Chapter 5 in this volume.

5 Lucia Battaglia Ricci, *Ragionare nel giardino: Boccaccio e i cicli pittorici del 'Trionfo della morte'* (Rome: Salerno, 2000).

6 Paolo da Certaldo, 'Libro di buoni costumi', in *Mercanti scrittori: ricordi nella Firenze tra medioevo e Rinascimento*, ed. by Vittore Branca (Milan: Rusconi, 1986), pp. 3–99. Author's translations of maxims 21, 50, 51, 66, 195, 223, 347.

7 Ronald F. E. Weissman, 'The Importance of Being Ambiguous: Social Relations, Individualism, and Identity in Renaissance Florence', in *Urban Life in the Renaissance*, ed. by Susan Zimmerman and Ronald F. E. Weissman (Newark: University of Delaware Press, 1989), pp. 269–80 (p. 272).

8 Stephen J. Milner, '"*Le sottili cose non si possono bene aprire in volgare*": Vernacular Oratory and the Transmission of Classical Rhetorical Theory in the Late Medieval Italian Communes', *Italian Studies*, 64.2 (2009), 221–44.

9 See also Chapter 3 in this volume on voicing and audiences across Boccaccio's fictional works.

10 Greta Olson, 'Reconsidering Unreliability: Fallible and Untrustworthy Narrators', *Narrative*, 11 (2003), 93–109 (p. 105).

11 Erich Auerbach, *Mimesis: The Representation of Reality in Western Literature*, trans. by Willard R. Trask (Princeton: Princeton University Press, 1968), pp. 203–31.

12 *Statuti della Repubblica Fiorentina*, ed. by Romolo Caggese, 2 vols (Florence: Galileiana, 1910–21), I, Book IV, Rubrics 21–9.

13 Christiane Klapisch-Zuber, '"Parenti, amici, vicini": il territorio urbano d'una famiglia mercantile nel XV secolo', *Quaderni storici*, 33 (1976), 953–82.

14 Henri de Lubac, *Medieval Exegesis: The Four Senses of Scripture*, 3 vols (Grand Rapids, MI: Eerdmans, 1998–2001), II, 1–39.

15 Päivi Mehtonen, *Obscure Language, Unclear Literature: Theory and Practice from Quintilian to the Enlightenment*, trans. by Robert MacGilleon (Helsinki: Academiae scientiarum Fennicae, 2003), pp. 60–75, 104–6.

16 Rita Copeland and Peter T. Struck, 'Introduction', in *The Cambridge Companion to Allegory*, ed. by Copeland and Struck (Cambridge: Cambridge University Press, 2010), pp. 1–11.

17 Dante Alighieri, *The Divine Comedy: Inferno*, trans. by Robin Kirkpatrick (London: Penguin, 2006), p. 47.

18 Deirdre Boden, 'People Are Talking: Conversation Analysis and Symbolic Interaction', in *Symbolic Interaction and Cultural Studies*, ed. by Howard S. Becker and Michal M. McCall (Chicago: University of Chicago Press, 1990), pp. 244–74.

19 Stephen J. Milner, 'Coming Together: Consolation and the Rhetoric of Insinuation in Boccaccio's *Decameron*', in *The Erotics of Consolation: Desire and Distance in the Late Middle Ages*, ed. by Catherine E. Léglu and Stephen J. Milner (New York: Palgrave, 2008), pp. 95–113.

7

F. REGINA PSAKI

Voicing gender in the *Decameron*

Over the *Decameron*'s long reception history, its sexual politics have been examined and interpreted from different points of view. Ostensibly dedicated to women unlucky in love, and with seven female narrators out of ten, the *Decameron* represents women in speaking roles to a degree extraordinary for a medieval author. This gesture, and the sympathetic admiration for women the Narrator claims, earned Boccaccio a reputation as a philogynist, a defender of women; by the same token his later turn towards Latin literature, and his venomously (to me, superficially) misogynous *Corbaccio*, were long interpreted as a conversion to a profound and sincere hostility towards women.[1] More recently, feminist analysis of the *Decameron* has spotlighted many narrative mechanisms Boccaccio used to explore the social and rhetorical structures defining the lived reality of women. At first feminist critics tended to look at relative advantages accorded to women in single or paired tales, such as verbal or strategic victories, or sexual or economic autonomy.[2] Current feminist and more broadly gender-based criticism tends to look more comprehensively at the rhetorical mechanisms underlying a sex/gender system in the whole book, with its different levels of speakers and audiences.[3]

From its very beginning, the *Decameron* privileges the question of sexual difference. The Proem posits a female audience, on the grounds that women are uniquely disadvantaged by social structures and custom as well as, apparently, by nature, which has given them less strength (Proem, 9–13). Boccaccio's Narrator thus installs one pillar of later feminist analysis, the distinction between biological sex and cultural constructions of gender. While critics disagree on whether the *Decameron* exposes the disadvantaged status of women in order to critique and correct it, or to endorse and reinforce it,[4] it is clear that Boccaccio, in Teodolinda Barolini's words, 'uses the status and condition of women to frame his ethical and social questions'.[5] He articulates the specific dilemmas and conditions of women in the *Decameron* through gender-specific utterances assigned to speakers both male and female. Therefore, 'voicing gender' in the *Decameron* means writing and thematizing the speech of men, as well as the speech of women.

The *Decameron* stages the production and the interpretation of language *in its social dimension* – as expression and interpretation among speaking subjects who occupy socially defined categories of class, occupation, geographic origin, religion, family, and, very pointedly, gender. The entire book pretends to capture spoken language: the Primary Narrator records the conversations and stories of seven women and three men, a sea of words supposedly recounted to him. It is hard to imagine such an intermediary narration literally occurring, and the historical author surely meant it to seem entirely implausible. Starting with such a broad wink to the audience gives us a neon-lit reminder of one of Boccaccio's most constant concerns, elaborated in Marilyn Migiel's essay in this volume (Chapter 11), that while concrete truth exists, our access to it is precarious, particularly when that truth is mediated through human language with its inherent distortions and slippages. Exploring the specifically gendered dimension of this creation and deciphering of human speech is one of the *Decameron*'s core agendas. Looking closely at which characters and narrators voice the utterances in individual tales gives us one tool to help us decide what Boccaccio is playing at in this most playful of books. Beyond this array of voices, though, we must still consider the explicit voice of the Primary Narrator and the implicit voice of the historical author. These various levels of gendered voicing correspond to various levels of gendered reception, as each utterance is aimed at one or more audiences.

Both men and women are made to speak, then, and both men and women are made to interpret speech. This parallel ends in the fact that men are the default gender, women the marked gender. Part of the intellectual patrimony of Aristotelian and Galenic science was a model of sexual difference within which human was male, and female was defective male. This paradigm was not accepted automatically, universally, and comprehensively; for one thing, it emerges from the delimited context of reproductive theory. As a global explanatory model it had detractors as well as supporters. At the same time, however, it had longevity and influence at levels both conscious and unconscious. Rather than a mental image of the two sexes as equal and different, it offers a pervasive mental image of the female sex as inferior to and contingent on, secondary to, the male. This in turn generated and legitimized the misogynous diatribe genre – the systematic inventory and denunciation of the failings of women – which Boccaccio explored, indeed interrogated, throughout his writing life.

What this means for the gendered speeches that Boccaccio writes for his *Decameron* is that any female character is simultaneously her specific (created) self and expressly *not-male*, whereas virtually every male character is solely himself, not expressly *not-female*. In this sex/gender system women's speech has the double burden of representing an individual woman and the entire female sex, whereas rarely if ever in the *Decameron* is the speech of a male character projected as 'typically male speech' – the speech of the male sex *qua* male. Monna Tessa's nagging harangue in IX. 5, 63–4 only partly characterizes her as an *individual* nag; here she nags because women, in misogynous convention, are nags. When she carps that her husband doesn't do his 'work' at home yet tries to 'play away', that she has wasted her love and fidelity on him, that pressed he wouldn't yield enough juice to make a sauce, she echoes not only other indignant *Decameron* wives (in II. 10, III. 6, V. 10), but also women in the misogynous diatribe. Her husband Calandrino's resentful harangue in VIII. 3. 52; 61–2, by contrast, is stupid because he is stupid – not because men, by some parallel misandrous convention, are stupid.

In IX. 9 the truculence of Giosefo's wife is shaded by the convention that women are rebellious and resentful of spousal authority, a convention laid out in elaborate length in Emilia's extended introduction to the tale (§§3–9). By contrast, Giosefo's savagery in beating his wife is not overlaid by a corresponding convention that by nature men are abusive and brutal – though individual men in the *Decameron* can indeed be so. That Giosefo's violence belongs to himself and not to his sex is shown by his opposite number in the tale, Melisso. Whereas Giosefo had asked Solomon 'how he should deal with his wife, who was the most perverse and stubborn woman on earth' (§12; p. 691), Melisso had asked 'what I must do to be loved' (§13; p. 691). Had Giosefo asked 'what I must do to be loved by my wife', he might have interpreted Solomon's advice less brutally.

Speech thus functions asymmetrically between the sexes in the *Decameron*, a fact often explicitly thematized: narrators and characters refer to the speech of women as inflected by, or inflecting, the entire sex; they do not do so with men. This essay explores some of the major categories of gendered speech and gendered silence in the *Decameron* tales and frame-tale, noting the major parallels and divergences between the speeches and silences assigned to men and women. It concludes by examining what Boccaccio undertook and what he accomplished in his encyclopaedic and kaleidoscopic, often fractal, collage of human stories.

When less is more: the soul of wit

Most tales of Days I and VI examine ways that speakers can use their wits, especially witty answers, to restabilize a relationship gone dangerously awry.

These verbal defences typically feature brevity – the soul of wit – rather than expansive or torrential speech; moreover, they usually function at two levels, literal and metaphorical, requiring the addressee to decode their meaning and to admit privately the justice of the coded reproof. In *Dec.*, I. 4, the monk threatened with punishment for lechery tells his abbot, 'you had failed until just now to show me that monks have women to support' (§21; p. 48); the abbot's guilty conscience supplies the gloss: 'I saw you do what you saw me do, and I can expose you.' The female narrators of I. 10, VI. 1, and VI. 3 lament that most modern women cannot deliver or understand witty lines: 'few if any women now remain who can produce a witticism at the right moment, or who, on hearing a witticism uttered, can understand its meaning' (VI. 1. 2–4; p. 446). (Here, the speech attributed to female characters also bears 'the weight of women' – the burden of representing the entire sex.) Yet we see female speakers deploy this concise and figurative discourse in the very tales whose narrators claim that they cannot (VI. 1 and VI. 3). Madonna Oretta in VI. 1 – a major metanovella of the collection – tactfully curtails an agonizingly bad narration by a witticism both deft and kind.

Similar brief and metaphorical ripostes in Days I and VI mirror the sudden and oblique threats which prompt them. When the King of France schemes to manoeuvre the Marchesana di Monferrato so as to bring 'his desires to fruition' (I. 5. 7–8; p. 49), he does not confess those desires, but only sends word that he will visit her en route to the Crusade. She must decipher his implied motivation: that 'he was being drawn thither by the fame of her beauty' (§9; p. 50). Because he has been indirect, she must be indirect as well. Rather than saying 'I don't know why you've decided to court *me*, when all women have pretty much the same thing on offer', by serving only chicken dishes, the Marchesana leaves the analogy implicit, thus strengthening her case for all its audiences: the king, the hearers, and the readers of the tale. (Even as the Marchesana states that women are all alike, she shows the opposite, revealing her unique wit and virtue by her carefully chosen menu.)[6] In other words, while the rubrics of these days highlight specific faults (lechery, foolish love, wicked hypocrisy, avarice, cowardice, conceit), the witticisms that unveil these faults simultaneously unveil the hypocrisy that had attempted to conceal them under an appearance of virtue.

The seed does not always fall on fertile ground: Cesca's uncle fails to curb his niece's vanity (VI. 8); Messer Betto must explain Guido Cavalcanti's urbane reproof to his rather slow posse (VI. 9). But most of the comebacks stand as powerful and successful speech acts which re-establish normalcy, and even outside of Days I and VI they often manage to push back against the abuse of power. When Monna Giovanna retorts, 'I would sooner have a gentleman without riches, than riches without a gentleman', her brothers must back down and accept her choice of a mate (V. 9. 42; pp. 431–2). A witty comeback which functions as only part of an expertly constructed discourse is that of Madonna Filippa, caught in adultery in VI. 7 and on trial for her life. When she urges the judge to ask her husband whether she had always fulfilled her marital obligations (§15), the unwary husband admits that she always has. He sets himself up for a rhetorical move he did not foresee: Filippa verbally transforms her excess sexual capacity into a concrete item which can not only be 'surplus' from her husband's consumption, but can actually go bad or be thrown to the dogs. She does this as a question: like every effective rhetorician she leads her interlocutor and listeners to an irresistible conclusion and then pulls back, letting them reach it on their own:

> if he has always taken as much of me as he needed and as much as he chose to take, I ask you, Messer Podestà, what am I to do with the surplus? Throw it to the dogs? Is it not far better that I should present it to a gentleman who loves me more dearly than himself, rather than allow it to turn bad or go to waste? (§17; p. 464)

While many critics judge that Boccaccio sets up Madonna Filippa as the butt of this *novella*,[7] the conclusion the audience reaches, after they had 'rocked with mirth', is that the lady 'was right and that it was well spoken' (§18; p. 464). The distinction between to 'be right' and 'speak well' is clear: it is not enough to be right if one does not also speak well, make one's case well, and sway one's listeners – here, by humour. The audience's laughter acknowledges the incongruity of Madonna Filippa's self-defence through self-incrimination – indeed, by embracing the cliché that the sexual capacity of women far exceeds that of men. Yet the result of Filippa's defence is that the 'bad law' that women be burned for adultery now applies only to commercial sex (obviously still a problematic conclusion).

When used by the abusive character, however, the neat and symmetrical rejoinder does not restore balance. Having made his wife eat her lover's heart unawares, Guglielmo Rossiglione jibes, 'I am not surprised to find that you liked it dead, because when it was alive you liked it better than anything else in the whole world' (§20; p. 351). His vengeful jab does not sway her; instead the grave eloquence of her short reproach prevails, convincing him that he has done wrong and prompting him to flee.

And more is less

If brevity is the soul of wit, some *Decameron* speeches are nonetheless sprawling rather than terse. For impossibly long, high-flown, and intricate utterances with (like their plots) no attempt at verisimilitude, we can consider the ominous family dynamic of IV. 1 and the hyperbolic 'altruism' of X. 8. The gendered speeches of these tales share a grandiloquent *gravitas* that leaves the reader more edified than moved. Indeed, these speeches do not aim to mimic orality, but rather ostentatiously stage the literary, the artful, in vernacular writing.

The tragic opening tale of Day IV sets out in oblique lines a paternal love which is both excessive and unsettling. Because Tancredi refuses to give his widowed daughter a second husband, Ghismonda chooses a secret lover of high merit but low birth. Inevitably and voyeuristically Tancredi discovers her liaison, and passionately accuses her of unchastity as well as of choosing a base lover (§27). Ghismonda is not moved by the reproach, which Tancredi intended to be noble; her lofty and scornful reply is fully four times as long (§§31–45):

> since you... fathered me, I am made of flesh and blood like yourself. Moreover, I am still a young woman. And for both these reasons, I am full of amorous longings, intensified beyond belief by my marriage, which enabled me to discover the marvellous joy that comes from their fulfilment... you reproach me more bitterly, not for committing the crime of loving a man, but for consorting with a person of lowly rank, thus implying that if I had selected a nobleman for the purpose, you would not have had anything to worry about.   (§§34–8; pp. 296–7)

As Tancredi takes on the role of 'a child who had been soundly beaten' (§29; p. 296), Boccaccio has Ghismonda assume the imposing mantle of parental authority, applying in her stern monologue the principles, reason, empirical evidence, and rhetorical refinement that make her own case unassailable and show her father's to be hysterical and untenable.

It does not end well. On being told, 'shed your tears among the women' and 'slaughter us both at one and the same time' (§45; p. 298), Tancredi has Guiscardo's heart delivered to Ghismonda in a golden goblet with this message: '"Your father sends you this to comfort you in the loss of your dearest possession, just as you have comforted him in the loss of his"' (§47; p. 299). Yet again, the compact and symmetrical riposte does not serve the aggressor: Tancredi fails to convince his daughter that his objections are benevolent and honourable. Ghismonda achieves verbal *gravitas* and appropriates the discourse of parental authority, but with it gains only her lover's death. As Fiammetta tells it, the blame for Ghismonda's failure lies with her father's excessive and unfatherly attachment to her. But at the same time, Fiammetta shows Ghismonda as too proud to try to move Tancredi, and so angry as to flay him verbally.

The narrator Fiammetta emphasizes that Ghismonda does not show 'contrition or womanly distress' (§31; p. 296), concealing the weakness prompted by her love under the 'will of iron' equally inspired by it (§46; p. 298). Her greatness of mind is countered by the weakness of mind Tancredi reveals in his uncontrollable weeping, overwrought denunciations, and vindictive mutilation of Guiscardo's offending body. When Ghismonda finally does weep she is deliberate and controlled, and only confirms her superhuman rationality. The text makes explicit the reversal of their gender roles: Ghismonda transcends women's 'sorrow', 'screaming and sobbing', and 'shattered spirits' in her love and her conviction (§§30–1; p. 296); Tancredi is unmanned by a love as excessive as it is transgressive. However we might interpret Tancredi's attachment, Guiscardo's single microscopic utterance, 'Neither you nor I can resist the power of Love' (§23; p. 295), reveals Tancredi as his equal and his rival in love, both helpless before love's force. If language that fails to persuade, fails, then Tancredi's passionate outburst and Ghismonda's extended, hypotactic, controlled, and cutting discourse are both rhetorical failures.

Rhetorically elaborate expression also characterizes Gisippo in *Decameron*, x. 8. Best friends Tito and Gisippo form the *novella*'s emotional core, although Tito's love for Sofronia threatens the male couple. Tito articulates his desire in rational utterance that deliberately echoes iv. 1: 'The laws of Love are more powerful than any others' (§16; p. 748); 'I am young, and youth is entirely subject to the power of Love' (§17; p. 748). Hearing of Tito's love, Gisippo, engaged to Sofronia, decides with stunning detachment to 'transfer' her to his best friend, explaining, 'I should not perhaps be so generous, if wives were so scarce and difficult to find as friends' (§38; p. 751). The emotional profiles of the two male friends are thoroughly canvassed in their monologues, although readers may remain both unconvinced and uninvested in this flat-line love triangle.

Hinge character Sofronia is silenced even more thoroughly than Guiscardo had been; she is assigned no direct discourse at all, and her objections are reported as petty and unreasonable: 'And having cast a withering look, first at one, then at the other, she burst into floods of tears, complaining bitterly of the trick Gisippus had played on her' (§52; p. 754). Sofronia did not realize that she was not the protagonist of her story. When it is borne in upon her that hers is a bit part, 'being a sensible girl, she made a virtue of necessity and soon accorded Titus the love she had formerly had for Gisippus' (§89; p. 760); she completes, in other words, the 'transfer' from one lover to the virtually identical other, whom Gisippo had called a 'second self' (§39; p. 752).

Boccaccio assigns direct discourse to certain characters and not to others as a way to position readers to understand and respond to them. Female characters silenced by uttering no direct discourse include the unnamed girl in I. 4, Madama Beritola in II. 6, the unnamed Traversari girl in V. 8, and Lisabetta in IV. 5. Everyone except Lisabetta speaks directly in IV. 5 – her brothers, the ghost of her lover in her dream, even her neighbours. Lisabetta's subjection to her restrictive, abusive brothers is re-enacted in the way her voice is sidelined in the tale, just as her will is overborne. In II. 7 Alatiel too displays a mimetic silence, representative of her inability to communicate during her four years of wandering captivity among alien peoples. Only when she encounters someone who knows her language does the narrator Panfilo quote her directly in the *novella*, and again call her by her name.

Gendered silences

In addition to characters who are assigned only indirect discourse, like Sofronia, the Traversari girl, and Lisabetta, the *Decameron* also features characters who are silent within the diegesis, that is, in the action of their tale. These silences too are asymmetrical. Silence is a strategic choice in the case of male characters; I cannot recall it being imposed on a male in the *Decameron*, except to conceal sexual impropriety. In III. 1, for example, Masetto feigns muteness to gain access to a convent of nuns, because he has diagnosed their reported behaviour as indicating frustrated sexual desire. He maintains his silence for as long as he can keep up with the desire he has unleashed; he speaks up when he runs out of steam. In III. 2 the unnamed groom of King Agilulf, hopelessly in love with Queen Teodolinda, adopts silence as his strategy: 'he had the good sense not to breathe a word about it to anyone' (§6; p. 200); 'Knowing that it would be quite futile to start either confiding in the Queen or writing letters to acquaint her with his love, he thought he would explore the possibility of entering her bed by means of a stratagem' (§11; p. 201). The groom is silent when he impersonates the king in her bed, and again when the king is seeking the man guilty of cuckolding him. King Agilulf too chooses silence when he finds the man whose heart is pounding from excitement and fear, and again when his attempt to identify that man publicly is thwarted by an intelligent ruse. The unnamed groom has in fact no direct discourse, and his two triumphs – the first in replacing the king, the second in thwarting him – are never to be repeated, as his class dooms him to subordinate status.

The groom's decision to conceal his identity by silence during a sexual encounter he has engineered parallels that of the possessive Catella of III. 6. Her admirer Ricciardo had lured her to the baths on the pretext that she would surprise her husband Filippello with Ricciardo's own wife. Catella remains silent throughout what she thinks is extended sexual intercourse with her own newly vigorous husband, then bursts into a torrent of blame which mimics the conventional discourse of women in the misogynous tradition:

> Alas! who have I been loving devotedly for all these years? A faithless cur, who thinks he has a strange woman in his arms, and lavishes more caresses and amorous attention upon me in the brief time I have spent with him here than in the whole of the rest of our married life. You unprincipled lout, I must say you have given a splendid display of manly vigour here today, in contrast with the feeble, worn-out, lack-lustre manner that you always adopt in your own house.
>   (§§35–6; pp. 233–4)

Upon learning that she has bedded her admirer, not her (innocent) husband, she swears to avenge herself. Ricciardo's subsequent persuasion and her own yielding to the *fait accompli* take place without further direct discourse from her.

This dance of deception and seduction, appearance and reality, is glossed throughout by the narrator Fiammetta:

> As is usually the way with people who suffer from jealousy, Catella immediately swallowed the whole story *without bothering to consider the kind of person who was telling it or whether he could be deceiving her*, and *began to connect this tale of Ricciardo's with certain things that had happened in the past.*
>   (§21; p. 231; emphasis added)

Fiammetta tells us explicitly that when we interpret the words of others, we need to consider the source, filter the utterance through the grid of the speaker's perspective ('the kind of person it was who was telling her these things') and intention ('the possibility of his deception'). Even knowing Ricciardo's desire for her (which should have made her question his neutrality and truthfulness), Catella believes him, because her own grid of perspective ('as is usually the way with people who suffer from jealousy') and intention ('began to connect this tale ... with certain things that had happened in the past') conditions what she will believe and how she will retrospectively revise events she had previously discounted. Boccaccio has Fiammetta address explicitly the problematic addressed by Migiel in her essay in this volume: that truth and lies are particularly difficult to distinguish when what is at issue is sex, and the sexes.

Speech on loan

Some *Decameron* characters deploy language with such success that they can lend their eloquence to others – for their own ends, of course. One of these is the dandy Zima in III. 5, who longs to win the love of Messer Francesco Vergellesi's unnamed wife. Hoping to take advantage of Messer Francesco's envy of his fine palfrey, Zima offers the horse in exchange for speech with the lady. Messer Francesco thinks he has prevented any seductive exchange of words by forbidding his wife to make any answer to Zima's declaration of love. Initially disconcerted, Zima hits on the solution: he will simply reply to himself, delivering the lines he wishes she would speak. The lady adopts the attitude Zima attributes to her, and in an interior monologue adds to his rationale some proofs of her own (§30). They meet repeatedly during Messer Francesco's absence, 'to the exquisite pleasure of both parties' (§33; p. 227).

Narrator Elissa sees the lady's wholehearted adoption of Zima's scenario as a triumph not at her expense, but rather at her husband's. Accepting a deal that put her on the same level as a horse, and trying to subvert Zima's attempt at persuasion pre-emptively, Messer Francesco underrated both her value and her autonomy. The lady has not merely shifted from being dominated by her husband to being dominated by Zima; her internal monologue shows that she has calculated what Zima and her husband can offer in terms of her own pleasure and well-being:

> What am I doing? Why am I throwing away my youth? This husband of mine has gone off to Milan and won't be returning for six whole months. When is he ever going to make up for lost time? When I'm an old woman? Besides, when will I ever find such a lover as Zima? (§30; p. 227)

Also, Zima had never proposed to *receive the lady* in exchange for the horse; his proposal was merely to be allowed to speak with her privately, and his intention to persuade, not overpower her. Zima's ventriloquism, his construction and loan of gendered discourse, parallels his greater sexual interest, generosity, regard, gratitude, and sheer availability; in comparison, Messer Francesco's imposed silence offers her very little of interest.

Similarly, the unnamed Florentine lady of III. 3, as cautious as Agilulf's groom, 'would not venture to declare her love by dispatching a maidservant or writing him a letter' (§7; p. 206). Without alerting the man she desires, she lends him her own amorous words through the unwitting intervention of their mutual acquaintance, a 'rotund, uncouth' priest whom she makes her confessor (§8; p. 207). In an intensifying series, she complains three times to the confessor that a 'close acquaintance' of his has 'laid siege' to her chastity

(§11; p. 207) – though the man does not even know her. Each time, the confessor promises to make the pursuit stop; each time he reproaches his innocent friend, who had immediately realized that the lady's campaign of reproaches is a campaign of seduction. By telling the confessor that her own feelings and schemes belong to the man she desires, the lady manipulates both men – as well as her innocuous husband, whose only offence is to be a 'woollen-draper' 'of low condition' and hence unworthy of her (§6; p. 206).

The lady's independence, initiative, shrewdness, and success seem to position her positively in the tale, until the climax: 'And then, each enjoying the other to the accompaniment of many a hilarious comment about the stupid friar's naïveté, and random jibes about such draperly concerns as slubbing and combing and carding, they gambolled and frolicked until they very nearly died of bliss' (§54; p. 215). By deceiving an inoffensive husband and by mocking him with her conquest, the lady joins the army of women in the misogynous tradition whose sexual impropriety is marked as actively cruel: the widow in the *Corbaccio*, and in the *Decameron* the lady in III. 4, Elena (VIII. 7), Peronella (VII. 2), Madonna Beatrice (VII. 7), and Lidia (VII. 9) – but not, we should note, Madonna Filippa (VI. 7). Their sexual pleasure is heightened by the ridicule and sometimes harm these ladies with their lovers heap upon their clueless husbands:

> My darling treasure, find yourself a good stout stick and go down to the garden. Make it appear that you were putting my fidelity to the test, pretend to think that Egano is me, shower him with abuse, and give him a sound thrashing with the stick. Just think of the wonderful joy and amusement it'll bring to us both! (VII. 7. 39; p. 523)

This paradigm too is asymmetrical, because there is no pattern of male characters mocking their unsuspecting wives in a way that increases their own sexual pleasure. The power advantage in a marriage lying with the husband, it seems, mocking him with a co-conspirator reifies and intensifies a wife's successful inversion of that power dynamic. Thus the model of speech on loan is also asymmetrical between the sexes.

Voicing women and men in the misogynous tradition

In textual precedents that Boccaccio not merely knew but carefully copied into his *Zibaldone Laurenziano* (Florence, Biblioteca Medicea Laurenziana, MS 29. 8), the litany of accusations against women rests stably on simultaneous crimes of sexual and linguistic impropriety. The claim that women are sexually insatiable yet coldly calculating and controlling in sexual matters parallels the claim that women are uncontrollably loquacious yet coldly calculating and manipulative in their use of language. Part of the liveliness of misogynous diatribes results from the ventriloquism by which these texts render the logorrhoea and manipulativeness of women's speech. Long 'quotations' of women's speech are part of the toolbox of Juvenal and Ovid, as well as of Walter Map and Jean de Meun,[8] and the *Decameron* follows these in the speech of the old woman encouraging the younger to sexual licence in v. 10. The 'Potiphar's wife' plot borrowed into II. 8 features the princess of France's disingenuous apology for overpowering sexual desire, which echoes claims typical of misogynous texts – such as that women have less strength than men to resist sexual desire (§15). Following the principle that the best defence is a good offence are the torrential pre-emptive verbal strikes of Peronella (VII. 2) and the unnamed wife of Pietro da Vinciolo (V. 10), who launch into attacks to deflect blame they have deserved. Jealous Catella (III. 6) harangues at length the man she thinks is her guilty husband, though the latter was quite innocent. The unnamed wife of Ricciardo di Chinzica (II. 10) pays him back for disguising his impotence as virtuous abstinence: her deft verbal excoriation appropriates his pretext of 'holidays' and 'working-days' (§10; p. 180) and turns it into an extended metaphor, magisterially reified and refined (§§32–4, 41, 42). Although his humiliation drives him to madness and death, his sexual moderation and his young wife's sexual excess do not gain him the moral high ground in the eyes of the narrator Dioneo or of the listening *brigata*. Borrowing in these speeches, however, Boccaccio does not borrow in the ideology of their textual sources; he multiplies viewpoints and circumstances in order to complicate that ideology, and to give depth and complexity to his characters.

Just as the *Decameron* inserts these and other speeches of women from the misogynous tradition into its narrative tapestry, it also imports from that textual matrix the boiler-plate speeches of male accusers. The plot of II. 9 rests on Ambruogiuolo's false accusation, first of all women and then of Bernabò's virtuous wife Zinevra:

> You told us yourself that your wife is a woman, made of flesh and blood like the rest, in which case her desires are no different from any other woman's, and her power to resist these natural cravings cannot be any greater . . . You can rest assured that the only chaste woman is either one who never received an improper proposal or one whose own proposals were always rejected.
>
> (§§17, 20; pp. 167–8)

The mere presence of standard misogynous accusations cannot be the metric by which we decide the historical author's opinion on this topic; there is too much evidence to the contrary within the diegesis itself.[9] For example, Ambruogiuolo's own rationale rests not on the sturdy resistance of men to sexual temptation, but rather on their *in*ability to resist it (echoing the Princess of France in II. 8) and their tenacity in mounting campaigns of seduction (§§15–17, 19–20). Similarly, Zinevra's virtue in the tale is spotless; she is a victim not only of Ambruogiuolo's stratagem to accuse her of adultery, but also of her own husband's credulity. Moreover, so far from being the vengeful harridan of misogynous cliché, she forgives Bernabò 'although he merited no such favour' (§71; p. 177).

The high point of misogynous discourse in the *Decameron* is of course VIII. 7, the longest *novella* in the collection and a major precursor of the *Corbaccio*. Millicent Marcus has explored how symptomatic of Boccaccio's putative misogyny this tale might or might not be.[10] Rinieri's overwrought indictments do reflect some of Elena's bad behaviour; she treats him with gratuitous cruelty. His diatribe does, however, move beyond a rational and balanced renunciation of erotic desire, into an irrational and unbalanced denunciation of all women on the basis of his one hyperbolic disappointment. Rinieri's hysterical overreaction, his sadistic revenge, his bizarre channelling of misogynous tropes that do not technically apply, and his unsettling blend of compassion, arousal, and vengefulness in planning her suffering, combine to discredit the discourse of misogyny as a basis for moral behaviour or belief. Boccaccio sets up Rinieri, like Ambruogiuolo, as a self-subverting speaker. The butt of VIII. 7 is not Elena, vain, naive, and unkind though she is. The butt is Rinieri, whose vituperation reveals his own participation in the faults the genre attributes to women, including logorrhea, *superbia*, unreason, obsession, vindictiveness, manipulation, lust tinged with sadism, intellectual dishonesty, and an arrogant desire for dominance. The *brigata*'s conclusion (as the Primary Narrator describes it) is that both characters were to blame, with the scholar's failings articulated in greater detail (VIII. 8. 2).

What can we conclude?

Voicing gender in the *Decameron*, as this overview suggests, is an undertaking with considerable overlap between male and female. Efficacious speech, eloquent speech, virulent speech, stupid speech, and silence are distributed between the sexes, in yet another example of the *Decameron* sometimes showing us the opposite of what it tells us. Female members of the *brigata* lament the inability of modern women to compose and deliver snappy answers, but female *Decameron* characters compose and deliver them with ease and verve. Women need men to guide them, says Filomena (Introduction to Day I, 74), but 'it is . . ., ladies, . . . your own good sense that has led us to this spot', says Dioneo (Introduction to Day I, 93; p. 20). We cannot confidently attribute either Filomena's opinion or Dioneo's to the historical author. The author has the Narrator parade contrasting points of view from unexpected sources – a woman indicts female nature as imperfect and dependent, a man defends female behaviour as intelligent and independent – and invites us to think it over, considering evidence both textual and extratextual. The misogynous tirades of Rinieri and Ambruogiuolo repeat common clichés about a universal female nature, but Boccaccio makes the *Decameron* women as varied in their characters and motivations as *Decameron* men.

However, the non-overlap or asymmetry between male and female in the gendered speech of *Decameron* characters is also considerable. The women speakers are most often either pushing back against some kind of sexual force or abuse, or reaching for an autonomy usually marked as sexual (or effected by means of sex, as in II. 5 and VIII. 10). The femaleness of a speaking subject, in other words, is almost never a neutral circumstance; gendered characteristics, or sexual behaviour, are nearly always in play. The sexed and gendered dimension of a male speaking subject, by contrast, is rarely explicitly thematized, and I think never universalized. Even when Catella is verbally shredding the man she thinks is her husband, she condemns him *as an individual*, not *as a male*: there is no reference to the deceptive infidelity of 'all you men', as there surely would be if the shoe were on the other foot. When men speak and act foolishly, the tales attribute this to a secondary characteristic such as age, intelligence, class, or rank – not to their sex. Friar Puccio (III. 4) is a 'prosperous, law-abiding citizen', but also 'a simple, well-intentioned soul' of 'a certain age' (§§4–6; p. 216); Ferondo in III. 8 is a 'very wealthy yeoman', an 'exceedingly coarse and unimaginative fellow', 'fatuous', and 'stupid' (§§5–6; p. 255). These traits create male characters, not the male sex.

Does this asymmetry in the *Decameron* argue an antipathy towards women? Or is Boccaccio 'willing to generalize about the lives of women – to universalize – in order to file his "class-action" suit on their behalf?'.[11] I believe the latter. Boccaccio inserts at various narrative levels the cliché that women are more able than men to satisfy multiple partners (III. 1; V. 10; II. 7), not to indict them as hopelessly carnal or debased, the inferior half of humanity, but to explore the consequences of this putative sexual difference: to answer the question, 'so what?'. The trope functions differently with each textual occurrence, but never in fact to delimit or degrade women overall. In VI. 7, it is the axiom which underpins Madonna Filippa's manifesto against waste and rot: 'Must I throw it to the dogs?'. That punchline crowns all of her rhetorical strategies to win over the judge. What triggers the roar from the crowd ('as with a single voice') that she is right, the law is wrong, and the law must be changed, is humour, the 'amusing question' (§18;

p. 464); but the witty question alone is not enough. Her wit is only one of many persuasive strategies, including her aesthetic appeal, nobility, dignity, composure, charm, strategic concession, rigorous logic, learning, strong secondary sources, beautiful and highly individualized voice, calculated variety of registers, courage, conviction, candour, passion, wit, shrewdly sequenced argument, and variety of evidence (from law, scripture, nature, and experience). If these sound like the ingredients of good writing, I believe that Boccaccio intended them to be so: he made Madonna Filippa an inset mirror of the *Decameron*.

I noted above that the Proem posits an ethical project of showing gratitude for consolation received, by passing such consolation on. In his Day IV Introduction, the Narrator extends his proemial discussion of his putatively female audience by deliberately calling his vernacular prose a narrative language 'most unassuming' (§3; 284). In the Conclusion, he returns to the ethics and the decorum of a literature putatively addressed to ladies and written in language both 'proper' and 'improper' for ladies: proper in that it is not Latin, improper in that it is racy. Kristina Olson explores the adoption and ennobling of the vernacular in late medieval Italy as a separation of the 'language of women' from the 'literature of men':

> Boccaccio's lifetime witnessed the project of attributing authority to the vernacular. From Dante onwards... such a project entailed distancing the vernacular from its 'maternal' origins and feminine usage and lending it to the crafting of the language of erotic material, as manipulated by male writers. It meant exploiting the spoken vernacular as the language used by women for moments when a fictive audience was required (as in the *Decameron*'s Proem), but restoring the written vernacular to the Muses.[12]

It is certainly possible to interpret such a project as a move ultimately either hostile or indifferent to women – to interpret the philogyny long seen in the *Decameron* as 'part of a rhetorical strategy to build vernacular authority within shifting textual communities' (Olson, p. 54), mere surface content empty of substance.

However, we can also interpret Boccaccio's project differently. I see his exploration of rhetorical decorum (oral and written, masculine and feminine) as part of a comprehensive and multifarious investigation into the nature of lived experience and the verbal representation of that experience. Male/female is the binary that Boccaccio uses to probe the analytical tool of binarism itself, and the array of other binaries that intersect or overlap with it: young/old, rich/poor, noble/humble, same/other, intelligent/foolish, lay/clerical, holy/sinful, compassionate/cruel. As Barolini puts it, Boccaccio's 'preferred mechanism for considering difference is gender', the 'vehicle for addressing his most pressing social and ethical concerns' of all kinds, standing in for an array of other categories in a monumental canvas of interpretation and representation, of particularity and generality.[13] The epistemological charge that gender bears in the *Decameron* (and in other writings) does not, however, empty it of literal content. Boccaccio's fascination with how our language both reflects and constitutes us as beings in the world encompasses how our language both reflects and constitutes us as *men and women* in the world.

Because 'the hearts of the ancients' are 'long since removed in death',[14] to interpret the *Decameron* we must resort to the interpretative strategies it lays out for us, which are analytical and comparative. Moreover, we must acknowledge the role that a reading preference plays in interpretation, as the *Decameron* repeatedly shows with regard to its characters, from Abram (I. 2) to Catella (III. 6) to Giosefo (IX. 9). Does the *Decameron* offer a clear pattern with a coherent moral message? Or does it ultimately upset every pattern it posits, and decline to articulate a unified message? Many possibilities lie between these two extremes, but most readers end up favouring one pole or the other. Which pole we choose may determine, or alternately it may result from, how we read Boccaccio's project of voicing gender in the *Decameron*.

NOTES

1 Robert Hastings, *Nature and Reason in the 'Decameron'* (Manchester: Manchester University Press, 1975), pp. 59–60.

2 Raymond Fleming, 'Happy Endings? Resisting Women and the Economy of Love in Day Five of Boccaccio's *Decameron*', *Italica*, 70.1 (1993), 30–45.

3 Marilyn Migiel, *A Rhetoric of the 'Decameron'* (Toronto: University of Toronto Press, 2003).

4 Marilyn Migiel, 'The Untidy Business of Gender Studies', in *Boccaccio and Feminist Criticism*, ed. by Thomas C. Stillinger and F. Regina Psaki (Chapel Hill: Annali d'Italianistica, 2006), pp. 217–33.

5 Teodolinda Barolini, 'Afterword', in *The 'Decameron'*, trans. by Mark Musa and Peter Bondanella (New York: Signet Classics, 2010), pp. 809–18 (p. 810).

6 Barolini, 'Afterword', p. 818.

7 Kenneth Pennington, 'A Note to *Decameron* 6. 7: The Wit of Madonna Filippa', *Speculum*, 52 (1977), 902–5; Migiel, *A Rhetoric*, pp. 119–22.

8 Excerpts are anthologized in *Woman Defamed and Woman Defended*, ed. by Alcuin Blamires, Karen Pratt, and C. W. Marx (Oxford: Oxford University Press, 1992).

9 Lisa Perfetti, *Women and Laughter in Medieval Comic Literature* (Ann Arbor: University of Michigan Press, 2003), p. 3.

10 Millicent Marcus, 'Misogyny as Misreading: A Gloss on *Decameron* VIII, 7', *Stanford Italian Review*, 4.1 (1984), 23–40; reproduced in *Boccaccio and Feminist Criticism*, pp. 129–43.

11 Barolini, 'Afterword', p. 814.

12 Kristina Olson, 'The Language of Women as Written by Men: Boccaccio, Dante, and Gendered Histories of the Vernacular', *Heliotropia*, 8–9 (2011–12), 51–78 (p. 55): www.heliotropia/org/08-09/olson.pdf.

13 Barolini, 'Afterword', pp. 811–12.

14 *Genealogia*, I, Preface I, 42; p. 11 (trans. by Osgood).

PART III

Boccaccio's Literary Contexts

8

GUYDA ARMSTRONG

Boccaccio and Dante

Boccaccio's intimate literary bond with Dante is foregrounded in the incipit to his most famous work, the *Decameron*, where the reference to *Inferno* v in the subtitle ('otherwise known as Prince Galahalt') immediately establishes the intertextual, vernacular, erotic key through which it is to be read. But this is merely the tip of the iceberg of their textual encounters. Boccaccio's engagement with the defining figure of the preceding literary generation is both extraordinary – in terms of its sophistication, intimacy, and extensiveness – and quite *ordinary*, rooted in his personal scribal and textual practices, and made material in his own books. His Dante is at once public and private. He is the subject of externally oriented statements, such as the public lectures on Dante Boccaccio gave in Florence in the last years of his life, and the autograph manuscripts of the *Comedy* he prepared for public consumption. But at the same time he is also a private presence in Boccaccio's studies, Dante's works carefully copied and edited from his youth onwards, and their forms and themes internalized and reworked in his own compositions, both Latin and vernacular. For Boccaccio, Dante is therefore both a foregrounded subject, and a constant background noise, as evidenced in the rich seams of Dantean intertextual allusions, structures, and models which run through his writings, both Latin and Italian.

This chapter will read Boccaccio's Dantean engagements through his copying and glossing practices, considering how his profound attachment is manifested materially. The first part of the chapter will deal with his manuscripts of Dante's works, while the second part will consider his writings *on* Dante: those which physically form part of his Dante manuscripts, such as his biography and paratextual summaries of the *Comedy*; and those outside them, such as his incomplete commentary on Dante, the *Esposizioni sopra la Comedia di Dante*. The final section outlines some of the ways in which Boccaccio deploys Dantean references in his own writings, examining the intertextual mechanisms within his characteristic combinatorial practices.

Boccaccio's Dante manuscripts

Boccaccio's engagement with Dante was not of course confined to the page and desk. Boccaccio was a Florentine, and Dante was a real presence in his family life, related as he was to Beatrice via his father's second wife. From childhood onwards, his education and travels brought him into contact with further individuals who had known Dante in person. The traces of these interactions, and his developing trajectory as a Dantist, can be followed through his manuscripts, the 'material facts' of his day-to-day engagement with his predecessor.

Boccaccio's parchment notebook, the *Zibaldone membranaceo* (now separated into two volumes), provides the earliest material testimony for his systematic lifelong engagement with Dante.[1] Most of it was written during a twenty-year period, from his youth in the second half of the 1320s up to about 1348, and thus provides a progressive account of Boccaccio's developing intellectual interests and textual methodologies, and a demonstration of his precocity as a *dantista* and the critical role he has played in Dante historiography. The dating of the material in the *Zibaldone* to the late 1330s and early 1340s (that is, before Boccaccio's return from Naples to Florence) materially locates Boccaccio's youthful Dantean interests in Neapolitan reading communities where Cino da Pistoia was a living link between the cultural milieux of Dante and the young Boccaccio.

The Dante texts in the parchment *Zibaldone* are a miscellany of first-person correspondence documents in Latin prose and verse, placed alongside writings by near-contemporary and contemporary authors. They include three letters by Dante (*Epistles* XI, III, and XII), and a letter by Boccaccio himself in imitation of Dante (*Epistle* IV); also present is the much-disputed *Letter of Ilaro*, a dedicatory letter to a presentation copy of the *Inferno*, addressed to Uguccione della Faggiuola, and Dante's poetic correspondence with Giovanni del Virgilio, also known as the *Eclogues*.[2] The enigmatic Ilaro letter is especially interesting as an account of Dante's travels in exile, and for evidence of the early circulation and glossing practices of the *Comedy*. If we are to believe the first-person account by 'the humble monk Ilaro', Dante himself gives a copy of the *Inferno* to the monk, instructing him to gloss it and to send it on to his noble patron, Uguccione. Ilaro's shock at reading Italian verses prompts Dante to explain that he had begun the poem in Latin hexameters, and cites the opening three lines.[3] Boccaccio will reprise the notion that Dante began the poem in Latin, quoting the same lines, in both the *Trattatello* and *Esposizioni*. Whether the letter is authentic or not (and scholarship seems to have settled that it is no longer to be considered an imaginative composition of Boccaccio's), it is clear that Ilaro can be read as a figure for what Boccaccio himself will become: the humble mediator who copies and glosses the poem, sends it on to a powerful patron (Petrarch), and debates the suitability of the vernacular as a vehicle for such work.

What can this small collection of Dantean texts, inscribed into Boccaccio's personal reference library ('un vero e proprio libro-biblioteca' [a veritable library in a book]), tell us about Boccaccio's early engagement with Dante?[4] First and foremost, it shows a desire, even at this relatively early stage of his career, to afford Dante the status of an *auctor* (authority), a consecration performed materially by locating these rare Dante documents alongside other scholarly authorities from the classical past to the present day. Dante is thus placed at the heart of a bi-cultural (both Latin and vernacular) literary continuum, one which also features the Bolognese Latinist Giovanni del Virgilio and which culminates naturally with the recently laureated Petrarch (memorialized here by Boccaccio's own tribute to Petrarch on his coronation, the *Notamentum*, which is followed by four of Petrarch's metrical epistles). The placing of Dante's works within a wider compilation of other contemporary authors, culminating with Petrarch, too, will be repeated materially in his last autograph Dante codex.

The most important documents of Boccaccio's work as a Dantist are the three autographs of the *Comedy* which he made between the mid-1350s and late 1360s, known as 'To' (Toledo, Biblioteca Capitular, Zelada 104.6), 'Ri' (Florence, Biblioteca Riccardiana, MS 1035), and 'Chig' (now in two volumes, Vatican City, Biblioteca Apostolica Vaticana, MS Chigi L. VI. 213 and MS Chigi L. V. 176). As book-objects, they are uniquely expressive of this intense literary relationship, and in their content, ambition, and innovations they embody Boccaccio's unique competencies as a Dantist and his ongoing negotiations with the poet and his legacy. Each manuscript contains the text of the *Comedy* plus an evolving suite of paratextual material which reflects Boccaccio's own developing vision of the poem and Dante's place in the vernacular literary canon. Philologically, all three manuscripts derive from the manuscript which Boccaccio gifted Petrarch between summer 1351 and May 1353, the so-called Vatican manuscript, 'Vat' (Biblioteca Apostolica Vaticana, MS Vat. lat. 3199), or an identical 'twin' manuscript in Boccaccio's possession: a large-format, decorated manuscript written in the typical Florentine two-column layout. Boccaccio is thought to have accompanied this generous gift with a bespoke Latin poem, in which he addresses Petrarch as *Ytalie iam certus honos* ('Already certain honour of Italy').[5] Praising Dante for the extraordinary achievement of his *Comedy*, it suggests that he, too, is an author worthy of the poetic laurels awarded to Petrarch. The poem is at once an endorsement of Dante's decision to write in the vernacular, and a subtle challenge to Petrarch to join Boccaccio in acknowledging this. Crucially, this invitation is expressed in material terms, as Boccaccio invites Petrarch to practise his textual criticism on Dante as he would a classical *auctor*: 'welcome, read attentively, join to your own, cultivate, and praise your learned fellow citizen and poet' (line 36).[6] This is another key document in his mediation of Dante: Boccaccio will resend it, slightly revised, to Petrarch in 1359 (in response to which Petrarch will write his famous letter *Familiares*, XXI. 15), and give it a prominent place in his final Dantean anthology, MS Chig. The version transcribed by Boccaccio into the Chigi codex is now thought to be the earliest surviving copy. The original gift letter and letter of 1359 are lost, and the version of the poem transcribed into MS Vat is written by a later hand. Boccaccio's invitation to Petrarch to 'read, join, cultivate' reflects his own textual engagement with this gift book. Working from yet another manuscript of the *Comedy*, now lost, he added many variant readings to the text in MS Vat, evidence that he was clearly working on the textual tradition of the *Comedy* even before he sent the manuscript to Petrarch in the early 1350s.

MS To, dated to 1352–5, is the first of Boccaccio's three surviving autograph Dante compilations. It contains the texts of all Dante's poetic works (the *Comedy*, *Vita nova*, and the fifteen 'canzoni distese' (extended *canzoni*)), framed by carefully constructed paratexts, in a form which presents Dante as the all-surpassing vernacular *auctor* and hence worthy of comparison with the classical greats. Boccaccio labels the *canzoni* in Latin as 'cantilene' in MS To, but uses the vernacular term 'canzoni distese' in MSS Ri and Chig.[7] This volume recalls the formats used for the works of classical authors, as well as some Dante manuscripts produced outside Tuscany: a medium-sized parchment manuscript, written in semi-gothic script in a single-column layout with ample margins for annotation.[8] Boccaccio's Dante compilation thus materially continues the authorizing work of Dante's earliest reading communities, institutionalizing the poet and his works with the introduction of classicizing paratextual elements such as a biography, summaries, rubrics, and glosses familiar from the *auctores*.

The volume opens with a text written specially for this anthology: Boccaccio's biography of the poet, known as the *Trattatello in laude di Dante* or *Life of Dante* (fols 1r–27r). The modern title is taken from the *Esposizioni*, where Boccaccio notes that 'I have already written a brief treatise in praise of him' (Accessus, 36; p. 44). This is followed by Dante's own *Vita nova* (fols 29r–46v), an alternative version of the 'Life', now autobiographical and written in the first person, then by the most significant text in the compilation, the *Comedy* (fols 52r–116v; 121r–187v; 191r–256r). The constituent parts of the poem are surrounded by conventional paratexts such as Latin incipits, explicits, and a vernacular prefatory verse summary (known as an *Argumentum*) before each cantica. The concluding section of the volume contains Dante's fifteen *canzoni* (fols 257r–266v), each introduced by a Latin rubric (which, like this ordering of the *canzoni*, already exist in the tradition, and are thus not of Boccaccio's composition). Throughout the manuscript, close attention is given to *making*: the systematic ordering of the texts is mirrored by the granularity and consistency of the material arrangement on the page, these elements conspiring together to argue for the elevated status of the poet.

The book as a whole proposes a trajectory through Dante's own poetic development and the apotheosis of his great poem. The *Comedy* is framed on both sides by lyric poetry, first Dante-*poeta*'s personal trajectory through the lyric tradition in the *Vita nova*, leading to the supreme poetic achievement of the gigantic cosmic poem, and concluded by the later poems in the generically elevated form of the *canzoni*. Because the focus is poetry, and not prose, the *Convivio* is not included in its entirety (although Boccaccio mentions it in the *Trattatello*), but the three *Convivio canzoni* are present in the final section in the order they appear in Dante's text. The volume is crowned by a recently discovered and highly suggestive element: a large portrait of Homer on the final leaf captioned 'Homero poeta sovrano' ('Homer, the supreme poet'), a quote from *Inferno* IV, where Virgil delineates the great poets, including Homer. If Boccaccio is the artist of this concluding portrait, as Marco Cursi and Sandro Bertelli suggest, then its meaning is surely clear: to accord Dante the vernacular author the status of his classical peers in Latin and Greek, in a volume inspired by classical 'editions' of Virgil, and bearing a portrait of Homer.[9] Indeed, Boccaccio makes this intention explicit in his *Trattatello* which opens the volume: 'this vernacular to my thinking he first exalted and brought into repute amongst us Italians, just as Homer did among the Greeks, or Virgil among the Latins' (first redaction, §84; p. 27).[10]

The presentation of the *Vita nova* is particularly innovative. Boccaccio visually foregrounds the poetic parts of the prosimetrum over the prose, moving Dante's own interpretative instructions (the 'divisions') out from the main text and into the margins of the page, and thereby foregrounding the lyric and autobiographical aspects of the text at the expense of its author-directed literary-critical function. With Dante's directions now accorded the visual status of glosses, Dante's authority is subtly subsumed to Boccaccio's own editorial aims by adopting the *mise-en-page* of a compilation of a classical author. It may well be that Dante's blending of narrative and interpretative functions within the prose sections of the *Vita nova* did not meet with Boccaccio's own view of book organization, but Boccaccio is at pains to tell the reader (fol. 29r) that he has made this editorial choice on the recommendation of 'persons of worthy faith', who told him that Dante himself regretted including the divisions later in his life.[11] As ever in Boccaccio, the formulation is ambiguous. This could be a historical fact, relayed to Boccaccio by one of Dante's relatives or acquaintances, but it is suggestive that the formulation 'persone di degna fede' recalls the narrator from the *Decameron* who claims he learned of the *brigata*'s meeting in Santa Maria Novella from a 'persona degna di fede' ('a person whose word can be trusted'; Introduction to Day I, 49; p. 13).

Dante's 'glosses' to the *Vita nova* lyrics are mirrored later in the manuscript by further marginal commentarial glosses in Italian in *Purgatorio* XI, which appear to derive from Pietro Alighieri's very recent commentary, and thus provide evidence once again of Boccaccio's participation in a cutting-edge, scholarly, Florence-based 'Dante club'.[12] The presence of these glosses (which could have been inserted by Boccaccio after he first copied the manuscript, of course), in the margins, can be seen as the first stages of Boccaccio's own commentary to the *Comedy*, which will culminate with his *Esposizioni* lectures, and Bertelli has recently suggested that, in fact, MS To is the one he used for his Dante lectures. Indeed, it seems likely that this first compilation was Boccaccio's working copy of the *Comedy*, which remained on his desk until his death.[13]

Boccaccio's second Dante compilation (Ri) is the shortest, comprising only the text of the *Comedy* and Dante's fifteen *canzoni*. In size and *mise-en-page*, it is similar to the first compilation, but the manuscript has been oriented further towards the vernacular tradition with the headings and rubrics translated from Latin into Italian. One new Latin element is added, a metrical explicit in red ink at the end of the *Paradiso* (fol. 178r), which will reappear in MS Chig. Wide margins to the outer and lower edges of the page suggest that, like MS To, it was designed to house textual and/or visual commentary, both of which are in fact included. Extensive marginal glosses (in a later hand) have been added in the *Purgatorio*, while the manuscript also contains seven illustrations in the first seventeen cantos of the *Inferno*, now thought to postdate Boccaccio rather than be in his hand.[14]

Boccaccio's third Dante compilation, MS Chig, is the most extensive, and is a wider-ranging glorification of the Italian vernacular lyric tradition, now exemplified by the twin 'crowns' of Dante and Petrarch. Like MS Ri, it dates from the 1360s (*c.* 1363–6), but in content it is more similar to MS To, containing the same editorial and primary texts, plus works by Guido Cavalcanti, Dino del Garbo, and Petrarch. As a witness to late Trecento philological and scribal practices, it is greatly important to both Dante and Petrarch's textual histories. Materially, this is the *ur*-object of Boccaccio's canon formation, the *making* of two crowns of the Italian lyric tradition by the author who by implication and by design would be the third.[15]

The manuscript is nowadays in two parts, and was probably dismembered by Boccaccio himself, as part of its reordering. However, a reconstruction of its contents shows that the first part (MS Chig L. V. 176) reprises the complex ordering strategies of the first compendium: it begins with a revised version of the *Trattatello* (fols 1r−13r), and is followed by the *Vita nova*, (13r−28v), Cavalcanti's poem *Donna mi prega* with Dino del Garbo's commentary (29r−32v), the revised version of *Ytalie iam certus honos* (34r), the fifteen Dante *canzoni* (34v−43r), and − a highly significant addition to this vernacular Pantheon − the only surviving copy of the second form (the so-called 'Forma Chigi') of Petrarch's lyric collection, the *Canzoniere*, here titled *Fragmentorum liber* (43v−79r). The other volume (MS Chig L. VI. 213), meanwhile, contains the text of the *Comedy*, accompanied once again by the *terza rima* verse summaries preceding each cantica, and now with longer prose rubrics in Italian before each canto. All but one of the prose *canzoni* rubrics have been cut, and thus the first one now serves as the sole framing paratext to the lyrics. The fasciculation emphasizes an organic continuity and forward progression (generic, chronological, teleological) between texts, where the works flow on from one another on the same page, rather than starting on the first page of a new booklet as previously. New editorial interventions emphasize this coherence seen, for example, in the passage between the *Trattatello* and the *Vita nova*, which now runs on in an unbroken single column (fol. 13r), the division between the two works marked by a rubricated passage which closes one and opens the next.

The placement of *Ytalie iam certus honos* shows a similar attention to genre and page design at this crucial moment of transition from Dante to Petrarch. Boccaccio's dedicatory poem, *about* Dante, *to* Petrarch, now serves as a bridge between Dante's most elevated lyric production and the consummate achievements of Petrarch's *Canzoniere*, a literal manifestation of Boccaccio's invitation to Petrarch to 'join' Dante to his own literary production. Before Boccaccio reordered the codex, the *Comedy* itself was the centrepoint of the collection and the pivot between pre- and post-Dante lyric production. In its separated state, however, the *Comedy* becomes a free-standing text, housed within its own Boccaccio-authorized commentarial framework, while the other volume can now be read as a history of the Italian lyric tradition from Dante to Petrarch via Cavalcanti, in which the narrative arc of the *Vita nova* (first in Boccaccio's *Trattatello*, then in Dante's prosimetrum, and Cavalcanti's generative *canzone* with commentary) is chiasmically mirrored and remade by Petrarch, the master of vernacular poetry and Dante's knowing, allusive heir.

Writing Dante with Dante

Boccaccio is thus supremely attentive to the forms of the book as a means of authorization. But his unsurpassed knowledge of Dante's writings (and the canons beyond them), adds an extra dimension to these productions. In texts such as the *Trattatello*, the *Argomenti* to the *Comedy*, the *Esposizioni*, and the late *Rime*, he enacts his profound internalization of Dante's words via his characteristic combinatorial mechanisms, creating a corpus of 'Dantean' writings which have a specificity and allusive resonance unparalleled in the many centuries of Dante criticism since.

The *Trattatello* is the only one of Boccaccio's texts for which we have two autograph manuscripts. Posterity has sometimes lost sight of its original function as an *accessus* – an entrance, or way in – to these two collections of Dante's works, MSS To and Chig, intimately bound into them not only by its physical location in the manuscripts but also by its allusive mechanisms, but it is crucial to understand it in its original production context. In the *Trattatello*, Boccaccio locates details from the *Vita nova* within a framework derived from classical literary models, chiefly the biographies of Virgil by Donatus and Servius. His acute desire to authorize Dante within contemporary debates, and to persuade Petrarch of Dante's worth, meanwhile, leads him to cite some of Petrarch's own letters for sensitive subjects such as the poet's exile from Florence, and the nature of poetry and its relation to theology.[16] Textually, as well as materially, then, the *Trattatello* is fundamental to Boccaccio's project to achieve for Dante the status of vernacular *auctor*.

Boccaccio reorients his Dante biography between his first and second autograph compilations, again probably with Petrarch in mind. The first version is the longest, while the second, revised version (known as the 'first compendium') found in MS Chig is about a third shorter. (A 'second compendium' survives in about 30 (non-autograph) manuscripts, and differs from the Chigi version in some minor textual variants.) The expansive Latin title of the first version (*De origine, vita, studiis et moribus viri clarissimi Dantis Alighierii Florentini poete illustris et de operibus compostis ab eodem* (Concerning the origins, life, studies and habits of that most great man and illustrious poet Dante Alighieri, and the works composed by him) is vernacularized for MS Chig as part of Boccaccio's definitive reframing of Dante towards Italian. All three versions cover essentially the same ground. The text begins with an exhortative proemial section invoking Dante's exile by the Florentines and presenting this text as restitution for this misdeed: a work written by Boccaccio, a fellow Florentine, writing like Dante in the Florentine language (and of course by implication, Boccaccio is a fellow master *auctor*, the maker of this neoclassical compilation). As befits an *auctor*'s biography, the principal theme of the text is poetry as the epitome of intellectual achievement, and Boccaccio frames the events of Dante's life through this lens. Biographical sections are interspersed with discursive passages, including a misogynist digression after a discussion of Dante's marriage, an invective against the city of Florence for exiling Dante (later toned down in MS Chig), and a separate discursive section on the nature of poetry and its relation to theology. Certain of Boccaccio's key Dante *topoi* are reprised, familiar from the dedicatory letter to Petrarch and *Zibaldone*, such as the defence of the decision to write the *Comedy* in the vernacular (citing again the 'abandoned' Latin verse opening from the *Letter of Ilaro*). The treatise closes with an expansion of the prophetic dream of Dante's mother which was briefly mentioned in the section on his origins (§§207–28), and which alludes to the dream of Virgil's pregnant mother recorded by Donatus.

Dante is present here not just as foregrounded subject, but in the very lexical structures of Boccaccio's language. From his very first literary experiments, Boccaccio's writing is characterized by a dense allusivity, an intertextual matrix of references to other texts which connect Boccaccio's texts to his wider literary system; a feature of his writings on Dantean subjects as much as his other fictions and works. The most obvious Dantean presence is naturally the *Vita nova*, whose plot points (on Dante's love for Beatrice and her death) are quickly paraphrased in a few paragraphs in the first part of the text. More suggestive are those allusions which derive from his global Dantean macro-text, particularly marked places in the *Comedy* which echo through into Boccaccio's world. So Dante's distress at the death of Beatrice in the *Trattatello* (first redaction, 41) is rendered not solely through reference to the *Vita nova* (*VN*, XXXI. 1–3), but with an additional amplification, where the cue of Dante's account of his weeping in the *Vita nova* triggers further allusions in Boccaccio to the sounds of the souls in Dante's Hell (*Inf.*, III. 22–4). Likewise, the anti-Florentine invective (§§92–109) personifies the negligent, exiling city as female, much as Dante does in his famous 'Ahi serva Italia' invective of *Purgatorio* VI, and Cacciaguida's eulogy to the good old days (*Paradiso*, XV–XVI), but its force is amplified by specific allusion to other locations in Dante, with Boccaccio's 'Oh ingrata patria' recalling Dante's own description of the Florentines as 'quello ingrato popolo' in Brunetto Latini's prophecy of his future exile in *Inferno*, XV. 61. The intertextual matrix is rich and assured, serving to embed Dante's words deeply into his own life story.

Boccaccio's verse *Argomenti* are his most ostentatiously visible exercise in formal Dantean collage. While still recognizably within the established

Dante commentary tradition of verse summaries (*capitoli*), in Boccaccio's hands they become a complex literary device akin to the acrostic key to the *Amorosa visione* (interestingly, another experiment in Dantean *terza rima*). Bookended by citations of the first and last lines of each cantica, and infused throughout by a dense concentration of Dante's own words, in Dante's own *terza rima* form, the *Argomenti* are a virtuoso performance of material function and intertextual allusion. While not strictly *centones* (a text made up entirely from citations from another), the resonating effect is striking, and showcases Boccaccio's naturally combinatorial compositional practice to the maximum. The *Inferno* and *Purgatorio* summaries have 226 lines each, and the *Paradiso* 181 lines. Their differing lengths are a function of the tight focus on the literal exposition (simply put, there are more encounters and plot points in *Inferno* and *Purgatorio*, and more lengthy – and hence compressible – discourses in *Paradiso*). As we will see, his predilection for the literal reading is displayed on a vast scale in the *Esposizioni*. As single self-contained *terza rima* summaries, they provide a unified (and almost comically accelerated) overview of each cantica. Generally two *terzine* (6 lines) are given to each canto, although some are longer (e.g. *Inferno*, III, XIII, VIII). Perhaps not accidently, these are privileged sites for Boccaccio's intertextual allusions (the entrance to Hell, the wood of the suicides, the wrathful in the Styx), whose Dantean locutions recur widely in his works. The *Argomenti* display Boccaccio's astonishing facility in manoeuvring within Dante's poem: a selective pan-and-zoom through the *Comedy*, oscillating between the macro overview while maintaining allusive closeness at the micro, word-level. Between the anchoring opening and closing lines, Boccaccio roams freely for allusions, often combining citations from the specific canto with others drawn from elsewhere in the poem.[17]

Boccaccio's vast unfinished commentary of Dante, the *Esposizioni*, stands as his culminating achievement as *dantista*. The autograph manuscript of the text of his lectures is now lost, but we know from the inheritance dispute at his death that it consisted of '24 notebooks and 14 memo books'.[18] Boccaccio gave about sixty public lectures on the poem between late October 1373 and January 1374, but they were suddenly suspended (for reasons which are still unclear), and the commentary text stops abruptly at *Inferno*, XVII. 17. But, although truncated, more than enough remains to show the scale and ambition of this work. Boccaccio's references to both 'listeners' and 'readers' in the *Esposizioni* indicate that he was directing the work at multiple audiences of varying levels of literacy, and therefore not only at the audience of his public lectures but also an eventual scholarly (written) readership.[19] The differing needs of these audiences are visible in the text itself, with its many abbreviations (perhaps intended to be glossed verbally), yet possessing a formidable density of scholarly reference. Although rough, they remain recognizably Boccaccian in their copiousness, narrative energy, and explicit focus on the theme of poetry and the status of the *auctor*. To this end Boccaccio reprises contextually appropriate passages from a lifetime of writing, with excerpts from the *Zibaldoni*, *Genealogia*, *De casibus*, *De mulieribus*, and *Trattatello*.

Boccaccio organizes his readings according to the standard scholastic method of textual division, formally separating the literal from the allegorical reading for each canto.[20] With his pronounced compilatory tendencies, Boccaccio shows a strong preference for literal readings over allegorical, even omitting the allegorical interpretation altogether in cantos x–xi and xv–xvi. As the work progresses, it accelerates and becomes more compressed, with the discussion of the first eight cantos alone taking up two-thirds of the text. His authorial intentions are, as ever, foregrounded in the opening (lengthy) *accessus*: 'the exposition of an artistic text, of multitudes of stories, and of the sublime meanings hidden beneath the poetic veil of our Dante's *Comedy*' (Accessus, 3; p. 39).

Here and in the allegorical commentary to Canto 1, Boccaccio once more reprises his notion of the poet as theologian: one who has access to the fundamental truths, but conceals them under the fictional veil of 'favoloso parlare' (fabulous speech) (*Esp.*, I. ii. 8). Dante the poet (not to mention his commentator Boccaccio) is thus the master of multiple meanings, whose 'rough' vernacular verse is in fact 'polysemous' (*Esp.*, I. ii. 18), housing precious truths. In fact, Boccaccio is the only Trecento commentator to use 'polysemous' to describe Dante's allegory, here and in the *Genealogia* (I. iii. 7), showing his knowledge of the *Epistle to Can Grande*.[21] Boccaccio here returns to Giovanni del Virgilio's poetic epitaph for Dante as 'Theologus poeta' (poet-theologian), which he had copied into the *Trattatello* in both versions.[22] The analogies with Boccaccio's own textual production are striking; Dante is the ostensible subject, but the features of his practice which Boccaccio chooses to highlight – polysemy, scholarliness, and surpassing prowess in vernacular composition – are those in which Boccaccio could in fact be argued to transcend his subject and poetic master (indeed, in so doing often using Dantean intertextual allusions as a subtextual shortcut to supply his deeper meanings).

Boccaccio's four late sonnets on Dante (*Rime* CXXII–CXXV) are often read as a recantation of his previous devotion to the poet, or at best as a weary acknowledgement of the pointlessness of expounding vernacular literature to the masses. But they are also a characteristically Boccaccian auto-defence of his engagement with taboo subjects (whether that be improper themes and female readers, or an unseemly debasement of the Muses via their association with vernacular literature, as here). Once again, these criticisms are allegedly levelled by unnamed critics, and are thus in keeping with other 'authorially voiced' parts of his corpus, for example, the Introduction to Day IV and Conclusion to the *Decameron*.

We may never know Boccaccio's underlying motivation for these sonnets, but their dense allusivity provides more evidence of his practice of writing Dante with Dante, which in turn points to a more nuanced position on Dante and Petrarch than is sometimes supposed. Like those other highly compressed verses, the *Argomenti*, these sonnets are constructed around some of Boccaccio's favourite Dantean loci. The accusation that Boccaccio has prostituted the Muses in the 'bordellos of the woeful masses' ('nelle fornice del vulgo dolente'), and 'foolishly revealed their hidden parts to the dregs of the lowest classes' ('e le lor parte occulte ho palesate | alla feccia plebeia scioccamente') (CXXII, 1–4) is richly resonant of Boccaccio's other statements on poetry, amplified further by the deployment of Boccaccio's own Dantean matrix of misogynist invective, as found in the *Corbaccio*.[23] Sonnet CXXIII ('If Dante weeps') deploys an iconic citation from Dante in line 2 ('del suo alto ingegno'; of his lofty genius), itself contextually linked to an invocation of the Muses for Dante's own poetic enterprise: 'O Muse, o alto ingegno' (*Inf.*, II. 7, 'O Muses, O lofty genius'), rhymed and contrasted in line 3 with the 'vulgo indegno' ('unworthy masses'), recalling the Dantean 'vulgo dolente' ('woeful masses') of sonnet CXXII.[24] Sonnet CXXIV contin- ues with an explicit, low-register citation from Cacciaguida's prophecy to Dante-personaggio in *Paradiso*, XVII. 127–9 'grattar della mia rogna' ('to scratch my itch'), where Cacciaguida steels Dante to continue writing poetic truths in the vernacular, against the criticisms of his naysayers. Boccaccio's literal incorporation of this passage into his own poetic account of his weari- ness with his authorization project shows both his meticulous command of Dante's poem, and an overriding desire for synthesis and lyric continuity in its redeployment in what is actually a very Petrarchan vehicle of exhaustion with the poetic project.

The last of the four so-called Dantean sonnets opens with a seafaring metaphor redolent of those found in the *Comedy* (*Purg.*, I.1–3; VI. 77; *Par.*, II. 1), and a reprise of the 'ingrato vulgo' ('ungrateful masses') allusion to Brunetto's prophecy of exile, also used in the *Trattatello*. Once again, the lexis and themes mix Dante and Petrarch, in which Dante's ambitions for his vernacular poem are framed within a pose of Petrarchan sorrow and weariness. The culmination of the self-reflective sonnets on poetry and posterity is Boccaccio's final sonnet on the death of Petrarch (CXXVI), 'Or sei salito, caro signor mio' ('Now you have ascended, my beloved master'). Here, Boccaccio places Petrarch in a Dantean poetic Elysium, able to gaze on his beloved Laura (and Boccaccio's Fiammetta), and dwelling beside Sennuccio (del Bene), Cino (da Pistoia), and Dante himself. The phrase 'mondo errante' in line 12 recurs twice in Dante (*Par.*, II. 94 and *Par.*, XX. 67), and twice in Petrarch (*RVF*, CCCXL VI. 7, and CCCL. 11). Bound together by shared intertextual items, Boccaccio's last poetic statement on his vernacular Pantheon is thus, too, a textual performance akin to that which he proposes in his first formal communication to Petrarch on Dante, the dedicatory poem *Ytalie iam certus honos* ('read attentively, join to your own');[25] and in his determined material juxtaposition of these two authors in his early *Zibaldone*, and then again in the Chigi codex. On their posthumous equivalence of status, Boccaccio has the last word.

Dante in Boccaccio

As we have seen, Dante permeates Boccaccio's literary works to an astonishing degree and in a number of different ways. Boccaccio favours a selective, accumulative, use of Dante, concentrating contextually appropriate (or comically inappropriate) allusions at certain points in his narratives. There is great consistency in his practice from his first literary experiments in the 1330s up to his final writings such as the *Esposizioni* and the late sonnets. His choice of *dantismi* is also notably consistent over the forty years or so of his writing: a core set of structurally marked sites in Dante's *Vita nova* and *Comedy*, with references from other works such as the *Monarchia*, and *De vulgari eloquentia*, if the occasion demands it. These allusive underpinnings are naturally most visible in his vernacular writings, but are also present to a considerable degree in the Latin works, as recently discussed by Simone Marchesi.[26]

Boccaccio's technique of *dantismo* by accumulation is probably the most brilliantly realized example of his general combinatorial practice. He has three main strategies, which are often combined for intensifying effect. The first is a structural or formal use, in which Boccaccio deploys structural elements or poetic forms derived from Dante's works as the macro-architecture of his own texts. The second is what might be loosely termed a 'thematic' or 'narrative' use of particular situations, characters, or locations from Dante; and the third a 'textual' (i.e. allusive and citational) use, whereby Boccaccio reuses words or phrases, most often from these key passages.

His adoption of Dante's literary forms begins very early in his writing career, in his intensely Dantean Neapolitan period. His so-called 'first fiction', the *Caccia di Diana*, comprises eighteen cantos of Dantean *terza rima*. If the verse form recalls the *Comedy*, the thematic inspiration is the *Vita nova*: in its celebration of fifty-nine noble ladies of Naples, led out on a fantastical hunt by the goddess Diana, the poem alludes to Dante's mention of his *sirventese* in the form of a letter to the sixty most beautiful women of Florence (*VN*, VI. 2). The *Caccia* also shows the earliest deployment of what will become key sites in Boccaccio's Dantean intertextual topography: not just the *Vita nova*, but also the cantos of the Earthly Paradise of *Purgatorio*, a primary source for the landscape; the infernal forest of *Inferno* XIII for the wild hunt; and St Bernard's prayer to the Virgin (*Par.* XXXIII) for the invocation to the divine female.

Boccaccio uses *terza rima* in two other early vernacular works: the *Comedia delle ninfe fiorentine* and the *Amorosa visione*. Both works are divided into fifty units, that is, exactly half the number of cantos in the *Comedy*. The *Comedia delle ninfe* advertises its Dantean affiliations in its titling as a 'comedy', and in its prosimetrum form (redolent of the *Vita nova* and *Convivio*), with nineteen of its fifty chapters in *terza rima* verse. The *Comedia delle ninfe* has general thematic similarities with Dante's *Comedy*, inasmuch as it is an account of the protagonist's allegorized journey towards spiritual enlightenment, and also contains clusters of textual *dantismi* similar to those deployed in the *Caccia*, with the addition of a character named Lia, described using allusions to Dante's own Lia of *Purgatorio* XXVII.

Boccaccio reworks many of these formal, thematic, and textual *dantismi* again in the *Amorosa visione*. As if the complex interlocking rhyme scheme was not enough, Boccaccio maps the whole text within a gigantic acrostic in the form of three sonnets dedicated to 'Fiamma', constructed with the first letter to each line of the poem. Dante himself had included small acrostics in his poem (*Purg.* XII. 25–58; *Par.* XIX. 115–41), and the creation of these three invocatory sonnets solves the problem of how to reflect Dante's tripartite division of the *Comedy* in fifty cantos. Other Dantean elements include the narrative voice, clearly modelled on Dante's presence as both poet and protagonist in the *Comedy*; the opening scene, likewise, recalls that of the *Comedy*, with the appearance of a guide-figure (here female) who promises to lead the author-protagonist to a better place. Situational similarities apart, the poem diverges quickly from the Dantean model of an afterlife journey in favour of a guided tour through a 'noble castle' (I. 59), with frescoed Triumphs depicting various qualities on the walls. Textual references to specific parts of Dante's poem cluster at certain points, not least in the first room of the castle, which is a rerun of the delineation of the inhabitants of Dante's Limbo in *Inferno* IV. Tellingly, Dante himself is included within this 'lovely school', the 'bella scola' of famed poets (*Inf.* IV. 94), which gives Boccaccio (as protagonist and narrator) the opportunity to perform his devotion to his poetic master, just as Dante-character does to Virgil in the

Comedy (*AV*, v. 79–88; vi. 1–24). The poetic tribute is replete with Dantean allusions, including the first instance of his criticism of Florence, deploying the same intertextual lexis of ingratitude used for this theme later in the *Trattatello* and late sonnets (*AV*, vi. 13–15). After the *Amorosa visione*, Boccaccio's compositions in *terza rima* will culminate in the supersaturated *dantismo* of his *Argomenti* to the *Comedy*, the most situationally specific example of his combinatorial skills.

Similar layering of Dantean references can be found in Boccaccio's other poetic and prose works. Key scenes and allusions are often reprised, such as the primal scene of erotic reading, Paolo and Francesca, which is reworked in the *Filocolo* when Florio and Biancifiore kiss after reading Ovid's *Ars amatoria*, and reappears in the subtitle to the *Decameron*, and the reference to the widow's erotic French reading matter in the *Corbaccio*. Another key site for Boccaccio is Dante-character's own primal love scene gazing at Beatrice in church, a literary antecedent which is redeployed in the *Filocolo*, *Elegia di madonna Fiammetta*, and *Corbaccio*. Formally, the *Decameron*'s 100 tales recall the underpinning structure of the *Comedy*, while other aspects of the narrative are framed through Dante: the comedic progression from tragedy to resolution is expressed through reference to the symbolic Dantean landscapes of *Inferno* I, then modelled again diegetically in the *brigata*'s escape from the infernal city to the serene countryside beyond. Specific textual allusions underpin the imitation of the Dantean authorial voices: the first-person author of the Proem evokes the shipwreck simile from *Inferno* I as he speaks of the task ahead of him, and then, at the beginning of the Introduction to Day I, evokes the horrors of Hell via his conventional shorthand of 'sighs' and 'tears' (*Inf.*, III. 22–4) to signal his 'bad beginning' (Introduction to Day I, 4). It is only by traversing this 'bad beginning' that the reader will ascend to the sun-bathed slopes beyond. By explicitly locating the narrative in the year 1348, when he himself was 35 years old, Boccaccio is able to set up a link between himself and his literary predecessor, who opens his *Comedy* at the same age, in the providential year 1300. There are many other Dantean allusions in the text, most famously in the tales of Nastagio degli Onesti (v. 8) and the Scholar and the Widow (VIII. 7), whose layering of evocative textual allusions is concentrated by further thematic links to the Dantean model of retribution, the *contrapasso*.

Boccaccio's 'last fiction', the *Corbaccio*, is famously his most Dantean – and arguably his most contentious – work. This short text is a tour de force of combinatorial prowess, a summa of the Latin antifeminist tradition framed within a Dantean afterlife landscape, where the unnamed narrator is instructed by a mysterious shady spirit he encounters in an infernal forest.

While the dense allusions of the central, misogynist section of the text are largely taken from the classical tradition, Dante as a source animates every part of this book. The doomed one-sided romance between the narrator and the widow draws heavily on the *Vita nova*, from his lovesick, suicidal misery in the chiasmic frame narrative, the flashbacks in the dream sequence to the widow flirting in church, through to the bitter explicit, in which the author announces he will curse this woman more than any man has ever done, an inversion of the laudatory conclusion of the *Vita nova*. The *Comedy*, meanwhile, supplies the infernal setting in which most of the action takes place, and the purgatorial landscape for the closing paragraphs; the model of the two-hander dialogue between lost narrator and omniscient guide; and most notoriously, the topography for the vast obscene portrait of the woman's vile body. Boccaccio's expert hand arrays his references with great precision: high-register allusions to the *Monarchia*, *De vulgari eloquentia*, the *Epistole*, and the *Paradiso* are found in the authorially marked spaces of the Proem, while the carefully mined scatological and obscene references find their natural home in the misogynist invective. But while Dante is the visible point of reference, the Petrarchan itinerary of the protagonist's journey once again stresses Boccaccio's successful synthesis of his two *auctores*. The *Corbaccio* is the extreme conclusion of Boccaccio's literary *dantismo*, a text which imaginatively remakes its sources whilst also succeeding in holding within itself Dante's words and the essence of his work. Just as the *Esposizioni* are the culminating achievement of Boccaccio's lifelong engagement with Dante as copyist, editor, and commentator, so the *Corbaccio* stands as a virtuoso performance of his literary *dantismo*. Throughout his writing career, Boccaccio consistently deploys Dantean references at moments of metaliterary reflection: in the authorial frames of his works, when discussing poetic inspiration, the ideal life of the poet, literary languages and genealogies, and the problems of posterity. In the *Corbaccio* he is able to harness his Dantean lexicon to his lifelong theme of the journey of the poet-scholar towards the fulfilment of his poetic vocation. Writing about writing, he builds his most enduringly provocative text through the words of his most profoundly internalized model.

NOTES

1 See List of manuscripts and Chapter 2 in this volume.
2 The *Zibaldone* also contains other texts by Giovanni del Virgilio: his eclogue addressed to Albertino Mussato, a fragment of epic poetry, and a poetic exchange with Guido Vacchetta. Boccaccio will also cite Giovanni del Virgilio's poetic epitaph for Dante, 'Theologus Dantis' (Dante Theologian) in the *Trattatello*.

3 Beatrice Arduini and H. Wayne Storey include a diplomatic transcription of the letter and Italian translation in their 'Edizione diplomatico-interpretativa della lettera di frate Ilaro (Laur. XXIX 8, c. 67r)', *Dante Studies*, 124 (2006), 77–89.

4 Stefano Zamponi, 'Nell'officina di Boccaccio: gli autori latini classici e medievali di una lunga iniziazione letteraria' (Scheda 56), in *Boccaccio autore e copista*, ed. by Teresa De Robertis and others (Florence: Mandragora, 2013), pp. 300–5 (p. 301).

5 See Giuseppe Velli, 'Moments of Latin Poetry (*Carmina*)', in *Boccaccio: A Critical Guide to the Complete Works*, ed. by Victoria Kirkham and others (Chicago: University of Chicago Press, 2013), pp. 53–61 (pp. 59–60).

6 I follow Martin Eisner's translation here: *Boccaccio and the Invention of Italian Literature: Dante, Petrarch, Cavalcanti, and the Authority of the Vernacular* (Cambridge: Cambridge University Press, 2013), p. 74.

7 Eisner, *Boccaccio and the Invention*, p. 163, n. 83. I use Eisner's English translation here.

8 Rhiannon Daniels, *Boccaccio and the Book: Production and Reading in Italy 1340–1520* (London: Legenda, 2009), p. 41; Marco Cursi, *La scrittura e i libri di Giovanni Boccaccio* (Rome: Viella, 2013), pp. 99–101.

9 Sandro Bertelli and Marco Cursi, 'Novità sull'autografo Toledano di Giovanni Boccaccio: una data e un disegno sconosciuto', *Critica del Testo*, 15 (2012), 287–95.

10 Cursi, *La scrittura e i libri*, p. 106.

11 Sandro Bertelli, 'La prima silloge dantesca: l'autografo Toledano' (Scheda 49), in *Boccaccio autore e copista*, pp. 266–8 (p. 267).

12 Carlo Pulsoni, 'Chiose dantesche di mano di Boccaccio', *Italia medioevale e umanistica*, 37 (1994), 13–26 (pp. 13; 25–6).

13 Bertelli, 'La prima silloge dantesca', p. 268.

14 Francesca Pasut, 'Boccaccio disegnatore', in *Boccaccio autore e copista*, pp. 51–9; Victoria Kirkham, 'A Visual Legacy: Boccaccio as Artist', in *Boccaccio: A Critical Guide*, pp. 321–40.

15 Bertelli, 'La prima silloge dantesca', p. 271.

16 Elsa Filosa, 'To Praise Dante, To Please Petrarch (*Trattatello in laude di Dante*)', in *Boccaccio: A Critical Guide*, pp. 213–20 (p. 218).

17 For examples, see Marco Baglio, 'Argomenti in *terza rima*', in *Boccaccio autore e copista*, pp. 277–80 (p. 278).

18 I follow Gilson's translation here: Simon Gilson, 'Modes of Reading in Boccaccio's *Esposizioni sopra la Comedia*', in *Interpreting Dante: Essays on the Traditions of Dante Commentary*, ed. by Paola Nasti and Claudia Rossignoli (Notre Dame: University of Notre Dame Press, 2013), pp. 250–82 (p. 253).

19 Gilson, 'Modes of Reading', p. 244.

20 Gilson, 'Modes of Reading', pp. 256–7.

21 Gilson, 'Modes of Reading', pp. 255, 276, n. 25.

22 First redaction, §91; second redaction, §65.

23 All quoted translations of the sonnets are from *Boccaccio's Expositions on Dante's 'Comedy'*, trans., with introduction and notes by Michael Papio (Toronto: University of Toronto Press, 2009), pp. 5–7; 33–34; Guyda Armstrong, 'Boccaccio and the Infernal Body: The Widow as Wilderness', in *Boccaccio and*

Feminist Criticism, ed. by Thomas C. Stillinger and F. Regina Psaki (Chapel Hill: Annali d'Italianistica, 2006), pp. 83–104.

24 I follow the Hollanders' translation here for *Inf.*, II. 7: Dante Alighieri, *The Inferno*, trans. by Robert Hollander and Jean Hollander (New York: Doubleday, 2000).

25 Eisner, *Boccaccio and the Invention*, p. 74.

26 Simone Marchesi, 'Boccaccio on Fortune (*De casibus virorum illustrium*)', in *Boccaccio: A Critical Guide*, pp. 245–54.

9

GUR ZAK

Boccaccio and Petrarch

At the beginning of Book VIII of the *De casibus virorum illustrium*, Boccaccio describes his weariness and indignation with the work he is writing, contemplating giving up his arduous task. Overcome by lethargy, Boccaccio lies down on his couch, when before his eyes appears a dignified man, wearing a crown of laurel (*De casibus*, VIII. 1. 5). That man, he soon realizes, is no other than his 'venerable teacher' Petrarch, who in a long speech reproaches Boccaccio for his sloth (p. 203). He reminds him that man 'was born to work' (p. 204), and above all justifies the merits of pursuing earthly glory by means of one's virtuous undertakings. Persuaded by his words, and no less by the 'strong proof of his life' (p. 206), Boccaccio is awakened to the right path of arduous labour and picks up his pen again.

Passages like this have long contributed to the scholarly emphasis on the crucial impact that Petrarch had on the life and works of Boccaccio. Although Boccaccio had been acquainted with some of Petrarch's works already in the 1330s, while he was still living in Naples, it was his personal encounter with Petrarch some twenty years later and the relationship that emerged afterward that truly altered, according to the scholarly commonplace, the course of his life and writings. Boccaccio first met Petrarch when the poet-laureate, then in his mid-forties and nine years Boccaccio's elder, passed through the city of Florence in 1350 on his way to Rome to celebrate the Jubilee declared by Clement VI. Following this first encounter, the two met in person a few more times, maintained an extensive correspondence, exchanged manuscripts, and cooperated on shared cultural projects, such as overseeing the first Latin translation of the Homeric epics. As a result of these close encounters, it is argued, Boccaccio was converted to Latin humanism, turning from the composition of amorous works in the vernacular to the writing of moralistic and historical ones in Latin, modelled after the fashion of Petrarch.[1]

In recent decades, scholars have revolted against the tendency to cast Boccaccio in the role of the passive disciple and to focus solely on Petrarch's impact on him. While not denying the transformative effect that the encounter with Petrarch had on Boccaccio, these scholars, led by Vittore Branca, have begun to seek evidence of Boccaccio's impact on Petrarch, discussing, for example, the possible influence of Boccaccio's vernacular works on Petrarch's *Canzoniere* (his collection of vernacular poems) and *Trionfi* (*Triumphs*),[2] or Boccaccio's contribution to Petrarch's Latin works.[3] Nonetheless, what remains constant in both scholarly traditions is the tendency to portray the relationship between the two authors as marked by a confluence of interests and ideas, and to regard the reciprocal influences between them as straightforward and unproblematic. The conflicts and tensions that often characterized their rapport tend to be brushed aside, or at best regarded as only a passing aberration in an otherwise harmonious and like-minded exchange. Furthermore, as Francisco Rico has argued, the tendency to regard the relationship between the two as solely rosy and benevolent led scholars to overestimate the level of familiarity of the two with each other's works, and thus also to exaggerate the actual impact their works had on each other's writings.[4]

This chapter will revisit the relationship between Boccaccio and Petrarch with the aim of further challenging some of the common assumptions about it. For that purpose, the chapter will begin with an examination of the nature and extent of the reciprocal influences between the two authors and will then turn to an analysis of conflicts and tensions that emerge from their correspondence. Although not denying the significance of the relationship between the two authors for the development of both, this chapter will at the same time show that their impact on each other's Latin writings was less pervasive than assumed, and that the instances in which they did rely upon each other's works are defined by a complex dynamic of both appropriation and transformation. Above all, this chapter will argue that following his meeting with Petrarch in 1350, Boccaccio continued to develop his ideas and convictions in ways that often contradicted Petrarch's views, thus advancing – vis-à-vis his dialogue with Petrarch – his own distinct cultural, artistic, and ethical vision.

There can be no doubt as to the shift that took place in Boccaccio's writing career following the early 1350s, when he turned most of his attention from vernacular to Latin composition. During this latter period, Boccaccio wrote several Latin works: two compendia of exemplary narratives – the *De casibus virorum illustrium* (1356–60) and the *De mulieribus claris* (1361–2); a massive moralistic exemplification of pagan mythology, the *Genealogia deorum gentilium* (1350–74); a classicized encyclopaedic account of geographical places and names, the *De montibus* (1355–64); and a collection of pastoral poems, the *Buccolicum carmen* (1342–72). While clearly not abandoning his interest in vernacular composition, he wrote during this period only two new works in the vernacular – the *Corbaccio* (probably early to mid-1350s) and the *Esposizioni sopra la Comedia di Dante* (1373–4). This shift in Boccaccio's career, as mentioned, has been widely attributed to the influence of Petrarch, and Boccaccio himself at times refers in his works to the way in which Petrarch ignited his desire to leave behind his 'vulgar song' (*Buccolicum carmen*, XII. 51) and to dedicate himself to 'other loves' suited to a 'higher age' (*Buccolicum carmen*, XII. 53–4; pp. 131–3).

Although Petrarch might have indeed influenced Boccaccio's turn to focus on Latin composition, this does not mean that Boccaccio was a slavish follower of Petrarch, and to determine the exact nature of Petrarch's impact on him we need to look closely at the extent to which Boccaccio actually relied upon Petrarch's works in his Latin writings and adhered to his ideas and styles within them. When we examine Boccaccio's Latin writings carefully, as Rico has shown, it becomes evident that his reliance upon Petrarch's works was rather limited.[5] Apart from drawing upon a few works of Petrarch that were generally known, such as some of his letters and his defences of poetry in his *Invective contra medicum* (*Invectives against a Physician*) and the *Collatio laureationis* (*Coronation Oration*), Boccaccio's major Latin prose writings do not quote directly or derive specific information from Petrarch's works. Even in cases in which Boccaccio specifically alludes to the impact of Petrarch's writing, as in his allusion to the influence of Petrarch's *De viris illustribus* (*On Illustrious Men*) in the preface to his own *De mulieribus claris*, or the possible reference to the title of *De viris illustribus* in his *De casibus*, the works themselves do not contain quotations or material drawn directly from Petrarch's *De viris*, or from any other of Petrarch's works for that matter – apart from the mentioned defences of poetry.[6]

Boccaccio's scarce utilization of Petrarch's works in his Latin writings, according to Rico, suggests that Petrarch – who was notorious for his reluctance to publish his works – never gave Boccaccio the opportunity to read, let alone copy, works such as *De viris illustribus*, *Africa*, or the *Secretum* (*The Secret*). Whatever knowledge Boccaccio had of these works was based on what Petrarch told him about them when they met in person. Petrarch's influence on Boccaccio's major Latin prose works, as a result, depended more on his personal example than his actual works, and consisted primarily of providing Boccaccio with general precepts for living and creativity – such as the emphasis on the merits of the pursuit of glory or of Latin composition – rather than any specific knowledge or scholarly information.[7]

While Boccaccio's scant utilization of Petrarch's works might indeed be a result of his lack of familiarity with Petrarch's writings, we should also pay attention to instances in which Boccaccio directly departs in his Latin works from Petrarch's positions. Already the *De casibus* and *De mulieribus* point to such a departure. Even if Boccaccio's knowledge of Petrarch's *De viris illustribus* was based only on what Petrarch told him about the work in person, it is hard to imagine that he was not aware of Petrarch's adamant focus on ancient figures in this work. Petrarch's scorn for his present age and neglect of contemporary examples, after all, is a common theme in his Latin works in general, evident, for example, in the *Collatio laureationis*. However, in opposition to Petrarch's strict reliance on examples drawn from antiquity, Boccaccio included in his exemplary narratives assembled in *De casibus* and *De mulieribus* both ancient *and* medieval figures up to his own day, thus following the model of Dante's *Comedy* and his own earlier works such as the *Amorosa visione*. Whereas Petrarch deplored and rejected in his Latin writings everything related to contemporary history, Boccaccio continued to insist in his later Latin works on the need to learn from both ancient and modern examples.

Boccaccio's departure from fundamental aspects of Petrarch's humanism is evident also in cases in which he undoubtedly draws directly upon Petrarch's writings, as in his defence of poetry in Books XIV and XV of the *Genealogia*. Answering accusations that poets are liars who weave meaningless fictions, in this work Boccaccio echoes Petrarch's discussions of poetry found in the *Collatio laureationis*, letter X. 4 of the *Epistolae familiares* (*Familiar Letters*), and *Invective contra medicum* – a work which Petrarch sent Boccaccio in 1357 following frequent requests. Like Petrarch, Boccaccio asserts that poets' fables contain valuable truths hidden under the veil of allegory, states that the Scriptures themselves employ figurative language, and argues that Plato did not intend to banish all poets from his republic – only the unworthy comic ones.[8]

Yet, Boccaccio's defence of poetry also departs from that of Petrarch's in crucial ways. In his discussions of the value of poetic fictions, Petrarch specifies that under the veil of allegory poets reveal truths which relate to three topics: history, morality, and natural phenomena. As he states in the *Collatio laureationis*: 'poets under the veil of fictions have set forth truths physical, moral, and historical'.[9] What is especially significant about this list of topics is the absence of theology; this amounts to a direct rebuke of Petrarch's poetic predecessor Dante, as he defends as worthy only classical poetry on classical and natural themes. In addition, Petrarch's concentration in his defence solely on classical poets demonstrates that in his view worthy poetry must be written in Latin.

In his defence of poetry in the *Genealogia*, Boccaccio directly departs from Petrarch's adamant classicism and ignores his exclusion of theology from the list of worthy poetic themes by including Dante's *Comedy* among the examples he gives for the value and truthfulness inherent in poets' fables. In his praise of Dante, Boccaccio specifically commends him for untying in his poetry the 'hard knots of theology' (*Genealogia*, XIV. 10; p. 53). Furthermore, whereas Petrarch aims his defence solely at classical Latin poetry, Boccaccio, again through the inclusion of the *Comedy*, extends his defence to vernacular poetry as well.

Boccaccio's simultaneous imitation of and departure from Petrarch's poetics is evident also in his poetic practice in the *Buccolicum carmen*. Petrarch's *Buccolicum carmen* was one of the few Latin works which Boccaccio read and copied during his visit to Petrarch's house in Milan in 1359. This reading – in addition to his earlier encounters with some of Petrarch's eclogues, which circulated already in the late 1340s – influenced Boccaccio's *Buccolicum carmen*, leading him to focus in his eclogues on political and moral themes. Boccaccio's eclogue 'Faunus', for example, which laments the death of King Robert of Naples, was clearly influenced by Petrarch's own lament of the death of the same king in his eclogue 'Argus'. In eclogue XII, as noted, Boccaccio directly refers to his desire to follow in the footsteps of Petrarch, declaring that he was converted to Latin poetry after hearing Petrarch and Virgil singing 'in rival song' (*Buccolicum carmen*, XII. 71; p. 133).

However, while manifesting his allegiance to Petrarch, Boccaccio also departs in his *Eclogues* from Petrarch's poetic practice in important ways. Here again he diverges by incorporating elements taken from Dante's *Comedy*. In his collection of bucolic poems, Petrarch remained overwhelmingly loyal to classical models, following the example of Virgil's eclogues in using allegory as a means of depicting moral, political, and poetic themes. Petrarch alludes to religious and theological themes only to contrast them in his first eclogue, or to attack the corruption of the Papacy in the sixth and seventh eclogues. These latter eclogues are thus essentially political. In contrast to Petrarch's firm classicism, in eclogues such as X and XIV, Boccaccio draws upon the example of Dante's *Comedy* to provide a depiction of both heaven and hell. Eclogue XIV, entitled 'Olympia', describes Boccaccio's meeting with his deceased daughter Violante, who descends from heaven in a manner similar to Beatrice, to inform him of the bliss of paradise. Violante's depiction of heaven in the eclogue, as Janet Smarr has noted, is modelled closely on cantos XXVIII–XXX of Dante's *Purgatorio*.[10] By directly imitating Dante's vernacular masterpiece in his classicized eclogues, Boccaccio departs from the model of Petrarch both thematically and stylistically, combining the ancient and the modern, the classical and the theological, to establish his own distinct poetic voice.

Boccaccio's very efforts to defend the value of poetry until the end of his life represent a departure from Petrarch's later convictions. Despite his early defences of poetry, in his later years Petrarch persistently claimed to have abandoned poetry. Even during his defence of poetry in his *Invective contra medicum*, completed in 1355, Petrarch declared that he had stopped reading poetry 'seven years ago' – associating all kinds of poetry – both Latin and vernacular – with youthfulness (III. 142). In his *Epistola ad posteritatem* (*Letter to Posterity*) (1350–74), Petrarch declared that although he had been inclined by nature to the study of 'moral philosophy and poetry', in the course of time he had 'abandoned poetry' (§11).[11] Boccaccio, as demonstrated by the *Genealogia*, remained, in contrast, adamantly loyal to the value of poetic fictions to the very end of his life, completely ignoring Petrarch's statements on the unworthiness of poetry. Significantly, in Boccaccio's recurring portraits of Petrarch in his later years, such as the one appearing in his letter to the aspiring poet Jacopo Pizzinga from 1371, Boccaccio continued to praise Petrarch especially for his poetic abilities and his revival of the 'poetic name' (*Epistles*, XIX. 29).[12] It is really only in Boccaccio's Petrarch that we receive an ideal of humanism that is unwaveringly poetic.

Thus far we have seen the limited impact that Petrarch's works had on Boccaccio's Latin writings, and the subversive nature that characterized the instances in which Boccaccio did draw upon Petrarch. When we turn to Boccaccio's possible impact on Petrarch, a similar picture emerges. The influence of Boccaccio's Latin compositions on Petrarch's Latin works appears to be minimal: Petrarch does not quote from Boccaccio's major Latin works in his writings, nor does he express any specific interest in them.[13] Furthermore, even in cases in which he does draw upon Boccaccio's minor Latin or vernacular works in his Latin writings, his use of his younger colleague's works is mostly defined by an attempt to correct what he sees as the flaws in Boccaccio's presentations.

One of Boccaccio's works upon which Petrarch might have drawn is Boccaccio's early biography of Petrarch, *De vita Petracchi*, written in 1341–2. Petrarch possibly used this early work in composing his own self-portrait in the *Epistola ad posteritatem* – drawing on the form of Boccaccio's biography. Like Boccaccio, Petrarch structures his self-portrait as a combination of a short chronological account of his life and a portrayal of his character and physical attributes. Nonetheless, even if Petrarch was influenced by Boccaccio's biography, it is clear that his aim in composing his self-portrait was to correct what he considered to be the flaws in Boccaccio's portrayal of him. Whereas Boccaccio focused in his biography especially on the development of Petrarch as a *poet* and celebrated the glory he won for his poetic achievements – providing a detailed description of Petrarch's coronation – Petrarch, as we have seen, specifically emphasized his disavowal of poetry in the *Epistola*, and downplayed the significance of his coronation, associating it with 'youthful elation' ('iuveniliter gloriabundus') (§27). In addition, Petrarch also much amplifies in his self-portrait his devotion to sacred letters, stating that he discovered later in life the hidden sweetness of the works he 'once despised' (§11).

A work of Boccaccio by which Petrarch was evidently affected is the closing story of the *Decameron*, that of 'patient Griselda'. His reading of the story, as Petrarch declares in the opening of *Seniles*, XVII. 3, motivated him to translate it into Latin, thus leading to the creation of one of his most influential compositions in early modern culture. Yet, this translation, as we shall see below, was prefaced by a highly disparaging assessment of Boccaccio's *Decameron*, and characterized as well by a complex process of both assimilation and transformation.

Boccaccio's influence on the course of Petrarch's vernacular compositions following their meeting in 1350 appears to have been more substantial. This impact relates in particular to Boccaccio's efforts to convince Petrarch to read Dante's *Comedy*. Despite the fact that Boccaccio adopted at times Petrarch's views of the inferiority of the vernacular tongue – as we have seen for example in eclogue XII – he clearly never abandoned his admiration for Dante's achievements in this language, and he repeatedly attempted to convince Petrarch to take Dante seriously. In 1351, Boccaccio sent Petrarch a copy of Dante's *Comedy*, accompanied by a Latin poem, *Ytalie iam certus honus*, in which Boccaccio praises Dante and urges Petrarch to read him carefully. It is undoubtedly significant that Petrarch began to compose his *Trionfi* – a vernacular work written in Dantean *terza rima* – not long afterwards.[14]

It was around the same time, in the early 1350s, that Petrarch also demonstrated a renewed interest in his vernacular poems and decided to gather them into a collection, sending the first version to Azzo da Correggio between 1356–8. In 1359 – around the same time that Boccaccio again sent him a copy of the *Comedy* (leading to Petrarch's highly ambiguous appraisal of Dante in *Familiares*, XXI. 15, addressed to Boccaccio) – Petrarch began working on the second version of the *Canzoniere*, now known as the 'Chigi' form.[15] The only surviving copy of this second form is written in Boccaccio's hand – copied probably during his meeting with Petrarch in Venice in 1363 – and preserved as the Chigi manuscript, in which Boccaccio also copied Dante's *Comedy* (see Chapter 8 in this volume). The fingerprints of

Boccaccio are thus apparent in the development of Petrarch's vernacular works in the period after 1350, counter-balancing Petrarch's role in Boccaccio's turn to Latin composition.

One of the most important aspects of the relationship between Boccaccio and Petrarch, and the central medium through which this relationship was enacted and sustained, is the elaborate correspondence the two maintained following their meeting in 1350. Boccaccio was the central correspondent of Petrarch's later years, with Petrarch addressing thirty-seven letters to him. Boccaccio wrote approximately twenty-two letters to Petrarch, though only six have survived. This rich exchange has been celebrated as a manifestation of the humanist revival of the ancient ideal of a friendship, which is enacted in letters written in the Ciceronian 'familiar' style.[16] This claim contains no doubt a lot of truth. The letters between the two often employ the ancient rhetoric of friendship – Petrarch tells Boccaccio in them that they share a 'single heart' ('unum cor'; *Seniles*, I. 5. 67; I. 26) – and they serve as a means to conduct intimate conversations.[17] Boccaccio's *Epistle* xv, in which he portrays his visit to Petrarch's house in Venice while the latter was absent and describes his meeting with Petrarch's granddaughter, who reminds him of his own deceased daughter, Violante, provides a particularly moving example of this fact (*Epistles*, xv. 10–12).

Yet at the same time, the correspondence between Boccaccio and Petrarch is also a site of ongoing tensions, conflicts, and mutual criticisms, as both authors often reproach each other in the letters for their actions and life-choices. These mutual criticisms are not only personal, but point to the divergent positions held by both poets on several crucial aspects. In the remaining part of this chapter, I would like to elaborate upon two central criticisms that emerge from their correspondence and the conflicts that underlie them: Boccaccio's ongoing critique of Petrarch's acceptance of patronage, and Petrarch's parallel reproaches of what he perceives as Boccaccio's 'weak' reactions to the blows of fortune. Whereas the first critique leads to an open debate between the two over the appropriate way of life for the man of letters, the second points to their differing positions on the Petrarchan ideal of self-cultivation.

Boccaccio's criticism of Petrarch's life-choices comes to the fore in his famous *Epistle* x, written in 1353 following Petrarch's decision to accept the invitation of the Lord of Milan, Giovanni Visconti, to move to the city and live there under his auspices. Two years beforehand, Boccaccio had presided over a similar invitation made to Petrarch by the city of Florence, inviting him to live in the city of his fathers and serve as the chair of rhetoric in the newly established Florentine *Studio*. Boccaccio was probably the one who drafted the celebratory letter of invitation and delivered it to Petrarch in person during their meeting in Padua in 1351. After some hesitations, Petrarch declined the Florentine invitation. Now, when he accepted the request of the Visconti, a dynasty which was in a state of war with Florence, Boccaccio was furious and responded with a harsh letter, written in the bucolic style, in which he bluntly accused Petrarch of submitting to a tyrant and sacrificing his humanist ideals.

Modern scholarship has often portrayed the conflict that emerges in this letter as a debate between republican freedom and submission to tyranny.[18] Yet this view is, to a large extent, anachronistic. When we look closely at Boccaccio's letter, it is evident that Boccaccio's complaint against Visconti rule did not reside with its autocratic nature *per se*, but rather with its expansionist tendencies, disturbing the peace among the Italian city-states ('the rustic Egone [i.e. Visconti]...took up arms, amassed robbers, and occupied the woods of Liguria'; x. 8). Boccaccio's ire, as a result, relates more to his local patriotic ties to Florence than to a republican ideology.[19] Moreover, what Boccaccio is mainly concerned about in this letter is the fact that by moving to serve the Visconti, Petrarch sacrifices his personal and creative freedom, incarcerating both himself and the Muses (§11). By accepting the patronage of the Visconti, according to Boccaccio, Petrarch betrays his ideal of 'honest poverty' ('paupertatem honestam'), which had characterized his solitary way of life thus far, and succumbs to the lure of 'dishonest riches' ('inhonestis...divitiis'; §27). The crux of the matter, in other words, is the question of the freedom and integrity of the man of letters, his ability to cultivate his writings freely, and Boccaccio assumes the position that by accepting patronage Petrarch inevitably sacrificed his humanist calling.

Petrarch did not answer Boccaccio's letter. At the time of his move to Milan several other Florentine friends wrote Petrarch letters expressing their discontent, which were evidently less harsh than Boccaccio's. Petrarch responded at the time with a series of letters to their mutual Florentine friend, Francesco Nelli, defending his position by stating that the Lord of Milan promised him 'perfect solitude and leisure' with no infringement upon his freedom. His former way of life, Petrarch insisted, did not change with his move to Milan, even though he acknowledged that nothing could guarantee that Visconti would keep his promise not to interfere with his studies (*Familiares*, XVI. 11. 9; II, 318).[20]

The correspondence between Petrarch and Boccaccio resumed two years after the incident, and by 1359 the storm had evidently passed, as Boccaccio went to visit Petrarch at his house in Milan. Yet, Boccaccio's criticism of Petrarch and the debate between the two over patronage continued until the very end of their lives and correspondence. Boccaccio, as is evident from letters Petrarch sent him in 1366 (*Seniles*, VI. 2), and 1372 (*Seniles*, XVII. 2), continued to criticize Petrarch for his submission to princes and the material gain he attained for his services. Petrarch kept insisting in response that he was with princes 'in name alone', able to maintain his liberty. While criticizing Petrarch, Boccaccio also represented himself in old age as jealously safeguarding the ideal of liberty. In a letter from 1371 to Niccolò Orsini, Count of Nola, Boccaccio rejected the former's offer of patronage and described the various similar offers he had rejected over the years. He stated that 'accustomed to living freely' he would not be able to 'subject his neck to the yoke' and added that his humble paternal estate in the village of Certaldo provided him with the little that he needed (*Epistles*, XVIII. 15–16). Although in the course of his career Boccaccio himself sought a position in courts – particularly in Naples – in his old age he thus portrays himself as living the ideal of autonomy and honest poverty which had characterized in his view the life of the young Petrarch. The true man of letters, Boccaccio kept insisting in opposition to Petrarch, should resist the temptations of patronage and maintain his autonomy at all costs.

In parallel to Boccaccio's ongoing criticism of Petrarch over his submission to patrons, in his letters to Boccaccio Petrarch assumed the role of the moral counsellor and repeatedly reproached Boccaccio for what he considered to be his feeble reactions to the vicissitudes of fortune. In *Familiares*, XVIII. 15, Petrarch tells Boccaccio that after reading his recent letters he reached the conclusion that Boccaccio is 'mentally disturbed' (a 'turbato animo'; *Familiares*, XVIII. 15. 1; III, 68), and reproaches him for letting certain unspecified arrows of fortune slip past the 'stronghold of reason'. Given that the letter was sent from Milan in 1355, it is plausible that Boccaccio's harsh *Epistle* X was on Petrarch's mind while writing the letter. In *Seniles*, I .5, Petrarch rebukes Boccaccio for what he describes as his 'all too usual' complaint about his financial constraints and tells him that this time he does not intend to offer him consolation (*Seniles*, I. 5. 67; I, 26).

While criticizing Boccaccio for his lack of virtue, Petrarch continually represents himself in his letters to Boccaccio as an exemplum of constancy. Already the first two prose letters Petrarch sent Boccaccio in 1350 focus on the theme of fortune, with Petrarch portraying his virile confrontations with its vicissitudes. In *Familiares*, XI. 1, written from Rome, Petrarch describes the horse accident he had on the way to the city, which caused a severe injury to his leg. In the course of the letter, Petrarch portrays the steadfastness with which he suffered the physical pain, and tells Boccaccio that the style of the letter stands to show him how he had 'patiently borne all these misfortunes and would bear much more serious ones if they should befall [him]' (*Familiares*, XI. 1.12; II, 86).

Petrarch's ongoing scolding of Boccaccio for his lack of virtue and his self-portrayals as a model of constancy point to the central ethical ideal that Petrarch advances in his Latin writings – that of Stoic virtue, the need to train oneself to accept the blows of fortune with complete equanimity and steadfastness. Petrarch often identifies this ideal of virtue with our 'true self', claiming that as long as we are removed from virtue we are bound to an endless experience of fragmentation and flux.[21] For Petrarch, moreover, this ideal is closely associated with the cultivation of masculinity; as he writes in a letter of consolation to his friend Donato degli Albanzani upon the death of his son in 1368: 'Just as it is human to miss [the departed], so it is womanish to weep . . . the mind has to be separated from the senses, and forced into those innermost recesses where invincible constancy and masculine thoughts dwell' (*Seniles*, X. 4. 18; III, 287).

Boccaccio, for his part, was much less inclined to this Stoic ideal and opted in his writings for a more nuanced and mild ideal of self-cultivation. Although we do not have a letter in which Boccaccio writes directly to Petrarch on the issue, his view of the Petrarchan ideal of virtue comes to the fore most explicitly in a letter he addressed to the Florentine nobleman Mainardo Cavalcanti in 1373. Boccaccio's letter to Cavalcanti is a response to a previous letter addressed to him by the latter, in which he professed his shame for the tears he shed upon reading about Boccaccio's recent ailments. In his reply, Boccaccio assured Cavalcanti of the nobility of his response, explaining that while 'loud lamentations and complaints' are 'characteristic of women' and are 'unbecoming of men', to shed some tears is a sign of a 'humane and compassionate heart' (*Epistles*, XXII. 9).[22] Boccaccio then states that while there are some who are able to overcome 'the limits of nature' and accept the blows of fortune with complete equanimity, we are justified in considering them 'no less stone-like and iron-hearted than strong' (*Epistles*, XXII. 10). In the same way, Boccaccio adds, we should consider those who do 'shed some tears' as 'humane and sensitive' beings ('homines et sensibiles se ostendunt'; *Epistles*, XXII. 10). As a result, in what might be seen as a response to the Petrarchan ideal of virtue and the repetitive reproaches Petrarch addressed to him in their correspondence, Boccaccio explicitly rejects in the letter to Cavalcanti this Petrarchan ideal, and advocates instead an ideal of being that combines self-control with sensitivity and compassion.

The question of the appropriate reaction to the vicissitudes of fortune – and Petrarch's repetitive critique of Boccaccio for his weak responses –

occupies a central role also in the remarkable Book XVII of Petrarch's *Seniles*, which serves as the conclusion to Petrarch's entire correspondence with Boccaccio (as well as to his letter writing as a whole). Consisting of four letters addressed solely to Boccaccio, the book revolves around Petrarch's translation of Boccaccio's Griselda story (*Decameron*, X. 10), and provides us with Petrarch's ultimate statement on his ideal of virtue, the role of literature in its pursuit, and his attitude towards his younger colleague Boccaccio.

The letters in Book XVII were written in response to a previous letter sent to Petrarch by Boccaccio, in which he apparently complained about his financial troubles and assumed for himself the role of the counsellor – advising Petrarch to slow down the pace of his studies in order to care for his deteriorating health. Petrarch divides his response in *Seniles*, XVII. 2 into two sections: first, he reclaims the position of the master and reproaches Boccaccio for complaining of his poverty, telling him that 'the virtuous man cannot justly complain about the lack of temporal goods' (XVII. 2. 4; II, 645). In the second part, he vehemently rejects Boccaccio's advice to give up his studies, stating that he feels as vigorous as ever and that nothing will deter him from his task of reviving ancient letters – a firm position that ostensibly contrasts with Boccaccio's complaints in his letter. To demonstrate his steadfastness, Petrarch tells Boccaccio that amidst his many cares, he recently managed to find the time to translate the closing story of his *Decameron*, that of patient Griselda, a translation he intends to attach in the ensuing letter.

Petrarch opens the following letter with a short preface to his translation, in which he presents a highly critical view of the *Decameron*, referring to it as a 'light' work written in the 'mother tongue' and directed to 'the common herd' ('ad vulgus...scriptus'; *Seniles*, XVII. 3. 1; II, 655). Insisting that he did not read the work, Petrarch admits that he did leaf through it, and that amidst the 'light-hearted fun' he managed to find some 'pious' passages – especially the description of the plague in the beginning and the story of Griselda in the end. This latter story so pleased and engrossed him that he decided to translate it into 'another style' ('stilo...alio'; *Seniles*, XVII. 3. 38; II, 668), i.e. his classicized Latin. Yet, as Petrarch immediately adds, in translating the story he took care to follow Horace's advice not to translate word for word, admitting to have altered the story here and there as he saw fit.

The alterations Petrarch indeed made to Boccaccio's story point primarily to his attempt to turn Griselda into an ultimate embodiment of his ideal of virtue, one who steadfastly accepts the twists and turns of fortune. To achieve this goal, Petrarch eliminates aspects of Boccaccio's original that might undermine the exemplary nature of Griselda's behaviour, such as the descriptions in the original of her struggle to control her emotions during her harsh trials. Thus, when describing Griselda's reactions to her third trial, in which her husband, the Marquis, Gualtieri, told her to leave his castle and go back to the hut in which she grew up, Boccaccio's narrator Dioneo states: 'The lady, hearing this, contained her tears, contrary to the nature of women, *though not without great unease*' ('*non senza grandissima fatica*'; *Decameron*, X. 10. 44; own translation and emphasis). In his translation, Petrarch completely omits this reference to Griselda's inner turmoil and struggle to control her tears, underscoring in this fashion her complete steadfastness.

In addition to such omissions, Petrarch also adds to Boccaccio's story descriptions that highlight Griselda's virtuosity. Near the beginning of his translation, Petrarch inserts a portrayal of Griselda's rustic upbringing, which does not appear in the original. The harsh conditions in which she was raised, according to Petrarch, shaped her 'virile' ('virilis') and 'wise' ('senilis') character (*Seniles*, XVII. 3. 10; II, 658). The translation of Boccaccio's story of Griselda from its vernacular origins to Petrarch's classicized Latin is thus accompanied by the transformation of the protagonist into an unequivocal model of Stoic virtue. Petrarch's translation, in this respect, demonstrates once again the dynamic of both appropriation and correction that characterizes his assimilation of Boccaccio's writings.

In the conclusion to his translation, Petrarch declares that his aim in retelling the story was to provide his (presumably male) readers with a model of virtuous constancy to imitate. The goal of such exemplary narratives, Petrarch insists, is to train readers to accept the blows of fortune with complete equanimity. And given the emphasis in the previous letter, *Seniles*, XVII. 2, on the weakness with which Boccaccio faced his own tribulations, we might assume that Petrarch directed the model first and foremost to its original author and intended first reader, Boccaccio. The translation of the Griselda story thus serves as the final incitement to virtue that Petrarch addresses to Boccaccio in their correspondence.

Nonetheless, this concluding statement is not the end of Book XVII and Petrarch's engagement with Boccaccio's story of Griselda. In the following letter, *Seniles*, XVII. 4, the attitude that dominated Petrarch's previous two letters dramatically shifts. In the beginning of the letter, Petrarch describes the reactions of two learned friends, one Veronese and one Paduan, to his translation. The Paduan, he writes, was so overwhelmed by emotions and tears that he had to stop reading, whereas the Veronese read the story through and claimed that it was simply unreliable. While severely criticizing the Veronese for his reaction, Petrarch praises the Paduan for his 'sensitivity' ('mitissimumque ... animum') and 'humanity' ('homo humanior ... nullus est') (*Seniles*, XVII. 4. 2; II, 669) – a praise which is closely reminiscent of Boccaccio's words to Cavalcanti in *Epistle* XXII, mentioned above, in which Boccaccio commended him for his own tearful reaction. Petrarch then adds a quotation from Juvenal's *Satire* XV, which explicitly praises the value of human softness and tears: 'Nature admits, she gives the human race the softest hearts ('mollissima corda'); she gave us tears, the best part of our feelings' (*Seniles*, XVII. 4. 2; II, 669). As a result, in opposition to the ideal of constancy which dominated *Seniles*, XVII. 2 and his translation of Boccaccio's Griselda story, Petrarch ends Book XVII with a 'Boccaccian' praise of the qualities of human sensitivity and compassion.

Furthermore, following his praise of the Paduan response in the first part of *Seniles*, XVII. 4, Petrarch goes on to describe his own unstable state of mind, portraying the indignation and impatience that he felt when he heard the news of the theft of the previous letters he sent to Boccaccio ('nemo me stomacantior, nullus *impatientior*'; *Seniles*, XVII. 4. 7; II, 670; emphasis added). In contrast to Griselda's remarkable patience, Petrarch emerges here as markedly impatient, unable to withstand a relatively minor incident such as the theft of his letter. Petrarch himself, as we learn, does not live up to his ideal of virtue, and the virile self-representation that characterized his letters to Boccaccio thus ends on this frail note. While Petrarch uses the letters of Book XVII of the *Seniles* to criticize Boccaccio once again for his weakness and to advance his ideal of virtue, his praise in *Seniles*, XVII. 4 of the Paduan emotional response and description of his own frailty thus question his own stated position in the previous two letters, and perhaps point to his ultimate concession to Boccaccio's own position – balancing his ideal of sturdy virtue with the praise of human sensitivity and compassion. At the very end of their lifelong exchange, it is Boccaccio, we might say, who had the final word.

In conclusion, the examination of the relationship between Boccaccio and Petrarch brings to light a dialogue that is marked by conflicts and mutual criticisms. Although both Boccaccio and Petrarch were affected by each other's works and convictions, their reliance upon each other's writings was less prevalent than assumed, as Boccaccio's acquaintance with Petrarch's Latin works was limited, and Petrarch expressed only minor interest in Boccaccio's writings. Furthermore, even in cases in which they evidently drew upon each other's works, this assimilation was characterized by a dynamic of both imitation and transformation. While the encounter with Petrarch motivated Boccaccio's turn to Latin composition, Boccaccio continued to develop in his Latin writings his own ideas and styles in a way that often challenged Petrarch's. He insisted on the absolute value of poetic fictions, combined both classical and modern – especially Dantean – themes and styles, called for the autonomy of the man of letters, and advocated an ideal of being which balances self-control with sensitivity and compassion. In all these respects, Boccaccio developed in his Latin writings his own distinct cultural, artistic, and ethical vision – the impact of which on the future of Renaissance humanism is worthy of much further investigation.

NOTES

1 Giuseppe Billanovich, *Petrarca letterato: lo scrittoio del Petrarca* (Rome: Edizioni di storia e letteratura, 1947), pp. 158–9.

2 Vittore Branca, *Boccaccio medievale*, 4th edn (Milan: Rizzoli, 2010), pp. 357–92; Marco Santagata, *Per moderne carte: la biblioteca volgare di Petrarca* (Bologna: Il Mulino, 1990), pp. 246–70; Giuseppe Velli, 'La poesia volgare del Boccaccio e i *Rerum vulgarium fragmenta*. Primi appunti', *Giornale storico della letteratura italiana*, 169 (1992), 183–99.

3 Vittore Branca, *Giovanni Boccaccio: profilo biografico*, rev. edn (Florence: Sansoni, 1997), pp. 173–4; Guido Martellotti, 'Momenti narrativi del Petrarca', *Studi petrarcheschi*, 4 (1951), 7–33; David Wallace, '*Letters of Old Age*: Love between Men, Griselda, and Farewell to Letters (*Rerum senilium libri*)', in *Petrarch: A Critical Guide to the Complete Works*, ed. by Victoria Kirkham and Armando Maggi (Chicago: University of Chicago Press, 2009), pp. 321–30.

4 Francisco Rico, *Ritratti allo specchio (Boccaccio, Petrarca)* (Padua: Antenore, 2012), pp. 23–5.

5 Rico, *Ritratti*, pp. 37–8.

6 Vittorio Zaccaria, *Boccaccio narratore, storico, moralista, e mitografo* (Florence: Olschki, 2001), pp. 161–5.

7 Rico, *Ritratti*, p. 37.

8 Zaccaria, *Boccaccio narratore*, pp. 165–70. See also Chapter 5 in this volume.

9 Translation from Ernest H. Wilkins, 'Petrarch's Coronation Oration', *PMLA*, 68 (1953), 1241–50 (p. 1246). See also *Africa*, IX. 131–5.

10 Giovanni Boccaccio, *Eclogues*, trans. by Janet Levarie Smarr (New York: Garland, 1987), pp. 253–5.

11 *Invectives*, trans. by David Marsh (Cambridge, MA: Harvard University Press, 2003), p. 121; *Posteritati*, ed. by Gianni Villani (Rome: Salerno, 1990).

12 Translations from the *Epistles* are my own.

13 Rico, *Ritratti*, p. 23.

14 Billanovich, *Petrarca letterato*, pp. 167–72.

15 Marco Santagata, *I frammenti dell'anima: storia e racconto nel 'Canzoniere' di Petrarca* (Bologna: Il Mulino, 1992), pp. 121–33; 243–6.

16 Gabriella Albanese, 'La corrispondenza fra Petrarca e Boccaccio', in *Motivi e forme delle 'Familiari' di Francesco Petrarca*, ed. by Claudia Berra (Milan: Cisalpino, 2003), pp. 39–84 (pp. 58; 60–7).

17 Petrarca, *Lettres de la vieillesse*, ed. by Elvira Nota, 5 vols (Paris: Les Belles Lettres, 2002–13); translation: *Letters of Old Age*, trans. by Aldo S. Bernardo, Saul Levin, and Reta A. Bernardo, 2 vols (Baltimore: Johns Hopkins University Press, 1992).

18 Branca, *Giovanni Boccaccio: profilo biografico*, pp. 151–2; Ugo Dotti, *Petrarca civile* (Rome: Donzelli, 2001), p. 186.

19 Francesco Bruni, *Boccaccio: l'invenzione della letteratura mezzana* (Bologna: Il Mulino, 1990), pp. 418–20.

20 Petrarch, *Le 'Familiari'*, 4 vols (Florence: Sansoni, 1933–42), I–III: ed. by Vittorio Rossi; IV: ed. by Umberto Bosco; translation: Petrarch, *Letters on Familiar Matters*, trans. by Aldo S. Bernardo, 3 vols (Albany: State University of New York, 1975–85).

21 Gur Zak, *Petrarch's Humanism and the Care of the Self* (New York: Cambridge University Press, 2010), pp. 37–8.

22 Timothy Kircher, *The Poet's Wisdom: The Humanists, The Church, and the Formation of Philosophy in the Early Renaissance* (Leiden: Brill, 2006), pp. 293–4.

TOBIAS FOSTER GITTES

Boccaccio and humanism

In 1339, the 26-year-old Boccaccio composed a letter, *Epistle* II, addressed to a 'valorous soldier of Mars' in which he describes himself wandering through Naples in the vicinity of Virgil's tomb when he was suddenly stricken, as though by lightning, with a vision of sensual beauty: a lady 'shaped to his desire'.[1] Often dismissed as a fumbling pastiche, a rhetorical exercise whose structure conforms to the medieval *ars dictaminis* and whose content draws heavily on two of Dante's letters (*Epistles* III and IV), this letter actually illustrates – at a very early point in his career – Boccaccio's great originality, his deft selection and artful integration of pre-existent literary matter (classical and medieval) into an essentially new creation. Whereas Dante, in his fourth epistle, describes himself as smitten by a carnal passion so strong that it eclipses his love for Florence, Boccaccio seems to suggest that in his case an analogous passion has diverted his attention from 'Virgil's Naples' and, more particularly, 'Virgil's tomb' (a metonym, perhaps, for the classical world as a whole). Reduced to an 'unordered mass' by this new passion, Boccaccio appeals to an unnamed sage in Avignon (almost certainly Petrarch) to restore order to his disordered psyche.

If the anchoring of this allegorical tableau to Virgil's Naples and tomb confirms the centrality of the classical world to Boccaccio's poetic self-image, his susceptibility to sensual seduction and dependence on Petrarch – whose erudition and stability he acknowledges to be superior – cast him as an intellectual subaltern, a disciple rather than a master. With the schematic concision of a medieval *Orbis terrarum* (world map), Boccaccio's letter plots the coordinates – as he sees them – of his professional trajectory: one whose intellectual ambitions are fundamentally poetic and humanistic (Virgil's tomb), whose distractions and dissipations are amorous (the spectral seductress), and whose guiding genius is Petrarch (the sage from Avignon).

Though conceived in his youth, and clearly influenced by literary models, this view of his poetic career is expressed time and again in his works and remains more or less consistent throughout his life.[2] It is no wonder that critical evaluations of Boccaccio's contribution to humanism often conform to this same pattern, casting Boccaccio as a gifted but erratic scholar, unlikely to have found the right path – or, having found it, too apt to wander off it – without the 'sweet yoke' of Petrarch's guiding presence.[3] Just as the autobiographical myths with which Boccaccio seeds his vernacular fictions – that, for instance, he was born of a Parisian noblewoman and in love with a Neapolitan princess – may contain some germ of truth, these critical assessments are not entirely without a foundation. However, the same critics who readily discount Boccaccio's family romance as pure poetic invention rarely think to question his far less flattering professional self-evaluation. Self-idealization and self-deprecation are two faces of the same coin, and it is well to treat both with some degree of scepticism. The critic who takes Boccaccio's self-assessments at face value has much in common with the good-willed, but too credulous, confessor of the brilliantly self-perjuring Cepparello of *Decameron*, I. I; when dealing with consummate masters of fiction, deeds are a more reliable standard of truth than words.

Giuseppe Billanovich, the scholar who, together with Vittore Branca, was most instrumental in debunking the long-accepted autobiographical fictions, has had the less auspicious role of casting doubt on Boccaccio's humanistic vocation and contribution to such humanistic activities as the tracking down and transcribing of classical texts.[4] The Boccaccio who emerges from Billanovich's philological laboratory is a sort of Petrarch manqué, whose sense of order is simply the pedantic rigour of scholasticism; whose scattered erudition reflects the desultory curriculum of an 'autodidact'; and whose imaginative brilliance, insufficiently disciplined by art, attests to the free-wheeling whimsy of a 'fantasist'.[5] Dazzled by the sheer mass of erudition marshalled in support of these views, it is easy to forget that Billanovich's re-evaluations of Boccaccio's role in inaugurating humanism are not certified truths, but suppositions, based on the preliminary findings of a philological investigation that, as Billanovich himself readily acknowledges, is still in its infancy. However, the whisper of authority often has the weight of truth, and recent assessments of Boccaccio's contribution to humanism indicate that Billanovich's qualified conjectures have hardened into facts, with the perverse consequence that Boccaccio is at risk of being excluded from the movement he was instrumental in founding.[6] Given this distressing state of affairs, it is not only useful, but necessary to provide a brief review of Boccaccio's 'deeds', his undisputed contribution to such essentially humanistic activities as the study, collection, transcription, translation, and imitation of the classics.

Study, collection, and transcription

In his pioneering study of Boccaccio's Latin works, Attilio Hortis declares that 'Boccaccio was, after Petrarch, the most erudite man of his age.'[7] Indeed, in thumbing one's way through the indices of the Mondadori critical edition of the *Genealogia deorum gentilium* and *Esposizioni sopra la Comedia di Dante Alighieri* one encounters not only such familiar authors as Virgil, Ovid, and Seneca, but numerous more obscure authors like Pomponius Mela, Solinus, and Justin, and, perhaps most unexpectedly, such Greek authors as Homer, Euripides, Plato, and Aristotle. Over forty classical works are directly cited, representing a range of ancient authors, subjects, and genres unprecedented in the scholarly works of Boccaccio's age and still impressive in our own.

Boccaccio's book-collecting activity is marked by a similar sweep and vigour and, Hortis assures us, fully justifies the claim that Boccaccio was, with Petrarch, among the first bibliophiles.[8] The most colourful, and frequently cited, account of Boccaccio's collecting activity is preserved for us by his friend, the acute commentarist Benvenuto da Imola, who tells us of Boccaccio's horror upon visiting Montecassino for the first time and discovering that so many of the monastery's precious manuscripts had been cut apart to fashion five-penny psalters, breviaries, and gospel books for young boys and women.[9] More concrete evidence of Boccaccio's extraordinary success as a collector is supplied by the scattered remains of his personal library, bequeathed to the convent of Santo Spirito in Florence, a collection, according to Antonia Mazza's meticulous reconstruction, which included such classical authors as Homer, Euripides, Plato, Aristotle, Terence, Cicero, Varro, Virgil, Horace, Livy, Ovid, Seneca, Columella, Pomponius Mela, Martial, Statius, Quintilian, Tacitus, Juvenal, Suetonius, Apuleius, Florus, Claudian, Justin, Macrobius, and Boethius.[10]

Our first glimpse of Boccaccio's activity as a copyist is provided in *Epistle* IV (*c.* 1339), where Boccaccio implores the letter's anonymous addressee to lend him a glossed copy of Statius's *Thebaid* so that he can transcribe the commentary. Even if, as some critics contend, this letter is most likely a rhetorical exercise, Boccaccio's decision to focus on this particular act – that of transcribing a commentary to a classical text – is certainly significant, for it reveals the essentially humanistic cast of his interests: his passion for classical texts, confidence in erudite commentary, and eagerness to make copies for his personal use.

Concerning Boccaccio's remarkable productivity as a copyist, there can be no doubt. His early fifteenth-century biographer Giannozzo Manetti, apparently no less impressed by Boccaccio's girth than by his scribal diligence, notes that 'it is really amazing, if one considers the quantity of books he transcribed, that a rather fat and corpulent man such as he was succeeded in copying on his own so many volumes'.[11] In an effusive letter thanking Boccaccio for sending him transcriptions of Varro's *De lingua latina* and Cicero's *Pro Cluentio*, Petrarch observes that this is by no means the first time Boccaccio has rendered him a service of this sort and adds that the texts are dearer to him for having been written by Boccaccio's own hand (*Familiares*, XVIII. 4). Even if such explicit testimonials were lacking, the many transcriptions of classical works in Boccaccio's hand that survive would amply suffice – and this without adding Boccaccio's transcriptions of works by St Thomas, Dante, Petrarch, Cavalcanti, and other medieval authors into the reckoning – to give substance to Manetti's claim: Martial's *Epigrams*; Boethius's *Consolation of Philosophy*; Terence's *Comedies*; Apuleius's *Golden Ass*, *Florida*, *Apologia*, and *On the God of Socrates*; Ovid's *Ibis* and *Amores*; Persius's *Satires*; the pseudo-Virgilian *Culex*, *Priapeia*, and *Dirae*; Calpurnius Siculus's and Nemesianus's eclogues; epitomes of Caesar, Sallust, Ovid, and Statius; excerpts from Cicero, Pliny, Martial, and Ausonius; a biography of Livy; a Senecan florilegium; a Greek alphabet; and the first recorded instance (in the Western world) of a Greek epigram copied directly from a monument.

Neither an occasional nor a casual copyist, Boccaccio was acutely aware of the challenges and responsibilities involved in transcribing an ancient text. In the epilogue of his geographical dictionary, *De montibus, silvis, fontibus, lacubus, fluminibus, stagnis seu paludibus et de diversis nominibus maris* (1355–74), he deplores the fact that copying work, once the province of professional scribes, is now entrusted to any ignoramus capable of forming letters and stringing them together (VII. 119). This is the lament of a conscientious scholar, not a Sunday scribbler.

Translation

In 1283, Lovato Lovati, the Paduan statesman and scholar whom Giuseppe Billanovich declares one of the 'unknown soldiers of the first humanism', used his authority in antiquarian matters to identify a recently discovered tomb as that of Padua's mythical founder Antenor, thereby forging a direct, material link to the classical world.[12] The effectiveness of this strategy for exalting a nation by tracing its foundation to a classical hero was not lost on the young Boccaccio who, in the *Comedia delle ninfe fiorentine* (c. 1339), nimbly replaces the traditional founder of Florence, Attalante (a descendant of Noah's son Japheth), with the Theban refugee Achaemenides – an individual, like Antenor, with a Virgilian pedigree to recommend him. No less remarkable than his decision to exchange a descendant of Noah for a pagan figure is his decision to assign Florence a Greek, in lieu of a Trojan, founder. The Theban Achaemenides is cast as a cultural mediator, a 'translator' of Hellenic language and culture to the Italian peninsula.[13] In writing this radically revised aetiology, Boccaccio not only grants Florence a new founding father, but implicitly makes himself founder of the Greek strand of humanism – a claim made explicit in the *Genealogia* where he declares: 'I too was the first who, at my own expense, called back to Tuscany the writings of Homer and of other Greek authors, whence they had departed many centuries before, never meanwhile to return' (xv. 7. 5; p. 120).

While I may rightly be accused of giving short shrift to Boccaccio's important role in the dissemination of classical culture through his own translations of Livy's third and fourth decades and even, perhaps, of Valerius Maximus's *Dicta factaque memorabilia*, there can be no question that his greatest achievement in the field of translation was not from Latin to vernacular, but from Greek to Latin: the first full translations of Homer's *Iliad* and *Odyssey* (1360–62) produced in the Latin West. Absurd though this claim may appear, for, it is true, Boccaccio's role was limited to the commissioning (with Petrarch) and superintendence of these translations, it seems equally clear that without Boccaccio's continuous pleadings, proddings, and supernatural patience, the actual translator – the notoriously surly and volatile Calabrian scholar Leonzio Pilato – would have neither begun nor finished the project.

Imitation

Critics have long noted Boccaccio's skill in drawing scattered fragments into a whole: a technique often likened to mosaic, intarsia, and the literary cento. Accurate as these descriptions are in conveying the superficial, formal characteristics of Boccaccio's compositive method, they tend to disguise, or even distort, what is certainly the most remarkable trait of his 'art of combination'. While the tessera does not evoke the marble slab, or the scrap of wood, the tree, the literary fragments used by Boccaccio do consistently call to mind the plots, themes, and characters of the works from which they are drawn. Equally misleading is the analogy of the cento, for the cento dismantles and destroys the text that it quarries. The structure of Virgil's *Bucolics*, *Georgics*, or *Aeneid* is no more visible in Proba's Virgilian cento than is that of the Colosseum in the buildings for which it supplied hewn stone and lime. Boccaccio's art does not consist in joining colours, shapes, forms, or scraps of metre, but meanings; and far from destroying these meanings, it conscripts their power to construct new meanings. As Giuseppe Velli points out, the constituent pieces have been placed in a new organizing structure with a new line of signification.[14]

The Latin works

Boccaccio's earliest Latin works (*c.* 1339) are those preserved in the Laurentian notebook (Florence, Biblioteca Medicea Laurenziana, MS 29. 8): four letters (*Epistles* I–IV), an elegy, *Verba puelle sepulte ad transeuntem* (better known as the *Elegia di Costanza*), and an opuscule titled *De mundi creatione* (more commonly referred to as the *Allegoria mitologica*). Once viewed as a precious record of Boccaccio's youthful life, these letters are now considered *dictamina* (rhetorical letter-writing exercises), and their content generally dismissed as a more or less indigestible pot-pourri of medieval (principally Dante) and classical (principally Ovid and Apuleius) sources. That this is an unfair evaluation should be evident even from the brief discussion of *Epistle* II that served as an introduction to this chapter. The elegiac *Verba puelle sepulte ad transeuntem* and the allegorical *De mundi creatione* have fared somewhat better, for the former, once considered a dry scholastic exercise modelled on the Roman epitaph to Claudia Homonoea (first century AD), has been revealed to be a prime example of Boccaccio's combinatory technique and a nursery for many peculiarly Boccaccian motifs, and the latter, once judged a servile imitation of Ovid (*Metamorphoses*, I and II), has been shown to be not only profoundly creative, but quick with probing philosophical concerns destined to recur with great consistency in his later works.[15] Readers who see these early Latin works as pastiches or centos of ancient Roman sources confirm their essentially classical impetus; those who see them as early examples of Boccaccio's art of combination, seeded with shadowy prefaces of motifs that would be more fully developed in later works, confirm their essentially creative quality. Finally, Boccaccio's familiarity with the epitaph of Homonoea, one apparently unknown to his contemporaries, attests to the early date and avant-gardism of his antiquarian interests.[16]

Several years later Boccaccio wrote the first of a series of sixteen eclogues, the *Buccolicum carmen*, that, as Boccaccio himself explains in his letter to Fra Martino da Signa (*Epistle* XXIII), follow neither the model of Theocritus, who did not use allegory, nor that of Petrarch, for whom every interlocutor clothed an allegory, but that of Virgil, who took a middle course, sometimes intending an allegorical sense, and at other times not. In this same letter, Boccaccio dismisses the first two eclogues of this collection, 'Galla' and 'Pampinea' (*c.* 1342), as having little importance, claiming that beneath the 'bark' of their literal level they contain what might almost be viewed as a chronicle of his youthful lusts. However, as Janet Smarr has pointed out, it is precisely in this erotic orientation that their importance lies, for by focusing on the sphere of erotic love Boccaccio effectively distances himself from his contemporaries Dante, Giovanni del Virgilio, and Petrarch – none of whom wrote erotic eclogues – and aligns himself with Virgil, thus introducing the possibility that these first two eclogues 'were intended as part of an ongoing project of classical revival'.[17]

Among Boccaccio's later Latin compendia, his imposing mythological encyclopaedia, the *Genealogia*, has long had an importance analogous to that granted the *Decameron* among the vernacular works. His other Latin compendia include two collections of moralized biographies – one, *De casibus virorum illustrium*, of famous men, and the other, *De mulieribus claris*, of famous women – and a geographical dictionary, *De montibus*. It was the striking eloquence and erudition of these Latin works that moved the prominent scholars and writers of his age – Coluccio Salutati, Franco Sacchetti, and Filippo Villani among others – to pronounce Boccaccio a founder, with Petrarch, of humanistic studies. It was this same cluster of Latin works that inspired the great nineteenth-century cultural historian Jacob Burckhardt to declare that Boccaccio had ushered in a new age, animated by a new spirit, and defined by a new relationship to the world of antiquity.[18]

That Boccaccio's most overtly humanistic works were produced shortly after he struck up a friendship with Petrarch in 1350 has, naturally enough, led critics to trace a causal relation between these two circumstances. While there can be no doubt that Petrarch's influence had a role in shaping Boccaccio's artistic choices, this does not support the further inference that Boccaccio's humanistic interests were first kindled and later sustained by Petrarch's flame, however brightly it may have shone. That this is not the case is proven not only by the overwhelming evidence of humanistic interests found in the early Latin compositions and classical miscellany in Boccaccio's notebooks, but by the ubiquitous, if too often ignored, presence of classical, humanistic features in even his earliest vernacular fictions. Since the classicism of the early Latin works has already been touched on, and that of the later Latin compendia is self-evident, it is the more elusive classicism of the vernacular fictions that will be considered in the following pages.

The vernacular works

It is a remarkable fact that even if none of Boccaccio's notebooks or Latin compendia had survived, an impressive catalogue of his favourite Latin authors could nonetheless have been reconstructed from his vernacular fictions. Cicero, Sallust, Virgil, Livy, Ovid, Valerius Maximus, Seneca, Lucan, Statius, Juvenal, Apuleius, and Boethius are among the classical authors whose texts Boccaccio mines for images, motifs, and verbal patterns. Since limitations of space prevent a complete survey of the classical traits of Boccaccio's vernacular production, a brief discussion of five representative texts will have to suffice: the *Filocolo*, the *Teseida*, the *Comedia delle ninfe fiorentine*, the *Ninfale fiesolano*, and the *Decameron*.

The 'Filocolo' (c. 1336–1338?)

According to the conceit presented in its first pages (I. 26), the *Filocolo* was written to dignify the memory of Florio and Biancifiore's great love, one whose survival had, for lack of a poet to exalt it in verse, long depended on the 'fantastical tales of the ignorant' (I. 26). Some of the more obvious ways in which the *Filocolo* sets about achieving this end are through the imposition of a classical historical framework, introduction of classical epic conventions, and application of a more general impasto of classical features drawn from the works of Sallust, Virgil, Ovid, Valerius Maximus, Lucan, Statius, and Boethius.[19] This new focus on Roman history, myth, and culture produces a strongly ethnographic cast, infuses the whole with a sense of historical realism, and projects an unmistakably humanistic appreciation of the classical world. One nineteenth-century scholar was moved to remark that the *Filocolo* is 'animated by a new spirit' – that of the classical renaissance – and that the youthful Boccaccio 'exults in the ancient world, aims to call all of its memories to mind, and to give a pagan colouring to the medieval romance'.[20] The unprecedented immediacy of Boccaccio's engagement with the classical world is clearest in the description of Filocolo's second tour of classical Naples (V. 5), where we are told that as Filocolo and his troupe walk about admiring the 'ancient marvels' of the city, their spirits, like those of the authors of these sublime works, 'become great'.[21] That an encounter with the ruins of classical antiquity should result in an elevation and dilation of the spirit would be no cause for wonder in a text by Byron or Shelley; that Boccaccio should describe a response of this sort is, however, remarkable and gives some substance to the claim made by his first biographer, Filippo Villani, that it was while contemplating Virgil's tomb that Boccaccio was inspired to dedicate his life to poetry.

Boccaccio famously ends the *Filocolo* with an apostrophe to his book, advising it to leave Virgil's great verses to robust minds, Lucan's and Statius's martial epics to those with a taste for battle, and Ovid's lyric poetry to successful lovers. Nor, he adds, should he presume an equal footing with Dante, but rather follow his measured verses reverently (*Filocolo*, V. 97. 5–6).

Humanism is not only because Petrarca's influence

This apostrophe, modelled, as critics have noted, on Statius's explicit in the *Thebaid*, is remarkable both for Boccaccio's elevation of a modern, Dante, to the ranks of the classical poets – thus inaugurating a career-long campaign to annex the moderns to the ancients – and for the conspicuous absence of Petrarch's name from this roster of the poets whom he most reveres. Had Boccaccio felt any debt to Petrarch at this early point in his career, he would certainly have seized the opportunity to place him in this noble company of poets, ancient and modern. Hence, it is probably safe to conclude that the striking classicism of the *Filocolo* owes nothing to Petrarch's influence.

The 'Teseida delle nozze d'Emilia'

By the time Boccaccio set his hand to writing the *Teseida* (*c.* 1339), his mind had apparently become adequately robust, and his taste for battle sufficiently keen, to enter the lists with Virgil, Statius, and the other poets of epic. The great Petrarch scholar E. H. Wilkins declares that 'the imitation, in some sense, of classic forms began with the *Teseida* of Boccaccio – which, though written in octaves, is definitely modelled upon the *Aeneid* and the *Thebaid*'.[22] In writing the *Teseida*, Boccaccio claims to be producing the first martial epic in the vernacular (XII. 84). If this objective is fulfilled in the fetishistic reproduction of the formal traits of Virgil's epic – not only does the first word of the title echo the title of Virgil's *Aeneid*, but it is divided into the same number of books and, even more remarkably, has the same number of lines – his decision to modulate from epic (*Teseida*) to romance (*le nozze d'Emilia*) has, at least since the nineteenth century, prompted a number of critics to question whether he actually achieved his declared objective.[23] However, to cast the *Teseida* as a renegade, or failed, epic is to overlook the fact – one vividly dramatized in Boccaccio's tale of Alatiel (*Decameron*, II. 7) – that the great political events are often sparked and driven by the erotic passions of individuals. Boccaccio's experimentation with epic form – in particular his organization of the plot according to a geometrically rigorous scheme that culminates in an amphitheatre, a highly charged space that circumscribes and unites the antithetical forces of Mars and Venus – suggests the desire to 'perfect' classical epic by revealing the essential interdependence and congruence of the two spheres, love and war, that classical epic generally casts in oppositional, conflictive terms.

One of the more peculiar traits of the autograph manuscript of the *Teseida* is that it includes a commentary, also composed by Boccaccio (Florence, Biblioteca Medicea Laurenziana, Acquisti e doni, 325). Unlike Rabelais, who memorably likens Accursius's glosses to excrement, Boccaccio clearly reveres the glossators, and views Servius, Donatus, Lactantius Placidus, and their ilk as intellectual crusaders, charged with illuminating the deepest reaches of the texts he most admires; when Boccaccio asks his anonymous friend to lend him a commentary to the *Thebaid*, it is because he despairs of understanding Statius's text 'without a master or a gloss' (*Epistles*, IV. 29). But clarity is not his sole objective, for by giving his text a gloss he has granted it instant authority, effectively placing it on the same shelf as the *Aeneid* or *Thebaid*. Boccaccio's *Teseida* does not merely imitate the classical forms, but goes further by attempting to reproduce the classical text as an object of reception, one already enshrined by an authoritative commentary.

The 'Comedia delle ninfe' and the 'Ninfale fiesolano'

Whereas in the *Filocolo* and the *Teseida* the classical features of the work sit, as it were, on the surface, other works present a subtler sort of classicism, one revealed neither through historical context nor through literary form, but through the adoption of Roman historiographical conventions. For instance, the *Comedia delle ninfe fiorentine* (c. 1341), a pastoral allegory, and the *Ninfale fiesolano* (1340s), an aetiological fable in verse, both present city-founding narratives that reflect the influence of Roman historians (particularly Livy) and poets (particularly Virgil) in the emphasis they place on the role of racial and cultural mixing in the constitution of new empires. Whereas the traditional foundation tales of Fiesole and Florence preserved in the medieval chronicles are characterized by a combination of historical naivety and racial chauvinism, Boccaccio's revised aetiologies reflect a more nuanced, progressive historical vision, one that readily acknowledges not only the presence, but the cultural and genetic contribution of indigenous peoples.[24] The cosmopolitan, ecumenical thrust of Boccaccio's historical vision is most vividly dramatized in the cultural, ethnic, and geographical heterogeneity of the *Decameron*.

The 'Decameron' (c. 1349–1351)

Observing that Boccaccio's habit of inserting 'translated' sections of classical verse into the *Decameron*'s prose had hitherto gone unnoticed, Ugo Foscolo, in his historical discourse of 1825, supplies the striking example of a passage from the *Decameron* Proem (§11) which follows *Heroides*, XIX. 5. 16 so closely that it may, he insists, be viewed as a vernacular translation of Ovid's text.[25] Curiously, Foscolo's important insight appears to have done little to encourage further investigation of the influence of classical authors on the *Decameron*. If better represented in the notes of Branca's critical edition of the *Decameron* (Mondadori, 1976), these authors are still very much on the margin – only cited when Boccaccio's text makes direct reference to classical figures, evokes conventional classical *topoi* (friendship etc.), or echoes classical epigrams or anecdotes. This is unfortunate, for while most contemporary readers will immediately recognize such names as Hippocrates, Quintilian, and Galen, and some, even without help from notes, will understand that the 'Tulio' to whom Boccaccio compares Frate Cipolla in VI. 10. 7 is Cicero, few – unless they happen to be thoroughly conversant in the classical texts dear to Boccaccio – are likely to notice the more subtle evidence of classical influence, the verbal and narrative patterns that have been so skilfully worked into the surrounding text that their contours can hardly be made out.

Whereas Foscolo saw this incorporation of classical verse as a purely aesthetic expedient, one of Boccaccio's strategies for enhancing the harmony of his prose, more recent criticism has focused on the semantic implications of these verbal pastiches or elements of plot drawn from the Latin poets, philosophers, and historians. Like the re-embodied souls of Ovid's *Metamorphoses*, narrative patterns preserve some memory, however faint, of their former lives, and the skilful author can harness these memory traces to animate and add nuance to a text: remembering Jupiter's deadly bolt, Cygnus, now a swan, shuns the sky (*Metamorphoses*, 11). 'Remembering' Ovid's incestuous Myrrha, Boccaccio's tale of Tancredi and Ghismonda (*Dec.*, IV. 1) sets the wholesome glow of natural love against the darkness of perverted passion; 'remembering' Dido's afflictions, Boccaccio's tale of Lisabetta (*Dec.*, IV. 5) invests the pathos of a commoner with a Virgilian sublimity of feeling. As critical studies continue to reveal, formal aesthetic considerations cannot alone account for the consistency and pertinence of these interpolated passages and literary schemes.

More elusive, because more abstract, are the classical values and philosophical perspectives that inform so much of the *Decameron*. Of the classical texts that shape the philosophical agenda of the *Decameron*, it is, arguably, Livy's *Ab urbe condita* that exercises the greatest influence. Though the formal resemblance of the *Decameron*'s prose (in particular its elegant periods) to Livy's prose style and diction has been noted and discussed at some length, the moral-philosophical similarity of Boccaccio's text to the *Ab urbe condita* – as well as its more general debt to the moral-philosophical writings of Aristotle, Cicero, and Seneca – has received far less attention, and is among the more promising areas for future research.

Our brief review of Boccaccio's contributions to humanism complete, it still remains to define with greater precision the essence of Boccaccio's humanism. Even those inclined to accept the thesis that Boccaccio's human-istic interests were sparked by Petrarch – despite the overwhelming evidence of his 'pre-Petrarchan' fascination with the classical world – must neverthe-less concede that the form taken by Boccaccio's classical interest is not in the least bit Petrarchan. Had Boccaccio truly fallen under Petrarch's spell before their meeting in 1350, the first evidence of his conversion to a Petrarchan brand of humanism would have been a wholesale rejection of the vernac-ular. Certainly, there is nothing remarkably Petrarchan about the works – Latin or vernacular – written between 1334 and 1350. Nor, significantly, did Boccaccio foreswear the vernacular after 1350. Not only did he produce two important vernacular works, the *Corbaccio* (*c.* 1365) and the *Espo-sizioni* (1373–74), after 1350, but about five years before his death, he took the time to recopy carefully and correct his *Decameron*. Boccaccio's insis-tence, moreover, on undertaking such anti-elitist projects as the translation and explication of classical texts, as well as his pronounced tendency to embrace genetic (in his aetiologies) and generic (in his poetic forms) bas-tardization – even in works written long after he began his close association with Petrarch – attest to his relative freedom from Petrarch's more fastidious strain of classicism, with its cultural elitism and emphasis on generic and linguistic purity.

What, then, are the distinctive traits of Boccaccio's humanism? What distinguishes it from the humanistic agenda and activities of the Paduan humanists and Petrarch? While admittedly reductive, it is nonetheless useful to consider Italian humanism as admitting of three distinct modes based on the very different ways that the Paduans, Petrarch, and Boccaccio concep-tualize their relation to the classical world. As critics have observed, Lovato Lovati and his circle view themselves as continuing an unbroken classical tradition, walking, as it were, 'in the footsteps of the ancients' ('Veterum vestigia vatum').[26] Petrarch, by contrast, is only too aware of the historical distance and cultural difference that separate the classical from the contem-porary worlds, and his disgust with the latter, exacerbated by his idealiza-tion of the former, fuels his nostalgic bid somehow to leap backwards to the Rome of Cicero and Seneca. In his 'Letter to Posterity' (*Seniles*, XVIII. 1), he explains that his study of antiquity is driven by a desire to transfer himself in spirit to the classical world, an impulse most vividly displayed in a series of letters addressed to classical authors (*Familiares*, XXIV. 3–12). Though by no means uncritical, Petrarch's engagement with the classical dead is nonetheless filled with veneration and an elegiac longing to inhabit their world. Of his own time, Petrarch bitterly observes that 'practically no age has been so poor in genius and virtue' (*Invective contra medicum*, II. 75).[27]

Boccaccio's humanism is of an entirely different cast, for unlike the Paduan humanists, he sees too radical a rupture between the cultural and religious values of the ancient and modern worlds to view himself as continuing an unbroken tradition, and unlike Petrarch, he neither idealizes the past nor deplores the present.[28] Whereas Petrarch would like to send his spirit back in time to mingle with the ancients, Boccaccio, as we have seen, views the monuments – literary and architectural – of the ancients as potentially magnifying the spirits of the moderns (*Filocolo*, v. 5). The first is an essentially retrospective, the second, a prospective, view. In the first, the present seeks to revive the classical past; in the second, the present is nourished and revived by the classical past.

Moreover, whereas Lovato's and Petrarch's humanism restricts its compass to the classical world, Boccaccio's progressive form of humanism is not defined by historical or cultural criteria, but by the more universal standard of human excellence. Just as Ovid cherishes the poets of his day (*Tristia*, IV. x. 41), Boccaccio eagerly acknowledges and celebrates the genius of Dante, Petrarch, and Giotto. Many of Boccaccio's works – ranging from a roster of famous men in the Magliabechian notebook (Florence, Biblioteca Nazionale Centrale, Banco Rari, 50) discretely expanded to include a few moderns, to the declamatory catalogue of *Genealogia*, xv. 6 – attest to his habit of annexing the outstanding men and women of his own age to the catalogues of ancient celebrities.[29] In his letter of 1371 to Iacopo Pizzinga (*Epistle* xix), Boccaccio declares that Dante was the first to restore the long-neglected discipline of poetry, not, importantly, by following the paths of the ancients ('veteres via'), but by taking alternate routes ('diverticula') untrodden by the ancients, and constraining the classical Muses to sing in his own, vernacular, tongue. Petrarch, by contrast, is described as following the path of the ancients ('vetus iter'), one, however, from which he must 'remove the thorn bushes and underbrush which human negligence had permitted to obstruct' (xix. 27). In the *Decameron*, Boccaccio tells us that Giotto's striking naturalism restored to light that art that had for many centuries lain 'buried... beneath the blunders of those who... aimed to bring visual delight to the ignorant rather than intellectual satisfaction to the wise' (vi. 5. 6; p. 457).

Of particular significance in these encomia to contemporary culture-heroes are the images of discontinuity, desuetude, and decay used to describe each artist's relation to the ancients. Dante does not follow the path of the ancients; Petrarch must clear the bramble-choked path of the ancients (thus, we are told, paving the way for his poetic successors); and Giotto finds it necessary to exhume the art of the ancients from a sort of cultural oubliette (the 'path' is apparently buried). The deplorable condition of the ancients' venerable path suggests that a quill, however sharp, would hardly suffice to follow in their footsteps: a pruning hook, pickaxe, or shovel would be a far better choice!

If Lovato and his fellow Paduans inaugurate humanism by walking 'in the footsteps of the ancients', Boccaccio supplies a theoretical basis for the notion of renaissance by recasting this new classicizing tendency in terms of rupture and rebirth. If Petrarch, from his transalpine refuge in the Sorgue valley, hopelessly pines for a restoration of the Augustan golden age, Boccaccio, his feet firmly planted in the public squares, merchant exchanges, and churches, is not only convinced that Florence has already inaugurated a golden age of its own, but that Dante, Giotto, and Petrarch play a central role in this renewal: Dante has done for the Florentine vernacular what Virgil did for Latin, and Homer for Greek (*Trattatello in laude di Dante*; first redaction, 84); Giotto is a new Apelles (*Genealogia*, XIV. 6. 7); and Petrarch is a new Virgil, Cicero, or Seneca (*Vita Petracchi*, 9; *Epistles*, VII. 10) whose coronation heralds a return of the golden age (*Vita*, 16).

Where, then, does Boccaccio himself fit into this elite crew of modern culture-heroes, tireless and intrepid restorers of the classical world? When speaking in his own name, he is most often Petrarch's humble disciple; when, however, he assumes the guise of a mythological double – Phaethon in the *De mundi creatione* and Daedalus, Prometheus, or Aesculapius in the *Genealogia* – he is far bolder, for he clearly sees himself as a vital member of this humanistic vanguard. This is particularly evident in the preface to the *Genealogia*, where Boccaccio explains that the damage of fires and floods, depredations of time's 'adamantine tooth', and the indifference – or even animosity – of the boorish mob have reduced classical literature to a dismembered corpse or an ancient wreck. Like Prometheus fashioning men from mud (I, Preface I, 41), or Aesculapius reassembling the scattered limbs of Hippolytus's body (I, Preface I, 50–1), Boccaccio is faced with the task of salvaging, and reducing to some sort of order, the *disjecta membra* of this blasted body: 'I will reduce them into a single corpus of genealogy, arranged to the best of my ability' (I, Preface I, 40).[30] Whether, like a 'new sailor', he directs his skiff into the trackless sea or, like another 'Daedalus', wings his way through the diaphanous aether (I, Preface I, 40), in pursuing this task, there are no precedents, no trails to follow.

Though, it is true, Boccaccio did not, like Dante, single-handedly restore a voice to the long-silent poetic Muses, or, like Petrarch, clear a passage through the weed-choked path of the ancients, or, like Giotto, resurrect a classical aesthetic of imitation from a dark grave, he may well have done something of no less importance: it may be that he invented the Renaissance.

NOTES

1 Unless marked with page numbers, translations are mine.

2 Boccaccio evaluates his poetic career in *Genealogia deorum gentilium*, XV. 10. He acknowledges Petrarch's guiding role in *Epistole* XVIII and XXIV. Other instances occur in *Buccolicum carmen* XV ('Phylostropos'); *De casibus*, VIII. 1 and IX. 27; and *Genealogia*, Proem, 1.

3 Giuseppe Billanovich, 'Da Dante al Petrarca e dal Petrarca al Boccaccio', in *Il Boccaccio nelle culture e letterature nazionali*, ed. by Francesco Mazzoni (Florence: Olschki, 1978), pp. 583-95 (p. 593). Examples of this tendency include Girolamo Tiraboschi's 'Vita di Giovanni Boccaccio', in *Decameron*, ed. by Giulio Ferrario (Milan: Società tipografica dei classici italiani, 1803), pp. xli–xlii; Giovanni Battista Baldelli Boni, *Vita di Giovanni Boccaccio* (Florence: Carli Ciardetti, 1806), p. 99; Edward Hutton, *Giovanni Boccaccio: A Biographical Study* (London: John Lane, 1910), p. 190; Giuseppe Billanovich, *Restauri boccacceschi* (Rome: Edizioni di storia e letteratura, 1947), pp. 192–6; Natalino Sapegno, *Storia letteraria del Trecento* (Milan: Riccardi Ricciardi, 1963), p. 330; and Vittore Branca, *Profilo biografico* (Milan: Sansoni, 1997), pp. 89–90.

4 See Giuseppe Billanovich, *Petrarca e il primo umanesimo* (Padua: Antenore, 1996), pp. 133–6.

5 See Billanovich, *Restauri*, p. 60 and p. 88; and 'Da Dante al Petrarca', pp. 590–5.

6 Ronald G. Witt, *In the Footsteps of the Ancients: The Origins of Humanism from Lovato to Bruni* (Leiden: Brill, 2003), p. 229.

7 Attilio Hortis, *Studi sulle opere latine del Boccaccio* (Trieste: Julius Dase, 1879), p. 363.

8 Hortis, *Studi*, p. 364.

9 See Benvenuto da Imola's comments to *Paradiso*, XXII. 73 in the Dartmouth Dante Project online edition of Benvenuto's late fourteenth-century *Comentum super Dantis Aldigherij Comoediam* (Florence: G. Barbèra, 1887): http://dante.dartmouth.edu.

10 Antonia Mazza, 'L'inventario della "parva libraria" di Santo Spirito e la biblioteca del Boccaccio', *Italia medioevale e umanistica*, 9 (1966), 1–74; now updated by Teresa De Robertis, 'L'inventario della *parva libreria* di Santo Spirito', in *Boccaccio autore e copista*, ed. by Teresa De Robertis and others (Florence: Mandragora, 2013), pp. 403–9.

11 Giannozzo Manetti, 'Life of Boccaccio', in his *Biographical Writings*, ed. and trans. by Stefano U. Baldassari and Rolf Bagemihl (Cambridge, MA: Harvard University Press, 2003), pp. 86–105 (p. 91).

12 Billanovich, 'Da Dante al Petrarca', p. 584, and Giuseppe Billanovich, *La tradizione del testo di Livio e le origini dell'umanesimo* (Padua: Antenore, 1981), pp. 4–5.

13 Tobias Foster Gittes, *Boccaccio's Naked Muse: Eros, Culture, and the Mythopoeic Imagination* (Toronto: University of Toronto Press, 2008), pp. 99–111.

14 Giuseppe Velli, 'Memoria', in *Lessico critico decameroniano*, ed. by Renzo Bragantini and Pier Massimo Forni (Turin: Bollati Boringhieri, 1995), pp. 222–48 (p. 224).

15 Pier Massimo Forni, 'La realizzazione narrativa in Boccaccio', in *Gli zibaldoni di Boccaccio: memoria, scrittura, riscrittura. Atti del Seminario internazionale di Firenze-Certaldo (26–28 aprile, 1996)*, ed. by Michelangelo Picone and Claude Cazalé Bérard (Florence: Cesati, 1998), pp. 415–23. For the *De mundi*, see Gittes, *Boccaccio's Naked Muse*, pp. 168–74.

16 See Giuseppe Velli, 'Moments of Latin Poetry (*Carmina*)', in *Boccaccio: A Critical Guide to the Complete Works*, ed. by Victoria Kirkham and others (Chicago: University of Chicago Press, 2013), pp. 53–61.

17 Giovanni Boccaccio, *Eclogues*, trans. by Janet Levarie Smarr (New York: Garland, 1987), p. xxxiii.

18 Jacob Burckhardt, *The Civilization of the Renaissance in Italy*, trans. by S. G. C. Middlemore (New York: Modern Library, 2002), p. 141.

19 Antonio Enzo Quaglio, 'Introduzione', in *Filocolo*, in *Tutte le opere*, I (1967), 47–970 (p. 51).

20 Adolfo Bartoli, *I precursori del Boccaccio* (Florence: Sansoni, 1876), p. 61.

21 Quaglio draws attention to the humanistic tenor of this passage in *Filocolo*, p. 914, n. [5] 8.

22 Ernest H. Wilkins, *The Invention of the Sonnet and other Studies in Italian Literature* (Rome: Edizioni di storia e letteratura, 1959), p. 173.

23 David Anderson, *Before the Knight's Tale: Imitation of Classical Epic in Boccaccio's 'Teseida'* (Philadelphia: University of Pennsylvania Press, 1988), pp. 1–37.

24 Gittes, *Boccaccio's Naked Muse*, pp. 77–140.

25 Ugo Foscolo, *Discorso storico sul testo del 'Decamerone'* (London: Pickering, 1825), pp. 66–7.

26 Ernst H. Wilkins, 'On the Nature and Extent of the Italian Renaissance', *Italica*, 27.2 (1950), 67–76; Giuseppe Billanovich, '"Veterum vestigia vatum" nei carmi dei preumanisti padovani', *Italia medioevale e umanistica*, I (1958), 155–243; and Witt, *In the Footsteps*.

27 Francesco Petrarca, *Invectives*, ed. and trans. by David Marsh (Cambridge, MA: Harvard University Press, 2003), p. 59.

28 Pamela D. Stewart, 'Boccaccio', in *The Cambridge History of Italian Literature*, ed. by Peter Brand and Lino Pertile, rev. edn (Cambridge: Cambridge University Press, 1999), pp. 87–8.

29 See Isabelle Heullant-Donat, 'Boccaccio lecteur de Paolino da Venezia', in *Gli zibaldoni*, pp. 37–52 (p. 43).

30 Trans. by Solomon, p. 19.

II

MARILYN MIGIEL

Boccaccio and women

Over the course of his career, Giovanni Boccaccio forged new ways to imagine women as existential subjects, as objects of desire, as participants in literary and philosophical conversations, and as guides for how to live. Still, because Boccaccio's narrators articulate a variety of views about women, including views that can be subtly or downright hateful, and because his female characters are, like most of us humans, a perplexing combination of virtuous behaviour and imperfection, any attempt to derive a unified stance on women from Boccaccio's writing or to mobilize representations of women for a programme of progressive change seems doomed to fail.

In the last fifteen years, there has been ever less desire to make Boccaccio speak with one voice, and ever less desire to upbraid him for the less enlightened views that we find in portions of his work. Regina Psaki has asserted that it is unlikely 'that we will ever be able to locate Boccaccio definitively at any point on a spectrum from philogyny to misogyny'; for Psaki, Boccaccio is not 'simply pro- or anti-feminist', but rather, he places 'the rhetorical moves of each stance in dynamic opposition with the other, to destabilize and problematize familiar claims'. Janet Smarr, while demonstrating the advances that Boccaccio made in portraying authoritative females, reiterates Psaki's caveat and cautions against seeing Boccaccio as 'feminist'. Jason Houston has stated categorically that 'trying to tie Boccaccio down to one authorial stance on gender is missing the point'.[1] In my work on the *Decameron*, I have argued against using categories like 'feminist' and 'misogynist', and have sought to understand how writers and readers together create and reinforce gender ideologies.[2] In particular, I have urged readers to recognize that literature, with its oblique portrayal of the world, is not always an obedient servant when we ask it to support our ideological and political agendas.[3]

Given the inadequacy of rigidly ideological categories, readers continue to investigate other ways to speak of Boccaccio's engagement with the figure of woman. As Thomas Stillinger and Regina Psaki observe, these attempts 'are bound to take strikingly different directions according to where, in the text, they start'.[4] The same obtains for Boccaccio's corpus as a whole. Taking this into consideration, I have decided to focus on several of Boccaccio's so-called 'minor' works that call attention to women's perceived virtues and defects. Although these works have often been mined for what they could tell us about women, I would propose instead that we maintain focus on their narrators and on the sources of information constructed as 'authoritative'. How should we judge the narrative of a woman such as Fiammetta in the *Elegia di madonna Fiammetta* when she details her own victimization while simultaneously skirting the questions of her own responsibility? How should we respond to the narrator of the *Corbaccio* when he recounts the anguish that results from his fixation on a widow he seeks out, determined to love, and then denigrates when she does not live up to his expectations? How much 'authority' do we accord the Spirit-Guide (also from the *Corbaccio*) who states he is the widow's husband come from Purgatory to aid the narrator, when there are a variety of indications that this Spirit-Guide is overly attached to worldly things and is moved by a spirit of revenge? What sort of investments in telling stories about women do we find in Boccaccio's *De casibus virorum illustrium*? Finally, to what extent do we consider authoritative the narrator of *De mulieribus claris*?

By adopting this approach, we set aside questions about 'positive' or 'negative' representations of women – a paradigm that threatens a fruitless calculation of misogyny quotients – and we focus instead on questions of what we find edifying, moving, credible, and persuasive. The narrators and authority figures in these works – even in the scholarly *De mulieribus* – never prove as reliable and consistent as we might like.

I would begin by calling our attention to several passages from *De casibus* that point to the complex struggle between men and women and expertly capture the difficulties we have in disentangling voices and in gauging tone in Boccaccio's writing. In *De casibus*, various historical figures appear in a dream-vision procession before the narrator, who then chooses an exemplary figure whose life he narrates, with a particular focus on unfortunate circumstances. Following the recounting of events, and especially in the earlier portion of the work, the narrator typically launches an invective against whomever or whatever he views as the cause: for example, disobedience, credulity, gluttony, fraudulence, riches, excessive desires, women, the stupid public, the prideful, spineless lawmakers, and so on.

Here is the opening of a chapter entitled 'Against Women', which follows the story of Samson's downfall, thanks to Fortune, his excessive confidence in himself, and a harlot named Delilah:

Sweet and deadly is the malady that is woman, which very few people realize before they have had the experience of it. Women, as if disregarding God's judgment, not only attempt to regain the status in society from which they were deservedly removed but they seek to dominate, and with their innate malice they almost all conspire against men. They realize that their objectives are much aided by the bright rosy colour of their faces, their large, deep and blue eyes, their blond and curly hair, their red mouths, their straight noses, their white necks which rise straightway from their rounded shoulders, their breast rising with two full and solid swellings, their long straight arms, their delicate hands, their elongated fingers, their graceful bodies, and their small feet. They nevertheless strive to use every means to obtain what they want by supplementing what nature has given them with other means that they have acquired through their industriousness. First of all they consult among themselves, and whatever appears excessive through a defect of nature they eliminate by means of art; and whatever is missing they add with remarkable shrewdness. They are able to get a young virgin who is too skinny to put on weight by eating sweet cakes and morsels, and by means of diets and vinegar they are able to turn the overweight girl into a reed; they can straighten out the one who is curved over by bending her in the other direction; they know how to lower shoulders that are too high and to lift up the ones that are too low; they can lengthen necks, make the short girl taller, and they even know how to get the lame girl to walk straight. And what should I say about swelling in the hands, freckles on the face, spots on the eyes, and defects in other parts of the body? Without any need to call upon Hippocrates, they are able to remedy these expertly.[5]　　　　　　　　　　　(*De casibus*, II. 18. 1–5)

The passage is striking for the multiple directions in which it tugs. Women are aesthetically pleasing, marked in body and mind by gross defects of nature, expertly accomplished, and morally disagreeable. The passage also pulls back the curtain on the male narrator: he begins by delivering commonplaces about woman that would have been considered acceptable in the fourteenth century and then goes just enough overboard to make us wonder whether indeed we should accept what he is saying.

It is this rhetorical and psychological complexity, I would argue, that is Boccaccio's ultimate objective in writing such a passage. He is a master at setting up narrators who offer categorical judgements, and then showing how they can trip themselves up. Even as the narrator denounces women as a 'deadly . . . malady' and as innately malicious conspirators against men, he provides a detailed catalogue of women's well-proportioned and dazzlingly coloured bodily features. Almost certainly, this constitutes evidence of why the 'malady' of woman is also 'sweet'. But how should we read this voice? Does the narrator document women's beauty because women are indeed beautiful or because he is under their sway? When he speaks of women's 'industriousness', their use of 'art', and their 'shrewdness', should we hear praise ('fine qualities!') or criticism ('fine qualities used to undermine men!')? Most curious is the narrator's account of women's achievements. When he suggests that high- and low-calorie diets can be used to alter girls' weight, his assertions seem within the realm of the plausible. As he continues, the women's accomplishments involve ever greater expertise (for example, the physical therapy techniques involved in bending a curved girl in the other direction, or lengthening necks), although certain achievements such as making a short girl taller might simply involve clever additions to a wardrobe. The quite outlandish claim that women 'even know how to get the lame girl to walk straight' strikes me as revealing more about the male narrator than it does about the women of whom he speaks.

As Boccaccio surely knew, the assertion that 'they even know how to get the lame girl to walk straight' brings to mind the opening of *Purgatorio* XIX. When a stuttering, ugly, and deformed woman, crooked on her feet, appears to the pilgrim Dante in a dream, his gaze warms and straightens her limbs, colours her sallow complexion, and transforms her into a beautiful, alluring Siren. Dante is liberated from her only after a 'holy woman' appears to rip open the Siren's clothes, bringing forth a loathsome stench. When the narrator of *De casibus* claims that women 'even know how to get the lame girl to walk straight', he is putting those women in the place of Dante-pilgrim whose gaze turns a loathsome object into a beautiful object of desire. What would not have been lost on Boccaccio is how the narrator, through the colouring of rhetoric, is involved in his own personal transformation of women, whether from naturally beautiful to defective, or naturally defective to alluring.

De casibus would not be a signature Boccaccian work if it did not provide leverage against its narrator. Consider a passage that appears not many chapters earlier, where the narrator comments on Theseus's downfall, attributed to his excessive credulity:

> Do you believe that there is but one point of view behind all statements? Certainly nothing is more foolish than to think so. The man who judges carefully ignores no one's ideas, but rather weighs each according to its merits, then considers the matter carefully so that he does not make a mistake by coming to too hasty a conclusion concerning things with which he is not familiar. In the watchtower of his mind, he uses balanced judgement as he observes who is speaking and to what end; he wants to know who speaks against whom, where things took place, when they happened, whether the speaker is angry or calm, enemy or friend, infamous or honourable.[6]
>
> (*De casibus*, I, II, 3–4)

Narratva Non credibile → donven?

The same method of evaluation could be applied to the narrator of the *De casibus*. Before we accept what he says about women, we should consider his subject-position and motives as well as how credible his report about women is.

Passages like these reveal how Boccaccio can sabotage his narrators. He crafts the text so that it includes contradictory information; if we accept what his narrators say in one place, we have to ignore what they say elsewhere. He expects his readers to be aware of how he handles subtexts, which frequently cast doubt on the narrators' assertions and enlighten us as to the central issues. And he is brilliant at manipulating shifting tonalities of voice, so that we can find ourselves hard put to disentangle praise from blame, the logical from the implausible, and what is fair and balanced from what is fanatical.

The difficulty of disentangling praise from blame is a primary challenge in the *Elegia di madonna Fiammetta*. The *Elegia* is a first-person narrative of a married Neapolitan woman who has had sexual relations with Panfilo, a Florentine whose return to his native city has caused her suffering and brought her to the brink of suicide, especially when she learns she has been replaced in his affections. There has been no easy consensus on how we should respond to Fiammetta's seemingly interminable lament, her classicizing serpentine prose, and her courageous persistence in an adulterous love that appears to have no future. In response to readers' ideological values, Fiammetta has garnered both supporters and fierce detractors. The *Elegia* disrupts easy judgements, however, and the most insightful readings of it remain attuned to the complexity of the ethical and psychological issues that it poses. Fiammetta is both seduced and seductress, both betrayed and betrayer, both self-aware and self-deceived, capable of delivering a useful lesson to us (though the lesson may not be the one she intends to deliver). Not everyone will have Fiammetta's specific experience or her specific reactions to it, but given that she is both *wronged* and *wrongdoer*, we face with her the problems we have when we must evaluate human beings who have suffered at the hands of others but who have themselves done foolish things: will we emphasize virtues or defects, innocence or culpability?

Janet Smarr, for example, discusses the limited frames of reference that Fiammetta uses to represent her experience (fortune, loss of worldly joy), arguing that Boccaccio would want readers to think also of 'the more serious fall from grace and of the human responsibility involved in that transgression'.[7] Smarr also shows how the classical allusions in the *Elegia* 'evok[e] associations of which Fiammetta seems naively or even willfully ignorant'; they prove to be 'a useful means for working into the text moral warnings beyond those uttered openly to Fiammetta or her nurse' (pp. 143–5). Noting that for Boccaccio, 'the proper use of rhetoric is to teach and move toward moral truth, not self-delusion', Smarr sees Fiammetta's rhetoric as operating otherwise: 'her careless readings lead her astray, and her art of persuasion is put to use to justify her own behavior to herself' (p. 146).

Whereas a reader like Smarr tends to privilege paradigms that Boccaccio himself would have used, Michael Calabrese encourages us to read the *Elegia* with dual paradigms in mind – Boccaccio's and those of our own culture – but cautions us against the grave pitfalls that await us if we anachronistically project terms like 'feminist' on to fictional women who are constructs of the medieval male imagination.[8] Paying particular attention to Fiammetta's lies (both about her sexual affair and about whether or not she consented to have sex with Panfilo), Calabrese makes the excellent argument that 'to maintain that Fiammetta is an "ardent and outspoken feminist" is to be forced to explain and apologize for such lies, or to find an absolving victimological explanation for them' (p. 23). Calabrese's detailed and incisive reading of the *Elegia* in light of Ovidian amatory literature (specifically the *Heroides* and the twelfth-century pseudo-Ovidian *Pamphilus de amore*) raises questions regarding female desire and sexual consent. Arguing that 'Boccaccio has imagined a woman who imagines date rape, who tries to free herself of responsibility by depicting herself as the victim of male deceit and male force', Calabrese goes on to show how the male-authored *Elegia* and its analogues 'depict the impossibility of female expression of desire . . . a woman cannot say yes to sex, lest she compromise her honor, and she cannot say no and be believed. So the only answer is "no" and its only meaning is "yes"' (pp. 34, 37).

In addition, it is important to consider, as Suzanne Hagedorn has, how Fiammetta's lament places the reader in a double bind. Hagedorn acknowledges the conflict between reason and desire in the *Elegia*, and allows for the moralizing readings advanced by Janet Smarr and Robert Hollander; but she argues for another possibility. In her view, 'Boccaccio forces his readers to experience a struggle between their own reason and desires as they interpret his text'; he thus brings us readers to 'better appreciate the divergence between theoretical moral frameworks and how human beings manage to apply them' and 'to understand how difficult it can be to make the "right" choices'.[9]

The *Corbaccio* provides, on the surface, the most explicitly misogynist of Boccaccio's works. In the main portion of the text, a male narrator dreams that he finds himself in a delightful landscape that soon turns infernal. Approached by a Spirit-Guide, the narrator recounts his suffering in love at the hands of his beloved. The Spirit-Guide, who happens to be the beloved's dead husband, responds with a sustained misogynist attack. Both narrator and Spirit-Guide progress through a purgatorial landscape, the Spirit-Guide disappears, and the narrator wakes up to find he is liberated from his suffering in love. He declares his intention to take revenge on the woman by writing about her, and offers his book as a guide to young men.

As in the *Elegia*, our reading of the *Corbaccio* depends on the level of destabilization we hear within the narrating voice. Once read as autobiographical and misogynist, the *Corbaccio* tends now to be read as an ironic fiction, an immense joke at the expense of those who would advance extreme misogynist views. Scholars such as Gian Piero Barricelli, Robert Hollander, Regina Psaki, and Guyda Armstrong have explored the fissures in the narratorial voices of male narrator and Spirit-Guide.[10]

In reading the scholarly commentaries on the *Corbaccio*, one might be tempted to conclude that it would be almost impossible to question the narratorial voices if one were not intimately familiar with Dantean subtexts and with a range of material from the classical and medieval misogynistic tradition. Still, while Boccaccio mobilizes other literary voices in a masterfully brilliant way, and while he would expect his learned readers to recognize the complex interplay of voices, he also takes care to create characters whose trustworthiness we are encouraged to question even if we are not already steeped in the literary tradition.

Consider, for example, the *Corbaccio*'s narrator when he describes what he heard about the widow from a neighbour and relative of the Spirit-Guide:

> Moved by who knows what sort of affection for her, he began to say amazing things, affirming that in matters of generosity there had never been a woman like her; and going beyond what concerns the innate ability of women, he did his best to show that she was an Alexander by recounting some of her generous deeds, which, so as not to take up time with storytelling, I won't bother to recount. Then, he said that she was endowed with more natural good sense than any other woman he had ever happened to meet; and furthermore, that she was also most eloquent, perhaps no less so than any expert and flowery orator had ever been; and furthermore (which pleased me very much, since I put complete faith in those words), he said that she was charming and gracious and possessed of all those manners which are commendable and praiseworthy in a great gentlewoman. As this person narrated these things, I confess that I said silently to myself, 'O happy is he to whom Fortune is kind enough to grant the love of such a lady!' (*Corbaccio*, 85–7; p. 16, translation modified)

The passage invites us to ask the questions that the narrator himself fails to ask. What moves the speaker to praise the widow? Why decline to report his words in direct discourse? Why place full faith in a report that sounds so hyperbolic?

Consider also the Spirit-Guide, as he speaks to women's malice and their use of ornamentation to dominate men:

> After they have reflected on their low and base condition, they put all their efforts into aggrandizing themselves with their abundant malice (which never makes amends for their fault, but always increases it). And first they set traps for men's liberty by painting themselves with a thousand ointments and colors, adding to that which nature has lent them in beauty or looks; and most of them make their hair, produced black from their pates, like spun gold.
>
> (*Corbaccio*, 136–7)

> Thinking they have climbed to a high station, though they know they were born to be servants, they at once take hope and whet their appetite for mastery; and while pretending to be meek, humble, and obedient, they beg from their wretched husbands the crowns, girdles, cloths of gold, ermines, the wealth of clothes, and the various other ornaments in which they are seen resplendent every day; the husband does not perceive that all these weapons are to combat his mastery and vanquish it. The women, no longer servants but suddenly equals, seeing their persons and rooms adorned like those of queens and their wretched husbands ensnared, contrive with all their might to seize control.
>
> (*Corbaccio*, 139–40; p. 25)

Ensuring that anything even vaguely positive is hemmed in by negative pronouncements, the Spirit-Guide emphasizes the pretence in women's appearance and behaviour; he indicates that women recognize their inferiority as a fact. At the same time, questions about his reliability bubble up, and not only on account of the strident tone and the exaggerations in number. How does the Spirit-Guide know what the women are thinking? Why does he slide from speaking about women and men to speaking about wives and husbands? Even if one thinks that women are not the equals of men, why should he designate wives as 'servants' and why should 'mastery' be accorded to husbands? He repeatedly emphasizes what women see and are aware of; if the men are indeed superior, why do they not perceive what is happening?

The Spirit-Guide's accusations will remind us of what the narrator of *De casibus* says about women, in other words, that seeking to dominate even though the natural order requires that they remain subjects, women will use every conceivable adornment to ensure their triumph. But subtle differences point to what Boccaccio seeks to achieve as he recycles misogynistic passages like these. As the narrator of *De casibus* rails against women, he reveals the subtle charms exercised by their physical presence. Indeed, his statements appear designed to draw attention to female beauty, to suggest (despite some protestations) that women's attractiveness might be authentic, and also to suggest (again, despite protestations) that men might themselves bear

Alghiel isn't the femme fatale she doesn't do anything

responsibility for the effects that women have on them. On the other hand, the passage in the *Corbaccio*, which draws attention to women's wickedness, suggests (despite the authoritative voice assumed by the Spirit-Guide) that there are gaps and slippages that undermine the claim to know. In both cases, Boccaccio invites us to see that disentangling truth from falsehood is easier said than done, especially when the other sex is involved, and in both cases, by portraying self-deception, he invites us to resist it.

In addition, if we read the *Corbaccio* together with the *Elegia*, we are able to see how the narrators' strategies for dealing with love woes are gendered. Whereas the strategies used by the female narrator reinforce her attachment to her love object, the strategies used by the male narrator prove successful in detaching him from his love object. Boccaccio explores how 'male reason' and 'male authority' can use a combination of praiseworthy and blameworthy strategies to free the male lover from love woes.

As the *Corbaccio* opens, the narrator is essentially a male Fiammetta.[11] Thanks to the gender transposition, however, he can overcome stasis and immobility. Male reason (in the form of the narrator's own inner thought that finds ways to create physical and psychological distance from the beloved) and male authority (in the form of the beloved's dead husband who uses the commonplaces of misogynistic discourse to portray the woman as abject) provide the means by which the narrator can 'move on'. That stasis and immobility should be characterized as female and that distancing movement should be characterized as male will certainly remind us of the characterization of men and women in love in the Proem to the *Decameron*. There women remain trapped within their rooms; men have ways to move beyond.

By comparing narratorial voices from various works (for example, Fiammetta with the narrator of the *Corbaccio*, and Fiammetta's nurse with the Spirit-Guide), we begin to see how Boccaccio understood gender difference to affect a narrator's authority and effectiveness. In his presentation of figures who articulate 'reasoned' arguments against persisting in unhappy love, Boccaccio asks us to reflect on the relative weight that these voices have, and why they succeed, or not, in directing their charges' attention away from love. Fiammetta's nurse presents compelling arguments about why Fiammetta should turn away from Panfilo. The nurse's arguments, as Eugenio Giusti has noted, represent an 'ideological shift' in the overall arc of Boccaccio's work, away from the logic of courtly love; they also, as Prudence Allen has argued, demonstrate that Boccaccio recognizes that there can be women who do present reasoned arguments about how to live life virtuously.[12] Yet when Fiammetta chooses not to follow the nurse's advice, the nurse cedes to her mistress's authority and does what she can to help

Fiammetta continue her pursuit of Panfilo. Thus the nurse may be wiser than Fiammetta, but she is ultimately defined by her subordinate position. On the other hand, the Spirit-Guide, whose investment in a vengeful rhetoric ought to be questioned, appears to command authority: he is a quasi-Virgilian figure, he speaks from experience, and he avails himself of anti-woman arguments that have wide currency. He calls on the narrator to place unwavering faith in him and easily deflects any questions that might cast doubt on his ability to speak authoritatively. Both the nurse and the Spirit-Guide serve to remind us that the success of arguments may depend on gender, class, cultural capital, claims to first-hand knowledge, and other social markers of authority.

If the problematic first-person narrators of the *Elegia* and the *Corbaccio* make it impossible to advertise the unwavering allegiance to women that many readers believe they should find in Boccaccio's works, then hope seems to lie with *De mulieribus claris*, a text that turns away from the framing devices and the fictional modes that Boccaccio could use in order to distance himself from his narrators. Dedicated to Andrea Acciaiuoli, Countess of Altavilla, and comprising 106 chronologically arranged portraits of women, both imaginary and historical, mainly from the Graeco-Roman era, *De mulieribus* is narrated by a male who is often assumed to express the views of Boccaccio himself. The assumption is buttressed by the fact that *De mulieribus* was composed in the latter part of Boccaccio's life, when he was largely dedicating himself to a variety of scholarly works (biographical, encyclopaedic, and so on) and seeking to emphasize his humanist credentials.

Many readers have expressed disappointment and befuddlement that *De mulieribus* does not speak to women's virtues as forcefully as they would like, or even as eloquently as the author would have appeared to have promised in the introductory dedication. Praise of women's accomplishments in the family sphere, in the public arena, and in the arts is often accompanied by accounts of their failings. Women are considered worthy when they are most manly and when they deny their sexuality. Their eloquence puts them in a 'double bind' because it both raises them above their sex and constitutes a threat to men; in several instances, their eloquence is best expressed when they are deprived of the ability to speak.[13]

Furthermore, Boccaccio seems determined to undermine his project by frustrating any women readers. As Pamela Benson points out, although the author offers the book as an aid to women, he writes in Latin, a language that very few women of the time could read. Moreover, the examples of famous women include comparisons between them and ordinary women, 'to the disadvantage of the ordinary woman', and the living woman honoured in the closing portrait (Giovanna, Queen of Sicily and Jerusalem) is someone his female readers could hardly hope to emulate.[14] Perhaps most puzzling is the dedication to Andrea Acciaiuoli, which is underhandedly discourteous. She appears to be a 'second-best' dedicatee; and as a woman who had had multiple husbands, she would, upon reading *De mulieribus*, be confronted with unforgiving criticism of widows who remarried.

Our readings have been hampered by our hesitancy to see ironic distance between Giovanni Boccaccio and the narrator of this work. Constance Jordan's view is representative. Although deeply puzzled by the 'obvious ambivalence in Boccaccio's treatment of his topic', she states that: 'it is unlikely that anyone as skilled in rhetorical procedures as the writer of the *Decameron* could remain unaware that he represents his subject with irony, yet this may have been the case with *De mulieribus*.'[15] Here I would recall Hollander's argument that the 'one rule . . . we can apply with confidence to *all* of Boccaccio's fiction is the following: Boccaccio never speaks openly *in propria persona*'.[16] Indeed, I would favour taking his argument further. I believe that even in works like *De mulieribus*, which purports to be scholarly rather than fictional, we should question whether the narrator is the same as the historical author Boccaccio.

If we stop looking simply for markers of praise and blame, we start hearing another story: *a story about how stories are told*. *De mulieribus* brings us to reflect on what sort of information we have available to us, how we determine what is reliable information, how we select what to emphasize, how we deal with contradictory information, how we may wilfully ignore information that doesn't suit us, how we use data in order to draw our conclusions (including contradictory conclusions from the very same data!), and what strategies we may use to justify our ideological views.

The narratorial voice of *De mulieribus*, like the narratorial voices of many a Boccaccian work, offers a variety of views that do not always mesh easily. Stephen Kolsky writes of a 'shifting movement' between two genres of historical narrative and moralizing commentary, 'each competing for control over the other'.[17] He also identifies a tension between the narrator's meticulous evaluation of sources (especially when the sources provide conflicting or inconclusive evidence), and the narrator's assertions that are 'not supported by any evidence' (pp. 134–5). In the end, however, I sense that Kolsky, like many a reader of *De mulieribus*, is unsettled by a narrator who is inexplicably careless as well as exceedingly careful, for Kolsky declines to draw too much attention to the narrator's peccadilloes, preferring to focus primarily on the commitment to scholarly ideals or the commitment to a coherent moralizing vision.

Evidently, we like not to think that authoritative secular scholarship (particularly when it regards subjects of supreme interest) can be interwoven with wilful assertions not based on the material evidence, can be the ground for moralizing statements, and can even be subject to lapses in logic. Boccaccio has his narrator repeatedly foreground his judicious handling of sources, but he also has his narrator draw attention to the sometimes wilful process that he uses to arrive at conclusions.

This wilfulness becomes especially evident when the narrator moves from dispassionate narration of conflicting views, to mild approbation of a single view, to wholesale embrace of that single view. Early on, in the portrait of Ceres, the narrator stages a dilemma that is at the heart of our experience in reading all of Boccaccio's works, and especially when they deal with women: what to praise and what to blame? Writing about Ceres' contribution to agriculture, he foregrounds his own uncertainty: 'I hardly know whether to praise or condemn their ingenuity' (v. 6; p. 15). First, he offers reason not to condemn ('Who will condemn the fact that wild, nomadic men were led out of the woods and into cities?'), then he considers the downside ('On the other hand, who will praise the fact that . . . ?') (v. 6–8; pp. 15–16). Then he notes that these agricultural practices 'opened the doors to vices still latent', thus leading to private property, division of labour, poverty, servitude, wars, envy, laziness, leisure, sexual desire, starvation, disease, and death (v. 9; p. 16). And he concludes: 'After considering these and many other issues, I am tempted to believe – indeed I do believe – that those golden centuries, even if they were rude and uncivilized, are greatly to be preferred to our own iron age, refined though it is' (v. 13; pp. 16–17).

In this conclusion, both ponderous and precipitous, the narrator documents his detailed study of the many aspects of the question, and shows the amazing rapidity with which his initial preference becomes a conviction: 'I am tempted to believe – indeed I do believe.' Boccaccio would have us ask: if we are tempted to believe something, how long before we find ourselves forgetting our initial uncertainty, casting aside all doubts in favour of a position now 'greatly . . . preferred', and perhaps even selecting the arguments that will support the belief we have espoused?

The narrator even suggests that wilfully subjective responses, based solely on personal preference, are completely legitimate. In the portrait of Artemisia, Queen of Caria, he again emphasizes how facts can be marshalled in favour of conclusions we want: 'Some sources . . . report . . . To prove their point, they adduce the fact that . . . But I agree with those who believe that . . . Whoever my readers are, let them believe what they prefer' (LVII. 19; p. 119).

We need to remember that when *De mulieribus* was distributed in manuscript, it appears, as Rhiannon Daniels has shown, 'to have commanded the most consistently cultured and wealthy owners, supporting the impression given by the critical responses that this work enjoyed a higher status than many of the vernacular works'. Also of import is Daniels's insight into how our 'individual relationship with humanism' affects our response to Boccaccio's works.[18] Because the narrator of *De mulieribus* has long been credited with a kind of scholarliness consistent with our own proclaimed ideals of integrity in data-gathering and argumentation, it is not easy to perceive the fissures in his logic, and it is even less easy to hear the ironic undertones. We need to understand, however, that even the mature and scholarly Boccaccio would not have wanted us to accept everything an author says, even when he himself is that author.

Throughout his writings, especially when questions about women arise, Boccaccio reminds us: the truth is out there, but there is no easy way to arrive at it. The signposts to truth are generally not marked. Statements made by human beings require that we carefully weigh the inevitable distortions, be they trivial or significant, unwitting or intentional, innocent or malicious. So even when Boccaccio's narrators offer themselves as reliable guides, they are pointing towards a sign that says: 'Good luck – because you are on your own.'

NOTES

1 F. Regina Psaki, 'Boccaccio and Female Sexuality: Gendered and Eroticized Landscapes', in *The Flight of Ulysses: Studies in Memory of Emmanuel Hatzantonis*, ed. by Augustus A. Mastri (Chapel Hill: Annali d'Italianistica, 1997), pp. 125–34 (p. 127); F. Regina Psaki, '"Women Make All Things Lose Their Power": Women's Knowledge, Men's Fear in the *Decameron* and the *Corbaccio*', *Heliotropia*, 1.1 (2003): www.heliotropia.org; Janet Levarie Smarr, 'Speaking Women: Three Decades of Authoritative Females', in *Boccaccio and Feminist Criticism*, ed. by Thomas C. Stillinger and F. Regina Psaki (Chapel Hill: Annali d'Italianistica, 2006), pp. 29–38; Jason Houston, 'Giovanni Boccaccio', in *Women and Gender in Medieval Europe: An Encyclopedia*, ed. by Margaret Schaus (New York: Routledge, 2006), pp. 77–8 (p. 78).

2 Marilyn Migiel, *A Rhetoric of the 'Decameron'* (Toronto: University of Toronto Press, 2003); Migiel, 'Figurative Language and Sex Wars in the *Decameron*', *Heliotropia*, 2.2 (2004): www.heliotropia.org; Migiel, 'The Untidy Business of Gender Studies: Or, Why It's Almost Useless to Ask if the *Decameron* is Feminist', in *Boccaccio and Feminist Criticism*, pp. 217–33; Migiel, 'New Lessons in Criticism and Blame from the *Decameron*', *Heliotropia*, 7.1–2 (2010), 5–30: www.heliotropia.org.

3 Migiel, 'The Untidy Business of Gender Studies'.

4 Thomas C. Stillinger and F. Regina Psaki, 'Introduction', in *Boccaccio and Feminist Criticism*, pp. 1–12 (p. 4).
5 My translation; compare translation by Brewer Hall, pp. 41–2.
6 My translation; compare translation by Brewer Hall, p. 24.
7 Janet Levarie Smarr, *Boccaccio and Fiammetta: The Narrator as Lover* (Urbana: University of Illinois Press, 1986), p. 134.
8 Michael Calabrese, 'Feminism and the Packaging of Boccaccio's Fiammetta', *Italica*, 74 (1997), 20–42.
9 Suzanne C. Hagedorn, *Abandoned Women: Rewriting the Classics in Dante, Boccaccio and Chaucer* (Ann Arbor: University of Michigan Press, 2004), p. 128.
10 Gian Piero Barricelli, 'Satire of Satire: Boccaccio's *Corbaccio*', *Italian Quarterly*, 18 (1975), 95–111; Robert Hollander, *Boccaccio's Last Fiction: 'Il Corbaccio'* (Philadelphia: University of Pennsylvania Press, 1988); F. Regina Psaki, 'The Play of Genre and Voicing in Boccaccio's *Corbaccio*', *Italiana*, 5 (1993), 41–54; Guyda Armstrong, 'Boccaccio and the Infernal Body: The Widow as Wilderness', in *Boccaccio and Feminist Criticism*, pp. 83–104.
11 Robert Hollander, *Boccaccio's Two Venuses* (New York: Columbia University Press, 1977), p. 48.
12 Eugenio Giusti, '*Elegia di Madonna Fiammetta*: First Signs of an Ideological Shift', in *Boccaccio and Feminist Criticism*, pp. 69–82; Sister Prudence Allen, RSM, *The Concept of Woman*, 2 vols (Grand Rapids: Eerdmans, 2006), II: *The Early Humanist Reformation, 1250–1500*, p. 290.
13 Constance Jordan, 'Boccaccio's In-Famous Women: Gender and Civic Virtue in the *De mulieribus claris*', in *Ambiguous Realities: Women in the Middle Ages and Renaissance*, ed. by Carole Levin and Jeanie Watson (Detroit: Wayne State University Press, 1987), pp. 25–47 (p. 32).
14 Pamela J. Benson, *The Invention of the Renaissance Woman: The Challenge of Female Independence in the Literature and Thought of Italy and England* (University Park: Pennsylvania State University Press, 1992), pp. 18, 19, 28.
15 Jordan, 'Boccaccio's In-Famous Women', p. 27.
16 Hollander, *Boccaccio's Last Fiction*, p. 25.
17 Stephen Kolsky, *The Genealogy of Women: Studies in Boccaccio's 'De mulieribus claris'* (New York: Peter Lang, 2003), p. 139.
18 Rhiannon Daniels, *Boccaccio and the Book: Production and Reading in Italy 1340–1520* (London: Legenda, 2009), p. 172.

PART IV

Transmission and Adaptation

12

BRIAN RICHARDSON

Editing Boccaccio

How can we publish texts of Boccaccio's works that are faithful to what he wrote, while taking account of the needs of present-day readers? This is the key question facing editors of Boccaccio, but it also needs to be considered by anyone with a serious interest in the author, since reliable and accessible texts are prerequisites for the interpretation of his writings. It is a question to which the answers are complex, are still not fully resolved, and have aroused controversy. Many of Boccaccio's works are lengthy and were copied frequently, so that variations tended to be introduced at an early stage. In order to reconstruct accurate texts, editors must examine surviving manuscripts and the early printed editions that were based on manuscripts now lost, and then decide impartially on how best to use these testimonies. They must judge whether any manuscripts are written in Boccaccio's own hand, while remembering that even an author's copies may contain unintentional errors, and whether there is any evidence that Boccaccio revised a work. They need to decide how far to respect fourteenth-century spelling. According to the nature of their edition, they may also wish to assist readers by adding paratexts such as an introduction, annotations, and indexes. At the same time, editors have to work within practical constraints, including those of the demands of their publishers and the expectations of their anticipated readers.

This essay surveys the main developments in editing Boccaccio since the first collection of his vernacular works was printed in the early nineteenth century. Just as in the case of studying translations of Boccaccio across time, so comparing successive editions can tell us both about how the author was understood and appreciated in different periods and about tendencies in methodology. Italy has produced no Edizione Nazionale for the works of Boccaccio, whereas one was instituted for those of Dante in 1889 and for those of Petrarch in 1904, and this may reflect a historical unease about some aspects of his writings. We can also take the case of a canonical author such as Boccaccio as a microhistory that reflects the evolution of editorial practices in Italian studies in response to changing influences.

Nineteenth-century editions: locating and using manuscripts

Writing in 1827, less than a decade after Leopardi's call to honour great Italians of the past in 'Sopra il monumento di Dante che si preparava a Firenze', the editor-publisher Ignazio Moutier introduced the first volume of his Florentine series of Boccaccio's *Opere volgari* by lamenting Italy's neglect of the full range of works by the *tre corone*. While Italians already had correct editions of Dante's *Comedy*, Petrarch's *Canzoniere*, and Boccaccio's *Decameron*, the texts of these authors' other works were, he argued, in a sorry state. As regards Boccaccio, Moutier was broadly correct to distinguish between the scholarly attention given to the *Decameron* and the relative neglect of the 'minor' vernacular works. The series of Italian classics published by the Società Tipografica de' Classici Italiani in Milan had by then included, of Boccaccio's writings, only the *Decameron* with one version of the *Vita di Dante* and a few letters (1803); the 'Biblioteca scelta di opere italiane antiche e moderne', published by Silvestri in the same city, included only the *Decameron* (1816), the *Teseida* (1819), and the *Vita di Dante* (1823); and the *Teseida* was the only work of Boccaccio's to appear in the 'Parnaso italiano' (Venice, 1820). Moutier's pioneering collection, on which he began work in 1819 and which allowed Florence to outdo the Milanese enterprises, was the first coordinated attempt to put all Boccaccio's vernacular works on a sound editorial footing. His preface identified three obstacles that had to be overcome: the need to consult many manuscripts in order to use the readings of the best, lack of time, and lack of money.[1]

As for the first problem, Moutier set out in his opening preface a 'constant system' of editing that in reality left considerable uncertainty. He would use only manuscripts or early printed editions faithful to manuscripts. In selecting 'the best and most original reading', his criterion was that of reason. He preferred not to emend the text where it appeared wrong, although he removed uneducated expressions ('idiotismi') and spelling errors; to vary the text capriciously would be to lack respect for the benefit of the ever-spreading Enlightenment ('i lumi'). Moutier's later prefaces reiterated his belief that old-fashioned spellings and evident errors of early manuscripts should be rejected, while on the other hand expressions no longer in use must never be replaced with modern ones. In editing the *Decameron*, Moutier followed the then conventional view that the text should be based primarily on that of MS 42. 1 of the Biblioteca Medicea Laurenziana of Florence, copied by Francesco d'Amaretto Mannelli in 1384 and now known as Mn. He rejected, however, the method of the Lucca edition of 1761, which had aimed to follow Mn exactly; instead, he used other sources wherever Mn was considered corrupt. In fact, Moutier simply adopted, with some emendations from other printed editions, the text edited by Michele Colombo for the Parma edition of 1812–14, which had been based on the Milanese edition of 1803, itself derived from the 'London', but actually Livorno, edition of 1789–90. Moutier ignored the Venetian edition of 1813, which had largely followed Mn but adopted a spelling based on modern Tuscan popular pronunciation. This choice had also been rejected as anachronistic by Ugo Foscolo in the *Discorso* that preceded his relatively conservative London text of 1825.

Moutier explicitly reproduced only one other recent printed text, basing the *Rime* on Giovanni Battista Baldelli Boni's first edition of Livorno, 1802. All the title pages of the *Opere volgari* up to volume XIV refer to correction made on the basis of manuscripts from Florentine libraries. The *Corbaccio* was printed 'according to the reading of the Mannelli text', in other words the copy that followed the *Decameron* in Laurenziana MS 42. 1. A few manuscripts from the Biblioteca Riccardiana were used for the *Fiammetta* and the *Filocolo* printed in 1829, and Moutier claimed to have turned to similar sources for most of the other works. Sometimes he underlined the advance that his edition represented. His *Teseida*, based on 'the best reading' of 'good and authoritative manuscripts', clearly improved on the Milanese edition of 1819, which had followed a hybrid eighteenth-century manuscript. Fra Luigi Baroni had used a manuscript of the *Filostrato* dating from 1393 for his Paris edition of 1789 and had compared it with others from Florence, but Moutier claimed to have restored the poem to its original state by consulting no fewer than eleven manuscripts from the Riccardiana and Laurenziana libraries. For the *Amorosa visione*, the rival edition was that published in Palermo, 1818, by Pietro Notarbartolo, duke of Villarosa, the first edition to be printed since 1558 and the first not to be based on Girolamo Claricio's edition of 1521. Notarbartolo had acknowledged that ideally an editor would select from various manuscripts and early printed editions and would form a model text by 'reuniting the best [readings] with the guide of enlightened and wise judgement'. Yet, he wrote, few had the fortune to be able to do this, and he had followed just one source, MS 1066 of the Riccardiana. Moutier argued that this copy was careless and that his own edition, based on two other copies from the Riccardiana with some recourse to one from the Biblioteca Magliabechiana, followed the author's intention. However, Moutier never explained why he had selected certain manuscripts and why he sometimes expressed a preference for one or more of them. The suspicion remains, too, that he used printed editions as the basis of his copy text to a greater extent than he admitted.

For Moutier, interpretation of his texts was of far lower importance than establishing their readings, the sole topic of his introductions. Like Colombo, he provided only a few notes on the *Decameron*, consisting of alternative readings, comments on usage, and explanations of unusual terms. His editions of other works contain no annotations or variants. The readers that Moutier appears to have had principally in mind were 'students of our language', as he put it in his *Filostrato*, those interested above all in bettering their knowledge of Trecento usage. In this he resembled other publishers of his period who addressed costly editions to 'the lover of good Italian language' (*Filostrato*, 1789) or 'the enthusiasts ["cultori"] of our tongue' (*Teseida*, 1819). This *Teseida* was on sale at 3.5 lire, more than twice the daily wage of a Milanese mason or carpenter; the four-volume *Decameron* of 1803 cost 26.5 lire.[2] However, the *Decameron* of Pietro Dal Rio (Florence, 1841–4) contained paratexts intended to help 'studious Youth' ('[la] studiosa Gioventù'). Dal Rio replaced Tiraboschi's life of Boccaccio, offered by Colombo, with the more recent biography composed by Giovanni Battista Baldelli Boni, and his annotations combined many new ones with those of others from Mannelli to Colombo.

The *Decameron* edited by Pietro Fanfani was published twelve times in Florence by Le Monnier between 1857 and 1926. Its unprecedented success can be explained by the mainly original annotations that sought to explain 'obscure and difficult passages... to any reader', as well as by its economical and handy octavo format. Like Moutier and Dal Rio, Fanfani chose the Parma edition as the model for his text, checking it against Mn, whose importance had, he believed, been overrated by previous editors. He claimed to have drawn on a few other manuscripts and early printed editions, but did not explain his methodology. Fanfani did not believe there had been two original versions of the *Decameron*, as suggested by Florentine editors in 1573; in fact, Boccaccio probably did not leave even one original, because he detested 'his past follies'. In 1859 Fanfani edited the *Fiammetta* and the letter to Pino de' Rossi. He accused Moutier of making poor use of manuscript sources of the *Fiammetta*, but preferred to base his own text merely on the Florentine edition of 1826 compared with the editions of 1472 and 1533.

At the antipodes of Fanfani's cavalier approach was the longer version of the *Vita di Dante* edited by Francesco Macrì-Leone (Florence: Sansoni, 1888), one of the first Italian editions to introduce the relatively new technique, associated with the German scholar Karl Lachmann (1793–1851), of classifying source texts in a genealogical tree or 'stemma' according to the significant errors that they shared. Justifying his own methodology with references to Gaston Paris's edition of *La Vie de saint Alexis* (1872) and the teaching of Pio Rajna, Macrì-Leone derived his text from agreement between three groups of Florentine and Venetian manuscripts; where consensus was lacking, preference was given to the manuscript considered oldest. Macrì-Leone's edition pointed the way towards a more rigorous approach to editing Boccaccio, but it would be some time before his example was followed by others.

The first half of the twentieth century: from arbitrary selection towards the 'new philology'

In the early twentieth century, two publishing series issued some of Boccaccio's vernacular works. Between 1907 and 1912, the 'Bibliotheca romanica', pocket-sized texts published in London and Strasbourg, included the *Decameron*, the *Fiammetta*, the *Filostrato*, and the *Corbaccio*. The respective editors – Gustav Gröber, Giuseppe Gigli, Paolo Savj-Lopez, and Luigi Sorrento – provided brief introductions, but their texts were unannotated and derived from editions already published: Fanfani's *Decameron* and *Fiammetta*, Moutier's *Filostrato* and *Corbaccio*. The Boccaccio volumes in the 'Collezione di classici italiani' produced in Turin by UTET included annotations and made contributions to the editing of the texts that were original but speculative. Aldo Francesco Massèra intended his edition of the *Caccia di Diana* and the *Rime* (1914) as the start of a 'reprinting' of the minor vernacular works that would not claim to offer critical texts except in these two cases. He had derived the *Caccia* from a 'good manuscript' whose whereabouts were, however, now unknown to him. For the *Rime*, he followed his own critical edition of the same year (Bologna: Romagnoli-Dall'Acqua). Massèra relied too heavily on one manuscript, and his organization of Boccaccio's lyric verse was determined by the romanticizing of the author's biography that endured until the 1940s.[3] He arranged the 126 poems that he considered authentic into a series of groups ordered chronologically, in which the first sixty-six told the story of Boccaccio's supposed love for 'the blonde countess' Fiammetta. This was followed by an appendix of twenty-nine sonnets probably by Boccaccio. This scheme set a pattern that, as we shall see, other twentieth-century editions were unable to escape. Massèra's edition of the *Ninfale fiesolano* (1926) took as its starting point the critical edition of Berthold Wiese (Heidelberg, 1913), based on thirty-six manuscripts. Massèra claimed to have improved Wiese's text with the use of manuscripts (though it is not clear that he consulted any directly) and of some conjectures, re-establishing, subjectively of course, 'the harmony of the verse'. In editing the *Filocolo* for this series, Ettore de Ferri stated with even greater imprecision that he had followed Moutier's edition (1829) but also those of 1530 and 1593 'where the Trecento expression is rendered fresher and more persuasive'.

The first major initiative of unified Italy in editing Boccaccio was the set of texts, both vernacular and Latin, that appeared among the 'Scrittori d'Italia' published by Laterza between 1918 and 1955. When Benedetto Croce announced this series in 1909, he stated that, like the Oxford Classical Texts, it would offer 'very accurate critical texts' without notes or commentaries.[4] However, there was no consistent understanding of what a critical text was, and discussion of the constitution of the text was relegated to a concluding 'Nota'. A first group of works by Boccaccio appeared while Fausto Nicolini was general editor. Domenico Guerri's editing of the life of Dante (1918) marked a considerable step forward. He derived the longer version from the Toledo manuscript that Michele Barbi had identified as written in Boccaccio's hand (Toledo, Biblioteca Capitular, Zelada 104. 6), and Guerri used the similarly autograph Chigi manuscript for the shorter of the two summary versions (Vatican City, Biblioteca Apostolica Vaticana, MS Chigi L. V. 176 and L. VI. 213), with footnotes giving variants from the longer summary version that Enrico Rostagno had edited in 1899 from unreliable sources.[5] (Barbi had shown in 1913 that the summary versions constituted a second redaction.) Guerri's text of Boccaccio's commentary on Dante was based on a comparison of three Florentine manuscripts from the early fifteenth century.

For the *Decameron* published in 1927, Massèra relied above all on MS Hamilton 90 of the Berlin Staatsbibliothek, Preussischer Kulturbesitz, known as B, which scholars had concluded in the late nineteenth century to be the source of Mn. He had recourse to Mn and the first printed edition of about 1470 in passages where B is incomplete or where he believed it to be in error. Massèra's use of B as well as of Mn, the source most revered in editions since the 1570s, was undoubtedly a step in the right direction, but the principles on which his edition was based were immediately contested by Barbi, the most authoritative living textual critic of medieval Italian literature. Barbi argued that a correct text could not be derived from B and Mn alone, that it was not proven that Mn had been copied directly from B, and that an editor should therefore consider the whole manuscript tradition, including the independent MS It. 482 of the Bibliothèque Nationale, Paris, copied by Giovanni d'Agnolo Capponi probably around 1360. Apropos of a variant of Mn, Barbi asked in conclusion whether there might not be two copies of the *Decameron* in Boccaccio's hand: on this question, too, further study was needed.[6]

Massèra also edited Boccaccio's *Opere latine minori* (1928). He derived the text of the *Buccolicum carmen* from the autograph MS 1232 of the Riccardiana, aiming to present the last of what he believed to be three phases of composition, while adopting modern spelling conventions.

The remaining editions in the Laterza series began to appear after a gap of nine years, when the series was directed by Luigi Russo. By then the influence of Barbi was felt more strongly, and it was reinforced by the publication in 1938 of a collection of his essays on the textual criticism of Italian authors, *La nuova filologia*. Barbi doubted, he explained in his introduction, whether most people knew what a critical edition should be, and he cited the resistance to his proposal that an edition of Dante's *Commedia* should be based on an examination of the whole textual tradition. He defended the primacy of Lachmann's method of grouping manuscripts. As an example of the maltreatment of an earlier author because of preconceptions about his style, he cited Massèra's *Ninfale fiesolano*.

In the Laterza series, a greater degree of rigour became apparent in Vincenzo Pernicone's edition of the *Filostrato* and *Ninfale fiesolano* (1937). He assigned manuscripts of the former work to three families and based his text on the agreement of any two groups against the third. Pernicone criticized both Wiese's and Massèra's editions of the *Ninfale*, while acknowledging that for his own he had consulted only manuscripts that he could see within a short time and that he followed principally one Florentine manuscript with checks from another. In his edition of *L'elegia di madonna Fiammetta* (1939), Pernicone concluded that the available manuscripts derived from a single source that contained errors. Most manuscripts fell into two groups, and his text was derived from the best representatives of each group and the independent sources. Salvatore Battaglia's *Filocolo* (1938) similarly improved on previous editions in respect of the range of sources consulted (ten manuscripts), but Battaglia did not explain how he had used them other than to say that he had derived from them 'a correct and, one may say, critical reading'.

Vittore Branca's long and distinguished career as an editor of Boccaccio began in 1939 with his Laterza edition of the *Rime*, the *Amorosa visione*, and the *Caccia di Diana*. For the *Rime*, Branca reluctantly kept Massèra's ordering, since he felt an alternative sequence would have been just as arbitrary, but he compared the manuscripts afresh and added thirteen poems excluded by Massèra. The texts of the two works in *terza rima* were based on a full survey of the manuscripts. In each case, three groups were identified and the texts were based on agreement between them. Branca discussed the question of whether the text of the Milanese printing of 1521 had been reworked by its editor Claricio or represented a version revised by the author himself.

At this stage, Branca limited himself to the suggestion that it would not be surprising if the latter were the case. However, the edition of the *Amorosa visione* that he then prepared for the Accademia della Crusca (1944) repro-duced Claricio's text as a second authorial redaction dating from about 1355–65, even though there is no manuscript evidence for this version. Branca's bold step reflected a contemporary interest in studying authors' variants, seen also in the work of the classical scholar Giorgio Pasquali and in Barbi's *La nuova filologia*.[7] The publication of the two texts of the *Amorosa visione* provoked a lively critical debate among scholars such as Pernicone (the main dissenter from Branca's views), Giuseppe Billanovich, and Gianfranco Contini. Much later, in a context of developing awareness of the procedures of early printers and editors, Lida Maria Gonelli compared copies of the 1521 edition and showed that many corrections made during printing reveal Claricio in the act of adding 'improvements' to his version of the text.[8] This evidence suggests that elsewhere, too, Claricio was revising the text according to his own tastes, as did other early Cinquecento editors of Boccaccio.

Nicola Bruscoli's edition of *L'Ameto, Lettere, Il Corbaccio* in the La-terza series (1940) had more limited ambitions. Bruscoli based his *Ameto*, or *Comedia delle ninfe fiorentine*, mainly on the agreement between two and sometimes three manuscripts from the Laurenziana, preferring one in cases of disagreement and referring to others when the reading was obscure. The *Corbaccio* was derived from Mannelli's copy, corrected on occasion from other sources. The *Teseida* edited by Aurelio Roncaglia (1941) had much more solid foundations. In 1938, an edition of the poem by Battaglia had appeared in the Crusca's series of 'Autori classici'. Battaglia had used the Laurenziana manuscript (Acquisti e doni 325) that Giuseppe Vandelli had shown in 1929 to be in the author's hand, but Battaglia had also con-sulted the rest of the tradition. His critical apparatus included variants from one of the two groups of manuscripts, which he believed probably derived from an earlier authorial original. Roncaglia was able to examine some further manuscripts and to improve Battaglia's text and its punctuation, including the introduction of diereses to interpret the metre of Boccaccio's verse.

Two further Boccaccio editions appeared in the 'Scrittori d'Italia' series in the post-war period. Vincenzo Romano based his text of the *Genealogie deorum gentilium libri* (1951) on MS 52. 9 of the Laurenziana, written and corrected by Boccaccio. Romano believed this text to be later than the most commonly diffused or 'vulgate' version and to date from Boccaccio's very last years. Finally, another *Decameron*, edited by Charles S. Singleton, was published in 1955. Singleton classified fifty-one manuscripts and five early printed editions. Some variants, he believed, were found throughout the tradition and could originate from the author. He divided the texts into three principal groups on the basis of these possible revisions; they might have descended from three distinct copies but, since such variants were few in number (just eleven were listed as possibly authorial), it was more probable that they stemmed from a single copy revised at different times. Singleton's critical text was based mainly on what he considered the two most significant manuscripts of one of the groups, B and MS 42. 3 of the Laurenziana, dating from the third quarter of the Quattrocento. Many years of preparation had gone into the preparation of this final edition in the Laterza series, but before long its results were to prove invalid.

From the second half of the twentieth century: the Mondadori series and beyond

Not long before the appearance of Singleton's *Decameron*, Vittore Branca had brought out an edition of the same work in two volumes for Le Monnier (1951–2). He selected for comparison eleven manuscripts, out of eighty-five identified by him, together with two early printed editions. Several readings characteristic of B and Mn were excluded. Branca stressed that the hypothesis of a second version of the *Decameron* could not, on its own, explain the sheer number of variants in a tradition that for him was characterized by discontinuity and freedom, with manuscripts being produced above all in bourgeois and mercantile environments. (Later research, especially by Marco Cursi, showed the need to modify this view.)[9] On the other hand, it was very probable, Branca argued, that Boccaccio did revise his work at least once, and some less successful readings, not found in the definitive 'vulgate' text that Branca aimed to present, were probably evidence of earlier versions. Branca's text was based on fuller evidence and firmer principles that that of Singleton, but it, too, was destined to be superseded before long.

The first of two volumes of annotated works by Boccaccio published by Ricciardi was edited by Enrico Bianchi, Carlo Salinari, and Natalino Sapegno (Milan and Naples, 1952). It offered little that was new as regards the text of the *Decameron*: Branca's text was adopted with the most plausible corrections suggested by other scholars. The volume was completed with the Laterza texts of the *Filocolo*, the *Ameto*, and the *Fiammetta*. The second volume, however, containing the *Opere in versi*, *Corbaccio*, *Trattatello in laude di Dante*, *Prose latine*, and *Epistole* (1965), was much more enterprising and formed part of a new wave of Boccaccio editing. The scholar responsible, Pier Giorgio Ricci, took a fresh look at textual evidence for some of the texts, with the guiding principle of restoring 'with caution and an attentive historical sense'. He also showed a fresh awareness of changes over time in Boccaccio's spelling, both vernacular and Latin, that has become a feature of modern editing of his works. For the *Teseida*, Ricci made some modifications to Roncaglia's text. More radically, he turned his back on Mannelli's transcription of the *Corbaccio* and used instead five manuscripts that he judged more authentic and that allowed him, he claimed, to restore the text for the first time to its genuine form. The *Trattatello* (previously published as the *Vita di Dante*) was derived from the Toledo manuscript, with necessary corrections. For his selections from the *De mulieribus claris*, Ricci used Laurenziana MS 90 sup. 98[1], which he had identified as autograph and dated to Boccaccio's last years.[10] His extracts from the *De casibus virorum illustrium* used just two manuscripts and was hence described as provisional. Ricci chose to use manuscripts of the 'vulgate' version of the *Genealogia deorum gentilium* which, inverting Romano's view, he judged to be later than the autograph manuscript. He consulted manuscripts of the Rossi letter that were not known to Bruscoli.

Ricci's edition made good use of the wide-ranging survey of manuscripts in the first volume of Branca's study of the tradition of Boccaccio's works.[11] Branca's researches also laid the foundations for the landmark series of *Tutte le opere* that was published under his general editorship between 1964 and 1998, within the prestigious 'Classici italiani' established by Arnoldo Mondadori and launched in 1935. Each work was to have an introduction and annotations, as well as a detailed 'Nota al testo'. The collection was planned in twelve volumes, but the last two, intended to contain respectively *Volgarizzamenti* and *Chiose, scritti e documenti vari, scritti attribuiti, indici e glossari*, were not published. The first volume to appear (vol. II, 1964) opened with the *Filostrato*, for which Branca made some corrections to Pernicone's Laterza edition. Alberto Limentani's text of the *Teseida delle nozze di Emilia* was based on Battaglia's edition but took Roncaglia's into account. For the *Comedia delle ninfe fiorentine*, Antonio Enzo Quaglio followed the critical text that he had published in the previous year in the Crusca series. Here, as well as restoring the original title in place of *Ameto*, he had widened the scope of his survey of manuscript and printed texts and used his sources more rigorously. The manuscripts, he showed, fell into two groups, but he excluded the likelihood of authorial revisions. Taking Barbi's editing of Dante's *Vita nova* as a model for dealing with a manuscript tradition divided into two groups, Quaglio based his choices on philological rather than arbitrary criteria; where one of the two readings was not clearly wrong, he preferred the group that seemed more faithful to the original source or archetype. The Crusca edition also included an important appendix on the textual innovations created for the Milanese *Ameto* of 1520 by Claricio, described here as a forger ('falsario'). However, in an essay first published in 1997, Giorgio Padoan was later to put forward the hypothesis that Claricio's edition of this work, like that of the *Amorosa visione*, used a text that had come, via Mannelli, from a second authorial redaction.[12]

For his text of the *Esposizioni sopra la comedia di Dante* (vol. VI, 1965), Padoan explained that he sought to remain as faithful as possible to the manuscripts, selecting readings objectively and using conjectural emendation only where necessary. The *Caccia di Diana*, already edited by Branca together with the *Rime* in 1939 and in an annotated edition of 1958, was presented by him once more in Volume I of the Mondadori series (1967). This volume also contained a *Filocolo* for which Quaglio had surveyed the entire manuscript and printed tradition. He criticized Battaglia's text of 1938 for not having freed itself entirely from the printed editions. Quaglio's version was based on agreement between two groups of manuscripts or, in other cases, on stylistic and other considerations, with a preference for the group considered more trustworthy. In the same year the *De mulieribus claris* appeared (vol. X): here Vittorio Zaccaria followed the autograph manuscript discovered by Ricci except where Boccaccio had manifestly made errors.

In Volume III (1974), Branca reproduced his two texts of the *Amorosa visione* with minor corrections and a renewed defence of his view that Claricio's text was based on a second redaction. Armando Balduino, on the other hand, found no evidence that Boccaccio had revised the *Ninfale fiesolano*. He divided forty-eight manuscripts into two groups, of which one was judged more reliable in cases where their readings differed. As a result, Pernicone's text was improved in several places. The volume concluded with both redactions of the *Trattatello in laude di Dante* edited by Ricci. Each was based on the surviving autograph manuscripts. Ricci did not attempt to produce a critical text of the B version of the shorter redaction, but he listed its most notable variants.

Volume IV (1976) was devoted to the *Decameron*, edited again by Branca. The text reproduced his critical edition published in the same year by the Accademia della Crusca, following the exciting recent confirmation that the scribe of the Berlin manuscript was none other than Boccaccio. This discovery had actually been made many years earlier, in 1933, by Barbi, who inspected B at first hand with his assistant Alberto Chiari. But, strangely, the attribution was announced only much later by Chiari, first in a journalistic piece of 1948, then in a brief article of 1955 that had little impact.[13] The high number of errors in B made it hard to accept that its hand was Boccaccio's without fuller evidence. In 1962, Ricci and Branca examined B directly and demonstrated that Boccaccio had indeed copied it, towards the end of his life.[14] Singleton transcribed it in an 'edizione diplomatico-interpretativa' (Baltimore, 1974) that received a scathing review by Branca.[15] Branca's own Florentine 'edizione critica secondo l'autografo Hamiltoniano' adopted modern punctuation and spelling, and used Mn to complete the sections missing in B. Branca later made minor modifications to his text in editions published by Einaudi of Turin.

For Volume IX of the Mondadori series (1983), Ricci took on the task of editing the *De casibus virorum illustrium*. He offered a text, described by him as reliable ('attendibile') rather than critical, of the second redaction, with some samples of the first. Volume V appeared in two tomes (1992 and 1994). For the first, Branca updated his 1958 edition of the *Rime* (in which he had added eight new poems to the text of 1939), taking account of suggestions by Domenico De Robertis.[16] The tome was completed by the *Carmina*, edited by Giuseppe Velli; the Latin and vernacular letters, edited by Ginetta Auzzas; the lives of Petrarch, Pier Damiani, and Livy, edited by Renata Fabbri; and the *De Canaria*, edited by Manlio Pastore Stocchi. In the second tome, the most innovative texts were those of the *Fiammetta* and the *Corbaccio*. Franca Ageno had produced in 1954 an edition of the *Fiammetta*, 'the fruit of a careful revision' of Pernicone's text of 1939, using five manuscripts thought to depend on a common ancestor; its spelling followed the model of the autograph manuscript of the *Teseida*, composed about the same time. Soon afterwards, an extensive study of the textual tradition had been published by Quaglio.[17] Carlo Delcorno now surveyed seventy-two manuscripts of the *Fiammetta* and divided them into two groups. His edition was based on agreement between them; where they differed, he preferred the reading of the more correct group, unless the other was clearly superior. He favoured the linguistic forms of one manuscript, except where it diverged from Boccaccio's usage in his autograph manuscripts.

As for the *Corbaccio*, one of the most problematic vernacular texts for editors, we saw that in 1965 Ricci had moved away from the manuscript copied by Mannelli. So, too, had Tauno Nurmela in an edition of 1968 that sought to identify two groups of manuscripts and preferred the group to which Mannelli's text did not belong. Nurmela saw no evidence for the suggestion, made by Ricci in an article first published in 1962, that there were two authorial versions.[18] For the Mondadori edition, Padoan returned to Mannelli's text and treated it with even more respect than in the past. The discovery that the Berlin copy of the *Decameron* (closely related to the version found in Mn and, it is now thought, very possibly derived from the same source) was autograph showed, according to Padoan, that Mannelli was an exceptionally faithful scribe. Padoan believed that Boccaccio had transcribed the *Corbaccio* more than once with slight modifications, and a late rewriting was witnessed by Mn.[19] This tome included the *Consolatoria a Pino de' Rossi*, edited by Giuseppe Chiecchi, the *Buccolicum carmen*, edited by Giorgio Bernardi Perini (whose text was close to Massèra's), and the *Allegoria mitologica*, edited by Pastore Stocchi.

The final volumes of the Mondadori series (VII and VIII, 1998) contained the *Genealogia*, edited by Zaccaria, and the *De montibus, silvis, fontibus, lacubus, fluminibus, stagnis seu paludibus et de diversis nominibus maris*, edited by Pastore Stocchi. Zaccaria had earlier confirmed that the 'vulgate' text of the *Genealogia* was later than the autograph manuscript, which he dated to 1365–70. His approach went beyond that of Ricci (1965) since he investigated more manuscripts and was able to show how the 'vulgate' had passed through phases of revision; his text represented its last stage. Editing the *De montibus* was an altogether different kind of task: there is no autograph, around seventy manuscripts are known, and the encyclopaedic nature of the text made it unusually prone to alterations by scribes. Pastore Stocchi's pragmatic and provisional solution was to attempt to create a version of the text as it was probably read *c.* 1400, on the basis of six representative manuscripts.

During the period in which the Mondadori series appeared, two other Milanese publishing houses produced editions of Boccaccio that were more affordable yet still helpfully annotated. After Mursia had published a volume of *Opere* in 1963 including the *Decameron*, the *Rime*, the *Filostrato*, the *Fiammetta*, the *Ninfale*, and the *Corbaccio*, all these works except the *Rime* appeared separately in its 'Grande Universale' series, in some cases with very full notes. Mario Marti's four-volume edition of the *Opere minori* for Rizzoli (1969–72) reproduced what he considered the best available texts of the vernacular works, with some improvements and brief annotations. This was followed by a *Decameron* edited by Marti for Rizzoli (1974) with Singleton's text of 1955 and notes by Elena Ceva Valla.

The question of Boccaccio's possible revisions of the *Decameron* was taken up by Aldo Rossi in an edition of 1977. He believed that a first phase of the work was best represented by MS It. 482 of the Bibliothèque Nationale (P), which he wrongly thought to be in Boccaccio's hand. There followed an intermediate phase whose most important witness was said to be the Laurenziana MS 42. 3. As evidence of the final version, Rossi attached importance not only to the Berlin manuscript but also to Mannelli's copy, which he believed to derive from B in spite of its variants. Rossi's critical text took B as its foundation but included within angle brackets readings found in neither B nor Mn that were described as probable errors of the author as scribe, deriving from the first and intermediate phases of composition. From the mid-1990s, Branca put the discussion on a much more solid footing by showing that P did indeed contain authorial variants, which he considered to constitute a first redaction of the work, and then by analysing Boccaccio's methods of revision in collaboration with Maurizio Vitale.[20]

New texts of the *Decameron*, edited by Maurizio Fiorilla, were published in 2011 and 2013. Fiorilla judged that several of the readings in Branca's texts were errors in the Berlin autograph, and to correct them he used other manuscripts wherever possible. The layout of his texts reflected Boccaccio's use of coloured capital letters to indicate different levels of narration. The edition of 2013, issued by Rizzoli to mark the septcentenary of Boccaccio's birth, was enriched by introductions and analytical material by Amedeo Quondam and Giancarlo Alfano. However, there is still a need for a critical edition of Boccaccio's masterpiece that provides full information on the variants of the text and its stages of evolution.

Many anthologies of tales from the *Decameron* and selections from the minor works have been published since the eighteenth century. They have often been aimed at younger readers, and in this case they have excluded stories considered unsuitable for them. Although some cuts were made for reasons of space, others reflected a long-standing tension between the promotion of the *Decameron* as a linguistic model and the anxiety that some stories would be sexually titillating or presented the clergy in a bad light. The bestsellers of the nineteenth century were selections of thirty stories, sometimes with specifications of the readership such as 'mainly for the use of modest youths and students of Tuscan' or 'for the use of schools'. Among the most successful of the many anthologies of the twentieth century were those edited by Giuseppe Rua (1910 onwards), Attilio Momigliano (1924 onwards), and Natalino Sapegno (1937 onwards).

Several previously published texts of Boccaccio are available online, for instance on the Decameron Web (www.brown.edu/Departments/Italian_Studies/dweb/texts), in Giuseppe Bonghi's Biblioteca dei Classici Italiani (www.classicitaliani.it), and in the Biblioteca Italiana (www.bibliotecaitaliana.it). Raul Mordenti launched a hypertextual critical edition of one of the miscellanies of texts copied by Boccaccio, the *Zibaldone Laurenziano*, MS 29. 8 of the Biblioteca Medicea Laurenziana (rmcisadu.let .uniroma1.it/boccaccio). This project covers at present only a small proportion of the sections of the manuscript, but it suggests an alternative way of approaching the editing of Boccaccio's own works in the future.

NOTES

1 'Ai lettori l'editore Ignazio Moutier', in Giovanni Boccaccio, *Opere volgari corrette su i testi a penna*, ed. by Ignazio Moutier, 17 vols (Florence: Magheri and Ig. Moutier, 1827–34), I, v–xiv (p. ix). Bibliographies of editions of Boccaccio's works are found in Alberto Bacchi della Lega with Francesco Zambrini, *Serie delle edizioni delle opere di Giovanni Boccacci latine, volgari, tradotte e trasformate* (Bologna: Romagnoli, 1875); Vittore Branca, *Linee di una storia della critica al 'Decameron' con bibliografia boccaccesca completamente aggiornata* (Milan: Società Anonima Editrice Dante Alighieri, 1939), pp. 79–103; Enzo Esposito with Christopher Kleinhenz, *Boccacciana: bibliografia delle edizioni e degli scritti critici (1939–1974)* (Ravenna: Longo, 1976), pp. 13–21.

2 Mario Romani, *Storia economica d'Italia nel secolo XIX, 1815–1914*, 2 vols (Milan: Giuffrè, 1968–76), I, 235.

3 Vittore Branca, *Boccaccio medievale*, rev. edn (Florence: Sansoni, 1970), pp. 191–249; Giuseppe Billanovich, *Restauri boccacceschi* (Rome: Edizioni di Storia e Letteratura, 1947).

4 Benedetto Croce, 'Gli Scrittori d'Italia', in *Pagine sparse*, 3 vols (Bari: Laterza, 1960), I, 173–8 (p. 176); Gianfranco Folena, 'Benedetto Croce e gli "Scrittori d'Italia"', in *Critica e storia letteraria: studi offerti a Mario Fubini*, ed. by Vittorio Enzo Alfieri and others, 2 vols (Padua: Liviana, 1970), II, 123–60.

5 See List of manuscripts in this volume.

6 Michele Barbi, 'Sul testo del *Decameron*' (1927), in *La nuova filologia e l'edizione dei nostri scrittori da Dante al Manzoni* (Florence: Sansoni, 1938; repr. 1973), pp. 35–85.

7 Boccaccio's variants are discussed in Giorgio Pasquali, *Storia della tradizione e critica del testo* (Florence: Le Monnier, 1954; 1st edn 1934), pp. 427, 443–8. Pasquali was more cautious about authorial variants in the 1954 edition, pp. xxi–xxii.

8 Lida Maria Gonelli, 'Esercizi di bibliografia testuale sulla *princeps* dell'*Amorosa Visione* (1521)', *Filologia italiana*, 2 (2005), 147–60.

9 Marco Cursi, *Il 'Decameron': scritture, scriventi, lettori. Storia di un testo* (Rome: Viella, 2007).

10 Pier Giorgio Ricci, *Studi sulla vita e le opere del Boccaccio* (Milan and Naples: Ricciardi, 1985), pp. 115–24.

11 Vittore Branca, *Tradizione delle opere di Giovanni Boccaccio*, 2 vols (Rome: Storia e Letteratura, 1958–91).

12 Giorgio Padoan, *Ultimi studi di filologia dantesca e boccacciana*, ed. by Aldo Maria Costantini (Ravenna: Longo, 2002), pp. 69–121 (esp. pp. 86–104).

13 Alberto Chiari, 'Ancora dell'autografia del codice berlinese del Decameron, Hamilton 90', *Convivium*, n.s., 23 (1955), 352–6.

14 Vittore Branca and Pier Giorgio Ricci, *Un autografo del Decameron: codice hamiltoniano 90* (Florence: Olschki, 1962).

15 In *Studi sul Boccaccio*, 8 (1974), 321–9.

16 In his edition of 2010, Antonio Lanza revised Branca's text, reassessed the authenticity of poems attributed to Boccaccio, and allocated the 127 judged authentic to seven groups according to their style. An edition by Roberto Leporatti was published in 2013.

17 Antonio Enzo Quaglio, 'Per il testo della *Fiammetta*', *Studi di filologia italiana*, 15 (1957), 5-205.

18 Ricci, *Studi sulla vita*, pp. 87-96 (pp. 94-5). Ricci (pp. 97-114) later dismissed Nurmela's edition as unsatisfactory.

19 See also Padoan, *Ultimi studi*, pp. 61-77.

20 Maurizio Vitale and Vittore Branca, *Il capolavoro del Boccaccio e due diverse redazioni*, 2 vols (Venice: Istituto veneto di scienze, lettere ed arti, 2002).

13

CORMAC Ó CUILLEANÁIN

Translating Boccaccio

Some of the problems facing translators today are best understood in a historical perspective. A backward glance at translations of Boccaccio throws up some intriguing practices, and helps to clarify persistent questions about the methodology, legitimacy, and utility of translating texts from another time.

A sideways glance may also help. Our main focus here is on how translators have set about shifting Boccaccio, particularly the *Decameron*, from Italian to English, but this interlingual activity is one strand among several related practices. Not only straight translation but various interpretative responses – paraphrases, retellings, adaptations, imitations, even critical essays – can form vital parts of a writer's afterlife. Boccaccio's *Decameron* continues to inspire new work; contemporary authors sometimes build explicitly on his foundations, foregrounding groups of storytellers as a model for social interaction and communal understanding – as in Julia Voznesenskaya's *The Women's Decameron* (1986), Christopher Whyte's *The Gay Decameron* (1998), or Fay Weldon's *The Spa Decameron* (2007) – although none of these exactly mirror Boccaccio's original framing conventions, their dynamic interplay of characters and stories being more reminiscent of Chaucer's *Canterbury Tales*. Other writers omit *Decameron* from their titles but present recognizable Boccaccian patterns: examples include Jane Smiley's *Ten Days in the Hills* (2007) and Douglas Coupland's futuristic *Generation A* (2009), where the five protagonists, held incommunicado by an evil scientist, reorient themselves by telling each other a series of horrific, trashy, or apocalyptic tales. One of the five claims that 'we turned the world back into a book'.[1] It's a necessary book: as in the *Decameron*, the cumulative process of storytelling establishes some tenuous hope for the continuation of life on earth.

Glancing at the history of translations and adaptations, we see the range of creative reactions available at different historical moments, and can better appreciate the context in which these interpretations happen if we pay attention to prevailing linguistic, social, cultural, political, and commercial factors. For example, a text moving between two European vernaculars may sometimes pass through another intermediate language. A Latin text might not seem to require translation at all, being written in the lingua franca of an erudite elite – yet it does get translated, and can then serve new purposes in a new culture (which may demand cuts, amplifications, changes of register or medium). Translated texts stimulate further translations and new creative works, inspiring literary chains of migration where somebody's translation becomes someone else's 'source text'.[2]

Translation practices vary, in fact, according to the purposes for which translations are commissioned, so our contemporary feelings about translating Boccaccio need to be contextualized according to different historical needs. That said, the historical coverage of the present essay will be sporadic, not to say spotty, as the aim is to elucidate issues that remain live today, rather than to dispute or duplicate the pioneering work of H. G. Wright, G. H. McWilliam, Guyda Armstrong, and other scholars.[3]

While transfers across languages remain the most visible instance of translation, Roman Jakobson's classic essay 'On Linguistic Aspects of Translation' locates interlingual translation (*'translation proper'*) between two other types of transfer: those that occur within a language ('intralingual translation or *rewording'*) and transfers of linguistic meaning into a non-verbal system of symbols ('intersemiotic translation or *transmutation'*).[4]

These categories certainly apply to Boccaccio, whose intralingual rewordings include the *Decamerone di Giovanni Boccaccio* (1990), rewritten in modern Italian by Aldo Busi, a contemporary Italian novelist. Busi made damaging cuts – the reactions and interactions of the frame-story are completely eliminated, thereby suppressing a vital dimension of the book – and his reworded Italian degrades Boccaccio's elegant prose to a tedious effusion of cliché. In a brief preface, he explains that his translation (and he does say *traduzione*) 'makes absolutely no claim to be a transliteration or a re-creation or a different thing from the original: it is the original *today*'.[5] This statement highlights, among other things, one of the perennial paradoxes of translation: every version inevitably displaces the original that it claims to preserve.

Boccaccio is also widely represented in Jakobson's third category of 'intersemiotic translation', with brilliant visual renderings of his work dating back to the fourteenth century, taking in painters such as Botticelli (c. 1445–1510) and Rubens (1577–1640), and reaching into the present time with various movie versions, notably Pasolini's *Decameron* film of 1972 (on which see Chapter 14 in this volume); the tradition of transmutation even includes a foray into light opera with Franz Suppé's *Boccaccio, oder Der Prinz von*

Palermo (Boccaccio, or the Prince of Palermo), based on a previous stage play, and first performed in Vienna in 1879. Some of the finest intersemiotic 'translators' were the anonymous miniaturists who illuminated the early Boccaccio manuscripts with a unique combination of visual and narrative skills. The early illustrations reinforce the point that a book's status is radically altered by changes in its language or its intended audience. Vittore Branca's researches suggested that in Italy the *Decameron*, although ostensibly addressed to ladies, circulated largely as a book for the merchant classes, whereas in France, translated into French, it became a text for the aristocracy, elegantly copied and illustrated at vast expense.[6] There could be no more gorgeous demonstration of this social apotheosis than the work of the copyists and artists who worked on the French manuscripts, and in a recent study, Anne D. Hedeman brilliantly assembles a circumstantial case, drawing on 'scattered but compelling' evidence, to show that Boccaccio's first French translator prescribed in some detail a cycle of illustrations that ought to appear in any well-made manuscript of *De casibus virorum illustrium*.[7] Thus the translator becomes not just a technical contractor but a scholar and cultural mediator, a gatekeeper and promoter, the person at the heart of a process that shapes the presentation and reception of the texts that pass through his hands.

Boccaccio, translator and writer

Boccaccio had it coming to him. If his *Decameron* and some other works have been much translated and at times traduced, that is entirely appropriate, as he was himself a linguistic adventurer, writing in Latin and the vernacular, promoting the importation of Greek culture into Italy, and drawing tales from everywhere. In the *Decameron* and elsewhere he proved an inveterate compiler, improver, and expander, working with classical and vernacular sources that ranged from Ovid and Apuleius (acquired through what Jonathan Usher calls his 'extraordinarily indiscriminate reading' and eclectic way of amassing knowledge), to the French *fabliaux* which (again according to Usher) he would have picked up orally, along with French romances and Byzantine culture, during his youthful years in Naples.[8] Indiscriminate reading, and a well-stocked but unsystematic mind, can be a great boon to the working translator, or the creative writer.

Boccaccio was free in his writing practices. J. H. Whitfield has shown how Boccaccio took an 'unconvincing bare page' from Petrus Alphonsus's twelfth-century collection of short texts for training priests, and turned that schematic Latin tale of a faithless wife outwitting her suspicious husband into 'six pages which move with unflagging verve through detail which seems too rich to be invented'. This is the seemingly realistic tale of Tofano (*Dec.* VII. 4), set in the local town of Arezzo and written in racy vernacular with bursts of convincing dialogue. Boccaccio has grafted living flesh on to the dry bones of his source. Unlike the schematic story from Petrus Alphonsus, 'all has sprung into a homely life which Boccaccio seems to know.'[9] Much of Boccaccio's realism, in fact, comes from adding lifelike detail to skeletal plots. The Perugia and Naples that provide plausible contemporary settings for adulterous intrigues in *Decameron*, V. 10 and VII. 2 are seamlessly superimposed on to two tales borrowed from a Latin novel written some 1200 years previously, Apuleius's *Golden Ass* – the eponymous ass even getting a small walk-on part in *Decameron*, V. 10, accidentally trampling the fingers of the young lover who hides in a chicken-coop from his mistress's homosexual husband. G. H. McWilliam notes that the tale 'is probably set in Perugia because of the town's homophile reputation', but the modern reader would never think to question the setting, hypnotized as we are into accepting Boccaccio's free translation as an original text.[10] David Damrosch has argued that world literature is 'an elliptical refraction of national literatures; world literature is writing that gains in translation; world literature is not a set canon of texts but a mode of reading... works become world literature by being received *into* the space of another culture'.[11] The *Decameron* qualifies here on several grounds: not only does it continue to gain in translation, but before it was ever translated it already gained much, as an original text, from its author's own creative reading and translation skills.

Boccaccio's early translators: rewriting, reshaping, compiling

Adaptation or rewriting, rather than straight translation, was the main channel through which European readers got to know Boccaccio. At first, his Latin compilations had a longer reach than his vernacular works, as few foreign writers or readers knew Tuscan. In English, the direct transmission of his vernacular started with Chaucer, who visited Italy more than once. Herbert G. Wright comments on

> the wonderful good fortune for English literature that its first great poet was sent on missions in the course of which he could hear the tongue of Boccaccio and obtain the manuscripts of the *Teseida* and the *Filostrato* which inspired the *Knightes Tale* and *Troilus and Criseyde*. But it was not until the sixteenth century was well advanced that a greater proficiency in Italian became more usual, though even then French still served as an intermediary.[12]

Although Chaucer's *Troilus and Criseyde* owes a subterranean debt to Dante's poetry (and includes some memorable lines from Petrarch), its main plot structure comes from Boccaccio's *Filostrato*, which itself is largely a refashioning of episodes from the *Roman de Troie* by the twelfth-century French poet Benoît de Sainte-Maure. Shakespeare and others later took up the story. Freedom in developing the *Filostrato* from its Boccaccian version is licensed by the fact that its core goes back at least to Homer's *Iliad*, more than two millennia before Boccaccio. Translation fits into a long line of transmission.

In the *Canterbury Tales*, Chaucer uses Petrarch's Latin version as an intermediate text when he takes the 'Clerk's Tale' from *Decameron*, x. 10, while his 'Knight's Tale' and 'Franklin's Tale' are particularly brilliant examples of creative adaptation based directly on Boccaccian vernacular texts. The 'Knight's Tale' is masterfully condensed from Boccaccio's immensely long *Teseida* (which had to wait until 1974 for its first complete translation into English), while the 'Franklin's Tale' is an enhanced reworking of a story that Boccaccio told twice: in his early *Filocolo* and in *Decameron*, x. 6. Chaucer's version is better than either, as it invents a powerful narrative 'lock' between the wife's concern for her husband and her wish to stave off her aspiring lover: no longer does the lover merely have to hire a magician to conjure up a May garden in January to win his lady's favours (the magic garden being admittedly a neat metaphor, as far as it goes). Instead, the lover's magician must conjure away the black rocks that threaten the husband's safe return by ship after a long and troubling absence. The psychological ramifications of that change may resonate with the modern reader more than with Chaucer's contemporaries; but a little anachronism is traditional when reading translations, and meanings are gained as well as lost over time. In the 'Franklin's Tale', Chaucer's enterprising approach to plot design is not unlike Boccaccio's attitude to some of his own sources, which he lays out anew with the aplomb of a Hollywood script doctor; indeed W. P. Ker suggested that 'the intuition of the right lines of the story was what Chaucer learned from Boccaccio'.[13] (Chaucer, oddly, never acknowledged any debts to Boccaccio.)

Of course this sense of freedom to adapt and develop the source material is very far from the normal practice of a modern translator, but as Jean Delisle and Judith Woodsworth point out, 'for Chaucer, as for other early vernacular writers, there was an overlap between translation, compilation, rewriting and original authorship'.[14] The same is true of Boccaccio, who could be categorized not just as a creative writer, but as an encyclopaedist, a mediator and, to quote Kenneth Clarke, 'a man whose laudable *intentio* is to provide relief and enjoyment to women . . . as *compilator*, rather than author of the original tales'.[15] And when translating a compilation, especially one carrying important ideological messages, the translator may feel some responsibility to reshape the story, to revisit the original compiler's sources in order to amplify the information content. Things that we might relegate to introductions or footnotes could thus be woven into the text.

Laurent de Premierfait and John Lydgate: amplification, national perspectives, translation through intermediate versions

Invention, enlargement, and enhancement can become a legitimate, even essential, part of the translator's task. Some late medieval translation processes have recently been brought out in Hedeman's study of Boccaccio's first French translator, Laurent de Premierfait, who produced two distinct versions, in 1400 and 1409, of *De casibus virorum illustrium*, Boccaccio's Latin compilation concerning famous men overtaken by disaster. Laurent's translation was made for aristocratic patrons, who saw *De casibus* as a history packed with moral teachings peculiarly relevant to the lives and (sometimes precarious) fortunes of minor French royalty. Laurent's work later migrated across the English Channel, being used as raw material for John Lydgate's *Fall of Princes*.

While suppressing some original paratexts, Laurent personalized Boccaccio's book by emphasizing its historical coverage 'from Adam and Eve to King John the Good of France, . . . father of Duke John of Berry, the man for whom the text was made'.[16] Boccaccio's original *De casibus* ended (IX. 27. 3) with the recent downfall of the same King John II, captured at the Battle of Poitiers (1356) by the marauding English – a useless, cowardly and worthless crew ('ab Anglis, inertissimis atque pavidis et nullius valoris hominibus'; p. 866) – and deported to London as a prisoner of his enemy King Edward. The brief reference in the original was enthusiastically expanded by Laurent, the English now being charged with appalling inhumanity, as Nigel Mortimer notes:

> Their infamous character ('des angloys hommes faillis et vains & de nulle valleur') is carefully translated, but John II's compatriot strengthens the account with the addition of a lengthy description of the battle of Poitiers, of the captivity of the king, and of the payment of the ransom . . . The whole concludes with an energetic assertion that John was shamefully murdered at the hands of his English captors.[17]

Laurent's English confrère, John Lydgate, does not agree, and twits 'Bochas' for not having attended the battle to fight on behalf of his beloved King

John. Lydgate's *Fall of Princes*, written in the 1430s, supersizes Boccaccio's reasonably concise prose work into possibly the longest poem in the English language (36365 lines); it enjoyed wide circulation and prestige (though modern critics have been unkind) and was apparently believed by many readers to be a direct translation from Boccaccio's Latin, not from French.[18]

Laurent had set out not just to translate *De casibus* as it stood, but also to flesh out some stories that Boccaccio had summarized so briefly that 'he scarcely puts in anything but the names' (Translator's Prologue, 9).[19] Drawing on the same ancient historians whom Boccaccio used, Laurent will repair the gaps that Boccaccio had left, not out of ignorance or indolence (Laurent hastens to add) but

> because he had them so promptly in hand and so firmly in memory, he assumed they were as common and well known to others as to himself. Thus in order that the book will have all its parts and be complete in itself, I will put them down briefly without deviating much from the text of the author.
>
> (Translator's Prologue, 10)[20]

Amplification, then, is not falsification but scrupulous restoration, using original materials, to give a more complete account to the work's new audience. The idea that Boccaccio's brevity could have been aimed at artistic balance does not seem to have occurred to Laurent, but his refusal to fetishize an untouchable original might appeal to our relativistic age.

Once the translator has made good those gaps that were purely related to the book's original readership, the text will be as clear to the new audience as it might have been in its own time. This recalls the late Eugene Nida's idea that a communicative translation should follow the principle of equivalent effect, or 'dynamic equivalence', where the new version

> aims at complete naturalness of expression, and tries to relate the receptor to modes of behavior relevant within the context of his own culture; it does not insist that he understand the cultural patterns of the source-language context in order to comprehend the message.[21]

Such 'dynamic equivalence' also describes the cultural and political agenda that Hedeman discerns in the manuscripts translated or overseen by Laurent, whose amplifications, both visual and textual, 'claimed the history of the Bible and of antiquity (most notably the history of Rome) as a prehistory of France'.[22]

Boccaccio's French reputation grew throughout the fifteenth century, when (to quote Patricia Gathercole) readers 'could enjoy in French six books of Boccaccio: *De Claris, De Casibus, Decameron, De Genealogia Deorum, Il Filostrato, La Teseide*, and also the stories of Griseldis and Ghismonda'.[23]

We notice that the most popular stand-alone stories from the *Decameron* foregrounded Boccaccio's solemn side.

The translator of the complete *Decameron* was once again Laurent de Premierfait, whose prologue contains a striking admission: as a Frenchman born and bred he lacks full knowledge of the Florentine language, so he made an arrangement with a Franciscan friar, Antonio from Arezzo, well versed in both his mother tongue and Latin. Antonio provided, for a suitable fee, a complete intermediate translation (now lost) of the *Decameron* from Florentine to Latin. The French translator's role is therefore a secondary or subsequent one, although he took the liberty of expanding where the original was too concise.[24]

More than 100 years later, Queen Marguerite of Navarre commissioned a new French *Decameron* from her secretary Antoine Le Maçon (1545), and subsequently cited Boccaccio at the start of her own *Heptaméron*, a related collection of stories in which she enriched the *novella* tradition with some compelling female perspectives that not even Boccaccio, with all his appreciation of women, had imagined.

Consuming the *Decameron*: all at once or bit by bit?

Apart from the different approaches to translation and transmission, already noted, we should also be aware of two contrasting visions of the *Decameron* that appear across the centuries, in Italy and abroad. The book can either be swallowed whole, or readers may sample individual stories or sequences. England got its first complete version in 1620, based partly on Le Maçon's French translation, and partly on Salviati's censored Counter-Reformation edition (1582); the English translator added some anti-Papist propaganda.[25] Other 'complete' editions followed: the anonymous 1702 and 1741 versions, some offshoots of these, and the Victorian version by W. K. Kelly (1855). These full English Boccaccios were pockmarked with censorship, religious and sexual material being rigorously pruned. McWilliam catalogues some of the weirder cuts, shrewdly remarking that as erotic and profane aspects of Boccaccio were toned down for centuries, his enduring popularity can hardly be attributed to those features.[26] The censorious holes were finally plugged by the truly complete but magniloquently inaccessible translation by John Payne (1886). Payne's addiction to archaic diction, his snobbish marketing style, and the eye-watering price he charged for his limited edition, still conspired to keep the unexpurgated *Decameron* out of common circulation.[27]

The other main approach to the book has involved selective anthologizing. Tales are often grouped in a purposeful way, their selection and wording being dictated by the aims of the publication. Painter's *Palace of Pleasure* (1561) presented sixteen representative (and mostly respectable) Decameronian *novelle*. The first issue of *Playboy* magazine (1953) offered nude photographs of Miss Marilyn Monroe and 'a humorous tale of adultery' from the *Decameron*, while a Stakhanovite *Playboy* employee 'screened submissions, edited those chosen for publication, wrote photo captions and subscription pitches, reviewed books and movies, and "retold" Ribald Classics from Boccaccio and Balzac'.[28] There is enough variety in the *Decameron* to offer any anthologist a choice of suitable tales, and many readers will have encountered their first Boccaccio tale as a single sample, having no way of knowing how typical that story might be.

Individual stories develop their own separate lines of transmission and readership. Petrarch himself had canonized Boccaccio's Griselda by Latinizing her. Other early favourites included Titus and Gisippus (X. 8), a tale that some today might find tedious, and Ghismonda's tragic suicide (IV. 1). In all, between the fourteenth and sixteenth centuries, there were thirty-eight Latin and thirty-one vernacular Italian rewritings of individual tales from the *Decameron*.[29] In Victorian England, Griselda became a girl's name, and featured in children's literature, such as *The Cuckoo Clock* (1877) and *The Child's Own Book* (1901) by Mrs Molesworth.

Even when the full book was available in translation, readers were still free to make their own choice of stories to retell, in the same language or another. In the mid-nineteenth century, someone left an English *Decameron* on a small island off the west coast of Ireland, and within a few years individual tales were circulating orally in the Irish language, adapted to local circumstances. Instead of Andreuccio travelling from Perugia to the horse fair in Naples, only to fall into bad company and end up stealing the dead bishop's ring (II. 5), Seán na dTubaiste visits Tralee, an Irish country town somewhat smaller than Naples, for a similar adventure. Some decades later, a Danish linguist found a variant of the same story on another Irish-speaking island.[30] Using Damrosch's definition, these are instances of 'world literature' in the making – a work, or a fragment thereof, being received into the space of another culture.

Translating Boccaccio today

Since the 1890s, according to Guyda Armstrong, Boccaccio's reception in English falls into two distinct strands: the erotic Boccaccio (including a multitude of popular and expensive illustrated editions) and the scholarly Boccaccio (extending from J. M. Rigg's 1903 translation up to the modern 'classic' editions).[31] Several trends have dictated the recent flowering of Boccaccio translations (not just the *Decameron*), including the growing academic book market, the need to study translations in cross-disciplinary academic courses, the growing acceptability of translation as a form of PhD research, the activities of niche publishers like Garland of New York, and the marketing of world literary classics by general trade publishers. Admirable bibliographical surveys by F. S. Stych, Armstrong, and Robin Healey document how partial or fragmentary translations gave way to complete annotated translations of major Boccaccio texts, produced by twentieth-century scholars.[32] Particularly towards the end of the century, works that had never appeared in English, or were available in antiquated versions, were translated afresh, sometimes more than once: Bernadette Marie McCoy's *Ameto* (1971) 'versus' Judith Serafini-Sauli's *Ameto* (1985); McCoy's *Teseida* (1974) 'versus' Vincenzo Traversa's *Teseida* (2002); *De mulieribus claris* by Guido Guarino (1963) 'versus' Virginia Brown (2001); the *Corbaccio* by Anthony K. Cassell (1975) 'versus' Normand R. Cartier (1977); the *Fiammetta* by Mariangela Causa-Stendler and Thomas Mauch (1990) 'versus' Roberta L. Payne and Alexandra Hennessey Olson (1992); and the whole *Filocolo* translated by Rocco Carmelo Blasi (1974) and again by Donald Cheney with Thomas G. Bergin (1985) – although the thirteen questions of love had been extracted from the *Filocolo* and translated into English several times before then. Apart from choice, these academic translations offer some fine examples of scholarly collaboration and research: for example, the *Caccia di Diana* translated by Anthony K. Cassell and Victoria Kirkham (1991).

Commercial publishers, meanwhile, produced multiple *Decameron*s, mostly translated by academics. Penguin Classics commissioned Harry McWilliam, both of whose editions (1972, 1995) provided valuable scholarly material and a well-modulated text. New American Library's translation by Peter Bondanella and Mark Musa (1982) has gone through several well-received paperback reprints; the translators have left perceptive comments on problems in rendering Boccaccio's speech varieties, for example, their argument against ill-judged archaism.[33] Oxford's choice (1993) was Guido Waldman, a London publishing executive and novelist, who had translated classic and contemporary texts from Italian, French, and Spanish; his lively text was accompanied by an incisive introduction and notes by Jonathan Usher. Oneworld Classics (2008) chose J. G. Nichols, poet, critic, and prizewinning translator of Italian texts from Dante to Lampedusa; this eloquent version (published with support from the Italian Ministry of Foreign Affairs) is issued in America by Random House, and should achieve wide and sustained circulation. My own *Decameron* version for Wordsworth Classics of World Literature (2004) was based on John Payne's 1886 text. This text had been reissued many times, and had been re-edited and copiously annotated by Charles S. Singleton for a handsome three-volume edition from the University of California Press (1982). Singleton's editing had, however, tended towards the archaic, and I felt there was room for a complete rewrite.

With all these texts available, critics may debate which translation is best, or we might simply enjoy the coincidence of so many possible versions, each with its own distinctive take on the original. (For commercial and copyright reasons, we rarely get this multifaceted perspective on contemporary foreign authors.) The new translator may, however, feel constrained by the proliferation of existing versions. The craft of translation is always constrained – perhaps more so now than it was 600 years ago. Free adaptation is no longer accepted if you call your work a translation, and accuracy is subject to stern cross-checking. With Boccaccio, the usual dilemmas – whether to prioritize formal faithfulness or communicability; how to match differences of tone in the original with comparable gaps in the translation; how to map original sentence and paragraph structures on to equivalent English rhythms; how to compensate inevitable translation losses with potential translation gains; how to do jokes and other effects that must trigger immediate reader reactions – are complicated by the antiquity and status of the source text, and the presence of so many competing versions. To consult one's competitors, or not? To annotate, or not? (Classic texts tend to be annotated. Fun reading tends not to be.) To illustrate, or not? (The Internet affects this decision.) To censor, or not? (Censorship is evil – but Boccaccio himself sometimes preferred to communicate through sly half-references.) Most crucial of all, whether to update Boccaccio's language: should his book appear contemporary with its own time or contemporary with ours? There is no simple right answer to these questions; one can only aspire to consistency and self-awareness.

Paratexts and story titles

In the 'Translator's Note' prefacing his Oxford *Decameron*, Guido Waldman states that just as Boccaccio's avowed purpose in writing the stories was to provide solace and entertainment, 'my principal aim in translating them for the English-speaking reader has been to convey the pleasure and the vigour of good story-telling' (p. xxxiii). One of Waldman's distinctive translation choices involves altering the rubrics introducing some stories, so that the ending is not given away. In deference to contemporary tastes, this alteration preserves the element of surprise, at the cost of altering Boccaccio's emphasis on how the story is told, rather than leaving the reader to wonder what it will contain. Certainly Boccaccio's procedure is odd and deflating by our standards of storytelling, but it also forms part of his defence of the book in the author's conclusion, when he argues that no-one is forced unwittingly to read an indecent story (Conclusion, 18–19) as (to quote Waldman's translation) 'to avoid leading anyone astray, each story is introduced by a description of what lies hidden within it.'[34] Boccaccio expressed this through a bodily metaphor whereby one almost has to look these fair and ladylike *novelle* in the eye: 'tutte nella fronte portan segnato quello che esse dentro dal loro seno nascose tengono' ('each of the stories bears on its brow the gist of that which it hides in its bosom': Conclusion, 19; trans. by McWilliam (1995), p. 801).

Other modern translators give the full descriptive title for each story. McWilliam, for example, repeats the descriptive titles in the list of contents at the start of the book, while the Nichols contents page only mentions days, somewhat detracting from the reader's thematic overview of the stories. I myself followed a hybrid procedure, whereby each story carries Boccaccio's informative description at its head, but the list of contents offers a one-phrase summary of what the story is about. These are personal interpretations, delivered in the style of a cinema strapline: Day VIII is headed 'tricks by women on men, men on women, men on men' and includes such stories as 'A mercenary soldier and a mercenary wife', 'The preposterous cleric and the ugly maid', 'A judge debagged', 'Conjugal love outside the box', and 'A Florentine merchant outwits a shady lady from Palermo'. These glib headings, reminiscent (I fear) of those proposed by Aldo Busi in his intralingual 'translation', are best appreciated after reading the stories, and could conceivably serve as a mnemonic device for locating tales that have been found enjoyable.[35]

Why keep translating Boccaccio?

It can be amusing, and conducive to a genuine understanding of Boccaccio's original, to compare some *Decameron* passages across various English versions to see how different translators convey aspects of the writing. For example, how many versions catch the link between the heavy punishment faced by the randy young monk (I. 4), and the heavy weight that causes the heavyweight abbot to position himself beneath the girl rather than on top of her? Which Ghismonda do you see as she launches into her fatal speech (IV. 1)? Rigg's Ghismonda (first published 1903): 'Wherefore, not as a woman stricken with grief or chidden for a fault, but unconcerned and unabashed, with tearless eyes, and frank and utterly dauntless mien, thus answered she her father'? Or Waldman's (1993): 'So there was nothing of the broken-hearted maiden, no hangdog expression in Ghismonda, indeed she looked unconcerned and indomitable, dry-eyed, straightforward, totally in control as she replied to her father'?[36] How should we question our own personal inner translations of the scene? For a third example, in describing his servant Guccio, Friar Onyon in the 1620 text rivals Boccaccio's original with a fine rhythmic outburst (VI. 10. 17):

> Boyes I have knowne, and seene,
> And heard of many:
> But,
> For Lying, Loytring, Lazinesse,
> For Facing, Filching, Filthinesse;
> For Carelesse, Gracelesse, all Unthriftinesse,
> My Boy excelleth any.[37]

Are such effects available to the modern translator? Here is the Nichols version (2008): 'I shall tell you: he is lazy and lying and dirty; disobedient, unhelpful and shirty; he is neglectful, forgetful and disrespectful.' How does this version reflect Boccaccio?[38]

Access to multiple translations allows foreign students to relativize Boccaccio's meanings and avoid accepting any one translation as the definitive text. Apart from the educational advantage, there are research possibilities: a digitized corpus of translations can be analysed to yield new understandings of language and translation. Cultural history is also served: the life of a classic involves being read, and if every translation is an act of reading as well as an act of writing, we gain a distinctive record of how a book was perceived at a given moment. In fact, perhaps the best argument for repeated translation is the one based on time. A translation of Boccaccio brings us into direct contact with the writer of the late Middle Ages whose sense of contemporary life is astonishingly vivid. When we read this through a translation made in our own day, the time lapse is clear and inescapable, forcing us to project ourselves back into another culture. If, however, we read a Victorian translation, we will spend more of our time trapped in a slightly different time-warp – very laudable if our purpose is to study Victorian culture, but not quite as useful if we wish to place ourselves in relation to the Middle Ages. One last psychic benefit of multiplicity may be extrapolated from a 'pluralist' argument put forward by Edith Grossman: 'Translation always helps us to know, to see from a different angle, to attribute new value to what once may have been unfamiliar. As nations and as individuals, we have a critical need for that kind of understanding and insight.'[39] More is better.

Subjectively speaking, there are many reasons to go on translating. Because it's there. Because we're paid. Because we feel some imagined affinity with the author or the text. Because we want to work alongside other translators, in a joint enterprise of transmission that goes back through our elders and betters to those whose versions have been lost, or those whose very names have been forgotten.

NOTES

1 Douglas Coupland, *Generation A* (London: Heinemann, paperback, 2010), p. 297.

2 Itamar Even-Zohar, 'The Position of Translated Literature within the Literary Polysystem', in *The Translation Studies Reader*, ed. by Lawrence Venuti, 3rd edn (London: Routledge, 2012), pp. 162–7.

3 H. G. Wright, *Boccaccio in England from Chaucer to Tennyson* (London: Athlone Press, 1957); G. H. McWilliam, 'Translator's Introduction', in Giovanni Boccaccio, *The 'Decameron'* (Harmondsworth: Penguin, 1972), pp. 21–43 (his revised introduction to the second edition of his Penguin translation (1995; repr. 2003) omits his pungent survey of previous translations); Guyda Armstrong, *The English Boccaccio: A History in Books* (Toronto: University of Toronto Press, 2013).

4 Roman Jakobson, 'On Linguistic Aspects of Translation', in *The Translation Studies Reader*, ed. by Venuti, pp. 126–31 (p. 127).

5 Aldo Busi, *Il Decamerone di Giovanni Boccaccio*, new edn (Milan: Rizzoli, 2010), p. 6.

6 More revisionist work now points to a wider readership than the merchant classes, for example: Marco Cursi, *Il 'Decameron': scritture, scriventi, lettori. Storia di un testo* (Rome: Viella, 2007).

7 Anne D. Hedeman, *Translating the Past: Laurent de Premierfait and Boccaccio's 'De Casibus'* (Los Angeles: J. Paul Getty Museum, 2008), p. 72.

8 Jonathan Usher, 'Introduction to Giovanni Boccaccio', in *The 'Decameron'*, trans. by Guido Waldman (Oxford: Oxford University Press, 1993), pp. xvi–xvii.

9 J. H. Whitfield, *A Short History of Italian Literature*, 2nd edn, rev. by J. R. Woodhouse (Manchester: Manchester University Press, 1980), p. 68.

10 *Decameron*, trans. by G. H. McWilliam, 2nd edn (Harmondsworth: Penguin Books, 1995), p. 836.

11 David Damrosch, *What is World Literature?* (Princeton: Princeton University Press, 2003), pp. 281, 283.

12 Wright, *Boccaccio in England*, pp. 479–80.

13 W. P. Ker, *Essays on Mediaeval Literature* (London: Macmillan, 1905), p. 69.

14 *Translators through History*, ed. by Jean Delisle and Judith Woodsworth, rev. edn (Amsterdam: John Benjamins/UNESCO, 2012), p. 61.

15 K. P. Clarke, 'A Good Place for a Tale: Reading the *Decameron* in 1358–1363', *Modern Language Notes*, 127 (2012), 65–84 (p. 83).

16 Hedeman, *Translating the Past*, p. 20.

17 Nigel Mortimer, *John Lydgate's 'Fall of Princes': Narrative Tragedy in its Literary and Political Contexts* (Oxford: Clarendon Press, 2005), p. 39.

18 Mortimer, *John Lydgate*, pp. 40, 1, 242.

19 *Laurent de Premierfait's 'Des cas des nobles hommes et femmes', Book I: Translated from Boccaccio, a Critical Edition Based on Six Manuscripts*, ed. by Patricia M. Gathercole (Chapel Hill: University of North Carolina Press, 1968), p. 90.

20 *Laurent de Premierfait's 'Des cas'*, ed. by Gathercole, p. 90; Hedeman, *Translating the Past*, p. 13.

21 Eugene Nida, 'Principles of Correspondence', in *Translation Studies Reader*, ed. by Venuti, pp. 141–55 (p. 144).

22 Hedeman, *Translating the Past*, p. 211.

23 Patricia M. Gathercole, 'The French Translators of Boccaccio', *Italica*, 46 (1969), 300–9 (pp. 307–8).

24 Hedeman, *Translating the Past*, pp. 13, 255, n. 21.

25 H. G. Wright, *The First English Translation of the 'Decameron' (1620)* (Uppsala: Lundequistska bokhandeln, 1953), pp. 41–6; McWilliam, 'Translator's Introduction' (1972), pp. 34–6.

26 McWilliam, 'Translator's Introduction" (1972), p. 42.

27 For the character of John Payne, prodigiously gifted linguist, logophile, minor poet, and miserable individual, see my 'Introduction' to Giovanni Boccaccio, *Decameron: A New English Version by Cormac Ó Cuilleanáin based on John Payne's 1886 Translation* (Ware: Wordsworth Editions, 2004), pp. liii–lxviii.

28 Steven Watts, *Mr Playboy: Hugh Hefner and the American Dream* (Hoboken, NJ: Wiley, 2008), pp. 72, 88.

29 Martin McLaughlin, 'Translation or Rewriting? Beroaldo's Version of *Decameron* x. 8', in *Caro Vitto: Essays in Memory of Vittore Branca*, ed. by Jill Kraye and Laura Lepschy, *The Italianist*, 27 (2007), Special Supplement 2, pp. 150–73 (p. 150), citing Michela Parma's exhaustive list of rewritings of *novelle*.

30 Ó Cuilleanáin, 'Introduction' to the Wordsworth Editions *Decameron*, pp. xlviii–liii.

31 Guyda Armstrong, 'Translations as Cultural "Facts": The History of Boccaccio in English', in *Translation: Transfer, Text and Topic*, ed. by Pierluigi Barrotta and Anna Laura Lepschy (Perugia: Guerra, 2012), pp. 53–67 (p. 61); and her *The English Boccaccio*. For all topics in the present essay, this book is the ideal *approfondimento*.

32 F. S. Stych, *Boccaccio in English: A Bibliography of Editions, Adaptions and Criticisms* (Westport, CT: Greenwood Press, 1995), now with web supplement to 2005 by Michael Buckland: http://people.ischool.berkeley.edu/~buckland/bocsupa.htm; Guyda Armstrong, 'A Bibliography of Boccaccio's Works in English Translation: Part I. The Minor Works', *Studi sul Boccaccio*, 38 (2010), 167–204; Robin Healey, *Italian Literature before 1900 in English Translation: An Annotated Bibliography 1929–2008* (Toronto: University of Toronto Press, 2011).

33 Quoted in Healey's compilation, *Italian Literature before 1900*, p. 537; and Peter Bondanella, 'Translating *The Decameron*', in *The Flight of Ulysses: Studies in Memory of Emmanuel Hatzantonis*, ed. by Augustus A. Mastri (Chapel Hill: Annali d'Italianistica, 1997), pp. 111–24.

34 Waldman, p. xxxiii; p. 685.

35 Armstrong quotes some snappy running headers from an edition of 1712 in *The English Boccaccio*: 'The feign'd Paralytick', 'The Dumb Gardner, 'The She-Hypocrite' (p. 229).

36 *Decameron*, trans. by Rigg (London: Navarre Society, [1921]), p. 269; *Decameron*, trans. by Waldman, p. 259.

37 *The 'Decameron'*, 2 vols (London: Isaac Jaggard, 1620), II, 14.

38 *Decameron*, trans. by J. G. Nichols (London: Oneworld Classics, 2008), p. 376.

39 Edith Grossman, *Why Translation Matters* (New Haven and London: Yale University Press, 2012), p. xi.

14

MASSIMO RIVA

Boccaccio beyond the text

The late medieval period: 'inter-expressivity' and material culture

Boccaccio belongs to that elite group of classic authors whose legacy transcends the written word. In the Conclusion to his masterpiece, the *Decameron*, Boccaccio writes: 'no less latitude should be granted to my pen than to the brush of the painter' – a sentence that can be read as both a straightforward defence of vernacular storytelling (a writer should have the same leeway as a painter) and a more subtle praise of the figurative power of words (Conclusion, 6; p. 799). In his introduction to the essential reference work about the visual dimension of Boccaccio's legacy, *Boccaccio visualizzato*, Vittore Branca speaks of 'interespressività' (or 'inter-expressivity') as an intrinsic feature of Boccaccio's literary art.[1] Trying to capture, in one short chapter, the whole range of this unique capacity to give tangible and colourful expression to human actions and passions, inspiring artists across centuries, cultures, and different media, is clearly impossible (Branca's *Boccaccio visualizzato* alone stretches over three hefty volumes). I will focus therefore on what might be considered as the main threads of a truly hypermedia tapestry.

Indeed, it is not too far-fetched to view the evolution of Boccaccio's *opus* as a 'trans-medial' phenomenon. Over the centuries, it has morphed through many stages of concretization and visualization, from manuscript to numerous printed editions, from miniature and etching to painting, from theatre to film and now the internet, all along adapting to the tastes of different audiences. The *Decameron* is indeed a living web of words, images, and other media, all radiating from its ideal centre: Boccaccio's text. From the evolutionary perspective of our contemporary media ecology, Horace's famous sentence describing his own poems, 'I have built a monument more lasting than bronze' (*Odes*, III. 30. 1) could perhaps be rephrased as: 'I have built a document more malleable than words.' This is precisely Boccaccio's achievement, again judging from the number of visualizers, imitators, emulators, or creative adapters who have taken inspiration from his writing. The evolution of this literary and visual corpus (which, of course, also includes the large, encyclopaedic body of Boccaccio criticism) began with Boccaccio himself and the first 'glossators' or commentators who wrote or drew on the margins of *Decameron* manuscripts (among the first of these being the copyist of MS Mn, Francesco d'Amaretto Mannelli, in 1384).[2]

In his introduction to *Boccaccio visualizzato*, Branca underlines the inter-expressive dimension already embedded in the first *Decameron* codices such as the Capponi and Hamilton manuscripts, generally considered the models with their drawings in the margins. This inter-expressivity is thus directly linked both to the work's narrative thrust and to its target audience.[3] This view has been recently reaffirmed by Richard F. Kuhns, who writes: '[Boccaccio's] assertions about painters and poets, his examples of poetic and painterly powers, construct an armature for the activity of storytelling' (p. 37).[4] Just as contemporary digital formats (blogs, tweets, etc.) shape the language in which they are written, Boccaccio's *novella*, as a cultural form, helped create a new vernacular literacy. The immediacy of the eloquent image and the mental decoding of silent reading (St Augustine) seem to find in it a common ground, an almost direct translation of the oral into the written word. According to Branca, Boccaccio's narrative force (stylistically confirmed by his visual glosses as the first illustrator of his own text, as shown in the autograph manuscripts of the *Teseida* and *Decameron*, among others) thus finds a direct parallel in the practical realization of the *biblia pauperum* and *laicorum litteratura*, the scenes from the Bible, the New Testament, or the lives of Saints (such as Jacopo da Voragine's *Legenda aurea*) illustrated by Giotto and his followers. In other words, the effort to give realistic expression to actions and gestures, through and in iconic and exemplary figures and colloquial storytelling, drives the inner dynamism of the *Decameron* text.[5] The catchword drawings of the Hamilton codex, a gallery of small, almost caricature-like cameo portraits, exemplify the work's key ideas (Fortune, Ingenuity) as well as the characters which are meant to embody or perform them, in an expressionistic vein which will further develop in the works of Chaucer and Rabelais, and flourish much later in the work of such modernist masters as James Joyce and Carlo Emilio Gadda.[6] The recent attribution to Boccaccio of a portrait of Homer drawn on the concluding flyleaf of the Toledo autograph manuscript of Dante's *Comedy* (Toledo, Biblioteca Capitular, Zelada 104. 6), confirms the important role of illustration in the complex web of authorial (self)-representation.

While at the end of the fourteenth century image and word still by and large belong to separate technical and artistic realms, Boccaccio's writings also contribute to the birth of a late-Gothic figurative tradition which departs from the Giotto–Michelangelo mainstream: a profane, fantastic, and mythological mode, appealing to the tastes of the new aristocracy (such as the Florentine Medici), whose main interpreters were Paolo Uccello, Ghirlandaio, and Sandro Botticelli. In this new phase, during which other works by Boccaccio (such as the *Teseida, Filocolo, De casibus,* and *De mulieribus*) enjoyed varied fortune, within the humanistic milieu and across the diversified European geography of book production, this 'other-Renaissance' line began to find concrete visual and social expression.[7]

Alongside a unique precious manuscript of the *Decameron,* such as the codex illuminated by Taddeo Crivelli for Teofilo Calcagnini (now Oxford, Bodleian Library, MS Holkham misc. 49), we thus have, in the same period in Italy, remarkable examples of Boccaccio in domestic art: the nuptial *cassoni* (dowry chests) and the *deschi da parto* (wooden birth trays), which played a utilitarian as well as celebratory role in commemorating a wedding and a child's birth.[8] These symbolic artefacts made reference to the 'fantastic' as well as to the 'moral' *Decameron*: the *novella* of Messer Torello, X. 9 (the *cassone* of the Cini collection at the Bargello); the *novella* of Alatiel, II. 7 (the *cassone* at the Museo Correr, in Venice); the *novella* of Ginevra, II. 9 (the *cassone* at the National Gallery of Scotland in Edinburgh); the *novella* of Griselda, X. 10 (Apollonio di Giovanni's *cassone* in the Este gallery in Modena); and the *novella* of Nastagio degli Onesti, V. 8, painted by Botticelli (the *spalliera* panels in the Prado Museum, in Madrid, perhaps the most famous of them all).[9] Together, they provide compelling evidence of the wide circulation and dissemination of Boccaccio's storytelling and its deep penetration within the social body and in material culture, particularly in Italy. In recent years, the systematic study of the manuscript and print tradition and reception has revised Branca's influential representation of the *Decameron* as a status symbol of a well-established mercantile class that recognizes in its stories its own epic world-view.[10] Within this modified perspective, the *cassoni* can perhaps also provide stylistic evidence of a more complex dialectic at work within a mercantile culture increasingly influenced by aristocratic aspirations.

Of these transmedial forms of visualization, perhaps none is more suggestive than the façade of the house in Stein am Rhein in the canton of Schaffhausen, Switzerland, painted with allegorical figures and references to *Decameron,* V. 6 and IV. 7 by Thomas Schmidt (1490–1550/60).[11] With this example, we move towards a tridimensional scenography, a new and concrete graphic interface – a kind of augmented reality which projects bi-dimensional book illustration, or the miniature tridimensionality of *cassoni* painting, from a private interior into a public, urban space. The façade of the Stein am Rhein house looks like the page of a thoroughly miniatured codex, only enlarged from the proportions of an object meant for a library or a bedroom, to those of an entire building – a public statement, indeed, and an example of architectural virtual reality. As evidence of the capacity of Boccaccio's art to interface with reality well beyond the confines of the printed word, the Stein am Rhein house also evokes, of course, a theatrical dimension. We will use this example of locative art as a historical springboard in order to jump to a period closer to us: the beginning of the late age of print, when the illustrated word was still the main cultural engine in the dissemination of Boccaccio's legacy. But as we shall see, it will slowly be displaced by other popular media.

Early modernity, multimedia revivals

In the period between the sixteenth and eighteenth centuries, illustrated editions and visualizations of the *Decameron* spread across an ever-expanding geographical area (Spain, France, Flanders and the Low Countries, Germany and England). Andreina Griseri has thoroughly outlined this itinerary in the modern age, showing how recurring topics or literary *topoi* correspond to the most widely illustrated *novelle*. The visual frequency of these stories provides evidence of which themes from Boccaccio's masterpiece struck the imagination of his readers. Let's take a cursory look. The *Decameron* frame-story, linked to the *topos* of the Garden of Love (as seen, for example, in the *Filocolo*) and its evolution into the garden in the Villa, providing a stark contrast to the City corrupted by the plague, provides the architectural and symbolic setting to many frontispiece illustrations. As we will see, the ideal microcosm of naturalistic storytelling will find widespread success in the Romantic period.

Let's focus, now, on some of the most representative *novelle*. In the iconographic popularity of the story of Cimon and Iphigenia (v. 1), from Rubens's nudes in the preparatory drawings of his painting now at the Kunsthistorisches Museum in Vienna, to the neoclassical paintings by Sir Joshua Reynolds and Angelica Kaufmann, we find a reference to another side of nature, the humanistic *topos* of the forest as the venue of an aesthetic revelation. Gazing at the naked body of Iphigenia, Cimon undergoes a metamorphosis from wild man and brute into a civilized human being, inspired by 'heroic furor' (Griseri, p. 168). In the story of Ghismonda (IV. 1), who affirms her right to choose freely her lover Guiscardo, only to succumb to her father's morbid jealousy, and dies pronouncing a most eloquent and moving indictment of patriarchal feudalism, we have the tragic theatre of the virtuous heroine represented in a series of exemplary illustrations, from Francesco Furini to William Hogarth. To these traditional humanistic topics, the somewhat more frivolous eighteenth-century tastes will add the suggestive 101st *novella* as retold by La Fontaine, *Les Oies de Frère Philippe* (Brother Philippe's Geese; Introduction to Day IV) in the lively Arcadian sketches by François Boucher and Nicolas Lancret. Finally, the dissemination of the book as a domestic object of (libertine) pleasure, a sort of 'pocket micro-stage' ('micro-palcoscenico tascabile') as Griseri puts it (p. 190), finds two different visual iconographies in Romain de Hooge's witty classicist 'close-ups', in his 1697 illustrations, and in the 1747 and 1757 Paris–London editions of the *Decameron*, illustrated by Hubert François Gravelot.

Throughout this time, the social life of the *Decameron* continues to develop in both a private and a public (or semi-public) dimension. Comedy, satire, and humanistic eloquence, as well as a form of aesthetic erotica, are part of its lasting appeal for aristocratic and bourgeois tastes alike. And again, the social penetration of Boccaccio's works is not limited to books, but extends also to other kinds of domestic objects, in which a playful dimension interfaces with a more symbolic or allegorical one: as, for example, in eighteenth-century Venetian playing cards which feature famous women, recalling the *De mulieribus* (Griseri, p. 197).

A parallel discourse can be extended to the performing arts; we will only mention here the singular fortune of Griselda, the enigmatic, Job-like heroine of *Decameron*, X. 10. A recent international symposium explored the wide European dissemination of Griselda's story (in versions often more indebted to Petrarch's humanist and Christian interpretation than Boccaccio's more ambiguous treatment): from her Parisian debut in 1395 (*Istoire de Griseldis*) to her appearances in a Tuscan *sacra rappresentazione* in the fifteenth century, then in German drama (from Hans Sachs to Gerhart Hauptmann) and Spanish drama (Lope de Vega), and in various tragedies and tragicomedies from the Baroque and Elizabethan age up to the Napoleonic age, in Italy, Poland, and Russia.[12] Within this context, we should note Griselda's particular popularity in eighteenth-century Venetian melodrama, when Apostolo Zeno's libretto (1701) was set to music by Antonio Pollarolo, and later by Alessandro Scarlatti, Tommaso Albinoni, Giovanni Bononcini, and finally, Antonio Vivaldi, after a young and inexperienced Carlo Goldoni revised the libretto for him in 1735.[13]

It is not by chance that literary adaptations and visual interpretations of Boccaccio's work surge again during the medieval revival in the Romantic period. The transmediality of Boccaccio's prose is a major source of inspiration for the English Romantics, in their re-imagination of the past. Here's how Samuel Taylor Coleridge presents his own idyllic vision of the Garden of Boccaccio (1828):

> Like Flocks adown a newly-bathed Steep
> Emerging from a mist: or like a Stream
> Of music soft that not dispels the Sleep,
> But casts in happier moulds the Slumberer's Dream,
> Gaz'd by an idle Eye with silent might
> The Picture stole upon my inward Sight.
>
> (lines 19–24)[14]

The *brigata* in the garden is one of the most suggestive representations of the period, as shown by Franz Xavier Winterhalter's painting *The Decameron* (1837): the frame-story becomes the daydream of another place, another time, in which a group of refined young people, men and women, share a cultural, fashionable, and aesthetic utopia.[15] As for the erotic-comic or satirical ambivalence of Boccaccio's legacy, perhaps the most representative case is the continuing popularity of the neoclassical *novella* of Cimon and Iphigenia, which a young John Everett Millais paints in 1847–8, just before embracing Keats and the Pre-Raphaelite brotherhood. The well-known story, adapted into English verse by Dryden and later performed on stage by the great actor David Garrick in the leading role, had already been a subject chosen by major painters such as Rubens, Reynolds, and Benjamin West. A later rendition by F. L. Leighton (1884), however, makes clear the somewhat subversive appeal that this story had for the Victorian mind: 'the parable of beauty soothing the savage breast inverts the standard Victorian cultural myth (painted by Burne-Jones and others) of Sleeping Beauty in which a man awakens a young woman to sexuality and adulthood; in this case, the woman's beauty', portrayed in the sensual fashion of Ingres's odalisque, 'causes a radical change, a metamorphosis, in the male figure in the story'.[16] Evidently, the power of love has a somewhat ambivalent meaning for sixteenth- and seventeenth-century humanists and Romantic and late Romantic artists.

Of the poetic remakes of Boccaccio's prose, none is more famous than John Keats's *Isabella, or The Pot of Basil* (1818), a rewriting of the sombre and macabre tale told in *Decameron*, IV. 5, in which Lisabetta's secret, lower-class lover, Lorenzo, is killed and buried by her brothers, and where she develops a fatal fetishistic attachment to his head, severed from his corpse and kept in a flower pot that she waters with her tears. Even in Keats's poem, Romantic love and social critique are both present. Notoriously, George

Bernard Shaw claimed that Keats's virulent indictment of the cruel brothers' capitalist exploitation in stanzas XIV–XVIII anticipated Karl Marx.[17] Perhaps a trace of this is detectable in the painting *Isabella* (1848) by the young John Everett Millais, now in the Walker Art Gallery in Liverpool, a somewhat ominous banquet scene inspired by the story setting.[18] The Pre-Raphaelites were particularly enthralled by Keats, as shown in a series of other paintings, including William Holman Hunt's *Isabella and the Pot of Basil* (1867), now in the Laing Art Gallery in Newcastle-upon-Tyne, inspired by the fifty-third stanza of Keats's poem. This painting makes visually explicit the mixture of erotic 'orientalism' and melancholic naturalism (obviously also indebted to the 'other-Renaissance' of Botticelli and co.) which informs most of the Pre-Raphaelite re-imaging of Boccaccio's Renaissance.[19]

Among the many other paintings and illustrations inspired by this tale and Keats's rewriting of it between the end of the nineteenth and the beginning of the twentieth century, we can mention those by the late Pre-Raphaelites John Melhuish Strudwick (1879) and J. H. Waterhouse (1907); the American symbolist painter John White Alexander (1897), and Arthur Trevethin Nowell (1904); and the edition illustrated by W. J. Neatby (1899). The subject was also painted by women artists such as Henrietta Ratcliffe Rae and Mary Lizzie Macomber (1908). Isabella's portrait by Hunt follows in the footsteps of Dante Gabriele Rossetti's *Bocca baciata* (1859), a female portrait which marks Rossetti's turn to a more voluptuous, Venetian (Titianesque) rather than Florentine, Botticelli-inspired imagery.[20] Its title is a quote from Boccaccio's longest tale, the proverb which seals Alatiel's adventures (with a happy ending) in *Dec.*, II. 7. 122: 'Bocca baciata non perde ventura, anzi rinuova come fa la luna' (A kissed mouth doesn't lose its freshness: like the moon it turns up new again'; pp. 147–8). We can take Alatiel's proverb as a leitmotif also for Boccaccio's alternate fortunes and misfortunes in the transition to another form of visualization, and popularization, of his fictional world at the turn of the twentieth century.

Boccaccio's stardust: the *Decameron* and the moving image

If we look back over the history of cinematic adaptations of the *Decameron*, we find the erotic component increasingly prevails over all others, in quantity, if not in quality. Yet, this prevalence of the 'decamerotic' theme (as the genre came to be known a few decades later) does not apply to Boccaccio's presence in early cinema. At a time when cinema was trying to gain respect as both a legitimate art form and a form of popular pedagogy by adapting classic works from national traditions (Dante and Shakespeare, for example), two of the Boccaccian main ingredients, eros and satire, were too risqué for the times. Only comedy and romance fared well, within certain limits. This situation lasted into the period between the two world wars in Italy. The Fascist regime in power at that time was certainly sympathetic to the mining of historic periods for the purposes of popular culture (we need only think of its attempts to cloak itself in the trappings of the Roman Empire), but the Fascist idea of the Middle Ages was dependent on an ideologically strict and morally stern message (the age of communes viewed through a proto-nationalist perspective), which left no room for bawdy Boccaccio.

During the silent era in Italy, if we ignore the slightly futurist plot of the bizarre *Il telefono nel Medioevo* (Telephone in the Middle Ages, 1907), the only adaptations we find are *Una novella di Boccaccio* (aka *Boccaccio*, 1910?), *Decamerone* (1912), and *Il Decamerone* (1921).[21] We do not know much about *Una novella di Boccaccio* (A Story by Boccaccio) also produced in Turin by Ernesto Maria Pasquali (the director of *Il telefono*), other than its definition as a comedy. Of the first *Decamerone* (1912), directed by Gennaro Righelli (also the film's star) and produced by Vesuvius Films of Naples, we know that it was somewhat more ambitious and included three *novelle*: the classic Neapolitan tale of Andreuccio da Perugia (II. 5), the *novella* of the count of Antwerp (II. 8), and the *novella* of the groom and King Agilulf (III. 2). The stories were presented within a framework thus described in the extant materials: 'During an elegant gathering of ladies and gentlemen, three guests read three stories from Boccaccio which create the three episodes of the film, each exemplifying a genre: the comic, the dramatic and the farcical.'[22] The film is a clear example of how early cinema based its exploration of different genres on the literary and theatrical tradition: Boccaccio's prose, in its episodic structure, encompassed them all. Another interesting example of adaptation between the two world wars is a musical film made in Nazi Germany in 1936, *Liebesgeschichten von Boccaccio* (Love-stories from Boccaccio), aka *Boccaccio*; a clip from the film is visible on the internet, a sort of Fred Astaire–Ginger Rogers singing–dancing number on a set which resembles the *loggia* of a Renaissance palace.[23] To conclude this very short treatment of Boccaccio's limited fortune in early cinema, we should at least mention one further curiosity: *Boccaccio's Liebesnächte* (Boccaccio's Love Nights; Austria–Italy, 1920), aka *Boccaccio*, directed by the Hungarian director Michael Kertesz, who later moved to Hollywood, where, as Michael Curtiz, he directed *Casablanca*.

The erotic theme begins to impose itself definitively in the cinema of the post-Second World War period. One early example is *Decameron Nights*, produced by RKO Films in 1953 and directed by the Argentinian director

Hugo Fregonese. The plot of this caper movie features Boccaccio (Louis Jourdan, in his first Hollywood starring-role) who, in pursuit of his beloved Fiammetta (Joan Fontaine), arrives in the country villa where she has taken refuge from the plague. Here, he is asked to entertain a merry *brigata* with his storytelling. A 'pursuit of love' begins in which Boccaccio and Fiammetta take turns in telling three stories, only to displease one another. The episodes are respectively based on *Decameron*, II. 10 (Ricciardo and Paganino, told by Boccaccio, with Fontaine in the role of the elderly Ricciardo's unhappy younger wife, Bartolomea, and Jourdan playing the pirate Paganino who kidnaps her and makes her happy); *Decameron*, II. 9 (told by Fiammetta, with Jourdan in the role of Giulio-Ambruogiuolo, who deceives Bernabò about the infidelity of his wife Ginevra, played by Fontaine, only to be unmasked by her, after various adventures); and *Decameron*, III. 9 (told by Boccaccio, with Fontaine in the role of Gilette of Narbonne, who cures the King of France and is rewarded with the hand of the playboy Bertrand of Roussillon, played by Jourdan). This story also inspired William Shakespeare's *All's Well That Ends Well*, another example of the broad appeal of Boccaccio's storytelling across the centuries. In the movie, as in the book, Bertrand first repudiates Gilette, issuing her what seems like an impossible challenge, only to be outwitted and conquered by her after she sleeps with him in the guise of a maid he wants to seduce (who is played in the movie by Joan Collins), stealing his ring and bearing his child along the way, as Bertrand had challenged her to do. The happy ending of this 'daring romance', as a contemporary advertisement described it, shows Boccaccio and Fiammetta finally putting aside their quarrels and embracing each other.

Even a brief history of cinematic adaptations of Boccaccio must establish a clear distinction between the only authorial adaptation worthy of its title, Pier Paolo Pasolini's *Decamerone* (1971), and the anarchic, anything-goes adaptations, typical of Italian comedy of the 1960s and 1970s (the 'Decamerotica' genre). The latter tends to use the *Decameron* merely as a pretext for titillation, although there are exceptions, including *Boccaccio 70*, based on an idea by Cesare Zavattini and comprising four uneven but nevertheless interesting episodes by major directors of the time (Mario Monicelli, Federico Fellini, Luchino Visconti, and Vittorio De Sica). The *Boccaccio 70* episodes do not adapt any specific *novella* from Boccaccio's book, but adapt instead the spirit of Boccaccio to the Italy of the so-called economic boom (the film came out in 1962). Pasolini's film, instead, is an entirely different story.

More than an adaptation, Pasolini's *Decamerone* is both a transformative remake and an original, critical interpretation of its model, with strong, albeit somewhat arbitrary, links to the philological tradition of mimesis (their arbitrary nature is in fact a hallmark of Pasolini's versatile creative personality as a poet, filmmaker, and critic).[24] Inspired by Gramsci's ideas about popular culture and the revival of those ideas in 1960s ethnological studies such as those by Ernesto De Martino, Pasolini's screenplay eliminates the *brigata* frame-story entirely, with its idealized aesthetic setting, which was so integral to early modern aristocratic-bourgeois visualizations. Instead, Pasolini replaces the frame-story with a double frame, featuring the story of Ser Ciappelletto (I. 1), in the first half of the film, and Giotto (VI. 5) and 'Giotto's disciple' in the second, perhaps in order to emphasize the ambivalent personality of the artist as a representative of humankind. (Pasolini himself acts in the role of both Giotto and 'Giotto's disciple' and his *alter ego* actor, Sergio Citti, plays Ciappelletto). The artist's dark side is represented by Ciappelletto, a murderer, a thief, and a liar, in short the ugliest man who ever lived (notoriously described by Boccaccio also as a homosexual: 'Of women he [i.e. Ciappelletto] was as fond as dogs are fond of a good, stout stick; in their opposite, he took greater pleasure than the most depraved man on earth': I. 1. 14; p. 26), and the artist's bright side is represented instead by Giotto, the keen observer of reality, full of empathy, humanity, and wit, capable of laughing (like Boccaccio) at a joke mocking his own ugliness, and able to conjure up the most spiritual of visions. Pasolini's *Decamerone* sets the book in a southern framework and is above all a subversive rediscovery of the erotic charge of popular Mediterranean culture: a playful translation of the Florentine vernacular world of Boccaccio into Neapolitan, Sicilian, and Pugliese dialect, accompanied by popular songs and figuratively based on a dual vision inspired by northern and southern masters, Brueghel along with Giotto. This joyous rediscovery, however, was later rejected by Pasolini himself, who disavowed his whole *Trilogy of Life* (including his cinematic appropriations of *The Canterbury Tales* and the *Arabian Nights*) when he became convinced that, in the media-saturated environment of the 1970s, the so-called 'sexual revolution' was no more than a side-effect of the neo-capitalist commodification of the body.[25]

In an ironic confirmation of Pasolini's pessimistic view, the proliferation of *Decamerotica* reaches astonishing proportions around this time, peaking in the year immediately following the release of Pasolini's film, but extending its reach well into the 1990s. It should be remembered that Pasolini's *Decameron* was passed by Italy's censorship committee (with some obligatory cuts), but then received more than eighty denunciations for 'offence to public morality' and obscenity. Its final release constituted a victory for free artistic expression and opened the gates for the immediate flood of exploitative by-products, which had almost nothing to do with artistic expression: as Michele Giordano and Daniele Aramu write in their *La commedia erotica italiana: vent'anni di cinema sexy made in Italy* (Rome: Gremese, 2000), in 1972 alone, thirty-one 'soft porn' *Decameron* films were produced, thirteen in 1973, five in 1974, one in 1975. The trend quickly fizzled out, and yet the erotic comedy genre continued to flourish, moving from a medieval to other settings, as in one example that might be worth remembering: *The Black Decameron*, directed by Piero Vivarelli in 1973 and set in Senegal, based on Leo Frobenius's work. To dismiss this sub-genre entirely would be to ignore perhaps the most remarkable mass exploitation of a literary work of art in modern times: a phenomenon that not only predates post-modernist parody but also foreshadows more recent trends in our mass-media culture (the sexual role-playing of fan fiction, for example).

What would Boccaccio have to say about all this? He said it quite well, in self-defence, in the Introduction to Day IV, 40:

> For whatever happens, my fate can be no worse than that of the fine-grained dust, which, when a gale blows, either stays on the ground or is carried aloft, in which case it is frequently deposited upon the heads of men, upon the crowns of kings and emperors, and even upon high palaces and lofty towers, whence, if it should fall, it cannot sink lower than the place from which it was raised.

(p. 290)

Contemporary mass culture, between TV and the movies

How much has this 'lightness', which Boccaccio underlines in his dusty metaphor (and as Calvino famously wrote in one of his *Six Memos for the Next Millennium*), and the inter-expressive richness of the *Decameron* actually contributed to its continuing fortunes through the centuries, in 'high' as well as 'low' spheres of culture? To be sure, in order to capture the whole spectrum of its late modern or post-modern metamorphoses, we have to cast our net wide.

At the high end of the spectrum, we find the *Decameron* illustrated by such major figures of the twentieth-century avant-garde as Marc Chagall and Salvador Dalí.[26] At the (much) lower end, we stumble upon diverse media market products such as for example, Italian political satirist Daniele Luttazzi's *Decameron, politica, sesso, religione e morte* (*Decameron*, politics, sex, religion and death), which is worth mentioning as an example of how Boccaccio has been used within the context of TV-dominated Italian culture in the age of Berlusconi. The controversial show quickly disappeared from Italian TV after a short run on La7, back in 2007, but is still viewable in seven instalments on YouTube. The title of this programme (the reference to the *Decameron* is meant to warn as much as entice the audience) indeed suggests a direct link to Boccaccio, filtered through Pasolini: both, after all, were deeply concerned with the intersection of power, sexuality, religiosity, and mortality, within the sombre framework of a literal or symbolic plague. As Luttazzi himself explains, however, his programme drew its broad inspiration from Boccaccio, mainly as a kind of 'comicità dura per tempi insaziabili' (hard comedy for insatiable times) – heavy political satire fit for Italy in the age of Berlusconi, with its tawdry sexual scandals. Even this kind of explicit satirical treatment of Italian domestic 'porno-politics' can be viewed as part of a long-standing tradition which (*mutatis mutandis*) counts Dante, Boccaccio, and Pasolini among its most illustrious practitioners.

An alternative example of what we may call free-adaptation is the film *Decameron Pie* (aka *Virgin Territory* or *Decameron: Angels and Virgins*), a US–British production which also appeared in 2007. Advertised in Italy as a loose remake in medieval costume of the semi-cult movie *American Pie*, the film is set against the pseudo-Romantic, brochure-perfect backdrop of a Tuscan country villa (on-location scenes include views of contemporary Florence, magically emptied of tourists). Its cast of handsome, scantily but elegantly dressed American and British teen actors is vaguely reminiscent of certain Pre-Raphaelite visualizations of the *Decameron*'s *brigata*. A better definition can be found in a user review (a new critical genre) on the Internet Movie Database (IMDB): 'Anybody who thought this was a soft core porn movie would be forgiven . . . the movie is not set in present times so perhaps we shouldn't judge the women within it on a modern standard, supposing nuns no longer [fall] for a good looking gardener' (a reference to the story of Masetto (III. 1), the young gardener who, pretending to be mute, penetrates behind the walls of a nunnery and enjoys many fruitful liaisons with the inhabitants).

In a sad footnote, Boccaccio scholars and fans were briefly excited to hear that Woody Allen was working on a film entitled *Bop Decameron*, set in Rome and starring Roberto Benigni – only to learn that the title had been changed at the last minute to *Nero Fiddled* (the film was finally released under the title *To Rome, With Love*). The official online explanation for the change said that *Decameron* is no longer a recognizable word, and though Allen claimed the film had no real connection to Boccaccio's *novelle*, he was also shocked at how few people had ever heard of Boccaccio's masterpiece.

A quick look at the future (perfect)

Our short (and incomplete) history of Boccaccio adaptations beyond the text, has finally reached the present day. Textual *mouvance* or variance – the mobility and variability of texts – already a well-debated philological issue in medieval studies – now extends its reach from scribal and print to web culture.[27] Boccaccio is at the centre of some of the most interesting experiments in digital philology, such as that focused on the *Zibaldone laurenziano*, the work of Raul Mordenti, in close collaboration with other prominent Boccaccio scholars (Claude Cazalé Bérard and the late Michelangelo Picone).[28] In this and other similar experiments, the very notion of authorship, as crystallized by print culture, is questioned (although by no means dismissed) from a new perspective no longer tied to strictly textual dimensions. Indeed, while contemporary forms of textual mobility also encompass, as in the Middle Ages, authorial anonymity, collective rewriting, and influences from the oral tradition, in the ongoing evolution from an analogue to a digital mode of cultural production, the text not only becomes more mobile but also radically changes its hierarchical relationship to image and sound. Simply consider how common it is today to release a narrative work simultaneously across multiple platforms (print, film, TV, animation, games, fanzines, and so on), all conveying, often as part of a single powerful franchise, a variation on the same story (or set of stories). Harry Potter immediately comes to mind as a prime example of what Henry Jenkins has called 'transmedia storytelling' in a 'convergence culture': a culture in which readers, enabled by digital tools, become writers and writers become players who rewrite or replay, or 'reperform', their model, adapting it to their tastes, identities, languages, skills, sexual orientations, and so on.[29]

From a historical point of view, the afterlife of the *Decameron* definitely anticipates some of the features of this contemporary evolution of the literary work of art. Perhaps, among our literary classics, only Dante's *Comedy* has met with comparable, non-academic fortune in terms of adaptation in modern media, from the cinema (the *Inferno* was adapted to the screen as early as 1911) to video games. In a sense, my students and I envisioned such a scenario when we first conceived of the Decameron Web, mainly as a collaborative learning tool, back in the mid-1990s.[30] Our focus was not on rewriting but on interpretation and annotation as legitimate components of the adaptation of a literary work of art to a changing environment, that is, from analogue to digital. The 'combinatorial' and 'social' nature of Boccaccio's *Decameron*, with its complex framing devices and its multiple internal cross-references, make of this literary work of art an example of the hyper-novel *ante litteram*. Only with the more recent advent of the Web 2.0 and social networks, however, has this scenario begun to fulfil its full potential. Today, simply googling the word 'Decameron' (perhaps no longer a recognizable word) gives a sense of the continued widespread presence of Boccaccio's transmedial legacy in contemporary culture: a culture where the distinction between high- and low-brow has practically disappeared, and where the *Decameron* has moved well beyond the confines of the scholarly community, and the letter of Boccaccio's text.

NOTES

1 Vittore Branca, 'Introduzione: il narrar boccacciano per immagini dal tardo gotico al primo rinascimento', in *Boccaccio visualizzato: narrare per parole e per immagini fra Medioevo e Rinascimento*, ed. by Branca, 3 vols (Turin: Einaudi, 1999), I, 5–37 (p. 3).
2 Florence, Biblioteca Medicea Laurenziana, MS 42. 1 (Mn); see List of manuscripts in this volume.
3 Paris, Bibliothèque Nationale, MS It. 482 (Capponi MS); Berlin, Staatsbibliothek Preussischer Kulturbesitz, MS Hamilton 90, and see Chapter 2 and the List of manuscripts in this volume.
4 Richard F. Kuhns in his *Decameron and the Philosophy of Storytelling: Author as Midwife and Pimp* (New York: Columbia University Press, 2005), p. 37.
5 Branca, 'Introduzione', pp. 5–6.
6 For reproductions of these catchword drawings see Branca, 'Introduzione', pp. 15–18.
7 Branca, 'Introduzione', p. 22.
8 Images of this manuscript can be viewed at http://bodley30.bodley.ox.ac.uk: 8180/luna/servlet/view/all/what/MS.+Holkham+misc.+49. Note, however, that the first partially or fully illustrated *printed* editions of the *Decameron* are published outside Italy, in France and Germany (*Livre des cent nouvelles*, trans. by Laurent de Premierfait, printed in Paris by Jean Dupré for Antoine Vérard in 1485; *Cento novelle: Das seind die hundert neuen Fabelen*, trans. by Arigo [Heinrich Schlüsselfelder?], printed in Augsburg by Anton Sorg in 1490). The first Italian illustrated *Decameron* is printed by the brothers Giovanni e Gregorio de Gregori in Venice in 1492.
9 www.museodelprado.es/coleccion/galeria-on-line/galeria-on-line/zoom/2/obra/ la-historia-de-nastagio-degli-onesti-iii/oimg/0; *Boccaccio visualizzato*, I, 22–25. See the online exhibition on domestic art in Renaissance Italy at the Metropolitan Museum in New York: www.metmuseum.org/toah/hd/dome/hd_dome.htm.
10 Marco Cursi, *Il 'Decameron': scritture, scriventi, lettori. Storia di un testo* (Rome: Viella, 2007); Rhiannon Daniels, *Boccaccio and the Book: Production and Reading in Italy 1340–1520* (London: Legenda, 2009).
11 Andreina Griseri, 'Di fronte al *Decameron*: l'età moderna', in *Boccaccio visualizzato*, I, 155–211 (pp. 157–9).
12 *Griselda: metamorfosi di un mito nella società europea. Atti del Convegno internazionale a 80 anni dalla nascita della Società per gli studi storici della Provincia*

di Cuneo, Saluzzo, 23–24 aprile 2009, ed. by Rinaldo Comba and Marco Piccat (Cuneo: Società per gli studi storici, archeologici ed artistici della Provincia di Cuneo, 2011).

13 Maria Teresa Muraro, 'Primi appunti sulla fortuna del *Boccaccio* nei libretti per musica', *Studi sul Boccaccio*, 5 (1968), 265–73; Gabriele Muresu, 'Goldoni e il *melodramma*: il rifacimento della Griselda di Apostolo Zeno', in his *La parola cantata: studi sul melodramma del Settecento* (Rome: Bulzoni, 1982).

14 *The Collected Works of Samuel Taylor Coleridge*, ed. by Kathleen Coburn, 16 vols (Princeton: Princeton University Press, 1968–), XVI: *Poetical Works, I, Poems (Reading Text)*, ed. by J. C. C. Mays (Princeton: Princeton University Press, 2001), pp. 1089–95 (p. 1092).

15 Griseri, 'Di fronte al *Decameron*', p. 201.

16 Exhibition catalogue: Angus Trumble, *Love and Death: Art in the Age of Queen Victoria* (Adelaide: Art Gallery of South Australia, [n.d.]): www.victorianweb.org/painting/leighton/paintings/16.html.

17 George Bernard Shaw, 'Keats', in *The John Keats Memorial Volume*, ed. by G. C. Williamson (London, 1921), pp. 173–6.

18 For a reproduction, see: www.liverpoolmuseums.org.uk/walker/collections/19c/millais.aspx.

19 Sarah Wootton, 'Keats' Poetry as a Common Thread in English and American Pre-Raphaelitism', in *Worldwide Pre-Raphaelitism*, ed. by Thomas J. Tobin (Albany: SUNY University Press, 2005), pp. 279–301.

20 *The Pre-Raphaelites*, ed. by Leslie Parris (London: Tate Gallery, 1984), p. 25. For a reproduction, see the Rossetti Archive: www.rossettiarchive.org/docs/s114.rap.html.

21 *Il telefono nel Medioevo* is a comic short movie (75 metres), by Ernesto Maria Pasquali, in which a character named Trovatore tries to communicate with a damsel through a long tube stretched under her window, only to be discovered by her father and sprayed with water.

22 Aldo Bernardini and Vittorio Martinelli, *Il cinema muto italiano: 1912*, 3 vols (Pisa: Nuova Eri, 1995), I, 134–6.

23 www.fdb.cz/film-trailery/69598-boccaccio.html.

24 Simone Villani, *Il Decameron allo specchio: il film di Pasolini come saggio sull'opera di Boccaccio* (Rome: Donzelli, 2004).

25 Patrick A. Rumble, *Allegories of Contamination: Pier Paolo Pasolini's Trilogy of Life* (Toronto: University of Toronto Press, 1995).

26 The watercolours of Marc Chagall were a graphic supplement for the art magazine *Verve*, no. 24, *Contes de Boccace 'Decameron'* (Paris: Tériade, 1950).

27 Jerome J. McGann, *Radiant Textuality: Literature after the World Wide Web* (New York: Palgrave, 2001).

28 http://rmcisadu.let.uniroma1.it/boccaccio and Raul Mordenti, *Per l'edizione ipertestuale dello Zibaldone Laurenziano di Boccaccio* (Rome: Accademia Nazionale dei Lincei, 1999).

29 Henry Jenkins, 'Transmedia Storytelling: Moving Characters from Books to Films to Video Games Can Make Them Stronger and More Compelling', *Technology Review*, 15 January 2003: http://www.technologyreview.com/news/401760/transmedia-storytelling; Henry Jenkins, *Convergence Culture: Where Old and New Media Collide* (New York: New York University Press, 2006).

30 http://www.brown.edu/Departments/Italian_Studies/dweb/index.php; Michael Papio and Massimo Riva, 'The Decameron Web: Ten Years Later', in *Teaching Foreign Languages and Literatures Online*, ed. by Ian Lancashire (New York: Modern Language Association, 2009), pp. 343–57.

ה

GUIDE TO FURTHER READING

Key studies in English

Almansi, Guido, *The Writer as Liar: Narrative Techniques in the 'Decameron'* (London: Routledge, 1975)

Armstrong, Guyda, *The English Boccaccio: A History in Books* (Toronto: University of Toronto Press, 2013)

Bergin, Thomas, *Boccaccio* (New York: Viking, 1981)

Branca, Vittore, *Boccaccio: The Man and his Works*, trans. by Richard Monges and Dennis J. McAuliffe (New York: New York University Press, 1976)

Cervigni, Dino S., ed., *Boccaccio's 'Decameron': Rewriting the Christian Middle Ages, Annali d'Italianistica*, 31 (2013)

Ciabattoni, Francesco and Pier Massimo Forni, *The Decameron Third Day in Perspective* (Toronto: University of Toronto Press, 2014)

Cottino-Jones, Marga, *Order from Chaos: Social and Aesthetic Harmonies in Boccaccio's 'Decameron'* (Washington, DC: University Press of America, 1982)

Daniels, Rhiannon, *Boccaccio and the Book: Production and Reading in Italy 1340–1520* (London: Legenda, 2009)

Dombroski, Robert S., ed., *Critical Perspectives on the 'Decameron'* (London: Hodder and Stoughton, 1976)

Eisner, Martin, *Boccaccio and the Invention of Italian Literature: Dante, Petrarch, Cavalcanti, and the Authority of the Vernacular* (Cambridge: Cambridge University Press, 2013)

Forni, Pier Massimo, *Adventures in Speech: Rhetoric and Narration in Boccaccio's 'Decameron'* (Philadelphia: University of Pennsylvania Press, 1996)

Gittes, Tobias Foster, *Boccaccio's Naked Muse: Eros, Culture, and the Mythopoeic Imagination* (Toronto: University of Toronto Press, 2008)

Hollander, Robert, *Boccaccio's Two Venuses* (New York: Columbia University Press, 1977)

Boccaccio's Last Fiction: 'Il Corbaccio' (Philadelphia: University of Pennsylvania Press, 1988)

Boccaccio's Dante and the Shaping Force of Satire (Ann Arbor: University of Michigan Press, 1997)

Kirkham, Victoria, *The Sign of Reason in Boccaccio's Fiction* (Florence: Leo S. Olschki, 1993)

Fabulous Vernacular: Boccaccio's 'Filocolo' and the Art of Medieval Fiction (Ann Arbor: University of Michigan Press, 2001)

Kirkham, Victoria, Michael Sherberg, and Janet Levarie Smarr, eds, *Boccaccio: A Critical Guide to the Complete Works* (Chicago: University of Chicago Press, 2013)

Marcus, Millicent Joy, *An Allegory of Form: Literary Self-Consciousness in the 'Decameron'* (Saratoga: Anma Libri, 1979)

Mazzotta, Giuseppe, *The World at Play in Boccaccio's 'Decameron'* (Princeton: Princeton University Press, 1986)

McGregor, James H., ed., *Approaches to Teaching Boccaccio's 'Decameron'* (New York: Modern Language Association of America, 2000)

Migiel, Marilyn, *A Rhetoric of the 'Decameron'* (Toronto: University of Toronto Press, 2003)

Ó Cuilleanáin, Cormac, *Religion and the Clergy in Boccaccio's 'Decameron'* (Rome: Edizioni di storia e letteratura, 1984)

Potter, Joy Hambuechen, *Five Frames for the 'Decameron': Communication and Social Systems in the 'cornice'* (Princeton: Princeton University Press, 1982)

Sherberg, Michael, *The Governance of Friendship: Law and Gender in the 'Decameron'* (Columbus: Ohio State University Press, 2011)

Smarr, Janet Levarie, *Boccaccio and Fiammetta: The Narrator as Lover* (Urbana: University of Illinois Press, 1986)

Stone, Gregory B., *The Ethics of Nature in the Middle Ages: On Boccaccio's Poetaphysics* (New York: St. Martin's Press, 1998)

Usher, Jonathan, 'Boccaccio's "Ars morendi" in the Decameron', *Modern Language Review*, 81.3 (1986), 621–32

'Boccaccio on Readers and Reading', *Heliotropia*, 1.1 (2003) http://www.heliotropia.org

'Monuments More Enduring than Bronze: Boccaccio and Paper Inscriptions', *Heliotropia*, 4.1 (2007) http://www.heliotropia.org

'"Sesto fra cotanto senno" and Appetentia primi loci: Boccaccio, Petrarch and Dante's Poetic Hierarchy', *Studi sul Boccaccio*, 35 (2007), 157–98

Wallace, David, *Giovanni Boccaccio: Decameron* (Cambridge: Cambridge University Press, 1991)

Weaver, Elissa B., ed., *The 'Decameron' First Day in Perspective* (Toronto: University of Toronto Press, 2004)

Key studies in Italian

Battaglia Ricci, Lucia, *Boccaccio* (Rome: Salerno, 2000)

Bragantini, Renzo, and Pier Massimo Forni, eds, *Lessico critico decameroniano* (Turin: Bollati Boringhieri, 1995)

Branca, Vittore, *Boccaccio medievale e nuovi studi sul 'Decameron'*, 4th edn (Milan: BUR Rizzoli, 2010)

Bruni, Francesco, *Boccaccio: l'invenzione della letteratura mezzana* (Bologna: Il Mulino, 1990)

Bruno Pagnamenta, Roberta, *Il 'Decameron': l'ambiguità come strategia narrativa* (Ravenna: Longo, 1999)

Cardini, Franco, *Le cento novelle contro la morte: Giovanni Boccaccio e la rifondazione cavalleresca del mondo* (Rome: Salerno, 2007)

De Robertis, Teresa, Carla Maria Monti, Marco Petoletti, Giuliano Tanturli, and Stefano Zamponi, eds, *Boccaccio autore e copista* (Florence: Mandragora, 2013)

Fido, Franco, *Il regime delle simmetrie imperfette* (Milan: Franco Angeli, 1988)

Getto, Giovanni, *Vita di forme e forme di vita nel 'Decameron'* (Turin: Petrini, 1986)

Marchesi, Simone, *Stratigrafie decameroniane* (Florence: Olschki, 2004)

Natali, Giulia, *Boccaccio e le controfigure dell'autore* (L'Aquila: Japadre, 1991)

Quondam, Amedeo, Maurizio Fiorilla, and Giancarlo Alfano (eds), *Giovanni Boccaccio: 'Decameron'* (Milan: BUR Rizzoli, 2013)

Surdich, Luigi, *Boccaccio* (Rome: Laterza, 2001)

Medieval textual production and the language arts

Alexander, J. G., *Medieval Illuminators and their Methods of Work* (New Haven: Yale University Press, 1992)

Bertolo, Fabio M., Paolo Cherubini, Giorgio Inglese, and Luisa Miglio, *Breve storia della scrittura e del libro* (Roma: Carocci, 2005)

Brown, Michelle P., *A Guide to Western Historical Scripts from Antiquity to 1600* (Toronto: University of Toronto Press, 1993)

Cerquiglini, Bernard, *In Praise of the Variant: A Critical History of Philology*, trans. by Betsy Wing (Baltimore: Johns Hopkins University Press, 1999)

Clemens, Raymond and Terry Graham, *Introduction to Manuscript Studies* (Ithaca, NY: Cornell University Press, 2007)

Copeland, Rita and Ineke Sluiter, eds, *Medieval Grammar and Rhetoric: Language Arts and Literary Theory, AD 300–1475* (Oxford: Oxford University Press, 2009)

Cursi, Marco, *Il 'Decameron': scritture, scriventi, lettori. Storia di un testo* (Rome: Viella, 2007)

—— *La scrittura e i libri di Giovanni Boccaccio* (Rome: Viella, 2013)

De la Mare, Albinia C., *The Handwriting of Italian Humanists* (London: Oxford University Press, 1973)

De Hamel, Christopher, *Scribes and Illuminators* (Toronto: Toronto University Press, 1992)

Lubac, Henri de, *Medieval Exegesis: The Four Senses of Scripture*, 3 vols (Grand Rapids, MI: Eerdmans, 1998–2001)

Mehtonen, Päivi, *Old Concepts and New Poetics: 'Historia', 'Argumentum', and 'Fabula' in the Twelfth- and Early Thirteenth-Century Latin Poetics of Fiction* (Helsinki: Societas Scientiarum Fennica, 1996)

Minnis, Alastair, *Medieval Theory of Authorship: Scholastic Literary Attitudes in the Later Middle Ages*, 2nd edn (Philadelphia: University of Pennsylvania Press, 2010)

Minnis, A. J., and A. B. Scott, with David Wallace, eds, *Medieval Literary Theory and Criticism c. 1100–c.1375*, 2nd edn (Oxford: Clarendon Press, 1991)

Petrucci, Armando, *Writers and Readers in Medieval Italy: Studies in the History of Written Culture*, trans. by C. M. Radding (New Haven: Yale University Press, 1995)

Richardson, Brian, *Printing, Writers and Readers in Renaissance Italy* (Cambridge: Cambridge University Press, 1999)

Social, cultural, and historical contexts

Branca, Vittore, ed., *Mercanti scrittori: ricordi nella Firenze tra medioevo e Rinascimento* (Milan: Rusconi, 1986)

Brucker, Gene A., *Florentine Politics and Society 1343–1378* (Princeton: Princeton University Press, 1962)

Klapisch-Zuber, Christiane, *Ritorno alla politica: i magnati fiorentini 1340–1440* (Rome: Viella, 2009)

Milner, Stephen J., 'Communication, Consensus and Conflict: Rhetorical Precepts, the *ars concionandi* and Social Ordering in Late Medieval Italy', in *The Rhetoric of Cicero in its Medieval and Renaissance Commentary Tradition*, ed. by Virginia Cox and John O. Ward (Leiden: Brill, 2006), pp. 411–60

'The Italian Peninsula: Reception and Dissemination', in *Humanism in Fifteenth-Century Europe*, ed. by David Rundle (Oxford: The Society for the Study of Medieval Languages and Literatures, 2012), pp. 1–30

Najemy, John M., *A History of Florence 1200–1575* (Oxford: Blackwell, 2006)

Trexler, Richard C., *Public Life in Renaissance Florence* (Ithaca: Cornell University Press, 1991)

Wallace, David, *Chaucerian Polity: Absolutist Lineages and Associational Forms in England and Italy* (Stanford: Stanford University Press, 1997)

Weissman, Ronald F. E., 'The Importance of Being Ambiguous: Social Relations, Individualism, and Identity in Renaissance Florence', in *Urban Life in the Renaissance*, ed. by Susan Zimmerman and Ronald F. E. Weissman (Newark: University of Delaware Press, 1989), pp. 269–80

Witt, Ronald, *In the Footsteps of the Ancients: The Origins of Humanism from Lovato to Bruni* (Boston: Brill, 2003)

Literary contexts

Alfano, Giancarlo, Teresa D'Urso, and Alessandra Perriccioli Saggese, eds, *Boccaccio angioino: materiali per la storia di Napoli nel Trecento* (Brussels: Peter Lang, 2012)

Anderson, David, 'Which are Boccaccio's Own Glosses?', in *Gli zibaldoni di Boccaccio: memoria, scrittura, riscrittura. Atti del Seminario internazionale di Firenze-Certaldo (26–28 aprile 1996)*, ed. by Michelangelo Picone and Claude Cazalé Bérard (Florence: Cesati, 1998), pp. 327–31

Anselmi, Gian Mario, Giovanni Baffetti, Carlo Delcorno, and Sebastiana Nobili, eds, *Boccacccio e i suoi lettori: una lunga ricezione* (Bologna: Il Mulino, 2013)

Armstrong, Guyda, 'Heavenly Bodies: The Presence of the Divine Female in Boccaccio', *Italian Studies*, 60 (2005), 134–46

Barański, Zygmunt G., and Theodore J. Cachey Jr., eds, *Petrarch and Dante: Anti-Dantism, Metaphysics, Tradition* (Notre Dame: University of Notre Dame Press, 2009), pp. 114–73

Barolini, Teodolinda, 'The Wheel of the Decameron', *Romance Philology*, 36.4 (1983), 521–39

Barsella, Susanna, 'Boccaccio, Petrarch, and Peter Damian: Two Models of the Humanist Intellectual', *Modern Language Notes*, 121 (2006), 16–48

Baxter, Catherine, 'Turpiloquium in Boccaccio's Tale of the Goslings (*Decameron*, Day IV, Introduction)', *Modern Language Review*, 108 (2013), 812–38

Billanovich, Giuseppe, *Restauri boccacceschi* (Rome: Edizioni di storia e letteratura, 1947)

Clarke, K. P., *Chaucer and Italian Textuality* (Oxford: Oxford University Press, 2011)

Cornish, Alison, *Vernacular Translation in Dante's Italy: Illiterate Literature* (Cambridge: Cambridge University Press, 2011)

Eisner, Martin, 'Petrarch Reading Boccaccio: Revisiting the Genesis of the Triumphi', in *Petrarch and the Textual Origins of Interpretation*, ed. by Teodolina Barolini and H. Wayne Storey (Leiden: Brill, 2007), pp. 131–46

Enenkel, Karl, 'Modelling the Humanist: Petrarch's Letter to Posterity and Boccaccio's Biography of the Poet Laureate', in *Modelling the Individual: Biography and Portrait in the Renaissance*, ed. by Karl Enenkel, Betsy de Jong-Crane, and Peter Liebregts (Amsterdam: Rodopi, 1998), pp. 11–49

Ferrante, Joan M., 'Politics, Finance and Feminism in *Decameron*, II, 7', *Studi sul Boccaccio*, 21 (1993), 151–74

Gibaldi, Joseph, 'The *Decameron cornice* and the Responses to the Disintegration of Civilisation', *Kentucky Romance Quarterly*, 24 (1977), 349–57

Gittes, Tobias Foster, 'St. Boccaccio: The Poet as Pander and Martyr', *Studi sul Boccaccio*, 30 (2002), 133–57

Giusti, Eugenio, *Dall'amore cortese alla comprensione: il viaggio ideologico di Giovanni Boccaccio dalla 'Caccia di Diana' al 'Decameron'* (Milan: LED, 1999)

Hagedorn, C. Suzanne, *Abandoned Women: Rewriting the Classics in Dante, Boccaccio and Chaucer* (Ann Arbor: University of Michigan, 2004)

Janssens, Marcel, 'The Internal Reception of the Stories within the *Decameron*', in *Boccaccio in Europe: Proceedings of the Boccaccio Conference, Leuven, December 1975*, ed. by Gilbert Tournoy (Leuven: Leuven University Press, 1977), pp. 135–48

Kirkham, Victoria, 'An Allegorically Tempered *Decameron*', *Italica*, 62.1 (1985), 1–23

Kriesel, James C., 'The Genealogy of Boccaccio's Theory of Allegory', *Studi sul Boccaccio*, 36 (2009), 197–226

Lummus, David, 'Boccaccio's Three Venuses: On the Convergence of Celestial and Transgressive Love in the *Genealogie Deorum Gentilium*', *Medievalia et Humanistica*, 37 (2011), 65–88

'Boccaccio's Hellenism and the Foundations of Modernity', *Mediaevalia*, 33 (2012), 101–67

'Boccaccio's Poetic Anthropology: Allegories of History in the *Genealogie Deorum Gentilium Libri*', *Speculum*, 87.3 (2012), 724–65

Marchesi, Simone, '"Sic me formabat puerum": Horace's *Satire* I, 4 and Boccaccio's Defense of the *Decameron*', *Modern Language Notes*, 116.1, (2001), 1–29

'Boccaccio's Vernacular Classicism: Intertextuality and Interdiscoursivity in the *Decameron*', *Heliotropia*, 7 (2010), 31–50

McLaughlin, Martin L., *Literary Imitation in the Italian Renaissance: The Theory and Practice of Literary Imitation in Italy from Dante to Bembo* (Oxford: Clarendon Press, 1995)

Mercuri, Roberto, 'Genesi della tradizione letteraria italiana in Dante, Petrarca e Boccaccio', in *Letteratura italiana: storia e geografia*, dir. by Alberto Asor Rosa, 3 vols (Turin: Einaudi, 1987), I: *L'età medievale*, pp. 229–455

Milner, Stephen J. 'Coming Together: Consolation and the Rhetoric of Insinuation in Boccaccio's *Decameron*', in *The Erotics of Consolation: Desire and Distance in the Late Middle Ages*, ed. by Catherine E. Léglu and Stephen J. Milner (New York: Palgrave, 2008), pp. 95–113

La novella italiana: atti del convegno di Caprarola, Roma, 2 vols (Rome: Salerno, 1989)

Rico, Francisco, *Ritratti allo specchio (Boccaccio, Petrarca)* (Padua: Antenore, 2012)

Storey, H. Wayne, 'Following Instructions: Remaking Dante's *Vita nova* in the Fourteenth Century', in *Medieval Constructions in Gender and Identity: Essays in Honor of Joan M. Ferrante*, ed. by Teodolinda Barolini (Tempe: Arizona Center for Medieval and Renaissance Studies, 2005), pp. 117–32

'Contesti e culture testuali della lettera di frate Ilaro', *Dante Studies*, 124 (2006), 57–76

Velli, Giuseppe, *Petrarca e Boccaccio: tradizione, memoria, scrittura* (Padua: Antenore, 1995)

Gender

Armstrong, Guyda, 'Boccaccio and the Infernal Body: The Widow as Wilderness', in *Boccaccio and Feminist Criticism*, ed. by Stillinger and Psaki, pp. 83–104

'The Framing of Fiammetta: Gender, Authorship, and Voice in an Elizabethan Translation of Boccaccio', in *Elizabethan Translation and Literary Culture*, ed. by Gabriela Schmidt (Berlin: Walter de Gruyter, 2013), pp. 299–339

Barolini, Teodolinda, '"Le parole son femmine e i fatti sono maschi": Toward a Sexual Poetics of the *Decameron* (*Decameron* 2.9, 2.10, 5.10)', *Studi sul Boccaccio*, 21 (1993), 175–97, repr. in Barolini, *Dante and the Origins of Italian Literary Culture* (New York: Fordham University Press, 2006), 281–303

Blamires, Alcuin, Karen Pratt, and C. W. Marx, eds, *Woman Defamed and Woman Defended* (Oxford: Oxford University Press, 1992)

Calabrese, Michael, 'Feminism and the Packaging of Boccaccio's Fiammetta', *Italica*, 74 (1997), 20–42

Filosa, Elsa, *Tre studi sul 'De mulieribus claris'* (Milan: Edizioni Universitarie di Lettere Economia Diritto, 2012)

Franklin, Margaret, *Boccaccio's Heroines: Power and Virtue in Renaissance Society* (Aldershot: Ashgate, 2006)

Jordan, Constance, 'Boccaccio's In-Famous Women: Gender and Civic Virtue in the *De mulieribus claris*', in *Ambiguous Realities: Women in the Middle Ages and Renaissance*, ed. by Carole Levin and Jeanie Watson (Detroit: Wayne State University Press, 1987)

Kolsky, Stephen, *The Genealogy of Women: Studies in Boccaccio's 'De mulieribus claris'* (New York: Peter Lang, 2003)

Maclean, Ian, *The Renaissance Notion of Woman: A Study in the Fortunes of Scholasticism and Medical Science in European Intellectual Life* (Cambridge: Cambridge University Press, 1980)

Psaki, F. Regina, 'The Play of Genre and Voicing in Boccaccio's *Corbaccio*', *Italiana*, 5 (1993), 41–54

Stillinger, Thomas C. and F. Regina Psaki, eds, *Boccaccio and Feminist Criticism*, (Chapel Hill: Annali d'Italianistica, 2006)

Wallace, David, '*Letters of Old Age*: Love between Men, Griselda, and Farewell to Letters (*Rerum senilium libri*)', in *Petrarch: A Critical Guide to the Complete Works*, ed. by Victoria Kirkham and Armando Maggi (Chicago: The University of Chicago Press, 2009), pp. 321–30

Transmission and adaptation

Armstrong, Guyda, 'Paratexts and their Functions in Seventeenth-Century English *Decamerons*', *Modern Language Review*, 102 (2007), 40–57

'A Bibliography of Boccaccio's Works in English Translation: Part I. The Minor Works', *Studi sul Boccaccio*, 38 (2010), 167–204

Branca, Vittore, ed., *Boccaccio visualizzato: narrare per parole e per immagini fra Medioevo e Rinascimento*, 3 vols (Turin: Einaudi, 1999)

Daniels, Rhiannon, 'Controversy, Censorship and Boccaccio's Life of Pope Joan', *Studi sul Boccaccio*, 34 (2006), 185–98

'Rethinking the Critical History of the *Decameron*: Boccaccio's Epistle XXII to Mainardo Cavalcanti', *Modern Language Review*, 106 (2011), 423–47

Diffley, P. B., 'From Translation to Imitation and Beyond: A Reassessment of Boccaccio's Role in Marguerite de Navarre's *Heptaméron*', *Modern Language Review*, 90 (1995), 345–62

Hainsworth, Peter, 'Translating the *Decameron*: Some Problems and Possibilities', in '*Ciò che potea la lingua nostra*': *Lectures and Essays in Memory of Clara Florio Cooper*, ed. by Vilma De Gasperin, *The Italianist*, 30 (2010), Special Supplement, pp. 121–31

Hedeman, Anne D., *Translating the Past: Laurent de Premierfait and Boccaccio's 'De casibus'* (Los Angeles: J. Paul Getty Museum, 2008)

Jones, Nicola, 'The Importance of "Visualization": Re-viewing Branca on Manuscript Illustration', in *Caro Vitto: Essays in Memory of Vittore Branca*, ed. by Jill Kraye and Laura Lepschy, *The Italianist*, 27 (2007), Special Supplement 2, 28–48

Ó Cuilleanáin, Cormac, 'Not in Front of the Servants: Forms of Bowdlerism and Censorship in Translation', in *Literary Translation: Constraints and Creativity*, ed. by Jean Boase-Beier and Michael Holman (Manchester: St Jerome, 1999), pp. 31–44

'"Boccaccio Could be Better Served": Harry McWilliam and Translation Criticism', in *Italian Culture: Interactions, Transpositions, Translations*, ed. by Cormac Ó Cuilleanáin, Corinna Salvadori, and John Scattergood (Dublin: Four Courts Press, 2006), pp. 45–68

Richardson, Brian, *Print Culture in Renaissance Italy: The Editor and the Vernacular Text, 1470–1600* (Cambridge: Cambridge University Press, 1994)

Manuscript Culture in Renaissance Italy (Cambridge: Cambridge University Press, 2009)

'The Textual History of the Decameron', in *Boccaccio: A Critical Guide to the Complete Works*, ed. by Victoria Kirkham, Michael Sherberg, and Janet Levarie Smarr (Chicago: University of Chicago Press, 2013), pp. 41–49

Ricketts, Jill, *Visualizing Boccaccio: Studies on Illustrations of the 'Decameron', from Giotto to Pasolini* (Cambridge: Cambridge University Press, 1997)

INDEX

INDEX

Boccaccio, Giovanni (*cont.*)
Gualtieri 151; Guccio 215;
Lisabetta 165, 224–5; Lorenzo 224;
Masetto 95, 230; Nastagio 135, 221;
scholar and the widow 135; Tancredi
165, 222; Titus and Gisippus 211;
Tofano 206; Torello 221
Decameron, frame characters, *see also*
narrators: Dioneo 112, 113, 151;
Elissa 110; Emilia 39, 103; female
members of brigata 62, 63, 113;
Fiammetta 57, 78, 107, 109;
Filomena 56, 95, 113; Filostrato 57;
narrator 37, 39–40, 101, 126; Neifile
29, 56, 78; Pampinea 62, 93; Panfilo
93, 108; Licisca and Tindaro 18
Decameron sections: title 87, 92;
subtitle 15, 39, 47, 121, 135, *see also*
'Prencipe Galeotto' (Prince Galahalt):
cornice (frame) 63, 77, 85, 222, 224,
228; rubrics 87, 104, 213–14; Proem
39, 58–9, 62, 75, 77, 84, 87, 89, 101,
115, 135, 164, 168, 179; Intr. I 39,
62, 75, 87, 126, 135; Intr. IV 40, 41,
42, 44, 46, 59–61, 62, 75, 89, 115,
132, 223, 229; Conclusion 39–40, 41,
44, 45, 46, 61, 75, 76, 87, 96, 115,
132, 214, 219
Decameron Days and tales: [Day,
number]: Day I 56, 103, 104: I.1 85,
156, 228; I.2 116; I.3 56, 96; I.4 104,
108, 214; I.5 104; I.7 96; I.9 83; I.10
104; Day II 45, 56: II.3 83; II.4 83;
II.5 114, 226; II.6 108; II.7 55, 83,
108, 114, 163, 221, 225; II.8 83, 112,
113, 226; II.9 83, 96, 112–13, 221,
227; II.10 103, 112, 227; Day III 56,
79, 80: III.1 95, 108, 114, 230; III.2
95, 108, 226; III.3 95, 110–11; III.4
114; III.5 95, 110; III.6 96, 103, 109,
112, 116; III.7 96; III.8 114; III.9 83,
96, 227; Day IV 56, 57, 103, 104: IV.1
57, 106–7, 165, 211, 214, 222; IV.2
33, 88; IV.3 83; IV.5 108, 165, 224;
IV.7 222; IV.9 105; Day V 56, 57: V.1
83, 222, 224; V.4 57; V.6 222; V.8
108, 135, 221; V.9 222; V.10 103,
112, 114, 206; Day VI 103, 104: VI.1
43, 95, 96, 104; VI.2 88; VI.3 104;
VI.5 85, 228; VI.7 105, 114–15; VI.8
104; VI.9 85, 104; VI.10 27, 85, 215;
Day VII: VII.1 39, 95; VII.2 112,
205–6; VII.7 111, 113; VII.8 96; VII.9

33, 111; Day VIII 214: VIII.3 58, 85,
103; VIII.6 58, 85; VIII.7 85, 135;
VIII.9 85; VIII.10 114; Day IX 43: IX.3
58, 85; IX.4 78; IX.5 58, 78, 85, 103;
IX.6 86; IX.9 103, 116; Day X 56, 74:
X.3 83; X.6 207; X.8 106, 107–8, 211;
X.9 55, 83, 221; X.10 16, 151, 207,
221, 223
De Canaria 198
De casibus virorum illustrium 14, 17,
33, 38, 44, 45, 46, 47, 131, 139, 140,
161, 172–5, 196, 198, 221: 'Against
women' 172–3; Brunhilde, Queen of
Franks 41; French 208–9; narrator
40–1, 44, 173–5, 178; second
redaction 48; Theseus 174; Thyestes
and Atreus 41; Philippa of Catania 41
De montibus 14, 140, 158, 161, 199
De mulieribus claris 15, 16, 17, 48–9,
131, 140, 161, 172, 180, 197, 209,
212, 221, 223: Artemisia, Queen of
Caria 182; autograph 23, 196, 197;
Ceres 182; dedication to Andrea
Acciaiuoli 17, 48, 62, 180, 181;
dissemination in manuscript 183;
French 209; Giovanna, Queen of
Sicily and Jerusalem 17; narrator 172,
180, 181–2
De vita Petracchi 31, 144, 168
Elegia di Costanza 160
Elegia di madonna Fiammetta 15, 16,
45, 47, 70, 135, 175–6, 177, 189,
190, 191, 193, 195, 198, 199, 212:
adultery 175; classicizing allusions 74,
175; Fiammetta 172, 175–6; narrator
43, 179; nurse 175, 179–80
*Esposizioni sopra la Comedia di Dante
Alighieri* 121, 122, 124, 126, 128,
130–1, 133, 136, 141, 157, 166, 192,
197
Filocolo 14, 16, 42, 43, 45, 47, 70, 73,
135, 162–3, 167, 189, 192, 193, 195,
197, 207, 212, 221
Filostrato 67, 189, 190, 191, 193, 196,
199, 206, 207: dedication to
Filomena 44; French 209; narrator 43
Florio and Biancifiore 47, 68, 135:
narrator 37; 'Thirteen questions' 212;
see also (Cantare tradition)
Genealogia deorum gentilium 4, 14, 24,
42, 44, 45–6, 47, 48, 65, 77, 84,
90–2, 96, 131, 140, 157, 159, 161,
167, 194, 199: autograph 4, 194,

246

Cambridge Companions to...

AUTHORS

TOPICS